EVERYMAN, I will go with thee,

and be thy guide,

In thy most need to go by thy side

SIR THOMAS MALORY
(*fl.* 1470.)

Very little is known of him for certain. Some identify him with a Sir Thomas Malory of Warwickshire who fought successively on both sides in the Wars of the Roses, sat in Parliament 1444–5, and died in 1471. Another theory, attributed to Leland and followed by Sir John Rhys in this edition, would make Sir Thomas Malory a Welshman; but it is not now commonly held.

SIR THOMAS MALORY

Le Morte d'Arthur

IN TWO VOLUMES · VOLUME ONE

INTRODUCTION BY
SIR JOHN RHYS

DENT: LONDON
EVERYMAN'S LIBRARY
DUTTON: NEW YORK

This book if bound as a paperback is
subject to the condition that it may
not be issued on loan or otherwise
except in its original binding

No. 45   ISBN (if a hardback) 0 460 00045 4
No. 1045   ISBN (if a paperback) 0 460 01045 X

INTRODUCTION

SIR THOMAS MALORY has given us no account of himself or his family, but he has left his name and his work. The name Malory is found connected with estates in Yorkshire in the sixteenth century, and with estates in Leicestershire in that which follows. As the name of the knight to whom we owe the Morte Darthur, it is found written not only Malory or Malorye, but also Maleore. It occurred to me some years ago that this fact lent countenance to the statement ascribed to Leland and others, that Sir Thomas Malory was a Welshman; for Maleore reminded me of *Maylawr*, *Maelawr* or *Maelor*, the name of two districts on the confines of England and Wales: a 'Welsh Maelor' is included in the County of Denbigh, and an 'English Maelor' in that of Flint. How such a name could readily become a surname may be seen from the designation, for instance, of a lord of the two Maelors in the twelfth century, named *Gruffud Maelawr*. Literally rendered, this would mean 'Griffith of Maelor.' Similarly, the name of a Welsh poet of the fifteenth century, Edward ab Rhys Maelor, might now be rendered 'Edward Price of Maelor.'

Since then Dr. Sommer, in a Supplement to the second volume of his great edition of the Morte Darthur, has called attention to the following passage in Bale's *Illustrium Maioris Britanniæ Scriptorum*, fol. 208 verso :—

"Thomas Mailorius, Britannus natione, heroici spiritus homo, ab ipsa adolescentia uariis animi corporisque dotibus insigniter emicuit. Est Mailoria (inquit in *Antiquarum Dictionum Syllabo* Joannes Lelandus) in finibus Cambriæ regio, Deuæ flumini uicina. Quam et alibi a fertilitate atque armorum fabrefactura commendat. Inter multi plices reipublicæ curas, non intermisit hic literarum studia, sed succisiuis horis uniuersas disparsæ uetustatis reliquias, sedulus perquisiuit. Vnde in historiarum lectione diu uersatus, ex uariis autoribus undique selegit, de fortitudine ac uictoriis inclytissimi Brytannorum regis Arthurii."

The first edition of Bale's work was published at Ipswich in 1548, while Malory's Morte Darthur was only completed by him in 1469. These dates are not so far apart that we must suppose either Bale or Leland unable to obtain reliable information concerning Malory's history and origin. Bale's statement that Malory was *Britannus natione*, that is to say, Welsh, brings with it the solution of what was my difficulty,—to wit, the relation between the name *Malory* and the dissyllabic form *Maleore;* for one can hardly help seeing that while the latter postulates the Welsh place-name Maelor, the former more naturally connects itself with the derived Latin *Mailorius.*

Thus far of Malory's name: we now come to his work, which, as already mentioned, was finished in 1469. It was, however, not printed till 1485, when its publication was undertaken by Caxton. Then followed two editions by Wynkyn de Worde in 1498 and 1529, and before the middle of the seventeenth century four more editions appeared: all these seven were in black letter. The eighteenth century appears to have been content with what the three previous ones had done for the text of Malory; but the nineteenth century had already seen it edited no less than six times, notably by Southey, Wright, Sir E. Strachey, and H. Oskar Sommer. Dr. Sommer's edition is comprised in three stately volumes, published in London by David Nutt: the first volume, consisting of the Text, appeared in 1889; then followed a volume of Introduction in 1890, and one of Studies on the Sources in 1891. This edition marks an era in the history of the Morte Darthur, seeing that special pains have been taken to make it reproduce the Caxton original, which is not known to exist in more than two copies, one of which is not quite perfect. This latter copy belongs to the Althorp Library, while the other, the perfect copy, once belonged to the Harleian Library. As regards its later history, we are told that it was purchased by the Earl of Jersey for his library at Osterley Park, and that in 1885 it became the property of a citizen of the United States, Mrs. Abby E. Pope of Brooklyn.[1] Lastly, I must add that no trace of Malory's own manuscript has ever been found.

The question of the sources of Malory's work is no new one, and it had been to some extent discussed by M. Gaston Paris and M. J. Ulrich, in the introduction to their *Merlin*, edited from a manuscript belonging to Mr. Alfred Huth, London, and published in Paris in 1888 by the *Société des anciens Textes français;* but the exhaustive treatment of the subject was reserved for Dr. Sommer, who has devoted to it his third volume. The space at my disposal will only allow of my mentioning his conclusions in the briefest manner possible. Most of Malory's originals prove to have been romances written

[1] See Sommer's *Malory*, ii. 1-3.

in French, which he, as a rule, reduced greatly in length in the process of giving the work an English garb. His sources, however, were not exclusively French; thus, for instance, he used for his fifth book of the Morte Darthur, a poem composed by the Scotch poet Huchown, which is extant in a manuscript of Thornton's in the library of Lincoln Cathedral. Here and there Malory alters the sequence of the incidents given in his originals, and in some cases he interpolates facts not contained in them, while in other instances he omits certain incidents which he did not find to his purpose; but he is rarely found to have inserted entire chapters of his own. Taking the work as a whole, Dr. Sommer has succeeded in assigning with more or less precision the originals forming the groundwork of the whole, with one remarkable exception: I allude to Malory's seventh book, which relates the adventures of Sir Gareth, the story of his first coming to Arthur's court, of his being fed for a year in the kitchen, and of his receiving the nickname of Beaumayns at the hands of Syr Kay. Dr. Sommer admits that he has failed to trace any part of the contents of this book in any of the numerous manuscripts studied by him. He is inclined to regard it as a folk-tale which had no connection with the Arthurian cycle, until Malory, or some unknown writer before him, adapted it from a French poem now lost, as he conjectures.

After this brief reference to the works used by Malory, we come to a much larger and harder question of source, namely, the origin of the whole cycle of Arthurian stories and romances. For the most fruitful speculations on this subject in our day, one has to thank Dr. Zimmer, professor of Sanskrit in the University of Greifswald.[1] He believes the romances to be based on stories of Breton rather than of Welsh origin. Briefly described, his theory[2] sets out with the facts of the permanent conquest of a considerable tract of the east of Brittany by the Normans in the first half of the tenth century, and the intimate relationship which eventually grew up between the great families of Brittany and Normandy. Now, if we suppose the Bretons in their migration from Great Britain to their new country, called after them the Lesser Britain, to have

---

[1] Later professor of Celtic at Berlin.

[2] See Zimmer's review of the thirtieth volume of the *Histoire littéraire de la France* in the *Göttingische gelehrte Anzeigen* for October 1, 1890, pp. 802–4. But M. Loth in the *Revue Celtique*, xiii. 480–503, has justly charged Zimmer with underrating the Welsh element.

carried with them the stories current about Arthur in the southern districts of this country, it may be further supposed that, ages later, those of their descendants who submitted to the Normans in the eastern portion of Brittany must have translated their popular stories about Arthur into their adopted Norman French. Thus a channel would be opened for Breton stories to reach the ears of Normans and Frenchmen. It is natural, further, to infer that, in the transition from the one language to the other, the Celtic names of most importance in the stories would inevitably undergo a considerable modification of form. This would seem to be countenanced by the circumstance, that certain of these names in the romances cannot be identified with the Welsh ones by merely allowing for the errors in copying and reading incident to the manuscripts of the time in question. Such is the fact, for example, with *Galvain, Perceval, Calibor*,[1] as compared with the Welsh *Gwalchmei, Peredur*, and *Caletvwlch*. For my own part, I have found this to be much less marked in the case, for example, of the Grail legend, the proper names in which lend themselves, on the whole, more readily to identification with their originals in Welsh. In other words, Professor Zimmer's views led me to draw the following two-fold conclusion :—(1) The older romances relating chiefly to Arthur and his Men are of Breton rather than of Welsh origin, while (2) the reverse is the case with the Grail romances. The Welsh origin of the Grail legend has been discussed by me elsewhere,[2] so that I think it needless to endeavour to prove it here. But as to the alleged Breton origin of the romances about Arthur, it is to be observed that if the picture presented in them of Arthur and his Men be mainly Breton, one may expect to find those warriors represented differently in Welsh literature, especially such Welsh literature as one finds to be fairly free from the influence of the romances when they reached the Welsh. So one could, perhaps, not do better than devote the rest of this introduction to a review of the more important passages concerning Arthur in manuscripts which have come down to us from Welsh sources. I have, however, to confess at the outset that those of them which happen to be in Welsh, as most of them are, prove to be couched in very obscure language, so that my rendering must be regarded as only tentative.

[1] See Zimmer's review, *ibid.* p. 830.
[2] See my *Arthurian Legend*, pp. 300–27.

The first passage to demand attention is written in Latin, for it occurs in the *Historia Brittonum* with which the name of Nennius is associated. The year of the composition of the *Historia Brittonum* was, according to M. A. de la Borderie, no other than A.D. 822,[1] and the words relating to Arthur read as follows [2] :—

In illo tempore Saxones invalescebant in multitudine, et crescebant in Britannia. Mortuo autem Hengisto, Octha ejus filius transivit de sinistrali parte Brittanniæ ad regnum Cantiorum, et de ipso orti sunt reges Cantiorum. Tunc Arthur pugnabat contra illos in illis diebus cum regibus Brittonum, sed ipse dux erat bellorum. Primum bellum fuit in ostium fluminis quod dicitur Glein ; secundum, et tertium, et quartum, et quintum, super aliud flumen, quod dicitur Dubglas, et est in regione Linnuis. Sextum bellum super flumen quod vocatur Bassas. Septimum fuit bellum in Silva Celidonis, id est, Cat Coit Celidon. Octavum fuit bellum in castello Guinnion, in quo Arthur portavit imaginem Sanctæ Mariæ perpetuæ virginis super humeros suos, et pagani versi sunt in fugam in illo die, et cædes magna fuit super illos per virtutem Domini nostri Jesu Christi, et per virtutem Sanctæ Mariæ virginis genetricis ejus. Nonum bellum gestum est in Urbe Legionis. Decimum gessit bellum in littore fluminis, quod vocatur Tribruit. Undecimum factum est bellum in monte, qui dicitur Agned. Duodecimum fuit bellum in monte Badonis, in quo corruerunt in uno die nongenti sexaginta viri de uno impetu Arthur ; et nemo prostravit eos nisi ipse solus, et in omnibus bellis victor exstitit. Et ipsi, dum in omnibus bellis prosternebantur, auxilium a Germania petebant, et augebantur multipliciter sine intermissione, et reges a Germania deducebant, ut regnarent super illos in Brittannia, usque ad tempus quo Ida regnavit, qui fuit Eobba filius, ipse fuit primus rex in Beornicia, id est, in Berneich.

As regards a historical Arthur, the words here cited are very suggestive, for without explicitly saying that Arthur was one of the kings of the Brythons, they make him the general or *dux bellorum*, in whom one readily recognises the superior officer, known in the time of Roman rule as the *Comes Britanniæ*. This office, it may be presumed, was continued after the Roman forces left, with the only difference that the

[1] See *l'Historia Britonum attribuée a Nennius et l'Historia Britannica avant Geoffroi de Monmouth, par Arthur de la Borderie* (Paris and London, 1883), p. 20. Since the above was written Zimmer's work entitled *Nennius Vindicatus* (Berlin, 1893) has reached me, and in it he gives it as his conclusion, p. 82, that the *Historia Brittonum* was put together as early as the year 796.

[2] *Nennii Historia Britonum ad fidem codicum manuscriptorum recensuit Josephus Stevenson* (London, 1838), pp. 47-9.

man filling it would be himself supreme, having no longer any lord, such as the Roman emperor, over him. This position seems to have been Arthur's, and one has accordingly no difficulty in understanding how he came to fight battles at places so far apart from one another. For, though the majority of the twelve battles were fought in what we now call the North of England or the South of Scotland, some of them undoubtedly took place in the south of the Island, such as the battle of *Urbs Legionis*, which must have been either Chester on the Dee or Caerleon on the Usk; and still farther south must have been that of *Mons Badonis*. In a word, Arthur moved about in Britain just as Agricola or Severus would have done, and without necessarily being one of the kings of the Brythons, he would seem to have been over and above them. This must have been a position which would in time cause all kinds of heroic legends to be associated with the name of the man filling it. Add to this the numerous opportunities for the display of valour on behalf of a bleeding country provided by the invasions of Germanic tribes from the Continent, and by the incursions of Picts and Scots from the outlying portions of the British Isles, and we have the full explanation of no inconsiderable part of the wondrous fame of Arthur and his Men in subsequent ages.

The next references to Arthur, which deserve to be mentioned, occur in the *Annales Cambriæ*, the oldest existing manuscript of which was completed in 954 or 955.[1] The first entry occurs under the year 516, and reads as follows :—

Bellum Badonis in quo Arthur portauit crucem domini nostri Ihesu Christi tribus diebus et tribus noctibus in humeros suos et Brittones uictores fuerunt.

The next entry in point comes under the year 537, and runs thus[2]—

Gueith cam lann [i.e., *the Battle of Camlan*] *in qua Arthur et Medraut corruerunt. et mortalitas in Brittannia et in Hibernia fuit.*

The *Bellum Badonis* of the *Annales Cambriæ* is the same battle undoubtedly as Nennius' *bellum in Monte Badonis*. But the statement as to Arthur carrying the cross of Christ on his shoulders has been surmised to be a mistranslation of Welsh words representing him carrying a figure of the cross in his shield ; since the Welsh for shoulder would have been written

[1] See Phillimore's edition in the *Cymmrodor*, vol. ix. p. 144.
[2] *Ibid.* p. 154.

iscuit or *iscuid* which would also be spellings of the word for a shield.[1] This seems to shew that 'there was a Welsh tradition as to Arthur's personal appearance at one of his great battles. The other entry is remarkable as representing the death of Arthur and Medraut or Medrod (the Modred and Mordred of the romances) as an ordinary event of war.

The next two passages to be cited occur in the *Mirabilia* usually associated with the *Historia Brittonum;* and most of them are probably to be referred to the same date as the *Historia* itself.[2] The words in point read as follows:—

Est aliud miraculum in regione quæ dicitur Buelt. Est ibi cumulus lapidum, et unus lapis superpositus super congestum, cum vestigio canis in eo. Quando venatus est porcum Troit,[3] impressit Cabal, qui erat canis Arthuri militis, vestigium in lapide, et Arthur postea congregavit congestum lapidum sub lapide in quo erat vestigium canis sui, et vocatur Carn Cabal. Et veniunt homines et tollunt lapidem in manibus suis per spacium diei et noctis, et in crastino die invenitur super congestum suum.

Est aliud miraculum in regione quæ vocatur Ercing. Habetur ibi sepulchrum juxta fontem qui cognominatur Licat Amir, et viri nomen, qui sepultus est in tumulo, sic vocabatur. Amir[4] filius Arthuri militis erat, et ipse occidit eum ibidem, et sepelivit. Et veniunt homines ad mensurandum tumulum ; in longitudine aliquando sex pedes, aliquando novem, aliquando quindecim. In qua mensura metieris eum in ista vice, iterum non invenies eum in una mensura ; et ego solus probavi.

The *Porcus Troit* occupies a great place, as *Twrch Trwyth*, in the story of Kulhwch and Olwen, where *Cabal*[5] also occurs in its ordinary Welsh form of *Cavall;* but the lesson these two

---

[1] In later Welsh the words are *ysgwydd*, "a shoulder," and *ysgwyd*, "a shield."

[2] This is Zimmer's view in his *Nennius Vindicatus*, p. 115.

[3] Stevenson seems to have found two readings of this word, namely, *Troit* and *Troynt*, and he selected for his text the latter, which is gibberish : see his *Nennius*, p. 60. In Welsh literature the word has the two forms *Trwyd* and *Trwyth*.

[4] The same manuscript E, which reads *Troit*, and is supposed by Stevenson to have been written about the beginning of the thirteenth century, reads here *amirmur;* but, as was to be expected, he inserted in his text a *vox nihili*, namely *Anir: Amirmur=Amir mur* "the Great Amir," and in the Liber Landavensis, *Amir* is written *Amyr;* but a man's name *Amhyr* occurs also in that manuscript, while the name of Arthur's son in question is given as *Amhar* in the Welsh romance of *Gereint and Enid:* I do not recollect meeting with it elsewhere.

[5] It is to be noticed that *Cabal* with its *b* and single *l* belongs to the same school of orthography as the ninth century triplets beginning with *Noigrucosam:* see Skene's *Four anc. Books of Wales*, ii. 2.

passages in common teach us is, that at a comparatively early date Arthurian names had begun to figure in the topography of Wales.

Attention is next claimed by some of the references to Arthur in Welsh literature, and here the Black Book of Carmarthen is entitled to the first place. The manuscript may be supposed to have been written in the reigns of Stephen, Henry II., and Richard.[1] One of the allusions to Arthur in this manuscript consists of a triplet occurring in the Stanzas of the Graves, apprising the reader of the futility of looking for Arthur's grave, as follows[2] :—

> *Bet y march. bet y guythur.*
> *bet y gugaun cletyfrut.*
> *anoeth bid bet y arthur.*

A grave for March, a grave for Gwythur,
A grave for Gwgawn of the ruddy Sword,
Not wise (the thought) a grave for Arthur.[3]

It might be objected that these lines are of no value here, as the idea suggested by them might have been derived from the romances which represent Arthur departing to the Isle of Avallon to be healed of his wounds, and not dying at all. But it may as reasonably be regarded as an expression of the native belief fixed in various localities, that Arthur and his knights were slumbering in a cave awaiting the destined hour of their return. This prevailed among Arthur's countrymen from Cadbury to the Eildon Hills, and has never been more charmingly sung than by the poet Leyden, when he speaks of the enchanted sleep to be broken at length by somebody

" That bids the charmëd sleep of ages fly,
Rolls the long sound through Eildon's caverns vast,
While each dark warrior rouses at the blast,
His horn, his falchion, grasps with mighty hand,
And peals proud Arthur's march from Fairyland."

The time likewise is not long past when the shepherds of North Wales used to entertain one another with stories describing one

[1] See Mr. J. G. Evans' preface (p. xvi.) to his Autotype Facsimile of the Black Book, Oxford, 1888.

[2] *Ibid.* fol. 34ᵃ.

[3] I believe that such is the sense of the third line of the triplet, but I cannot attain to any certainty approaching the assurance with which Prof. Zimmer categorically declares that, "sie sagt bloss aus, dass man Arthur's Grab nicht kenne":—see the *Zeitschrift für französische Sprache und Litteratur*, xij. 238.

of their number finding his way to the presence of Arthur and his Men, all asleep in a Snowdonian cave resplendent with untold wealth of gold and other treasure : the armed sleepers were believed to be merely awaiting the signal for their return to take an active part in the affairs of this world. In South Wales an elaborate but popular story lodges Arthur and his Knights in a cave at Craig y Ddinas, in Glamorgan,[1] while the peasanty of South Cardiganshire, relating the same story, locate it elsewhere, and call the sleeping hero not Arthur but Owen,[2] a name the memory of which used to be kept fresh by ballad singers, who made country fairs ring with such strains as the following :—

> *Yr Owen hwn yw Harri 'r Nawfed,*
> *Sydd yn trigo ngwlad estronied.*

> This Owen is Henry the Ninth,
> Who lives in the land of strangers.

The Owen of the Cardiganshire legend is known as Owen Lawgoch or Owen of the Red Hand, and he is represented as a man of seven feet in stature with a right hand which was all red. The whole story reminds one of him of the red beard, Frederic Barbarossa. I mention this lest anyone should suppose such stories had anything originally to do with the historical Arthur. Some light is shed on their genesis by a passage in the writings of an ancient author who lived in the first century of our era, namely Plutarch. In his work *De Defectu Oraculorum*, xviij., he uses words to the following effect[3]—the Italics are mine :—

"Demetrius further said, that of the islands around Britain many lie scattered about uninhabited, of which some are named after deities and heroes. He told us also, that, being sent by the emperor with the object of reconnoitring and inspecting, he went to the island which lay nearest to those uninhabited, and found it occupied by few inhabitants, who were, however, sacrosanct and inviolable in the eyes of the Britons. Soon after his arrival a great disturbance of the atmosphere took place, accompanied by many portents, by the winds bursting forth into hurricanes, and by fiery bolts falling. When it was over, the

---

[1] The story is given in the *Brython* for 1858, p. 162.

[2] *Ibid.* p. 179. The editor, who was, I believe, no other than the Rev. Canon Silvan Evans, adds in a note that this sort of story might be found current also in Cumberland.

[3] For the original see the Didot edition of Plutarch, vol. iii. p. 511 (*De Defectu Oraculorum*, xviij.) ; it is also to be found printed in my *Arthurian legend*, p. 367.

islanders said that some of the mighty had passed away. For as a lamp on being lit, they said, brings with it no danger, while on being extinguished it is grievous to many, just so with regard to great souls, their beginning to shine forth is pleasant and the reverse of grievous, whereas the extinction and destruction of them frequently disturb the winds and the surge as at present ; oftentimes also do they infect the atmosphere with pestilential diseases. Moreover, there is there, they said, an island in which Cronus is imprisoned, with Briareus keeping guard over him as he sleeps ; for, as they put it, sleep is the bond forged for Cronus. *They add that around him are many deities, his henchmen and attendants.*"

To return to the Black Book, I may mention that another of the Stanzas of the Graves is worth citing here, though it does not name Arthur. It alludes, however, to Camlan, the Camelot of Malory and the romances, and that in the same strain of apparently historical definiteness as the entry in the *Annales Cambriæ* cited as mentioning Camlan. The lines in question run thus [1]—

> *Bet mab osvran yg camlan.*
> *gvydi llauer kywlavan.*
> *Bet bedwir in alld tryvan.*

> Osvran's son's grave (is) at Camlan,
> After many a slaughter,
> Bedwyr's grave (is) in Allt Tryvan. [2]

We next come to a poem headed *Gereint filius Erbin*, which describes a battle at a place called Llongborth. Gereint is the poet's hero, but he introduces Arthur as Gereint's superior and lord, as follows [3] :—

> *En llogporth y gueleise. y arthur*
> *guir deur kymynint a dur.*
> *ameraudur* [4] *llywiaudir llawur.*

> At Llongborth saw I of Arthur's
> Brave men hewing with steel,
> (Men of the) emperor,[4] director of toil.

---

[1] Evans' Facsimile, fol. 32[b].

[2] There are several mountain tops in the Snowdon district called *y Tryfan*, "the Tryvan," and *Moel Tryfan*, "the round-topped hill of Tryvan." Lady Charlotte Guest (*Mabinogion*, ii. 167) has been misled by somebody to indulge in the impossible spelling *Trivaen*.

[3] Evans' Facsimile, fol. 36[b].

[4] I am not certain what documents exactly Prof. Zimmer had in view when he wrote as to Arthur, "Nirgends führt er den Titel *amherawdyr*" ; or whether he would regard *ameraudur* here as a title or not : see the *Gött. gel. Anz.* for 1890, p. 524.

En llogporth y llas y gereint.
guir deur o odir diwneint.
a chin rillethid ve. llatysseint.

At Llongborth there fell of Gereint's
Brave men from the border of Devon,
And ere they were slain they slew.

In these triplets the position of Arthur seems to be very
clearly indicated : the men fighting on his side are Gereint's
men from Devon. That is to say, Arthur is Gereint's superior :
he fills in fact the rôle assigned him in the *Historia Brittonum*
when he is there termed a *Dux Bellorum*. This raises the
question of Arthur's title ; for passing on from the description
of him as a *Dux Bellorum*, we have him twice in the *Mirabilia*
called *Arthur Miles*. Further the *Vita Gildæ*, sometimes
ascribed to the twelfth century author, Caradoc of Llancarvan,
in giving the story of the carrying away of Guenever by
Melwas,[1] speaks of the latter as *rex*, or king, reigning over
the *Æstiva Regio* or Somerset, while it styles Arthur a
tyrannus. To this must be added the fact that in the story
of Kulhwch and Olwen the hero salutes Arthur as *Penteyrned
yr Ynys honn*, or "the Head of the Princes of this Island," and
one should notice that, in common with all these, the passage
last cited from the Black Book avoids calling Arthur a king.
On the other hand the word *ameraudur* which it applies
to Arthur is one of the forms given in Welsh to the
Latin word *imperator* borrowed ; but as it is used of him
commonly in the stories of Peredur, Owein, Gereint and others
which betray the influence of the French romances, it might
perhaps be supposed that its presence in Gereint's Elegy was
due to that influence. There is, however, no evidence, and the
way in which the word is used rather inclines me to regard it
as spontaneous on the part of the poet : I am only doubtful
whether instead of rendering, as I have done, " emperor,
director of toil," it would not have been more correct to write
" commander, director of toil " : that is to say, to suppose the
word to retain here the meaning which it had primarily in
Latin. In any case, the instances which have been adduced
will suffice, it seems to me, to shew that it was not due to
accident that other terms than that of king were thought more
suitable in speaking of Arthur. In that fact one seems to trace

[1] For the text of that story, see San-Marte's *Nennius et Gildas*, pp. 122,
3, also the *Romania*, vol. x. 491, where it is given by M. Gaston Paris.

one of the logical consequences of Arthur's having, as I have ventured to suppose, occupied the historical position of the *Comes Britanniæ*, in other words that of the *Imperator* himself, which it became when Britain ceased to form a part of the dominions of Rome.

We next have a poem consisting of a dialogue between Arthur and Glewlwyd Gavaelvawr, who in the Welsh stories about Arthur is represented as one of his chief porters; but here he seems to have a castle of his own, the gates of which he appears in no hurry to open for Arthur and his companions. He asks Arthur who he is and what followers he has, which Arthur is made to seize as an opportunity for describing some of them, especially Kei, Malory's Sir Kay the seneschal. Unfortunately, the poem is so obscure that I can only guess its meaning, as follows [1]:—

Pa gur yv y porthaur.	Who is the porter?
Gleuluid gauaeluaur.	Glewlwyd Gavaelvawr.
Pa gur ae gouin.	Who asks the question?
arthur. a chei guin. [2]	Arthur and worthy Kei.
Pa imda genhid.	What following (?) hast thou?
Guir goreu im bid.	The best of men are mine.
Ym ty ny doi.	To my house thou shalt not come
onys guaredi.	Unless thou plead (?) for them.
Mi ae guar[e]di.	I will plead (?) for them.
athi ae gueli.	And thou shalt see them :—
Vythneint elei.	Wythneint of Elei,
Assivyon ell tri.	And the wise men three—
Mabon am mydron.	Mabon son of Modron,
guas uthir pen dragon.	(Uther Pendragon's man)
Kysceint · mab · Banon.	Kyscaint son of Banon,
A guin godybrion.	And Gwyn Godyvrion.
Oet rinn vy gueisson	Sturdy would be my men
in amuin ev detvon.	In defence of their laws—
Manawidan ab llyr.	Manawydan son of Llyr,
oet duis y cusil.	Profound in counsel;

[1] Evans' Facsimile, fol. 47ᵇ—48ᵇ.

[2] *Guin*, now written *gwyn* means as a colour adjective *white*, but it is a very difficult word to render, one of its uses being somewhat like that of French *beau* in *beau pere*. On the banks of the Dovey in Mid-Wales a stepfather is respectfully called *tad gwyn*, literally " white father," and I surmise that it had a somewhat similar force here. It is to be borne in mind that Kei is, so far as I can remember, elsewhere called *Kei guin* only in the story of Kulhwch. See *Red Book Mabinogion*, p. 105, and for further remarks on *gwyn* see my *Hibbert Lectures*, pp. 527-8.

Neustuc manauid	(Manawyd brought home
eis tull o trywruid	A pierced buckler from Tryvrwyd).
A mabon am melld.	And Mabon son of Mellt
maglei guaed ar guelld.	Who stained the grass with gore ;
Ac anguas edeinauc.	And Angwas the Winged,
a lluch · llauynnauc.	And Llwch Llawynnawc,
Oetin diffreidauc	Who were protective
ar eidin cyminauc	Against Eidyn[1] the gashing.
Argluit ae llochei	His lord would shelter him,
my nei ymtiwygei	My nephew would amend (?),
Kei ae heiriolei.	Kei would plead for (?) them,
trae llathei pop tri	While slaying them three at a time.
Pan colled kelli.	When Kelli was lost
caffad cuelli.	Savagery was experienced.
Aseirolei kei	Kei would plead for them (?)
hid trae kymynhei.	Until he might hew them down.
Arthur ced huarhei	Though Arthur was playing
y guaed gouerei.	The blood was dripping.
In neuat awarnach	In Awarnach's hall
in imlat ew a gurach.	A-fighting with a hag,
Ew a guant pen palach.	He slew Pen-palach
in atodeu dissethach.	In the tasks (?) of Dissethach.
Ym minit eidin	On Eidyn's mountain
amuc · a · chinbin.	He combated with champions (?),
Pop cant id cuitin.	By the hundred they fell—
id cuitin · pop cant.	They fell a hundred at a time
rac beduir bedrydant.	Before Bedwyr . . .
Ar traethev trywruid.	On the shores of Tryvrwyd ;
in amuin a garvluid.	Combating with Garwlwyd.
Oet guythir y annuyd.	Victorious was his wrath
o cletyw ac yscuid.	Both with sword and shield.
Oet guaget bragad	It were vain to boast
vrth kei ig kad.	Against Kei in battle.
Oet cletyw ighad.	His sword in battle was
oe lav diguistlad.	Not to be pledged from his hand.
Oet hyneiw guastad	He was an equable lord
ar lleg ar lles gulad.	Of a legion for the state's good.
Beduir · A Bridlav.[2]	Bedwyr son of Bridlaw,
Nau cant guarandau.	Nine hundred to watch,

---

[1] Mention is made of this man in Triads i. 38, 39 ; iii. 47, 48 (*Myv. Arch.* vol. ii. 9, 65), where he is described as the slayer of the bard Aneurin.

[2] This should probably give the parentage of Bedwyr, and it is natural to suggest as an emendation *Beduir ab Bridlav ;* but in *Gereint and Enid* he is described as son of *Bedrawt:* see *Red Book Mab.* p. 265.

chuechant y eirthau.	Six hundred to attack
a talei y ortinav.	Was his onslaught (?) wo.th.
Gueisson am buyint	The young men I have—
oet guell ban uitint.	It is well where they are
rac rieu emreis.	Before the kings of Emrys
gueleise · kei ar uris.	Have I seen Kei in haste.
Preitev gorthowis.	Leader of the harryings,
oet gur hir in ewnis.	Long would he be in his wrath ;
Oet trum y dial.	Heavy was he in his vengeance ;
oet tost y cynial.	Terrible in his fighting.
Pan yuei o wual	When from a horn he drank
yuei urth peduar	He drank as much as four men ;
ygkad pan delhei.	When he came into battle
vrth cant id lathei.	He slew as would a hundred.
Ny bei duv ae digonhei.	Unless it should be God's act [1]
Oet diheit aghev kei.	Kei's death would be unachieved.
Kei guin a llachev.	Worthy Kei and Llacheu
digonint we kadev.	Used to fight battles,
kin gloes glas verev.	Before the pang of livid spears,
yguarthaw ystawingun.	On the top of Ystavingun
kei a guant nav guiton.	Kei slew nine witches. [2]
Kei win aaeth von	Worthy Kei went to Mona
y dilein lleuon.	To destroy lions.
y iscuid oet mynul	His shield was small
erbin cath paluc.	Against Palug's Cat.
Pan gogiueirch tud.	When people shall ask
Puy guant cath paluc.	"Who slew Palug's Cat?"
Nau ugein kinlluc.	Nine score . . .
a cuytei in y buyd.	Used to fall for her food
Nau ugein kinran	Nine score leaders
A . . .	Used to . . .

The manuscript is imperfect, and it breaks off just where one should have heard more about Cath Paluc, or "Palug's Cat," a monster, said in the Red Book Triads to have been reared by

[1] With this sentiment compare the following passage put into the mouth of Llew in the Mabinogi of Math son of Mathonwy : *Onym llad i duw hagen nyt hawd vy llad i.* "Unless God slay me, however, it is not easy to slay me." See the *Red Book Mabinogion*, p. 75, also Lady Charlotte Guest's *Mab.* iii. 242, where she imparts to her translation a Christian tone not to be detected in the original, thus : "But until Heaven take me I shall not easily be slain."

[2] This looks as if it might be the incident in which the story of Peredur makes that hero take a leading part; he encounters the witches of Caer Loyw at a castle on a mountain, and he together with Arthur and his Men afterwards kills them all at the end of the story : see the *Red Book Mab.*, pp. 210-1, 242-3, and Guest's *Mab.* i. 322-3, 369-70.

the Sons of Palug, in Anglesey. The contests here mentioned with monsters, hags and witches, form also a feature of the story of *Kulhwch and Olwen,* not to mention Irish stories, such as that of *Bricriu's Feast,*[1] which abound in them. Moreover, the majority of Arthur's followers in the Black Book poem, figure as such in the Kulhwch also, namely Glewlwyd, Kei, Mabon son of Modron, Gwyn Godyvron, Mabon son of Mellt, Angwas Edeinawc, Llwch Llawyniawc, Bedwyr, and Arthur's son Llacheu; not to mention Manawyddan, who is forced into Arthur's train in both poem and story. On the other hand, only two of Arthur's men enumerated in the former, evade identification elsewhere, namely, Wythneint and Kysceint.[2] Perhaps the most remarkable thing in the Black Book poem, is the position which it assigns to Kei, who there towers far above all the rest of the Arthurian train: he is, in fact, not to be conquered by man or beast, so that his death could only be attributed to the direct interference of the Almighty. The next in importance to Kei was Bedwyr, the Bedewere or Bedyuere of Malory's Morte Darthur, and the positions of both heroes are relatively the same in the Kulhwch story.

Another allusion to Arthur occurs in the Black Book, to wit in an elegy to Madog son of Meredydd, prince of Powys, who died in the year 1159. The poem is ascribed to Madog's contemporary, the well-known Welsh poet Cynddelw, who, in alluding to the mourning and grief among Madog's men, characterises the uproar as being—*Mal gavr toryw teulu arthur.*[3]

"Like the shout of the multitude of Arthur's host."

This leads, however, to no inference of any importance in this context. The same remark may be made concerning a mention of Arthur in a poem called *Gorchan Maelderw* in the Book of Aneurin, a manuscript of the latter part of the thirteenth or of the beginning of the fourteenth century: the passage is unfortunately obscure.[4]

[1] The Irish text is given at length in Windisch's *Irische Texte,* pp. 254–303.
[2] *Kysceint* is probably a miscopying of *Kysteint,* the Welsh form of *Constantius;* a name *Wytheint* appears in the Book of Taliessin, as that of one who fights with Gwydion son of Dôn, see Skene's *Four anc. Books of Wales,* ii. 158.
[3] Evans' Facsimile, fol. 52ᵃ.
[4] For the text see Skene's *Four anc. Books of Wales,* vol. ii. 106, and for the translation vol. i. 426. Both will also be found in Thomas

The next manuscript to be mentioned is one of approximately the same data as the last-mentioned : I allude to the Book of Taliessin, where an obscure poem occurs, headed *Kat Godeu*. There, near the end, we have the following couplet :—

derwydon doethur.	Druids erudite,
darogenwch y Arthur.	Prophesy for Arthur.

Another allusion to Arthur in the Book of Taliessin runs thus [1] :—

heilyn pascadur.	Heilyn of the Passover
treded dofyn doethur	One of three deeply wise
y vendigaw Arthur.	To bless Arthur.
Arthur vendigan	Arthur they will bless
ar gerd gyfaenat	In elaborate song.

Who the Heilyn mentioned here was does not appear, but he may be supposed to have been a priest or a bard.

Other references to Arthur occur in the Book of Taliessin, but the most important by far is the poem known as *Preiddeu Annwfn*, or the Harryings of Hades, which I subjoin, so far as it is in point, with an attempt to translate into English, as follows :—

> *Golychaf wledic pendeuic gwlat ri.*
> *py ledas y pennaeth dros traeth mundi.*
> *bu kyweir karchar gweir ygkaer sidi.*
> *trwy ebostol pwyll aphryderi.*
> *Neb kyn noc ef nyt aeth idi*
> *yr gadwyn tromlas kywirwas ae ketwi.*
> *A rac preideu annwfyn tost yt geni.*
> *Ac yt urawt parahawt yn bard wedi.*
> *Tri lloneit prytwen yd aetham ni idi.*
> *nam seith ny dyrreith o gaer sidi.*

I adore the noble prince and high king
Who extended his sway over the world's strand.
Perfect was the captivity of Gwair in Caer Sidi,
Through the warning [2] of Pwyll and Pryderi.

Stephens' *Gododin*, pp. 352–3 ; but I am convinced that the meaning of the words still remains to be discovered.

[1] See Skene, ii. 456: vol. i. 259, gives a translation differing considerably from the one proposed here with great diffidence.

[2] As to this meaning of the word *ebostol*, see *Llyvyr Agkyr Llandewivrevi* (in the *Anecdota Oxoniensia*), p. 159. It is *epistola* borrowed and sometimes confounded with *abostol* from *apostolus:* the sequence of meanings seems to have been a letter, a message or admonition by letter, a warning. See a note on the word by Prof. Powel in the *Cymmrodor*, ix. 199.

Before him no one entered into it,
Into the heavy dark chain a trusty youth guarded ;
And at the harryings of Hades grievously did he sing,
And till doom will he remain a bard afterwards.
Three freights of Prydwen went we into it—
Seven alone did we return from Caer Sidi.

> Neut wyf glot geinmyn cerd o chlywir.
> ygkaer pedryuan pedyr y chwelyt.
> vgkynneir or peir pan leferit.
> Oanadyl naw morwyn gochyneuit.
> Neu peir pen annwfyn pwy y vynut.
> gwrym am yoror a mererit.
> ny beirw bwyt llwfyr ny rytyghit.
> cledyf lluch lleawc idaw rydyrchit.
> Ac yn llaw leminawc yd edewit.
> Arac drws porth vffern llugyrn lloscit.
> Aphan aetham ni gan arthur trafferth lethrit.
> namyn seith ny dyrreith o gaer vedwit.

I am a seeker (?) of praise, if (my) song be heard :
In Caer Pedryvan . . .
. . . from the cauldron it would be spoken
By the breath of nine maidens it would be kindled.
The head of Hades' cauldron—what is it like ?
A rim it has, with pearls, round its border :
It boils not a coward's food : it would not be perjured.
The sword of Llwch Lleawc would be lifted to it.
And in the hand of Lleminawc was it left.
And before the door of Hell's gate lamps were burning,
And when we accompanied Arthur, a brilliant effort,
Seven alone did we return from Caer Veddwit.

> Neut wyf glot geinmyn kerd glywanawr.
> ygkaer Pedryfan ynys pybyrdor.
> echwyd amuchyd kymysgetor
> gwin gloyw eu gwirawt rac eu gorgord.
> Tri lloneit prytwen yd aetham ni ar vor.
> namyn seith ny dyrreith o gear rigor.

I am a seeker (?) of praise, (my) song being (?) heard :
At Caer Pedryvan in Quick-door Island,
At dusk and in the blackness (of night) they mix
The sparkling wine, their drink before their retinue.
Three freights of Prydwen went we on sea :
Seven alone did we return from Caer Rigor.

> Ny obrynafi lawyr llen llywyadu†
> tra chaer wydyr ny welsynt wrhyt arthur.

Tri vgeint canhwr a seui arymur.
oed anhawd ymadrawd ae gwylyadur.
tri lloneit prytwen yd aeth gan arthur.
namyn seith ny dyrreith o gaer golud.

I merit not the laurel of the ruler of letters—
Beyond the Glass Fort they had not seen Arthur's valour.
Three score hundreds stood on the wall:
Hard it was found to converse with their sentinel.
Three freights of Prydwen (were they that) went with Arthur,
Seven alone did they return from Caer Goludd.

Ny obrynaf y lawyr llaes eu kylchwy.
ny wdant wy py dyd peridyd pwy.
py awr ymeindyd y ganet cwy.
Pwy gwnaeth arnyt aeth doleu defwy.
Ny wdant wy yr ych brych bras ypenrwy.
Seith vgein kygwng yny aerwy.
A phan aetham ni gan arthur aurydol gofwy.
namyn seith ny dyrreith o gaer vandwy.

I merit not the laurel of them of the long shields (?):
They know not which is the ruler's day (or) who (he is),
At what hour of early day he was born (or) where (?),
Who made . . . went not . . .
They know not the Speckled Ox with the stout halter,
With seven score joints in his collar.
When we went with Arthur, anxious visit,
Seven alone did we return from Caer Vanddwy.

Ny obrynafy lawyr llaes eu gohen
ny wdant py dyd peridyd pen.
Py awr ymeindyd y ganet perchen.
Py vil a gatwant aryant y pen.
pan aetham ni gan arthur afyrdwl gynhen
namyn seith ny dyrreith a gaer ochren.

I merit not the laurel of those of long . . .
They know not which is the day of the ruler (and) chief,
At what hour of early day was born the owner,
(Or) what myriad guards the silver of the head.
When we went with Arthur, anxious contest,
Seven alone did we return from Caer Ochren.

Of the eight castles or strongholds mentioned in this poem not a single one has been identified with any real place, and the Isle of the Active Door belongs probably to the same sort of geography as *Annwvyn* or Hades, and *Uffern* or Hell. The poem evidently deals with expeditions conducted by Arthur by sea to the realms of twilight and darkness; but the one in quest of the cauldron of the Head of Hades reminds me of that described in the Kulhwch as having for its object the cauldron of Diwrnach the Goidel: Arthur sets out with a small number of men on board his ship Prydwen, and after severe fighting brought away the cauldron full of the money of the country, which was, however, according to the Kulhwch, not Hades but Ireland. But with this difference the stories agree, not to mention that *yr Ych Brych*, or "the Speckled Ox," of the poem figures also in the Kulhwch. To do justice to this part of the comparison, and to complete the outline which I have suggested, I should have here to append at length the story of Kulhwch; but as that is out of the question, I will only add that a translation of it into English will be found in the second volume of Lady Charlotte Guest's *Mabinogion*. The *Kulhwch* is contained in the Jesus College manuscript, the *Red Book of Hergest*, which belongs to the latter half of the fourteenth century; but the present version carries with it some evidence that it was copied from a manuscript written in the Kymric hand usual in Wales before the Norman Conquest and its influences had introduced another hand. On the whole, one cannot go far wrong in supposing that it was composed in the tenth century; and as to its contents, it has been pronounced purely [1] Kymric by Professor Zimmer,—that is to say, as contrasted with stories in which the influence of the romances cannot, as he thinks, be mistaken.

It is not to be supposed, however, that other manuscripts, whether belonging to the same period as that of the Kulhwch or to later dates, relate nothing concerning Arthur but the echo of incidents occurring in the French romances. Instances could readily be cited to the contrary: take for example the episode in which the Welsh Triads [2] bring Arthur in contact with Drystan the *gal-ofydd* or "war-leader" of March and the lover of Essyllt, that is to say, Malory's *Tristram, kynge Mark*, and *Isoud* respectively. Drystan is represented sending March's swineherd on an errand to Essyllt, Drystan in the meantime taking upon himself the charge of the swine. The story then makes Arthur, assisted by March, Kei and Bedwyr, attempt to get possession of some of the swine by every means in their

---

[1] In the *Göttingische gel. Anzeigen* for June 10, 1890, pp. 517, 523-4.
[2] Triads i. 30, ii. 56, iii, 101 : see the *Myv. Arch.*, vol. ii. pp. 6, 20, 72-3.

power, but all in vain, so that Drystan came to be styled one of "the Three stout Swineherds of the Isle of Britain." Or take another instance, namely the statement that Arthur had not one wife Gwenhwyvar, Malory's Guenever, but three wives in succession, all called Gwenhwyvar. This strange piece of information likewise comes from the Triads,[1] and I should be surprised to learn that it found its way into them from the French romances rather than from some far older source.

Speaking generally of the Arthur of Welsh literature, one may characterise him in few words :—His first appearance is found to conform itself with the rôle of a *Comes Britanniæ*, on whom it devolved to help the inhabitants of what was once Roman Britain against invasion and insult, whether at the hands of Angles and Saxons or of Picts and Scots : so we read of him acting for the kings of the Brythons as their *dux bellorum*. We next find his fame re-echoed by the topography of the country once under his protection, and his name gather-ing round it the legends of heroes and divinities of a past of indefinite extent. In other words, he and his men, especially Kei and Bedwyr, are represented undertaking perilous expedi-tions to realms of mythic obscurity, bringing home treasures, fighting with hags and witches, despatching giants, and destroy-ing monsters. How greatly this rude delineation of the triumph of man over violence and brute force differs from the more finished picture of the Arthur of Malory's painting, it would be needless to try to shew to any one bent on the pleasure of perusing the Morte Darthur. Such a reader may be trusted to pursue the comparison unassisted, in the fascinating pages of this incomparable book.

JOHN RHYS.

[1] Triad i. 59, ii. 16, iii. 109 : see the *Myv. Arch.*, vol. ii. pp. 12, 14, 73.

SELECT BIBLIOGRAPHY

The more important editions of the *Morte d'Arthur* have already been mentioned in the foregoing introduction (see p. vi). But since Sir John Rhys wrote it many popular reprints and volumes of selections and adaptations from Malory's romance have appeared. The best companion romance-book is *The Mabinogion*, No. 97 in Everyman's Library, translated by Thomas Jones and Gwyn Jones, 1949, to replace the version mentioned on p. xxiii *ante*. The most significant single fact in Malorian studies since *Le Morte d'Arthur* came out in Everyman was the discovery in 1934, in the library of Winchester College, Oxford, of a manuscript copy of the work; a "fair copy," by two different hands, neither of them the compiler (or translator), which nevertheless serves to explain certain discrepances between the text of Caxton's edition and the French and English poems which are its not distant source. E. Vinaver's *Malory's "Morte Darthur" in the Light of a recent Discovery*, 1935, will be found to contain most of the critical deductions that can be drawn from this find; he also wrote *Malory*, 1929, and *A Note on the Earliest Printed Editions of Malory's "Morte Darthur,"* 1939. On the question of the "author's" identity, consult G. L. Kittredge: *Sir Thomas Malory*, 1925, or Edward Hicks: *Sir Thomas Malory, his Turbulent Career*, 1926. There is also a biographical study by Sir E. K. Chambers, 1922, and by the same author a book on the Arthurian legend generally, called *Arthur of Britain*, 1927; on this subject see also W. J. C. Reid's *The Arthurian Legend*, 1938. As to the question of the historicity of Arthur, modern authors have in the main followed the lines traced in the foregoing Preface. The theme is developed in some detail in Collingwood and Myers's *Roman Britain and the English Invasions*, 1936, in A. G. Brodeur's *Arthur Dux Bellorum*, 1939, and in Trelawney Dayrell Reade's *Battle for Britain in the Fifth Century*, 1946.

CONTENTS

BOOK II

Contents

BOOK III

BOOK IV

Contents

Contents xxxiii

Contents

BOOK IX

Contents

BOOK X

CAXTON'S ORIGINAL PREFACE

AFTER that I had accomplished and finished divers histories, as well of contemplation as of other historical and worldly acts of great conquerors and princes, and also certain books of ensamples and doctrine, many noble and divers gentlemen of this realm of England came and demanded me, many and ofttimes, wherefore that I have not do made and imprinted the noble history of the Sangreal, and of the most renowned Christian king, first and chief of the three best Christian and worthy, King Arthur, which ought most to be remembered among us English men tofore all other Christian kings. For it is notoriously known through the universal world that there be nine worthy and the best that ever were. That is to wit three paynims, three Jews, and three Christian men. As for the paynims they were tofore the Incarnation of Christ, which were named, the first Hector of Troy, of whom the history is come both in ballad and in prose; the second Alexander the Great; and the third Julius Cæsar, Emperor of Rome, of whom the histories be well-known and had. And as for the three Jews which also were tofore the Incarnation of our Lord, of whom the first was Duke Joshua which brought the children of Israel into the land of behest; the second David, King of Jerusalem; and the third Judas Maccabæus: of these three the Bible rehearseth all their noble histories and acts. And sith the said Incarnation have been three noble Christian men stalled and admitted through the universal world into the number of the nine best and worthy, of whom was first the noble Arthur, whose noble acts I purpose to write in this present book here following. The second was Charlemagne or Charles the Great, of whom the history is had in many places both in French and English; and the third and last was Godfrey of Bouillon, of whose acts and life I made a book unto the excellent prince and king of noble memory, King Edward the Fourth. The said noble gentlemen instantly required me to imprint the history of the said noble king and conqueror, King Arthur, and of his knights, with the history of the Sangreal, and of the death and ending of the said Arthur; affirming that I ought rather to imprint his acts and noble feats, than of Godfrey of Bouillon, or any of the other eight, considering that he was a man born within this realm, and king and emperor of the same;

and that there be in French divers and many noble volumes of his acts, and also of his knights. To whom I answered, that divers men hold opinion that there was no such Arthur, and that all such books as be made of him be but feigned and fables, by cause that some chronicles make of him no mention nor remember him no thing, nor of his knights. Whereto they answered and one in special said, that in him that should say or think that there was never such a king called Arthur, might well be credited great folly and blindness ; for he said that there were many evidences of the contrary: first ye may see his sepulture in the Monastery of Glastonbury. And also in Polichronicon, in the fifth book the sixth chapter, and in the seventh book the twenty-third chapter, where his body was buried and after found and translated into the said monastery. Ye shall see also in the history of Bochas, in his book *De Casu Principum*, part of his noble acts, and also of his fall. Also Galfridus in his British book recounteth his life ; and in divers places of England many remembrances be yet of him and shall remain perpetually, and also of his knights. First in the Abbey of Westminster, at Saint Edward's shrine, remaineth the print of his seal in red wax closed in beryl, in which is written *Patricius Arthurus, Britannie, Gallie, Germanie, Dacie, Imperator*. Item in the castle of Dover ye may see Gawaine's skull and Craddock's mantle : at Winchester the Round Table : at other places Launcelot's sword and many other things. Then all these things considered, there can no man reasonably gainsay but there was a king of this land named Arthur. For in all places, Christian and heathen, he is reputed and taken for one of the nine worthy, and the first of the three Christian men. And also he is more spoken of beyond the sea, more books made of his noble acts than there be in England, as well in Dutch, Italian, Spanish, and Greek, as in French. And yet of record remain in witness of him in Wales, in the town of Camelot, the great stones and marvellous works of iron, lying under the ground, and royal vaults, which divers now living hath seen. Wherefore it is a marvel why he is no more renowned in his own country, save only it accordeth to the Word of God, which saith that no man is accept for a prophet in his own country. Then all these things foresaid alleged, I could not well deny but that there was such a noble king named Arthur, and reputed one of the nine worthy, and first and chief of the Christian men ; and many noble volumes be made of him and of his noble knights in French, which I have seen and read beyond the sea, which be not had in our maternal tongue, but in Welsh be many and also in French, and some in English, but no where nigh all. Wherefore, such as have late been drawn out briefly into English I have after the simple conning that God hath sent to me, under the favour and correction of all noble lords and gentlemen, emprised to imprint a book of the noble histories of the said King Arthur, and of certain of his knights, after a copy unto me delivered, which copy Sir Thomas Malory did take out of certain books of French, and reduced it into English. And I, according to my copy, have done set it in imprint, to the intent that noble men may see and learn the noble acts of chivalry, the gentle and virtuous deeds that some knights used in those days, by which they came to honour ; and how they that were vicious were punished and oft put to shame and rebuke ; humbly beseeching all noble lords and ladies, with all other estates, of what estate or degree they be of, that shall see and read in this said book and work, that they take the good and honest acts in their remembrance, and to follow the same. Wherein they shall find many joyous and pleasant histories, and noble and renowned acts of humanity, gentleness, and chivalries. For herein may be seen noble chivalry, courtesy, humanity, friendliness, hardiness, love, friendship, cowardice, murder, hate, virtue, and sin. Do after the good and leave the evil, and it shall bring you to good fame and renown. And for to pass the time this book shall be pleasant to read in ; but for to give faith and believe that all is true that is contained herein, ye be at your liberty ; but all is written for our doctrine, and for to beware that we fall not to vice nor sin ; but to exercise and follow virtue ; by which we may come and attain to good fame and renown in this life, and after this short and transitory life, to come unto everlasting bliss in heaven, the which he grant us that reigneth in heaven, the blessed Trinity. Amen.

Then to proceed forth in this said book, which I direct unto all noble princes, lords and ladies, gentlemen or gentlewomen, that desire to read or hear read of the noble and joyous history of the great conqueror and excellent king, King Arthur, sometime king of this noble realm, then called Britain. I, William Caxton, simple person, present this book following, which I have emprised to imprint ; and treateth of the noble acts, feats of arms of chivalry, prowess, hardiness, humanity, love, courtesy and very gentleness, with many wonderful histories and adventures. And for to understand briefly the content of this volume, I have divided it into twenty-one books, and every book chaptered as hereafter shall by God's grace follow. The first book shall treat how Uther Pendragon gat the noble conqueror King Arthur, and containeth twenty-eight chapters. The second book treateth of Balin the noble knight, and containeth nineteen chapters. The third book treateth of the marriage of King Arthur to Queen Guenever, with other matters, and containeth fifteen chapters. The fourth book, how Merlin was assotted, and of war made to King Arthur, and containeth twenty-nine chapters. The fifth book treateth of the conquest of Lucius the emperor, and containeth twelve chapters. The sixth book treateth of Sir Launcelot and Sir Lionel, and marvellous adventures, and containeth eighteen chapters. The seventh book treateth of a noble knight called Sir Gareth, and named by Sir Kay, Beaumains, and containeth thirty-six chapters. The eight book treateth of the birth of Sir Tristram the noble knight, and of his acts, and containeth forty-one chapters. The ninth book treateth of a knight named by Sir Kay, La Cote Male Taile, and also of Sir Tristram, and containeth forty-four chapters. The tenth book treateth of Sir Tristram and other marvellous adventures, and containeth eighty-eight chapters. The eleventh book treateth of Sir Launcelot and Sir Galahad, and containeth fourteen chapters. The twelfth book treateth of Sir Launcelot and his madness, and containeth fourteen chapters. The thirteenth book treateth how Galahad came first to King Arthur's court, and the quest how the Sangreal was begun, and containeth twenty chapters. The fourteenth book treateth of the quest of the Sangreal, and containeth ten chapters. The fifteenth book treateth of Sir Launcelot, and containeth six chapters. The sixteenth book treateth of Sir Bors and Sir Lionel his brother, and containeth seventeen chapters. The seventeenth book treateth of the Sangreal, and containeth twenty-three chapters. The eighteenth book treateth of Sir Launcelot and the queen, and containeth twenty-five chapters. The nineteenth book treateth of Queen Guenever and Launcelot, and containeth thirteen chapters. The twentieth book treateth of the piteous death of Arthur, and containeth twenty-two chapters. The twenty-first book treateth of his last departing, and how Sir Launcelot came to revenge his death, and containeth thirteen chapters. The sum is twenty-one books, which contain the sum of five hundred and seven chapters, as more plainly shall follow hereafter.

KING ART

BOOK I

CHAPTER I

It befell in the days of Uther Pendragon, when he was king of all England, and so reigned, that there was a mighty duke in Cornwall that held war against him long time. And the duke was called the duke of Tintagil. And so by means King Uther sent for this duke, charging him to bring his wife with him, for she was called a fair lady, and a passing wise, and her name was called Igraine. So when the duke and his wife were come unto the king, by the means of great lords they were accorded both : the king liked and loved this lady well, and he made them great cheer out of measure, and desired to have lain by her. But she was a passing good woman, and would not assent unto the king. And then she told the duke her husband, and said, I suppose that we were sent for that I should be dishonoured, where-fore, husband, I counsel you, that we depart from hence suddenly, that we may ride all night unto our own castle. And in like wise as she said so they departed, that neither the king nor none of his council were ware of their departing. All so soon as King Uther knew of their departing so suddenly, he was wonderly wroth. Then he called to him his privy council, and told them of the sudden departing of the duke and his wife. Then they asked the king to send for the duke and his wife by a great charge ; And if he will not come at your summons, then may ye do your best, then have ye cause to make mighty war upon him. So that was done, and the messengers had their answers, and that was this shortly, that neither he nor his wife would not come at him. Then was the king wonderly wroth. And then the king sent him plain word again, and bade him be ready and

.m and garnish him, for within forty days he would nim out of the biggest castle that he had. When the .e had this warning, anon he went and furnished and .irnished two strong castles of his, of the which the one hight Tintagil, and the other castle hight Terrabil. So his wife Dame Igraine he put in the castle of Tintagil, and himself he put in the castle of Terrabil, the which had many issues and posterns out. Then in all haste came Uther with a great host, and laid a siege about the castle of Terrabil. And there he pyght many pavilions, and there was great war made on both parties, and much people slain. Then for pure anger and for great love of fair Igraine the King Uther fell sick. So came to the King Uther, Sir Ulfius a noble knight, and asked the king why he was sick. I shall tell thee, said the king, I am sick for anger and for love of fair Igraine that I may not be hool. Well, my lord, said Sir Ulfius, I shall seek Merlin, and he shall do you remedy, that your heart shall be pleased. So Ulfius departed, and by adventure he met Merlin in a beggar's array, and then Merlin asked Ulfius whom he sought. And he said he had little ado to tell him. Well, said Merlin, I know whom thou seekest, for thou seekest Merlin; therefore seek no farther, for I am he, and if King Uther will well reward me, and be sworn unto me to fulfil my desire, that shall be his honour and profit more than mine, for I shall cause him to have all his desire. All this will I undertake, said Ulfius, that there shall be nothing reasonable but thou shalt have thy desire. Well, said Merlin, he shall have his entente and desire. And therefore, said Merlin, ride on your way, for I will not be long behind.

CHAPTER II

HOW UTHER PENDRAGON MADE WAR ON THE DUKE OF CORNWALL, AND HOW BY THE MEANS OF MERLIN HE LAY BY THE DUCHESS AND GAT ARTHUR

THEN Ulfius was glad, and rode on more than a paas till that he came to King Uther Pendragon, and told him he had met with Merlin. Where is he? said the king. Sir, said Ulfius, he will not dwell long; therewithal Ulfius was ware where Merlin stood at the porch of the pavilion's door.

And then Merlin was bound to come to the king. When King Uther saw him, he said he was welcome. Sir, said Merlin, I know all your heart every deal; so ye will be sworn unto me as ye be a true king anointed, to fulfil my desire, ye shall have your desire. Then the king was sworn upon the four Evangelists. Sir, said Merlin, this is my desire: the first night that ye shall lie by Igraine ye shall get a child on her, and when that is born, that it shall be delivered to me for to nourish there as I will have it; for it shall be your worship, and the child's avail as mickle as the child is worth. I will well, said the king, as thou wilt have it. Now make you ready, said Merlin, this night ye shall lie with Igraine in the castle of Tintagil, and ye shall be like the duke her husband, Ulfius shall be like Sir Brastias, a knight of the duke's, and I will be like a knight that hight Sir Jordans, a knight of the duke's. But wayte ye make not many questions with her nor her men, but say ye are diseased, and so hie you to bed, and rise not on the morn till I come to you, for the castle of Tintagil is but ten miles hence; so this was done as they devised. But the duke of Tintagil espied how the king rode from the siege of Terrabil, and therefore that night he issued out of the castle at a postern for to have distressed the king's host. And so, through his own issue, the duke himself was slain or-ever the king came at the castle of Tintagil. So after the death of the duke, King Uther lay with Igraine more than three hours after his death, and begat on her that night Arthur, and or day came Merlin came to the king, and bade him make him ready, and so he kissed the lady Igraine and departed in all haste. But when the lady heard tell of the duke her husband, and by all record he was dead or-ever King Uther came to her; then she marvelled who that might be that lay with her in likeness of her lord; so she mourned privily and held her peace. Then all the barons by one assent prayed the king of accord betwixt the lady Igraine and him; the king gave them leave, for fain would he have been accorded with her. So the king put all the trust in Ulfius to entreat between them, so by the entreaty at the last the king and she met together. Now will we do well, said Ulfius, our king is a lusty knight and wifeless, and my lady Igraine is a passing fair lady; it were great joy unto us all, an it might please the king to make her his queen. Unto that they all well accorded and moved it to the king.

And anon, like a lusty knight, he assented thereto with good will, and so in all haste they were married in a morning with great mirth and joy. And King Lot of Lothian and of Orkney then wedded Margawse that was Gawaine's mother, and King Nentres of the land of Garlot wedded Elaine. All this was done at the request of King Uther. And the third sister Morgan le Fay was put to school in a nunnery, and there she learned so much that she was a great clerk of necromancy, and after she was wedded to King Uriens of the land of Gore, that was Sir Ewain's le Blanchemain's father.

CHAPTER III

OF THE BIRTH OF KING ARTHUR AND OF HIS NURTURE

THEN Queen Igraine waxed daily greater and greater, so it befell after within half a year, as King Uther lay by his queen, he asked her, by the faith she owed to him, whose was the child within her body; then was she sore abashed to give answer. Dismay you not, said the king, but tell me the truth, and I shall love you the better, by faith of my body. Sir, said she, I shall tell you the truth. The same night that my lord was dead, the hour of his death, as his knights record, there came into my castle of Tintagil a man like my lord in speech and in countenance, and two knights with him in likeness of his two knights Brastias and Jordans, and so I went unto bed with him as I ought to do with my lord, and the same night, as I shall answer unto God, this child was begotten upon me. That is truth, said the king, as ye say; for it was I myself that came in the likeness, and therefore dismay you not, for I am father of the child; and there he told her all the cause, how it was by Merlin's counsel. Then the queen made great joy when she knew who was the father of her child. Soon came Merlin unto the king, and said, Sir, ye must purvey you for the nourishing of your child. As thou wilt, said the king, be it. Well, said Merlin, I know a lord of yours in this land, that is a passing true man and a faithful, and he shall have the nourishing of your child, and his name is Sir Ector, and he is a lord of fair livelihood in many parts in England and Wales; and this lord, Sir Ector, let him be sent for, for to come and speak with you, and desire him yourself, as he loveth you, that he will put his own child to nourishing to another woman, and that his wife nourish yours. And when the child is born let it be delivered to me at yonder privy postern unchristened. So like as Merlin devised it was done. And when Sir Ector was come he made fyaunce to the king for to nourish the child like as the king desired ; and there the king granted Sir Ector great rewards. Then when the lady was delivered, the king commanded two knights and two ladies to take the child, bound in a cloth of gold, and that ye deliver him to what poor man ye meet at the postern gate of the castle. So the child was delivered unto Merlin, and so he bare it forth unto Sir Ector, and made an holy man to christen him, and named him Arthur; and so Sir Ector's wife nourished him with her own pap.

CHAPTER IV

OF THE DEATH OF KING UTHER PENDRAGON

THEN within two years King Uther fell sick of a great malady. And in the meanwhile his enemies usurped upon him, and did a great battle upon his men, and slew many of his people. Sir, said Merlin, ye may not lie so as ye do, for ye must to the field though ye ride on an horse-litter : for ye shall never have the better of your enemies but if your person be there, and then shall ye have the victory. So it was done as Merlin had devised, and they carried the king forth in an horse-litter with a great host towards his enemies. And at St. Albans there met with the king a great host of the North. And that day Sir Ulfius and Sir Brastias did great deeds of arms, and King Uther's men overcame the Northern battle and slew many people, and put the remnant to flight. And then the king returned unto London, and made great joy of his victory. And then he fell passing sore sick, so that three days and three nights he was speechless : wherefore all the barons made great sorrow, and asked Merlin what counsel were best. There is none other remedy, said Merlin, but God will have his will. But look ye, all barons, be before King Uther to-morn, and God and I shall make him to speak. So on the morn all the barons with Merlin came before the king ; then Merlin said aloud unto King Uther, Sir, shall your son Arthur be king after your days, of this realm with all the appurtenance? Then Uther Pendragon turned him, and said in hearing of them all, I give him God's blessing and mine, and bid him pray for my soul, and righteously and worshipfully that he claim the crown upon forfeiture of my blessing; and therewith he yielded up the ghost, and then was he interred as longed to a king. Wherefore the queen, fair Igraine, made great sorrow, and all the barons.

CHAPTER V

HOW ARTHUR WAS CHOSEN KING, AND OF WONDERS AND MARVELS OF A SWORD TAKEN OUT OF A STONE BY THE SAID ARTHUR

THEN stood the realm in great jeopardy long while, for every lord that was mighty of men made him strong, and many weened to have been king. Then Merlin went to the Archbishop of Canterbury, and counselled him for to send for all the lords of the realm, and all the gentlemen of arms, that they should to London come by Christmas, upon pain of cursing; and for this cause, that Jesus, that was born on that night, that he would of his great mercy show some miracle, as he was come to be king of mankind, for to show some miracle who should be rightways king of this realm. So the Archbishop, by the advice of Merlin, sent for all the lords and gentlemen of arms that they should come by Christmas even unto London. And many of them made them clean of their life, that their prayer might be the more acceptable unto God. So in the greatest church of London, whether it were Paul's or not the French book maketh no mention, all the estates were long or day in the church for to pray. And when matins and the first mass was done, there was seen in the churchyard, against the high altar, a great stone four square, like unto a marble stone, and in midst thereof was like an anvil of steel a foot on high, and therein stuck a fair sword naked by the point, and letters there were written in gold about the sword that said thus :—Whoso pulleth out this sword of this stone and anvil, is rightwise king born of all England. Then the people marvelled, and told it to the Archbishop. I command, said the Archbishop, that ye keep you within your church, and pray unto God still; that no man touch the sword till the high mass be all done. So when all masses were done all the lords went to behold the stone and the sword. And when they saw the scripture, some assayed; such as would have been king. But none might stir the sword nor move it. He is not here, said the Archbishop, that shall achieve the sword, but doubt not God will make him known. But this is my counsel, said the Archbishop, that we let purvey ten knights, men of good fame, and they to keep this sword. So it was ordained, and then there was made a cry, that every man should essay that would, for to win the sword. And upon New Year's Day the barons let make a jousts and a tournament, that all knights that would joust or tourney there might play, and all this was ordained for to keep the lords and the commons together, for the Archbishop trusted that God would make him known that should win the sword. So upon New Year's Day, when the service was done, the barons rode unto the field, some to joust and some to tourney, and so it happened that Sir Ector, that had great livelihood about London, rode unto the jousts, and with him rode Sir Kay his son, and young Arthur that was his nourished brother; and Sir Kay was made knight at All Hallowmass afore. So as they rode to the jousts-ward, Sir Kay had lost his sword, for he had left it at his father's lodging, and so he prayed young Arthur for to ride for his sword. I will well, said Arthur, and rode fast after the sword, and when he came home, the lady and all were out to see the jousting. Then was Arthur wroth, and said to himself, I will ride to the churchyard, and take the sword with me that sticketh in the stone, for my brother Sir Kay shall not be without a sword this day. So when he came to the churchyard, Sir Arthur alit and tied his horse to the stile, and so he went to the tent, and found no knights there, for they were at jousting; and so he handled the sword by the handles, and lightly and fiercely pulled it out of the stone, and took his horse and rode his way until he came to his brother Sir Kay, and delivered him the sword. And as soon as Sir Kay saw the sword, he wist well it was the sword of the stone, and so he rode to his father Sir Ector, and said: Sir, lo here is the sword of the stone, wherefore I must be king of this land. When Sir Ector beheld the sword, he returned again and came to the church, and there they alit all three, and went into the church. And anon he made Sir Kay to swear upon a book how he came to that sword. Sir, said Sir Kay, by my brother Arthur, for he brought it to me. How gat ye this sword? said Sir Ector to Arthur. Sir, I will tell you. When I came home for my brother's sword, I found nobody at home to deliver me his sword, and so I thought my brother Sir Kay should not be swordless, and so I came hither eagerly and pulled it out of the stone without any pain. Found ye any knights about this sword? said Sir Ector. Nay, said Arthur. Now, said Sir Ector to Arthur, I understand ye must be king of this land. Wherefore I, said Arthur, and for what cause? Sir, said Ector, for God will have it so, for there should never man have drawn out this sword, but he that shall be rightways king of this land. Now let me see whether ye can put the sword there as it was, and pull it out again. That is no mastery, said Arthur, and so he put it in the stone, therewithal Sir Ector essayed to pull out the sword and failed.

CHAPTER VI

HOW KING ARTHUR PULLED OUT THE SWORD DIVERS TIMES

Now assay, said Sir Ector unto Sir Kay. And anon he pulled at the sword with all his might, but it would not be. Now shall ye essay, said Sir Ector to Arthur. I will well, said Arthur, and pulled it out easily. And therewithal Sir Ector knelt down to the earth, and Sir Kay. Alas, said Arthur, my own dear father and brother, why kneel ye to me? Nay, nay, my lord Arthur, it is not so, I was never your father nor of your blood, but I wot well ye are of an higher blood than I weened ye were. And then Sir Ector told him all, how he was bitaken him for to nourish him, and by whose commandment, and by Merlin's deliverance. Then Arthur made great doole when he understood that Sir Ector was not his father. Sir, said Ector unto Arthur, will ye be my good and gracious lord when ye are king? Else were I to blame, said Arthur, for ye are the man in the world that I am most beholden to, and my good lady and mother your wife, that as well as her own hath fostered me and kept. And if ever it be God's will that I be king as ye say, ye shall desire of me what I may do, and I shall not fail you, God forbid I should fail you. Sir, said Sir

Ector, I will ask no more of you, but that ye will make my
son, your foster brother, Sir Kay, seneschal of all your
lands. That shall be done, said Arthur, and more, by the
faith of my body, that never man shall have that office but
he, while he and I live. Therewithal they went unto the
Archbishop, and told him how the sword was achieved, and
by whom; and on Twelfth-day all the barons came thither,
and to essay to take the sword, who that would essay. But
there afore them all, there might none take it out but
Arthur; wherefore there were many lords wroth, and said it
was great shame unto them all and the realm, to be over-
governed with a boy of no high blood born, and so they fell
out at that time that it was put off till Candlemas, and then
all the barons should meet there again; but always the ten
knights were ordained to watch the sword day and night,
and so they set a pavilion over the stone and the sword,
and five always watched. So at Candlemas many more
great lords came thither for to have won the sword, but
there might none prevail. And right as Arthur did at
Christmas, he did at Candlemas, and pulled out the sword
easily, whereof the barons were sore agrieved and put it off
in delay till the high feast of Easter. And as Arthur sped
before, so did he at Easter, yet there were some of the
great lords had indignation that Arthur should be king, and
put it off in a delay till the feast of Pentecost. Then the
Archbishop of Canterbury by Merlyn's providence let purvey
then of the best knights that they might get, and such
knights as Uther Pendragon loved best and most trusted in
his days. And such knights were put about Arthur as Sir
Baudwin of Britain, Sir Kay, Sir Ulfius, Sir Brastias. All
these with many other, were always about Arthur, day and
night, till the feast of Pentecost.

CHAPTER VII

HOW KING ARTHUR WAS CROWNED, AND HOW HE MADE OFFICERS

AND at the feast of Pentecost all manner of men essayed
to pull at the sword that would essay, but none might
prevail but Arthur, and pulled it out afore all the lords and
commons that were there, wherefore all the commons cried
at once, We will have Arthur unto our king, we will put him

no more in delay, for we all see that it is God's will that he shall be our king, and who that holdeth against it, we will slay him. And therewith they all kneeled at once, both rich and poor, and cried Arthur mercy because they had delayed him so long, and Arthur forgave them, and took the sword between both his hands, and offered it upon the altar where the Archbishop was, and so was he made knight of the best man that was there. And so anon was the coronation made. And there was he sworn unto his lords and the commons for to be a true king, to stand with true justice from thenceforth the days of this life. Also then he made all lords that held of the crown to come in, and to do service as they ought to do. And many complaints were made unto Sir Arthur of great wrongs that were done since the death of King Uther, of many lands that were bereaved lords, knights, ladies, and gentlemen. Wherefore King Arthur made the lands to be given again unto them that owned them. When this was done, that the king had stablished all the countries about London, then he let make Sir Kay seneschal of England ; and Sir Baudwin of Britain was made constable; and Sir Ulfius was made chamberlain ; and Sir Brastias was made warden to wait upon the north from Trent forwards, for it was that time the most part the king's enemies. But within few years after, Arthur won all the north, Scotland, and all that were under their obeissance. Also Wales, a part of it held against Arthur, but he overcame them all, as he did the remnant, through the noble prowess of himself and his knights of the Round Table.

CHAPTER VIII

HOW KING ARTHUR HELD IN WALES, AT A PENTECOST, A GREAT FEAST, AND WHAT KINGS AND LORDS CAME TO HIS FEAST

THEN the king removed into Wales, and let cry a great feast that it should be holden at Pentecost after the incoronation of him at the city of Carlion. Unto the feast came King Lot of Lothian and of Orkney, with five hundred knights with him. Also there came to the feast King Uriens of Gore with four hundred knights with him. Also there came to that feast King Nentres of Garlot, with seven hundred knights with him. Also there came to the feast the king of Scotland with six hundred knights with him, and he was but a young man. Also there came to the feast a king that was called the king with the hundred knights, but he and his men were passing well bisene at all points. Also there came the king of Carados with five hundred knights. And King Arthur was glad of their coming, for he weened that all the kings and knights had come for great love, and to have done him worship at his feast, wherefore the king made great joy, and sent the kings and knights great presents. But the kings would none receive, but rebuked the messengers shamefully, and said they had no joy to receive no gifts of a beardless boy that was come of low blood, and sent him word they would none of his gifts, but that they were come to give him gifts with hard swords betwixt the neck and the shoulders : and therefore they came thither, so they told to the messengers plainly, for it was great shame to all them to see such a boy to have a rule of so noble a realm as this land was. With this answer the messengers departed and told to King Arthur this answer. Wherefore, by the advice of his barons, he took him to a strong tower with five hundred good men with him : and all the kings aforesaid in a manner laid a siege tofore him, but King Arthur was well victualed. And within fifteen days there came Merlin among them into the city of Carlion. Then all the kings were passing glad of Merlin, and asked him, For what cause is that boy Arthur made your king ? Sirs, said Merlin, I shall tell you the cause, for he is King Uther Pendragon's son, born in wedlock, gotten on Igraine, the duke's wife of Tintagil. Then is he a bastard, they said all. Nay, said Merlin, after the death of the duke, more than three hours, was Arthur begotten, and thirteen days after King Uther wedded Igraine ; and therefore I prove him he is no bastard, and who saith nay, he shall be king and overcome all his enemies ; and, or he die, he shall be long king of all England, and have under his obeissance Wales, Ireland, and Scotland, and more realms than I will now rehearse. Some of the kings had marvel of Merlin's words, and deemed well that it should be as he said ; and some of them laughed him to scorn, as King Lot ; and more other called him a witch. But then were they accorded with Merlin, that King Arthur should come out and speak with the kings, and to come safe and to go safe, such assurance there was made. So Merlin went unto King Arthur, and told him how he had done, and bade him fear not, but come out boldly and speak with them, and spare them not, but answer them as their king and chieftain, for ye shall overcome them all, whether they will or nill.

CHAPTER IX

OF THE FIRST WAR THAT KING ARTHUR HAD, AND HOW HE WON THE FIELD

THEN King Arthur came out of his tower, and had under his gown a jesseraunte of double mail, and there went with him the Archbishop of Canterbury, and Sir Baudwin of Britain, and Sir Kay, and Sir Brastias : these were the men of most worship that were with him. And when they were met there was no meekness, but stout words on both sides ; but always King Arthur answered them, and said he would make them to bow an he lived. Wherefore they departed with wrath, and King Arthur bade keep them well, and they bade the king keep him well. So the king returned him to the tower again and armed him and all his knights. What will ye do? said Merlin to the kings ; ye were better for to stynte, for ye shall not here prevail though ye were ten times so many. Be we well advised to be afeard of a dream-reader? said King Lot. With that Merlin vanished away, and came to King Arthur, and bade him set on them fiercely ; and in the meanwhile there were three hundred good men of the best that were with the kings, that went straight unto King Arthur and that comforted him greatly. Sir, said Merlin to Arthur, fight not with the sword that ye had by miracle, till that ye see ye go unto the worse, then draw it out and do your best. So forthwithal King Arthur set upon them in their lodging. And Sir Baudwin, Sir Kay, and Sir Brastias slew on the right hand and on the left hand that it was marvel ; and always King Arthur on horseback laid on with a sword, and did marvellous deeds of arms that many of the kings had great joy of his deeds and hardiness. Then King Lot brake out on the back side, and the king with the hundred knights, and King Carados, and set on Arthur fiercely behind him. With that

Sir Arthur turned with his knights, and smote behind and before, and ever Sir Arthur was in the foremost press till his horse was slain underneath him. And therewith King Lot smote down King Arthur. With that his four knights received him and set him on horseback. Then he drew his sword Excalibur, but it was so bright in his enemies' eyes, that it gave light like thirty torches. And therewith he put them on back, and slew much people. And then the commons of Carlion arose with clubs and staves and slew many knights; but all the kings held them together with their knights that were left alive, and so fled and departed. And Merlin came unto Arthur, and counselled him to follow them no further.

CHAPTER X

HOW MERLIN COUNSELLED KING ARTHUR TO SEND FOR KING BAN AND KING BORS, AND OF THEIR COUNSEL TAKEN FOR THE WAR

So after the feast and journey, King Arthur drew him unto London, and so by the counsel of Merlin, the king let call his barons to council, for Merlin had told the king that the six kings that made war upon him would in all haste be awroke on him and on his lands. Wherefore the king asked counsel at them all. They could no counsel give, but said they were big enough. Ye say well, said Arthur; I thank you for your good courage, but will ye all that loveth me speak with Merlin? ye know well that he hath done much for me, and he knoweth many things, and when he is afore you, I would that ye prayed him heartily of his best advice. All the barons said they would pray him and desire him. So Merlin was sent for, and fair desired of all the barons to give them best counsel. I shall say you, said Merlin, I warn you all, your enemies are passing strong for you, and they are good men of arms as be alive, and by this time they have gotten to them four kings more and a mighty duke; and unless that our king have more chivalry with him than he may make within the bounds of his own realm, an he fight with them in battle, he shall be overcome and slain. What were best to do in this cause? said all the barons. I shall tell you, said Merlin, my advice; there are two brethren beyond the sea, and they be kings both and

marvellous good men of their hands; and that one hight
King Ban of Benwick, and that other hight King Bors of
Gaul, that is France. And on these two kings warreth a
mighty man of men, the King Claudas, and striveth with
them for a castle, and great war is betwixt them: but this
Claudas is so mighty of goods whereof he getteth good
knights, that he putteth these two kings most part to the
worse; wherefore this is my counsel, that our king and
sovereign lord send unto the kings Ban and Bors by two
trusty knights with letters well devised, that if they will come
and see King Arthur and his court, and so help him in his
wars, that he will be sworn unto them to help them in their
wars against King Claudas. Now, what say ye unto this
counsel? said Merlin. This is well counselled, said the
king and all the barons. Right so in all haste there were
ordained to go two knights on the message unto the two
kings. So were there made letters in the pleasant wise
according unto King Arthur's desire. Ulfius and Brastias
were made the messengers, and so rode forth well horsed
and well armed, and as the guise was that time, and so
passed the sea and rode toward the city of Benwick. And
there besides were eight knights that espied them, and at a
straight passage they met with Ulfius and Brastias, and
would have taken them prisoners; so they prayed them that
they might pass, for they were messengers unto King Ban
and Bors sent from King Arthur. Therefore, said the eight
knights, ye shall die or be prisoners, for we be knights of
King Claudas. And therewith two of them dressed their
spears, and Ulfius and Brastias dressed their spears, and
ran together with great raundon, and Claudas' knights
brake their spears, and theirs to-held and bare the two
knights out of their saddles to the earth, and so left
them lying, and rode their ways. And the other six knights
rode afore to a passage to meet with them again, and so
Ulfius and Brastias smote other two down, and so passed on
their ways. And at the fourth passage there met two for
two, and both were laid unto the earth; so there was none
of the eight knights but he was sore hurt or bruised. And
when they come to Benwick it fortuned there were both
Kings Ban and Bors. And when it was told the kings that
there were come messengers, there were sent unto them two
knights of worship, the one hight Lionses, lord of the
country of Payarne, and Sir Phariance a worshipful knight

Anon they asked from whence they came, and they said from King Arthur, king of England; so they took them in their arms and made great joy each of other. But anon, as the two kings wist they were messengers of Arthur's, there was made no tarrying, but forthwith they spake with the knights, and welcomed them in the faithfullest wise, and said they were most welcome unto them before all the kings living. And therewith they kissed the letters and delivered them; and when Ban and Bors understood the letters, then they were more welcome than they were before. And after the haste of the letters, they gave them this answer, that they would fulfil the desire of King Arthur's writing, and Ulfius and Brastias tarry there as long as they would, they should have such cheer as might be made them in those marches. Then Ulfius and Brastias told the king of the adventure at their passages of the eight knights. Ha! ah! said Ban and Bors, they were my good friends. I would I had wist of them, they should not have escaped so. So Ulfius and Brastias had good cheer and great gifts as much as they might bear away, and had their answer by mouth and by writing, that those two kings would come unto Arthur in all the haste that they might. So the two knights rode on afore, and passed the sea, and come to their lord, and told him how they had sped, whereof King Arthur was passing glad. At what time suppose ye the two kings will be here? Sir, said they, afore All Hallowmass. Then the king let purvey for a great feast, and let cry a great jousts. And by All Hallowmass the two kings were come over the sea with three hundred knights well arrayed both for the peace and for the war. And King Arthur met with them ten mile out of London, and there was great joy as could be thought or made. And on All Hallowmass at the great feast, sat in the hall the three kings, and Sir Kay seneschal served in the hall, and Sir Lucas the butler, that was Duke Corneus' son, and Sir Griflet, that was the son of Cardol, these three knights had the rule of all the service that served the kings. And anon, as they had washen and risen, all knights that would joust made them ready. By when they were ready on horseback there were seven hundred knights. And Arthur, Ban, and Bors, with the Archbishop of Canterbury, and Sir Ector, Kay's father, they were in a place covered with cloth of gold like an hall, with ladies and gentlewomen, for to behold who did best, and thereon to give judgment.

CHAPTER XI

OF A GREAT TOURNEY MADE BY KING ARTHUR AND THE TWO
KINGS BAN AND BORS, AND HOW THEY WENT OVER THE SEA

AND King Arthur and the two kings let depart the seven hundred knights in two parties. And there were three hundred knights of the realm of Benwick and of Gaul turned on the other side. Then they dressed their shields, and began to couch their spears many good knights. So Griflet was the first that met with a knight, one Ladinas, and they met so eagerly that all men had wonder; and they so fought that their shields fell to pieces, and horse and man fell to the earth; and both the French knight and the English knight lay so long that all men weened they had been dead. When Lucas the butler saw Griflet so lie, he horsed him again anon, and they two did marvellous deeds of arms with many bachelors. Also Sir Kay came out of an embushment with five knights with him, and they six smote other six down. But Sir Kay did that day marvellous deeds of arms that there was none did so well as he that day. Then there come Ladinas and Gracian, two knights of France, and did passing well, that all men praised them. Then come there Sir Placidas, a good knight, and met with Sir Kay, and smote him down horse and man, wherefore Sir Griflet was wroth, and met with Sir Placidas so hard, that horse and man fell to the earth. But when the five knights wist that Sir Kay had a fall, they were wroth out of wit, and therewith each of them five bare down a knight. When King Arthur and the two kings saw them begin to wax wroth on both parties, they leapt on small hackneys, and let cry that all men should depart unto their lodging. And so they went home and unarmed them, and so to evensong and supper. And after, the three kings went into a garden, and gave the prize unto Sir Kay, and to Lucas the butler, and unto Sir Griflet. And then they went unto council, and with them Gwenbaus, the brother unto Sir Ban and Bors, a wise clerk, and thither went Ulfius and Brastias, and Merlin. And after they had been in council, they went unto bed. And on the morn they heard mass, and to dinner, and so to their council, and made many arguments what were best to do. At the last they were concluded, that Merlin should go with a token of King Ban, and that was a ring, unto his men and King Bors's; and Gracian and Placidas should go again and keep their castles and their countries, as King Ban of Benwick, and King Bors of Gaul had ordained them, and so they passed the sea and came to Benwick. And when the people saw King Ban's ring, and Gracian and Placidas, they were glad, and asked how the kings fared, and made great joy of their welfare and cordyng, and according unto the sovereign lords' desire, the men of war made them ready in all haste possible, so that they were fifteen thousand on horse and foot, and they had great plenty of victual with them, by Merlin's provision. But Gracian and Placidas were left to furnish and garnish the castles, for dread of King Claudas. Right so Merlin passed the sea well victualled both by water and by land. And when he came to the sea he sent home the foot men again, and took no more with him but ten thousand men on horseback, the most part men of arms, and so shipped and passed the sea into England and landed at Dover; and through the wit of Merlin, he led the host northward, the priviest way that could be thought, unto the forest of Bedegraine, and there in a valley he lodged them secretly. Then rode Merlin unto Arthur and the two kings, and told them how he had sped; whereof they had great marvel, that man on earth might speed so soon, and go and come. So Merlin told them ten thousand were in the forest of Bedegraine, well armed at all points. Then was there no more to say, but to horseback went all the host as Arthur had afore purveyed. So with twenty thousand he passed by night and day, but there was made such an ordinance afore by Merlin, that there should no man of war ride nor go in no country on this side Trent water, but if he had a token from King Arthur, where through the king's enemies durst not ride as they did tofore to espy.

CHAPTER XII

HOW ELEVEN KINGS GATHERED A GREAT HOST AGAINST KING ARTHUR

AND so within a little space the three kings came unto the castle of Bedegraine, and found there a passing fair fellowship, and well besene, whereof they had great joy, and victual they wanted none. This was the cause of the northern host: that they were reared for the despite and rebuke the six kings had at Carlion. And those six kings by their means, gat unto them five other kings ; and thus they began to gather their people ; and how they sware that for weal nor woe, they should not leave other, till they had destroyed Arthur. And then they made an oath. The first that began the oath was the Duke of Cambenet, that he would bring with him five thousand men of arms, the which were ready on horseback. Then sware King Brandegoris of Stranggore that he would bring five thousand men of arms on horseback. Then sware King Clariance of Northumberland he would bring three thousand men of arms. Then sware the king of the hundred knights, that was a passing good man and a young, that he would bring four thousand men of arms on horseback. Then there swore King Lot, a passing good knight, and Sir Gawain's father, that he would bring five thousand men of arms on horseback. Also there swore King Urience, that was Sir Uwain's father, of the land of Gore, and he would bring six thousand men of arms on horseback. Also there swore King Idres of Cornwall, that he would bring five thousand men of arms on horseback. Also there swore King Cradelmas to bring five thousand men on horseback. Also there swore King Agwisance of Ireland to bring five thousand men of arms on horseback. Also there swore King Nentres to bring five thousand men of arms on horseback. Also there swore King Carados to bring five thousand men of arms on horseback. So their whole host was of clene men of arms on horseback fifty thousand, and a-foot ten thousand, of good men's bodies. Then were they soon ready, and mounted upon horse and sent forth their fore-riders, for these eleven kings in their ways laid a siege unto the castle of Bedegraine ; and so they departed and drew toward Arthur, and left few to abide at the siege, for the castle of Bedegraine was holden of King Arthur, and the men that were therein were Arthur's.

CHAPTER XIII

OF A DREAM OF THE KING WITH THE HUNDRED KNIGHTS

So by Merlin's advice there were sent fore-riders to skim the country, and they met with the fore-riders of the north, and made them to tell which way the host came, and then they told it to Arthur, and by King Ban and Bors' council they let burn and destroy all the country afore them, where they should ride. The king with the hundred knights mette a wonder dream two nights afore the battle, that there blew a great wind, and blew down their castles and their towns, and after that came a water and bare it all away. All that heard of the sweven, said it was a token of great battle. Then by counsel of Merlin, when they wist which way the eleven kings would ride and lodge that night, at midnight they set upon them, as they were in their pavilions. But the scout-watch by their host cried, Lords! at arms! for here be your enemies at your hand!

CHAPTER XIV

HOW THE ELEVEN KINGS WITH THEIR HOST FOUGHT AGAINST ARTHUR AND HIS HOST, AND MANY GREAT FEATS OF THE WAR

THEN King Arthur and King Ban and King Bors, with their good and trusty knights, set on them so fiercely that they made them overthrow their pavilions on their heads, but the eleven kings, by manly prowess of arms, took a fair champaign, but there was slain that morrowtide ten thousand good men's bodies. And so they had afore them a strong passage, yet were they fifty thousand of hardy men. Then it drew toward day. Now shall ye do by mine advice, said Merlin unto the three kings: I would that King Ban and King Bors, with their fellowship of ten thousand men, were put in a wood here beside, in an embushment, and keep them privy, and that they be laid or the light of the day come, and that they stir not till ye and your knights have fought with them long. And when it is daylight, dress your battle even afore them and the passage, that they may see all your host, for then will they be the more hardy, when they see you but about twenty thousand men, and cause them to be the gladder to suffer you and your host to come over the passage. All the three kings and the whole barons said that Merlin said passingly well, and it was done anon as Merlin had devised. So on the morn, when either host saw other, the host of the north was well comforted. Then to Ulfius and Brastias were delivered three thousand men of arms, and they set on them fiercely in the passage, and slew on the right hand and on the left hand that it was wonder to tell.   When that the eleven kings saw that there was so few a fellowship did such deeds of arms, they were ashamed and set on them again fiercely ; and there was Sir Ulfius's horse slain under him, but he did marvellously well on foot.   But the Duke Eustace of Cambenet and King Clariance of Northumberland, were alway grievous on Ulfius.   When Brastias saw his fellow fared so withal, he smote the duke with a spear, that horse and man fell down. That saw King Clariance and returned unto Brastias, and either smote other so that horse and man went to the earth, and so they lay long astonied, and their horse knees brast to the hard bone.   Then came Sir Kay the seneschal with six fellows with him, and did passing well.   With that came the eleven kings, and there was Griflet put to the earth, horse and man, and Lucas the butler, horse and man, by King Brandegoris, and King Idres, and King Agwisance. Then waxed the medley passing hard on both parties. When Sir Kay saw Griflet on foot, he rode on King Nentres and smote him down, and led his horse unto Sir Griflet, and horsed him again.   Also Sir Kay with the same spear smote down King Lot, and hurt him passing sore.   That saw the king with the hundred knights, and ran unto Sir Kay and smote him down, and took his horse, and gave him King Lot, whereof he said gramercy.   When Sir Griflet saw Sir Kay and Lucas the butler on foot, he took a sharp spear, great and square, and rode to Pinel, a good man of arms, and smote horse and man down, and then he took his horse, and gave him unto Sir Kay.   When King Lot saw King Nentres on foot, he ran unto Melot de la Roche, and smote him down, horse and man, and gave King Nentres the horse, and horsed him again.   Also the king of the hundred knights saw King Idres on foot, then he ran unto Gwimiart de Bloi, and smote him down, horse and man, and gave King Idres the horse, and horsed him again ; and King Lot smote down Clariance de la Forest Savage, and gave the horse unto Duke Eustace.   And so when they had horsed the kings again they drew them all eleven kings together, and said they would be revenged of the damage that they had taken that day.   The meanwhile came in Sir Ector with an eager countenance, and found Ulfias and Brastias on foot, in great peril of death, that were foul defoyled under horse-feet.   Then King Arthur as a lion, ran unto King Cradelment of North Wales, and smote him through the left side, that the horse and the king fell down ; and then he took the horse by the rein, and led him unto Ulfius, and said, Have this horse, mine old friend, for great need hast thou of horse. Gramercy, said Ulfias. Then Sir Arthur did so marvellously in arms, that all men had wonder. When the king with the hundred knights saw King Cradelment on foot, he ran unto Sir Ector, that was well horsed, Sir Kay's father, and smote horse and man down, and gave the horse unto the king, and horsed him again ; and when King Arthur saw the king ride on Sir Ector's horse, he was wroth and with his sword he smote the king on the helm, that a quarter of the helm and shield fell down, and the sword carved down unto the horse's neck, and so the king and the horse fell down to the ground. Then Sir Kay came unto Sir Morganore, seneschal with the king of the hundred knights, and smote him down, horse and man, and led the horse unto his father, Sir Ector ; then Sir Ector ran unto a knight, hight Lardans, and smote horse and man down, and led the horse unto Sir Brastias, that great need had of an horse, and was greatly defoyled. When Brastias beheld Lucas the butler, that lay like a dead man under the horse's feet, and ever Sir Griflet did marvellously for to rescue him, and there were always fourteen knights on Sir Lucas ; then Brastias smote one of them on the helm, that it went to the teeth, and he rode to another and smote him, that the arm flew into the field. Then he went to the third and smote him on the shoulder, that shoulder and arm flew in the field. And when Griflet saw rescues, he smote a knight on the temples, that head and helm went to the earth, and Griflet took the horse of that knight, and led him unto Sir Lucas, and bad him mount upon the horse and revenge his hurts. For Brastias had slain a knight tofore and horsed Griflet.

CHAPTER XV

YET OF THE SAME BATTLE

THEN Lucas saw King Agwisance, that late had slain Moris de la Roche, and Lucas ran to him with a short spear that was great, that he gave him such a fall, that the horse fell down to the earth. Also Lucas found there on

foot, Bloias de La Flandres, and Sir Gwinas, two hardy
knights, and in that woodness that Lucas was in, he slew
two bachelors and horsed them again. Then waxed the
battle passing hard on both parties, but Arthur was glad
that his knights were horsed again, and then they fought
together, that the noise and sound rang by the water and
the wood. Wherefore King Ban and King Bors made
them ready, and dressed their shields and harness, and
they were so courageous that many knights shook and
bevered for eagerness. All this while Lucas, and Gwinas,
and Briant, and Bellias of Flanders, held strong medley
against six kings, that was King Lot, King Nentres, King
Brandegoris, King Idres, King Uriens, and King Agwisance.
So with the help of Sir Kay and of Sir Griflet they held
these six kings hard, that unnethe they had any power to
defend them. But when Sir Arthur saw the battle would
not be ended by no manner, he ferd wood as a lion, and
steered his horse here and there, on the right hand, and on
the left hand, that he stinted not till he had slain twenty
knights. Also he wounded King Lot sore on the shoulder,
and made him to leave that ground, for Sir Kay and Griflet
did with King Arthur there great deeds of arms. Then
Ulfius, and Brastias, and Sir Ector encountered against
the Duke Eustace, and King Cradelment, and King
Clariance of Northumberland, and King Carados, and
against the king with the hundred knights. So these
knights encountered with these kings, that they made them
to avoid the ground. Then King Lot made great dole for
his damages and his fellows, and said unto the ten kings,
But if ye will do as I advise we shall be slain and destroyed;
let me have the king with the hundred knights, and King
Agwisance, and King Idres, and the Duke of Cambenet,
and we five kings will have fifteen thousand men of arms
with us, and we will go apart while ye six kings hold medley
with twelve thousand; an we see that ye have foughten
with them long, then will we come on fiercely, and else
shall we never match them, said King Lot, but by this
mean. So they departed as they here devised, and six
kings made their party strong against Arthur, and made
great war long. In the meanwhile brake the embushment
of King Ban and King Bors, and Lyonses and Phariance
had the vanguard, and they two knights met with King
Idres and his fellowship, and there began a great medley of

breaking of spears, and smiting of swords, with slaying of men and horses, and King Idres was near at discomforture. That saw Agwisance the king, and put Lionses and Phariance in point of death; for the Duke of Cambenet came on withal with a great fellowship, so these two knights were in great danger of their lives that they were fain to return, but always they rescued themselves and their fellowship marvellously. When King Bors saw those knights put aback, it grieved him sore; then he came on so fast that his fellowship seemed as black as Inde. When King Lot had espied King Bors, he knew him well, then he said, O Jesu, defend us from death and horrible maims! for I see well we be in great peril of death; for I see yonder a king, one of the most worshipfullest men and one of the best knights of the world, is inclined unto his fellowship. What is he? said the king with the hundred knights. It is, said King Lot, King Bors of Gaul; I marvel how they come into this country without witting of us all. It was by Merlin's advice, said the knight. As for him, said King Carados, I will encounter with King Bors, an ye will rescue me when myster is. Go on, said they all, we will do all that we may. Then King Carados and his host rode on a soft pace, till that they come as nigh King Bors as bow-draught, then either battle let their horse run as fast as they might. And Bleoberis that was godson unto King Bors he bare his chief standard, that was a passing good knight. Now shall we see, said King Bors, how these northern Britons can bear the arms: and King Bors encountered with a knight, and smote him throughout with a spear that he fell dead unto the earth, and after drew his sword and did marvellous deeds of arms, that all parties had great wonder thereof; and his knights failed not, but did their part, and King Carados was smitten to the earth. With that came the king with the hundred knights and rescued King Carados mightily by force of arms, for he was a passing good knight of a king, and but a young man.

CHAPTER XVI

YET MORE OF THE SAME BATTLE

By then came into the field King Ban as fierce as a lion, with bands of green and thereupon gold. Ha! ha! said King Lot, we must be discomfited, for yonder I see the most valiant knight of the world, and the man of the most renown, for such two brethren as is King Ban and King Bors are not living, wherefore we must needs void or die; and but if we avoid manly and wisely there is but death. When King Ban came into the battle, he came in so fiercely that the strokes redounded again from the wood and the water; wherefore King Lot wept for pity and dole that he saw so many good knights take their end. But through the great force of King Ban they made both the northern battles that were departed hurtle together for great dread, and the three kings and their knights slew on ever, that it was pity on to behold that multitude of the people that fled. But King Lot, and king of the hundred knights, and King Morganore gathered the people together passing knightly, and did great prowess of arms, and held the battle all that day, like hard. When the king of the hundred knights beheld the great damage that King Ban did, he threst unto him with his horse, and smote him on high upon the helm, a great stroke, and astonied him sore. Then King Ban was wroth with him, and followed on him fiercely; the other saw that, and cast up his shield, and spurred his horse forward, but the stroke of King Ban fell down and carved a cantel off the shield, and the sword slid down by the hauberk behind his back, and cut through the trappings of steel and the horse even in two pieces, that the sword felt the earth. Then the king of the hundred knights voided the horse lightly, and with his sword he broched the horse of King Ban through and through. With that King Ban voided lightly from the dead horse, and then King Ban smote at the other so eagerly, and smote him on the helm that he fell to the earth. Also in that ire he felled King Morganore, and there was great slaughter of good knights and much people. By then came into the press King Arthur, and found King Ban standing among dead men and dead horse, fighting on foot as a wood lion, that there came none nigh him as far as he might reach with his sword but he caught a grievous buffet; whereof King Arthur had great pity. And Arthur was so bloody, that by his shield there might no man know him, for all was blood and brains on his sword. And as Arthur looked by him he saw a knight that was passingly well horsed, and therewith Sir Arthur ran to him, and smote him on the helm, that his sword went unto his teeth, and the knight sank down to the earth dead, and anon Arthur took the horse by the rein, and led him unto King Ban, and said, Fair brother, have this horse, for ye have great myster thereof, and me repenteth sore of your great damage. It shall be soon revenged, said King Ban, for I trust in God mine eure is not such but some of them may sore repent this. I will well, said Arthur, for I see your deeds full actual; nevertheless, I might not come at you at that time. But when King Ban was mounted on horseback, then there began new battle the which was sore and hard, and passing great slaughter. And so through great force King Arthur, King Ban, and King Bors made their knights a little to withdraw them. But alway the eleven kings with their chivalry never turned back; and so withdrew them to a little wood, and so over a little river, and there they rested them, for on the night they might have no rest on the field. And then the eleven kings and knights put them on a heap all together, as men adread and out of all comfort. But there was no man might pass them, they held them so hard together both behind and before, that King Arthur had marvel of their deeds of arms, and was passing wroth. Ah, Sir Arthur, said King Ban and King Bors, blame them not, for they do as good men ought to do. For, by my faith, said King Ban, they are the best fighting men, and knights of most prowess, that ever I saw or heard speak of, and those eleven kings are men of great worship; and if they were longing unto you there were no king under the heaven had such eleven knights, and of such worship. I may not love them, said Arthur, they would destroy me. That wot we well, said King Ban and King Bors, for they are your mortal enemies, and that hath been proved aforehand, and this day they have done their part, and that is great pity of their wilfulness. Then all the eleven kings drew them together, and then said King Lot, Lords, ye must other ways than ye do, or else the great oss is behind; ye may see what people we have lost, and what good men we lose, because we wait always on these foot-men, and ever in saving of one of the foot-men we lose ten horsemen for him; therefore this is mine advice, let us put our foot-men from us, for it is near night, for the noble Arthur will not tarry on the foot-men, for they may save themselves, the wood is near hand. And when we horsemen be together, look every each of you kings let make such ordinance that none break upon pain of death. And who that seeth any man dresse him to flee, lightly that he be slain, for it is better that we slay a coward, than through a coward all we to be slain. How say ye? said King Lot, answer me all ye kings. It is well said, quoth King Nentres; so said the king of the hundred knights; the same said the King Carados, and King Uriens; so did King Idres and King Brandegoris; and so did King Cradelment, and the Duke of Cambenet; the same said King Clariance and King Agwisance, and sware they would never fail other, neither for life nor for death. And whoso that fled, but did as they did, should be slain. Then they amended their harness, and righted their shields, and took new spears and set them on their thighs, and stood still as it had been a plompe of wood.

CHAPTER XVII

YET MORE OF THE SAME BATTLE, AND HOW IT WAS ENDED BY MERLIN

WHEN Sir Arthur and King Ban and Bors beheld them and all their knights, they praised them much for their noble cheer of chivalry, for the hardiest fighters that ever they heard or saw. With that, there dressed them a forty noble knights, and said unto the three kings, they would break their battle; these were their names: Lionses, Phariance, Ulfius, Brastias, Ector, Kay, Lucas the butler, Griflet le Fise de Dieu, Mariet de la Roche, Guinas de Bloi, Briant de la Forest Savage, Bellaus, Morians of the Castle of Maidens, Flannedrius of the Castle of Ladies, Annecians that was King Bors' godson, a noble knight, Ladinas de la Rouse, Emerause, Caulas, Graciens le Castlein, one Blois de la Case, and Sir Colgrevaunce de Gorre, all these knights rode on afore with spears on their thighs, and spurred their horses mightily as the horses might run. And the eleven kings with part of their knights rushed with their horses as fast as they might with their spears, and there they did on both parts marvellous deeds of arms. So came into the thick of the press, Arthur, Ban, and Bors, and slew down right on both hands, that their horses went in blood up to the fetlocks. But ever the eleven kings and their host was ever in the visage of Arthur. Wherefore Ban and Bors had great marvel, considering the great slaughter that there was, but at the last they were driven aback over a little river. With that came Merlin on a great black horse, and said unto Arthur, Thou hast never done, hast thou not done enough? of three score thousand this day hast thou left alive but fifteen thousand, and it is time to say Ho! For God is wroth with thee, that thou wilt never have done, for yonder eleven kings at this time will not be overthrown, but an thou tarry on them any longer, thy fortune will turn and they shall increase. And therefore withdraw you unto your lodging, and rest you as soon as ye may, and reward your good knights with gold and with silver, for they have well deserved it; there may no riches be too dear for them, for of so few men as ye have, there were never men did more of prowess than they have done to-day, for ye have matched this day with the best fighters of the world. That is truth, said King Ban and Bors. Also said Merlin, withdraw you where ye list, for this three year I dare undertake they shall not dare you; and by then ye shall hear new tidings. And then Merlin said unto Arthur, These eleven kings have more on hand than they are ware of, for the Saracens are landed in their countries, more than forty thousand, that burn and slay, and have laid siege at the castle Wandesborow, and make great destruction; therefore dread you not this three year. Also, sir, all the goods that be gotten at this battle, let it be searched, and when ye have it in your hands, let it be given freely unto these two kings, Ban and Bors, that they may reward their knights withal; and that shall cause strangers to be of better will to do you service at need. Also you be able to reward your own knights of your own goods whensomever it liketh you. It is well said, quoth Arthur, and as thou hast devised, so shall it be done. When it was delivered to Ban and Bors, they gave the goods as freely to their knights as freely as it was given to them. Then Merlin took his leave of Arthur and of the two kings, for to go and

see his master Bleise, that dwelt in Northumberland ; and
so he departed and came to his master, that was passing
glad of his coming ; and there he told how Arthur and the
two kings had sped at the great battle, and how it was ended,
and told the names of every king and knight of worship
that was there.   And so Bleise wrote the battle word by
word, as Merlin told him how it began, and by whom, and
in likewise how it was ended, and who had the worse.   All
the battles that were done in Arthur's days, Merlin did his
master Bleise do write ; also he did do write all the battles
that every worthy knight did of Arthur's court.   After this
Merlin departed from his master and came to King Arthur,
that was in the castle of Bedegraine, that was one of the
castles that stood in the forest of Sherwood.   And Merlin
was so disguised that King Arthur knew him not, for he was
all befurred in black sheep skins, and a great pair of boots,
and a bow and arrows, in a russet gown, and brought wild
geese in his hand, and it was on the morn after Candlemas
day ; but King Arthur knew him not.   Sir, said Merlin unto
the king, will ye give me a gift ?   Wherefore, said King
Arthur, should I give thee a gift, churl ?   Sir, said Merlin,
ye were better to give me a gift that is not in your hand than
to lose great riches, for here in the same place where the
great battle was, is great treasure hid in the earth.   Who
told thee so, churl ? said Arthur.   Merlin told me so, said
he.   Then Ulfius and Brastias knew him well enough, and
smiled.   Sir, said these two knights, it is Merlin that so
speaketh unto you.   Then King Arthur was greatly abashed,
and had marvel of Merlin, and so had King Ban and King
Bors, and so they had great disport at him.   So in the
meanwhile there came a damosel that was an earl's daughter :
his name was Sanam, and her name was Lionors, a passing
fair damosel ; and so she came thither for to do homage, as
other lords did after the great battle.   And King Arthur set
his love greatly upon her, and so did she upon him, and the
king had ado with her, and gat on her a child : his name
was Borre, that was after a good night, and of the Table
Round.   Then there came word that the King Rience of
North Wales made great war on King Leodegrance of
Cameliard, for the which thing Arthur was wroth, for
he loved him well, and hated King Rience, for he was
alway against him.   So by ordinance of the three kings
that were sent home unto Benwick, all they would depart

for dread of King Claudas; Phariance, and Antemes, and Gratian, and Lionses of Payarne, with the leaders of those that should keep the kings' lands.

CHAPTER XVIII

HOW KING ARTHUR, KING BAN, AND KING BORS RESCUED KING LEODEGRANCE, AND OTHER INCIDENTS

AND then King Arthur, and King Ban, and King Bors departed with their fellowship, a twenty thousand, and came within six days into the country of Cameliard, and there rescued King Leodegrance, and slew there much people of King Rience, unto the number of ten thousand men, and put him to flight. And then had these three kings great cheer of King Leodegrance, that thanked them of their great goodness, that they would revenge him of his enemies; and there had Arthur the first sight of Guenever, the king's daughter of Cameliard, and ever after he loved her. After they were wedded, as it telleth in the book. So, briefly to make an end, they took their leave to go into their own countries, for King Claudas did great destruction on their lands. Then said Arthur, I will go with you. Nay, said the kings, ye shall not at this time, for ye have much to do yet in these lands, therefore we will depart, and with the great goods that we have gotten in these lands by your gifts, we shall wage good knights and withstand the King Claudas' malice, for by the grace of God, an we have need we shall send to you for your succour; and if ye have need, send for us, and we will not tarry, by the faith of our bodies. It shall not, said Merlin, need that these two kings come again in the way of war, but I know well King Arthur may not be long from you, for within a year or two ye shall have great need, and then shall he revenge you on your enemies, as ye have done on his. For these eleven kings shall die all in a day, by the great might and prowess of arms of two valiant knights (as it telleth after), their names be Balin le Savage, and Balan, his brother, that be marvellous good knights as be any living. Now turn we to the eleven kings that returned unto a city that hight Sorhaute, the which city was within King Uriens', and there they refreshed them as well as they might, and made leeches search their wounds, and sorrowed greatly for the death of their people. With that there came a messenger and told how there was come into their lands people that were lawless as well as Saracens, a forty thousand, and have burnt and slain all the people that they may come by, without mercy, and have laid siege on the castle of Wandesborow. Alas, said the eleven kings, here is sorrow upon sorrow, and if we had not warred against Arthur as we have done, he would soon revenge us; as for King Leodegrance, he loveth Arthur better than us, and as for King Rience, he hath enough to do with Leodegrance, for he hath laid siege unto him. So they consented together to keep all the marches of Cornwall, of Wales, and of the North. So first, they put King Idres in the City of Nauntes in Britain, with four thousand men of arms, to watch both the water and the land. Also they put in the city of Windesan, King Nentres of Garlot, with four thousand knights to watch both on water and on land. Also they had of other men of war more than eight thousand, for to fortify all the fortresses in the marches of Cornwall. Also they put more knights in all the marches of Wales and Scotland, with many good men of arms, and so they kept them together the space of three year, and ever allied them with mighty kings and dukes and lords. And to them fell King Rience of North Wales, the which was a mighty man of men, and Nero that was a mighty man of men. And all this while they furnished them and garnished them of good men of arms, and victual, and of all manner of habiliments that pretendeth to the war, to avenge them for the battle of Bedegraine, as it telleth in the book of adventures following.

CHAPTER XIX

HOW KING ARTHUR RODE TO CARLION, AND OF HIS DREAM, AND HOW HE SAW THE QUESTING BEAST

THEN after the departure of King Ban and of King Bors, King Arthur rode unto Carlion. And thither came to him, King Lot's wife, of Orkney, in manner of a message, but she was sent thither to espy the court of King Arthur; and she came richly bisene, with her four sons

Gawaine, Gaheris, Agravine, and Gareth, with many other knights and ladies. For she was a passing fair lady, therefore the king cast great love unto her, and desired to lie by her; so they were agreed, and he begat upon her Mordred, and she was his sister, on his mother's side, Igraine. So there she rested her a month, and at the last departed. Then the king dreamed a marvellous dream whereof he was sore adread. But all this time King Arthur knew not that King Lot's wife was his sister. Thus was the dream of Arthur: Him thought there was come into this land griffins and serpents, and him thought they burnt and slew all the people in the land, and then him thought he fought with them, and they did him passing great harm, and wounded him full sore, but at the last he slew them. When the king awaked, he was passing heavy of his dream, and so to put it out of thoughts, he made him ready with many knights to ride a-hunting. As soon as he was in the forest the king saw a great hart afore him. This hart will I chase, said King Arthur, and so he spurred the horse, and rode after long, and so by fine force oft he was like to have smitten the hart; whereas the king had chased the hart so long, that his horse lost his breath, and fell down dead; then a yeoman fetched the king another horse. So the king saw the hart embushed, and his horse dead; he set him down by a fountain, and there he fell in great thoughts. And as he sat so, him thought he heard a noise of hounds, to the sum of thirty. And with that the king saw coming toward him the strangest beast that ever he saw or heard of; so the beast went to the well and drank, and the noise was in the beast's belly like unto the questyng of thirty couple hounds; but all the while the beast drank there was no noise in the beast's belly: and therewith the beast departed with a great noise, whereof the king had great marvel. And so he was in a great thought, and therewith he fell asleep. Right so there came a knight afoot unto Arthur and said, Knight full of thought and sleepy, tell me if thou sawest a strange beast pass this way. Such one saw I, said King Arthur, that is past two mile; what would ye with the beast? said Arthur. Sir, I have followed that beast long time, and killed mine horse, so would God I had another to follow my quest. Right so came one with the king's horse, and when the knight saw the horse, he prayed the king to give him the horse: for I have followed this quest this twelvemonth, and either I shall achieve him, or bleed of the best blood of my body. Pellinore, that time king, followed the questing beast, and after his death Sir Palamides followed it.

CHAPTER XX

HOW KING PELLINORE TOOK ARTHUR'S HORSE AND FOLLOWED THE QUESTING BEAST, AND HOW MERLIN MET WITH ARTHUR

SIR knight, said the king, leave that quest, and suffer me to have it, and I will follow it another twelvemonth. Ah, fool, said the knight unto Arthur, it is in vain thy desire, for it shall never be achieved but by me, or my next kin. Therewith he started unto the king's horse and mounted into the saddle, and said, Gramercy, this horse is my own. Well, said the king, thou mayst take my horse by force, but an I might prove thee whether thou were better on horseback or I. Well, said the knight, seek me here when thou wilt, and here nigh this well thou shalt find me, and so passed on his way. Then the king sat in a study, and bade his men fetch his horse as fast as ever they might. Right so came by him Merlin like a child of fourteen year of age, and saluted the king, and asked him why he was so pensive. I may well be pensive said the king, for I have seen the marvellest sight that ever I saw. That know I well, said Merlin, as well as thyself, and of all thy thoughts, but thou art but a fool to take thought, for it will not amend thee. Also I know what thou art, and who was thy father, and of whom thou wert begotten; King Uther Pendragon was thy father, and begat thee on Igraine. That is false, said King Arthur, how shouldest thou know it, for thou art not so old of years to know my father? Yes, said Merlin, I know it better than ye or any man living. I will not believe thee, said Arthur, and was wroth with the child. So departed Merlin, and came again in the likeness of an old man of fourscore year of age, whereof the king was right glad, for he seemed to be right wise. Then said the old man, Why are ye so sad? I may well be heavy, said Arthur, for many things. Also here was a child, and told me many things that meseemeth he should not know, for he was not of age to know my father. Yes, said the old man, the child told you truth, and more would he have told you an ye would have suffered him ; but ye have done a thing late that God is displeased with you, for ye have lain by your sister, and on her ye have gotten a child that shall destroy you and all the knights of your realm. What are ye, said Arthur, that tell me these tidings? I am Merlin, and I was he in the child's likeness. Ah, said King Arthur, ye are a marvellous man, but I marvel much of thy words that I must die in battle. Marvel not, said Merlin, for it is God's will your body to be punished for your foul deeds ; but I may well be sorry, said Merlin, for I shall die a shameful death to be put in the earth quick, and ye shall die a worshipful death. And as they talked this, came one with the king's horse, and so the king mounted on his horse, and Merlin on another, and so rode unto Carlion. And anon the king asked Ector and Ulfius how he was begotten, and they told him Uther Pendragon was his father and Queen Igraine his mother. Then he said to Merlin, I will that my mother be sent for, that I may speak with her ; and if she say so herself, then will I believe it. In all haste, the queen was sent for, and she came and brought with her Morgan le Fay, her daughter, that was as fair a lady as any might be, and the king welcomed Igraine in the best manner.

CHAPTER XXI

HOW ULFIUS IMPEACHED QUEEN IGRAINE, ARTHUR'S MOTHER, OF TREASON ; AND HOW A KNIGHT CAME AND DESIRED TO HAVE THE DEATH OF HIS MASTER REVENGED

RIGHT so came Ulfius, and said openly that the king and all might hear that were feasted that day, Ye are the falsest lady of the world, and the most traitress unto the king's person. Beware, said Arthur, what thou sayest ; thou speakest a great word. I am well ware, said Ulfius, what I speak, and here is my glove to prove it upon any man that will say the contrary, that this Queen Igraine is causer of your great damage, and of your great war. For, an she would have uttered it in the life of King Uther Pendragon, of the birth of you, and how ye were begotten, ye had never had the mortal wars that ye have had ; for the most part of your barons of your realm knew never whose son ye were, nor of whom ye were begotten ; and she that bare you of her body should have made it known openly in excusing of her worship and yours, and in likewise to all the realm, wherefore I prove her false to God and to you and to all your realm, and who will say the contrary I will prove it on his body. Then spake Igraine and said, I am a woman and I may not fight, but rather than I should be dishonoured, there would some good man take my quarrel. More, she said, Merlin knoweth well, and ye Sir Ulfius, how King Uther came to me in the Castle of Tintagel in the likeness of my lord, that was dead three hours tofore, and thereby gat a child that night upon me. And after the thirteenth day King Uther wedded me, and by his commandment when the child was born it was delivered unto Merlin and nourished by him, and so I saw the child never after, nor wot not what is his name, for I knew him never yet. And there Ulfius said to the queen, Merlin is more to blame than ye. Well I wot, said the queen, I bare a child by my lord King Uther, but I wot not where he is become. Then Merlin took the king by the hand, saying, This is your mother. And therewith Sir Ector bare witness how he nourished him by Uther's commandment. And therewith King Arthur took his mother, Queen Igraine, in his arms and kissed her, and either wept upon other. And then the king let make a feast that lasted eight days. Then on a day there come in the court a squire on horseback, leading a knight before him wounded to the death, and told him how there was a knight in the forest had reared up a pavilion by a well, and hath slain my master, a good knight, his name was Miles ; wherefore I beseech you that my master may be buried, and that some knight may revenge my master's death. Then the noise was great of that knight's death in the court, and every man said his advice. Then came Griflet that was but a squire, and he was but young, of the age of the King Arthur, so he besought the king for all his service that he had done him to give him the order of knighthood.

CHAPTER XXII

HOW GRIFLET WAS MADE KNIGHT, AND JOUSTED WITH A KNIGHT

THOU art full young and tender of age, said Arthur, for to take so high an order on thee. Sir, said Griflet, I beseech you make me knight. Sir, said Merlin, it were great pity to lose Griflet, for he will be a passing good man when he is of age, abiding with you the term of his life. And if he adventure his body with yonder knight at the fountain, it is in great peril if ever he come again, for he is one of the best knights of the world, and the strongest man of arms. Well, said Arthur. So at the desire of Griflet the king made him knight. Now, said Arthur unto Sir Griflet, sith I have made you knight thou must give me a gift. What ye will, said Griflet. Thou shalt promise me by the faith of thy body, when thou has jousted with the knight at the fountain, whether it fall ye be on foot or on horseback, that right so ye shall come again unto me without making any more debate. I will promise you, said Griflet, as you desire. Then took Griflet his horse in great haste, and dressed his shield and took a spear in his hand, and so he rode a great wallop till he came to the fountain, and thereby he saw a rich pavilion, and thereby under a cloth stood a fair horse well saddled and bridled, and on a tree a shield of divers colours and a great spear. Then Griflet smote on the shield with the butt of his spear, that the shield fell down to the ground. With that the knight came out of the pavilion, and said, Fair knight, why smote ye down my shield? For I will joust with you, said Griflet. It is better ye do not, said the knight, for ye are but young, and late made knight, and your might is nothing to mine. As for that, said Griflet, I will joust with you. That is me loath, said the knight, but sith I must needs, I will dress me thereto : of whence be ye ? said the knight. Sir, I am of Arthur's court. So the two knights ran together that Griflet's spear all to-shivered ; and therewithal he smote Griflet through the shield and the left side, and brake the spear that the truncheon stuck in his body, that horse and knight fell down.

CHAPTER XXIII

HOW TWELVE KNIGHTS CAME FROM ROME AND ASKED TRUAGE
FOR THIS LAND OF ARTHUR, AND HOW ARTHUR FOUGHT WITH
A KNIGHT

WHEN the knight saw him lie so on the ground, he alit, and was passing heavy, for he weened he had slain him, and then he unlaced his helm and gat him wind, and so with the truncheon he set him on his horse and gat him wind, and so betook him to God, and said he had a mighty

heart, and if he might live he would prove a passing good
knight. And so Sir Griflet rode to the court, where great
dole was made for him. But through good leeches he was
healed and saved. Right so came into the court twelve
knights, and were aged men, and they came from the
Emperor of Rome, and they asked of Arthur truage for this
realm, other-else the emperor would destroy him and his
land. Well, said King Arthur, ye are messengers, therefore
ye may say what ye will, other-else ye should die therefore.
But this is mine answer: I owe the emperor no truage, nor
none will I hold him, but on a fair field I shall give him my
truage that shall be with a sharp spear, or else with a sharp
sword, and that shall not be long, by my father's soul, Uther
Pendragon. And therewith the messengers departed passingly wroth, and King Arthur as wroth, for in evil time
came they then; for the king was passingly wroth for the
hurt of Sir Griflet. And so he commanded a privy man of
his chamber that or it be day his best horse and armour,
with all that longeth unto his person, be without the city or
to-morrow day. Right so or to-morrow day he met with his
man and his horse, and so mounted up and dressed his
shield and took his spear, and bade his chamberlain tarry
there till he came again. And so Arthur rode a soft pace
till it was day, and then was he ware of three churls chasing
Merlin, and would have slain him. Then the king rode
unto them, and bade them: Flee, churls! then were they
afeard when they saw a knight, and fled. O Merlin, said
Arthur, here hadst thou been slain for all thy crafts had I
not been. Nay, said Merlin, not so, for I could save myself
an I would; and thou art more near thy death than I am,
for thou goest to the deathward, an God be not thy friend.
So as they went thus talking they came to the fountain, and
the rich pavilion there by it. Then King Arthur was ware
where sat a knight armed in a chair. Sir knight, said
Arthur, for what cause abidest thou here, that there may no
knight ride this way but if he joust with thee? said the
king. I rede thee leave that custom, said Arthur. This
custom, said the knight, have I used and will use maugre
who saith nay, and who is grieved with my custom let him
amend it that will. I will amend it, said Arthur. I shall
defend thee, said the knight. Anon he took his horse and
dressed his shield and took a spear, and they met so hard
either in other's shields, that all to-shivered their spears.
Therewith anon Arthur pulled out his sword. Nay, not so,

said the knight; it is fairer, said the knight, that we twain run more together with sharp spears. I will well, said Arthur, an I had any more spears. I have enow, said the knight; so there came a squire and brought two good spears, and Arthur chose one and he another; so they spurred their horses and came together with all their mights, that either brake their spears to their hands. Then Arthur set hand on his sword. Nay, said the knight, ye shall do better, ye are a passing good jouster as ever I met withal, and once for the love of the high order of knighthood let us joust once again. I assent me, said Arthur. Anon there were brought two great spears, and every knight gat a spear, and therewith they ran together that Arthur's spear all to-shivered. But the other knight hit him so hard in midst of the shield, that horse and man fell to the earth, and therewith Arthur was eager, and pulled out his sword, and said, I will assay thee, sir knight, on foot, for I have lost the honour on horseback. I will be on horseback, said the knight. Then was Arthur wroth, and dressed his shield toward him with his sword drawn. When the knight saw that, he alit, for him thought no worship to have a knight at such avail, he to be on horseback and he on foot, and so he alit and dressed his shield unto Arthur. And there began a strong battle with many great strokes, and so hewed with their swords that the cantels flew in the fields, and much blood they bled both, that all the place there as they fought was overbled with blood, and thus they fought long and rested them, and then they went to the battle again, and so hurtled together like two rams that either fell to the earth. So at the last they smote together that both their swords met even together. But the sword of the knight smote King Arthur's sword in two pieces, wherefore he was heavy. Then said the knight unto Arthur, Thou art in my daunger whether me list to save thee or slay thee, and but thou yield thee as overcome and recreant, thou shalt die. As for death, said King Arthur, welcome be it when it cometh, but to yield me unto thee as recreant I had liefer die than to be so shamed. And therewithal the king leapt unto Pellinore, and took him by the middle and threw him down, and rased off his helm. When the knight felt that he was adread, for he was a passing big man of might, and anon he brought Arthur under him, and rased off his helm and would have smitten off his head.

CHAPTER XXIV

HOW MERLIN SAVED ARTHUR'S LIFE, AND THREW AN ENCHANT-
MENT ON KING PELLINORE AND MADE HIM TO SLEEP

THEREWITHAL came Merlin and said, Knight, hold thy
hand, for an thou slay that knight thou puttest this realm
in the greatest damage that ever was realm: for this knight
is a man of more worship than thou wotest of. Why, who
is he? said the knight. It is King Arthur. Then would
he have slain him for dread of his wrath, and heaved up his
sword, and therewith Merlin cast an enchantment to the
knight, that he fell to the earth in a great sleep. Then
Merlin took up King Arthur, and rode forth on the knight's
horse. Alas! said Arthur, what hast thou done, Merlin?
hast thou slain this good knight by thy crafts? There
liveth not so worshipful a knight as he was; I had liefer
than the stint of my land a year that he were alive. Care
ye not, said Merlin, for he is wholer than ye; for he is but
a-sleep, and will awake within three hours. I told you, said
Merlin, what a knight he was; here had ye been slain had
I not been. Also there liveth not a bigger knight than he
is one, and he shall hereafter do you right good service;
and his name is Pellinore, and he shall have two sons that
shall be passing good men; save one they shall have no
fellow of prowess and of good living, and their names shall
be Percivale of Wales and Lamerake of Wales, and he shall
tell you the name of your own son begotten of your sister
that shall be the destruction of all this realm.

CHAPTER XXV

HOW ARTHUR BY THE MEAN OF MERLIN GAT EXCALIBUR HIS
SWORD OF THE LADY OF THE LAKE

RIGHT so the king and he departed, and went unto an
hermit that was a good man and a great leech. So the
hermit searched all his wounds and gave him good salves;
so the king was there three days, and then were his wounds
well amended that he might ride and go, and so departed.
And as they rode, Arthur said, I have no sword. No force,
said Merlin, hereby is a sword that shall be yours, an I

may. So they rode till they came to a lake, the which was a fair water and broad, and in the midst of the lake Arthur was ware of an arm clothed in white samite, that held a fair sword in that hand. Lo! said Merlin, yonder is that sword that I spake of. With that they saw a damosel going upon the lake. What damosel is that? said Arthur. That is the Lady of the Lake, said Merlin; and within that lake is a rock, and therein is as fair a place as any on earth, and richly beseen; and this damosel will come to you anon, and then speak ye fair to her that she will give you that sword. Anon withal came the damosel unto Arthur, and saluted him, and he her again. Damosel, said Arthur, what sword is that, that yonder the arm holdeth above the water? I would it were mine, for I have no sword. Sir Arthur, king, said the damosel, that sword is mine, and if ye will give me a gift when I ask it you, ye shall have it. By my faith, said Arthur, I will give you what gift ye will ask. Well! said the damosel, go ye into yonder barge, and row yourself to the sword, and take it and the scabbard with you, and I will ask my gift when I see my time. So Sir Arthur and Merlin alit and tied their horses to two trees, and so they went into the ship, and when they came to the sword that the hand held, Sir Arthur took it up by the handles, and took it with him, and the arm and the hand went under the water. And so they came unto the land and rode forth, and then Sir Arthur saw a rich pavilion. What signifieth yonder pavilion? It is the knight's pavilion, said Merlin, that ye fought with last, Sir Pellinore; but he is out, he is not there. He hath ado with a knight of yours that hight Egglame, and they have foughten together, but at the last Egglame fled, and else he had been dead, and he hath chased him even to Carlion, and we shall meet with him anon in the highway. That is well said, said Arthur, now have I a sword, now will I wage battle with him, and be avenged on him. Sir, you shall not so, said Merlin, for the knight is weary of fighting and chasing, so that ye shall have no worship to have ado with him; also he will not be lightly matched of one knight living, and therefore it is my counsel, let him pass, for he shall do you good service in short time, and his sons after his days. Also ye shall see that day in short space, you shall be right glad to give him your sister to wed. When I see him, I will do as ye advise me, said Arthur. Then Sir Arthur looked on the sword, and liked it passing well. Whether liketh you better, said Merlin, the sword or the scabbard? Me liketh better the sword, said Arthur. Ye are more unwise, said Merlin, for the scabbard is worth ten of the swords, for whiles ye have the scabbard upon you, ye shall never lose no blood be ye never so sore wounded, therefore keep well the scabbard always with you. So they rode unto Carlion, and by the way they met with Sir Pellinore; but Merlin had done such a craft, that Pellinore saw not Arthur, and he passed by without any words. I marvel, said Arthur, that the knight would not speak. Sir, said Merlin, he saw you not, for an he had seen you, ye had not lightly departed. So they came unto Carlion, whereof his knights were passing glad. And when they heard of his adventures, they marvelled that he would jeopard his person so, alone. But all men of worship said it was merry to be under such a chieftain, that would put his person in adventure as other poor knights did.

CHAPTER XXVI

HOW TIDINGS CAME TO ARTHUR THAT KING RIENCE HAD OVER-
COME ELEVEN KINGS, AND HOW HE DESIRED ARTHUR'S BEARD
TO TRIM HIS MANTLE

THIS meanwhile came a messenger from King Rience of North Wales, and king he was of all Ireland, and of many isles. And this was his message, greeting well King Arthur in this manner wise, saying that King Rience had discomfited and overcome eleven kings, and every each of them did him homage, and that was this, they gave him their beards clean flayed off, as much as there was; wherefore the messenger came for King Arthur's beard. For King Rience had purfled a mantle with kings' beards, and there lacked one place of the mantle; wherefore he sent for his beard, or else he would enter into his lands, and burn and slay, and never leave till he have the head and the beard. Well, said Arthur, thou hast said thy message, the which is the most villainous and lewdest message that ever man heard sent unto a king; also thou mayest see my beard is full young yet to make a purfle of it. But tell thou thy king this: I owe him none homage, nor none of mine elders, but or it be long to, he shall do me homage on both his knees, or else he shall lose his head, by the faith of my body, for this is the most shamefulest message that ever I heard speak of. I have espied thy king met never yet with worshipful man, but tell him, I will have his head without he do me homage. Then the messenger departed. Now is there any here, said Arthur, that knoweth King Rience? Then answered a knight that hight Naram, Sir, I know the king well; he is a passing good man of his body, as few be living, and a passing proud man, and Sir, doubt ye not he will make war on you with a mighty puissance. Well. said Arthur, I shall ordain for him in short time.

CHAPTER XXVII

HOW ALL THE CHILDREN WERE SENT FOR THAT WERE BORN ON MAY-DAY, AND HOW MORDRED WAS SAVED

THEN King Arthur let send for all the children born on May-day, begotten of lords and born of ladies; for Merlin told King Arthur that he that should destroy him should be born on May-day, wherefore he sent for them all, upon pain of death; and so there were found many lords' sons, and all were sent unto the king, and so was Mordred sent by King Lot's wife, and all were put in a ship to the sea, and some were four weeks old, and some less. And so by fortune the ship drave unto a castle, and was all to-riven, and destroyed the most part, save that Mordred was cast up, and a good man found him, and nourished him till he was fourteen year old, and then he brought him to the court, as it rehearseth afterward, toward the end of the Death of Arthur. So many lords and barons of this realm were displeased, for their children were so lost, and many put the wyte on Merlin more than on Arthur; so what for dread and for love, they held their peace. But when the messenger came to King Rience, then was he woode out of measure, and purveyed him for a great host, as it rehearseth after in the book of Balin le Savage, that followeth next after, how by adventure Balin gat the sword.

Explicit Liber Primus

BOOK II

CHAPTER I

AFTER the death of Uther Pendragon reigned Arthur his son, the which had great war in his days for to get all England into his hand. For there were many kings within the realm of England, and in Wales, Scotland, and Cornwall. So it befell on a time when King Arthur was at London, there came a knight and told the king tidings how that the King Rience of North Wales had reared a great number of people, and were entered into the land, and burnt and slew the king's true liege people. If this be true, said Arthur, it were great shame unto mine estate but that he were mightily withstood. It is truth, said the knight, for I saw the host myself. Well, said the king, let make a cry, that all the lords, knights, and gentlemen of arms, should draw unto a castle called Camelot in those days, and there the king would let make a council-general and a great jousts. So when the king was come thither with all his baronage, and lodged as they seemed best, there was come a damosel the which was sent on message from the great lady Lile of Avelion. And when she came before King Arthur, she told from whom she came, and how she was sent on message unto him for these causes. Then she let her mantle fall that was richly furred; and then was she girt with a noble sword whereof the king had marvel, and said, Damosel, for what cause are ye girt with that sword? it beseemeth you not. Now shall I tell you, said the damosel; this sword that I am girt withal doth me great sorrow and cumberance, for I may not be delivered of this sword but by a knight, but he must be a passing good man of his hands and of his deeds, and without villainy or treachery, and without treason. And if I may find such a knight that hath all these virtues, he may draw out this sword out of the sheath, for I have been at King Rience's, it was told me there were passing good knights, and he and all his knights have assayed it and none can speed. This is a great marvel, said Arthur, if this be sooth; I will myself assay to draw out the sword, not presuming upon myself that I am the best knight, but that I will begin to draw at your sword in giving example to all the barons that they shall assay every each one after other when I have assayed it. Then Arthur took the sword by the sheath and by the girdle and pulled at it eagerly, but the sword would not out. Sir, said the damosel, you need not to pull half so hard, for he that shall pull it out shall do it with little might. Ye say well, said Arthur; now assay ye all my barons, but beware ye be not defiled with shame, treachery, nor guile. Then it will not avail, said the damosel, for he must be a clean knight without villainy, and of a gentle strain of father side and mother side. Most of all the barons of the Round Table that were there at that time assayed all by row, but there might none speed; wherefore the damosel made great sorrow out of measure, and said, Alas! I weened in this Court had been the best knights without treachery or treason. By my faith, said Arthur, here are good knights, as I deem, as any be in the world, but their grace is not to help you, wherefore I am displeased.

CHAPTER II

HOW BALIN, ARRAYED LIKE A POOR KNIGHT, PULLED OUT THE SWORD, WHICH AFTERWARD WAS THE CAUSE OF HIS DEATH

THEN fell it so that time there was a poor knight with King Arthur, that had been prisoner with him half a year and more for slaying of a knight, the which was cousin unto King Arthur. The name of this knight was called Balin, and by good means of the barons he was delivered out of prison, for he was a good man named of his body, and he was born in Northumberland; and so he went privily into the court, and saw this adventure, whereof it reysed his heart, and he would assay it as other knights did, but for he was poor and poorly arrayed he put him not far in press; but in his heart he was fully assured to do as well, if his grace happed him, as any knight that there was. And as the damosel took her leave of Arthur and of all the barons. so departing, this knight Balin called unto her, and said, Damosel, I pray you of your courtesy, suffer me as well to assay as these lords; though that I be so poorly clothed, in my heart meseemeth I am fully assured as some of these others, and meseemeth in my heart to speed right well. The damosel beheld the poor knight, and saw he was a likely man, but for his poor arrayment she thought he should be of no worship without villainy or treachery. And then she said unto the knight, Sir, it needeth not to put me to more pain or labour, for it seemeth not you to speed there as other have failed. Ah! fair Damosel, said Balin, worthiness, and good tatches, and good deeds, are not only in arrayment, but manhood and worship is hid within man's person, and many a worshipful knight is not known unto all people, and therefore worship and hardiness is not in arrayment. By God, said the Damosel, ye say sooth; therefore ye shall assay to do what ye may. Then Balin took the sword by the girdle and sheath, and drew it out easily; and when he looked on the sword it pleased him much. Then had the king and all the barons great marvel that Balin had done that adventure, and many knights had great despite of Balin. Certes, said the damosel, this is a passing good knight, and the best that ever I found, and most of worship without treason, treachery, or villainy, and many marvels shall he do. Now, gentle and courteous knight, give me the sword again. Nay, said Balin, for this sword will I keep, but it be taken from me with force. Well, said the damosel, ye are not wise to keep the sword from me, for ye shall slay with the sword the best friend that ye have, and the man that ye most love in the world, and the sword shall be your destruction. I shall take the adventure, said Balin, that God will ordain me, but the sword ye shall not have at this time, by the faith of my body. Ye shall repent it within short time, said the damosel, for I would have the sword more for your avail than for mine, for I am passing heavy for your sake; for ye will not believe that sword shall be your destruction, and that is great pity. With that the damosel departed, making great sorrow. Anon after, Balin sent for his horse and armour, and so would depart from the court, and took his leave of King Arthur. Nay, said the king, I suppose ye will not depart so lightly from this fellowship, I suppose ye are displeased that I have shewed you unkindness; blame me the less, for I was misinformed against you, but I weened ye had not been such a knight as ye are, of worship and prowess, and if ye will abide in this court among my fellowship, I shall so advance you as ye shall be pleased. God thank your highness, said Balin, your bounty and highness may no man praise half to the value; but at this time I must needs depart, beseeching you alway of your good grace. Truly, said the king, I am right wroth for your departing; I pray you, fair knight, that ye tarry not long, and ye shall be right welcome to me, and to my barons, and I shall amend all amiss that I have done against you. God thank your great lordship, said Balin, and therewith made him ready to depart. Then the most part of the knights of the Round Table said that Balin did not this adventure all only by might, but by witchcraft.

CHAPTER III

HOW THE LADY OF THE LAKE DEMANDED THE KNIGHT'S HEAD
THAT HAD WON THE SWORD, OR THE MAIDEN'S HEAD

THE meanwhile, that this knight was making him ready to depart, there came into the court a lady that hight the Lady of the Lake. And she came on horseback, richly bysene, and saluted King Arthur, and there asked him a gift that he promised her when she gave him the sword. That is sooth, said Arthur, a gift I promised you, but I have forgotten the name of my sword that ye gave me. The name of it, said the lady, is Excalibur, that is as much to say as Cut-steel. Ye say well, said the king, ask what ye will and ye shall have it, an it lie in my power to give it. Well, said the lady, I ask the head of the knight that hath won the sword, or else the damosel's head that brought it; I take no force though I have both their heads, for he slew my brother, a good knight and a true, and that gentlewoman was causer of my father's death. Truly, said King Arthur, I may not grant neither of their heads with my worship, therefore ask what ye will else, and I shall fulfil your desire. I will ask none other thing, said the lady. When Balin was ready to depart, he saw the Lady of the Lake, that by her means had slain Balin's mother, and he had sought her three years; and when it was told him that she asked his head of King Arthur, he went to her straight and said, Evil be you found; ye would have my head, and therefore ye shall lose yours, and with his sword lightly he smote off her head before King Arthur. Alas, for shame! said Arthur, why have ye done so? ye have shamed me and all my court, for this was a lady that I was beholden to, and hither she came under my safe-conduct; I shall never forgive you that trespass. Sir, said Balin, me forthynketh of your displeasure, for this same lady was the untruest lady living, and by enchantment and sorcery she hath been the destroyer of many good knights, and she was causer that my mother was burnt, through her falsehood and treachery. What cause soever ye had, said Arthur, ye should have forborne her in my presence; therefore, think not the contrary, ye shall repent it, for such another despite had I never in my court; therefore withdraw you out of my court in all haste ye may. Then Balin took up the head of the lady, and bare it with him to his hostelry, and there he met with his squire, that was sorry he had displeased King Arthur, and so they rode forth out of the town. Now, said Balin, we must depart, take thou this head and bear it to my friends, and tell them how I have sped, and tell my friends in Northumberland that my most foe is dead. Also tell them how I am out of prison, and what adventure befel me at the getting of this sword. Alas! said the squire, ye are greatly to blame for to displease King Arthur. As for that, said Balin, I will hie me in all the haste that I may to meet with King Rience and destroy him, either else to die therefore; and if it may hap me to win him, then will King Arthur be my good and gracious lord. Where shall I meet with you? said the squire. In King Arthur's court, said Balin. So his squire and he departed at that time. Then King Arthur and all the court made great dole and had shame of the death of the Lady of the Lake. Then the king buried her richly.

CHAPTER IV

HOW MERLIN TOLD THE ADVENTURE OF THIS DAMOSEL

At that time there was a knight, the which was the king's son of Ireland, and his name was Lanceor, the which was an orgulous knight, and counted himself one of the best of the court; and he had great despite at Balin for the achieving of the sword, that any should be accounted more hardy, or more of prowess; and he asked King Arthur if he would

give him leave to ride after Balin and to revenge the despite
that he had none. Do your best, said Arthur, I am right
wroth with Balin; I would he were quit of the despite that
he hath done to me and to my court. Then this Lanceor
went to his hostelry to make him ready. In the meanwhile
came Merlin unto the court of King Arthur, and there was
told him the adventure of the sword, and the death of the
Lady of the Lake. Now shall I say you, said Merlin; this
same damosel that here standeth, that brought the sword
unto your court, I shall tell you the cause of her coming:
she was the falsest damosel that liveth. Say not so, said
they. She hath a brother, a passing good knight of prowess
and a full true man; and this damosel loved another knight
that held her to paramour, and this good knight her brother
met with the knight that held her to paramour, and slew him
by force of his hands. When this false damosel understood
this, she went to the Lady Lile of Avelion, and besought
her of help, to be avenged on her own brother.

CHAPTER V

HOW BALIN WAS PURSUED BY SIR LANCEOR, KNIGHT OF IRELAND,
AND HOW HE JOUSTED AND SLEW HIM

AND so this Lady Lile of Avelion took her this sword that
she brought with her, and told there should no man pull it
out of the sheath but if he be one of the best knights of this
realm, and he should be hard and full of prowess, and with
that sword he should slay her brother. This was the cause
that the damosel came into this court. I know it as well as
ye. Would God she had not come into this court, but she
came never in fellowship of worship to do good, but always
great harm; and that knight that hath achieved the sword
shall be destroyed by that sword, for the which will be great
dommage, for there liveth not a knight of more prowess than
he is, and he shall do unto you, my Lord Arthur, great
honour and kindness; and it is great pity he shall not
endure but a while, for of his strength and hardiness I know
not his match living. So the knight of Ireland armed him
at all points, and dressed his shield on his shoulder, and
mounted upon horseback, and took his spear in his hand,
and rode after a great pace, as much as his horse might go;

and within a little space on a mountain he had a sight of
Balin, and with a loud voice he cried, Abide, knight, for ye
shall abide whether ye will or nill, and the shield that is
tofore you shall not help. When Balin heard the noise, he
turned his horse fiercely, and said, Fair knight, what will ye
with me, will ye joust with me? Yea, said the Irish knight,
therefore come I after you. Peradventure, said Balin, it had
been better to have holden you at home, for many a man
weeneth to put his enemy to a rebuke, and oft it falleth to
himself. Of what court be ye sent from? said Balin. I am
come from the court of King Arthur, said the knight of
Ireland, that come hither for to revenge the despite ye did
this day to King Arthur and to his court. Well, said Balin,
I see well I must have ado with you, that me forthynketh
for to grieve King Arthur, or any of his court; and your
quarrel is full simple, said Balin, unto me, for the lady that
is dead, did me great damage, and else would I have been
loath as any knight that liveth for to slay a lady. Make
you ready, said the knight Lanceor, and dress you unto me,
for that one shall abide in the field. Then they took their
spears, and came together as much as their horses might
drive, and the Irish knight smote Balin on the shield, that
all went shivers of his spear, and Balin hit him through the
shield, and the hauberk perished, and so pierced through
his body and the horse's croup, and anon turned his horse
fiercely, and drew out his sword, and wist not that he had
slain him, and then he saw him lie as a dead corpse.

CHAPTER VI

HOW A DAMOSEL, WHICH WAS LOVE TO LANCEOR, SLEW HERSELF
FOR LOVE, AND HOW BALIN MET WITH HIS BROTHER BALAN

THEN he looked by him, and was ware of a damosel that
came riding full fast as the horse might ride, on a fair
palfrey. And when she espied that Lanceor was slain, she
made sorrow out of measure, and said, O Balin, two bodies
thou hast slain and one heart, and two hearts in one body,
and two souls thou hast lost. And therewith she took the
sword from her love that lay dead, and fell to the ground in
a swoon. And when she arose she made great dole out of
measure, the which sorrow grieved Balin passingly sore, and
he went unto her for to have taken the sword out of her

hand, but she held it so fast he might not take it out of her hand unless he should have hurt her, and suddenly she set the pommel to the ground, and rove herself through the body. When Balin espied her deeds, he was passing heavy in his heart, and ashamed that so fair a damosel had destroyed herself for the love of his death. Alas, said Balin, me repenteth sore the death of this knight, for the love of this damosel, for there was much true love betwixt them both. And for sorrow he might not longer behold him, but turned his horse and looked toward a great forest, and there he was ware, by the arms, of his brother Balan. And when they were met they put off their helms and kissed together, and wept for joy and pity. Then Balan said, I little weened to have met with you at this sudden adventure; I am right glad of your deliverance out of your dolorous prisonment, for a man told me, in the castle of Four Stones, that ye were delivered, and that man had seen you in the court of King Arthur, and therefore I came hither into this country, for here I supposed to find you. Anon the knight Balin told his brother of his adventure of the sword, and of the death of the Lady of the Lake, and how King Arthur was displeased with him. Wherefore he sent this knight after me, that lieth here dead, and the death of this damosel grieveth me sore. So doth it me, said Balan, but ye must take the adventure that God will ordain you. Truly, said Balin, I am right heavy that my Lord Arthur is displeased with me, for he is the most worshipful knight that reigneth now on earth, and his love will I get or else will I put my life in adventure, for the King Rience lieth at a siege at Castle Terrabil, and thither will we draw in all haste, to prove our worship and prowess upon him. I will well, said Balan, that we do, and we will help each other as brethren ought to do.

CHAPTER VII

HOW A DWARF REPROVED BALIN FOR THE DEATH OF LANCEOR, AND HOW KING MARK OF CORNWALL FOUND THEM, AND MADE A TOMB OVER THEM

Now go we hence, said Balin, and well be we met. The meanwhile as they talked, there came a dwarf from the city of Camelot on horseback, as much as he might, and found the dead bodies, wherefore he made great dole, and pulled out his hair for sorrow, and said, Which of you knights have done this deed? Whereby askest thou it? said Balan. For I would wit it, said the dwarf. It was I, said Balin, that slew this knight in my defence, for hither he came to chase me, and either I must slay him or he me; and this damosel slew herself for his love, which repenteth me, and for her sake I shall owe all women the better love. Alas, said the dwarf, thou hast done great damage unto thyself, for this knight that is here dead was one of the most valiantest men that lived, and trust well, Balin, the kin of this knight will chase you through the world till they have slain you. As for that, said Balin, I fear not greatly, but I am right heavy that I have displeased my lord King Arthur, for the death of this knight. So as they talked together, there came a king of Cornwall riding, the which hight King Mark. And when he saw these two bodies dead, and understood how they were dead, by the two knights above said, then made the king great sorrow for the true love that was betwixt them, and said, I will not depart till I have on this earth made a tomb, and there he pyght his pavilions and sought through all the country to find a tomb, and in a church they found one was fair and rich, and then the king let put them both in the earth, and put the tomb upon them, and wrote the names of them both on the tomb. How here lieth Lanceor the king's son of Ireland, that at his own request was slain by the hands of Balin; and how his lady, Colombe, and paramour, slew herself with her love's sword for dole and sorrow.

CHAPTER VIII

HOW MERLIN PROPHESIED THAT TWO THE BEST KNIGHTS OF THE WORLD SHOULD FIGHT THERE, WHICH WERE SIR LANCELOT AND SIR TRISTRAM

THE meanwhile as this was a-doing, in came Merlin to King Mark, and seeing all his doing, said, Here shall be in this same place the greatest battle betwixt two knights that was or ever shall be, and the truest lovers, and yet none of them shall slay other. And there Merlin wrote their names upon the tomb with letters of gold that should fight in that place, whose names were Launcelot de Lake, and Tristram.

Thou art a marvellous man, said King Mark unto Merlin, that speakest of such marvels, thou art a boystous man and an unlikely to tell of such deeds. What is thy name? said King Mark. At this time, said Merlin, I will not tell, but at that time when Sir Tristram is taken with his sovereign lady, then ye shall hear and know my name, and at that time ye shall hear tidings that shall not please you. Then said Merlin to Balin, Thou hast done thyself great hurt, because that thou savest not this lady that slew herself, that might have saved her an thou wouldest. By the faith of my body, said Balin, I might not save her, for she slew herself suddenly. Me repenteth, said Merlin; because of the death of that lady thou shalt strike a stroke most dolorous that ever man struck, except the stroke of our Lord, for thou shalt hurt the truest knight and the man of most worship that now liveth, and through that stroke three kingdoms shall be in great poverty, misery and wretchedness twelve years, and the knight shall not be whole of that wound for many years. Then Merlin took his leave of Balin. And Balin said, If I wist it were sooth that ye say I should do such a perilous deed as that, I would slay myself to make thee a liar. Therewith Merlin vanished away suddenly. And then Balan and his brother took their leave of King Mark. First, said the king, tell me your name. Sir, said Balan, ye may see he beareth two swords, thereby ye may call him the knight with the two swords. And so departed King Mark unto Camelot to King Arthur, and Balin took the way toward King Rience; and as they rode together they met with Merlin disguised, but they knew him not. Whither ride you? said Merlin. We have little to do, said the two knights, to tell thee, but what is thy name? said Balin. At this time, said Merlin, I will not tell it thee. It is evil seen, said the knights, that thou art a true man that thou wilt not tell thy name. As for that, said Merlin, be it as it be may, I can tell you wherefore ye ride this way, for to meet King Rience; but it will not avail you without ye have my counsel. Ah! said Balin, ye are Merlin; we will be ruled by your counsel. Come on, said Merlin, ye shall have great worship, and look that ye do knightly, for ye shall have great need. As for that, said Balin, dread you not, we will do what we may.

CHAPTER IX

HOW BALIN AND HIS BROTHER, BY THE COUNSEL OF MERLIN,
TOOK KING RIENCE AND BROUGHT HIM TO KING ARTHUR

THEN Merlin lodged them in a wood among leaves beside the highway, and took off the bridles of their horses and put them to grass and laid them down to rest till it was nigh midnight. Then Merlin bade them rise, and make them ready, for the king was nigh them, that was stolen away from his host with a three score horses of his best knights, and twenty of them rode tofore to warn the Lady de Vance that the king was coming, for that night King Rience should have lain with her. Which is the king? said Balin. Abide, said Merlin, here in a straight way ye shall meet with him; and therewith he showed Balin and his brother where he rode. Anon Balin and his brother met with the king, and smote him down, and wounded him fiercely, and laid him to the ground; and there they slew on the right hand and the left hand, and slew more than forty of his men, and the remnant fled. Then went they again to King Rience and would have slain him had he not yielded him unto their grace. Then said he thus: Knights full of prowess, slay me not, for by my life ye may win, and by my death ye shall win nothing. Then said these two knights, Ye say sooth and truth, and so laid him on a horse-litter. With that Merlin was vanished, and came to King Arthur aforehand, and told him how his most enemy was taken and discomfited. By whom? said King Arthur. By two knights, said Merlin, that would please your lordship, and to-morrow ye shall know what knights they are. Anon after came the knight with the two swords and Balan his brother, and brought with them King Rience of North Wales, and there delivered him to the porters, and charged them with him; and so they two returned again in the dawning of the day. King Arthur came then to King Rience, and said, Sir king, ye are welcome: by what adventure come ye hither? Sir, said King Rience, I came hither by an hard adventure. Who won you? said King Arthur. Sir, said the king, the knight with the two swords and his brother, which are two marvellous knights of prowess. I know them not, said Arthur, but much I am beholden to them. Ah, said Merlin, I shall tell you: it is

Balin that achieved the sword, and his brother Balan, a good knight, there liveth not a better of prowess and of worthiness, and it shall be the greatest dole of him that ever I knew of knight, for he shall not long endure. Alas, said King Arthur, that is great pity; for I am much beholden unto him, and I have ill deserved it unto him for his kindness. Nay, said Merlin, he shall do much more for you, and that shall ye know in haste. But, sir, are ye purveyed, said Merlin, for to-morn the host of Nero, King Rience's brother, will set on you or noon with a great host, and therefore make you ready, for I will depart from you.

CHAPTER X

HOW KING ARTHUR HAD A BATTLE AGAINST NERO AND KING LOT OF ORKNEY, AND HOW KING LOT WAS DECEIVED BY MERLIN, AND HOW TWELVE KINGS WERE SLAIN

THEN King Arthur made ready his host in ten battles, and Nero was ready in the field afore the Castle Terrabil with a great host, and he had ten battles, with many more people than Arthur had. Then Nero had the vanguard with the most part of his people, and Merlin came to King Lot of the Isle of Orkney, and held him with a tale of prophecy, till Nero and his people were destroyed. And there Sir Kay the Seneschal did passingly well, that the days of his life the worship went never from him; and Sir Hervis de Revel did marvellous deeds with King Arthur, and King Arthur slew that day twenty knights and maimed forty. At that time came in the knight with the two swords and his brother Balan, but they two did so marvellously that the king and all the knights marvelled of them, and all they that beheld them said they were sent from heaven as angels, or devils from hell; and King Arthur said himself they were the best knights that ever he saw, for they gave such strokes that all men had wonder of them. In the meanwhile came one to King Lot, and told him while he tarried there Nero was destroyed and slain with all his people. Alas, said King Lot, I am ashamed, for by my default there is many a worshipful man slain, for an we had been together there had been none host under the heaven that had been able for to have matched with us; this fayter with his prophecy hath mocked me. All that did Merlin, for he knew well that an King Lot had been with his body there at the first battle, King Arthur had been slain, and all his people destroyed; and well Merlin knew that one of the kings should be dead that day, and loath was Merlin that any of them both should be slain; but of the twain, he had liefer King Lot had been slain than King Arthur. Now what is best to do? said King Lot of Orkney; whether is me better to treat with King Arthur or to fight, for the greater part of our people are slain and destroyed? Sir, said a knight, set on Arthur for they are weary and forfoughten and we be fresh. As for me, said King Lot, I would every knight would do his part as I would do mine. And then they advanced banners and smote together and all to-shivered their spears; and Arthur's knights, with the help of the knight with the two swords and his brother Balan put King Lot and his host to the worse. But always King Lot held him in the foremost front, and did marvellous deeds of arms, for all his host was borne up by his hands, for he abode all knights. Alas he might not endure, the which was great pity, that so worthy a knight as he was one should be overmatched, that of late time afore had been a knight of King Arthur's, and wedded the sister of King Arthur; and for King Arthur lay by King Lot's wife, the which was Arthur's sister, and gat on her Mordred, therefore King Lot held against Arthur. So there was a knight that was called the knight with the strange beast, and at that time his right name was called Pellinore, the which was a good man of prowess, and he smote a mighty stroke at King Lot as he fought with all his enemies, and he failed of his stroke, and smote the horse's neck, that he fell to the ground with King Lot; and therewith anon Pellinore smote him a great stroke through the helm and head unto the brows. And then all the host of Orkney fled for the death of King Lot, and there were slain many mothers' sons. But King Pellinore bare the wytte of the death of King Lot, wherefore Sir Gawaine revenged the death of his father the tenth year after he was made knight, and slew King Pellinore with his own hands. Also there were slain at that battle twelve kings on the side of King Lot with Nero, and all were buried in the Church of Saint Stephen's in Camelot, and the remnant of knights and of others were buried in a great rock.

CHAPTER XI

OF THE INTERMENT OF TWELVE KINGS, AND OF THE PROPHECY
OF MERLIN, AND HOW BALIN SHOULD GIVE THE DOLOROUS
STROKE

So at the interment came King Lot's wife Margawse with
her four sons, Gawaine, Agravaine, Gaheris, and Gareth.
Also there came thither King Uriens, Sir Ewaine's father,
and Morgan le Fay his wife that was King Arthur's sister.
All these came to the interment. But of all these twelve
kings, King Arthur let make the tomb of King Lot passing
richly, and made his tomb by his own ; and then Arthur let
make twelve images of laton and copper, and over-gilt it with
gold, in the sign of twelve kings, and each one of them held
a taper of wax that burnt day and night ; and King Arthur
was made in sign of a figure standing above them with a
sword drawn in his hand, and all the twelve figures had
countenance like unto men that were overcome. All this
made Merlin by his subtle craft, and there he told the king,
When I am dead these tapers shall burn no longer, and soon
after the adventures of the Sangreal shall come among you
and be achieved. Also he told Arthur how Balin the
worshipful knight shall give the dolorous stroke, whereof
shall fall great vengeance. Oh, where is Balin and Balan
and Pellinore? said King Arthur. As for Pellinore, said
Merlin, he will meet with you soon ; and as for Balin he
will not be long from you ; but the other brother will depart,
ye shall see him no more. By my faith, said Arthur, they
are two marvellous knights, and namely Balin passeth of
prowess of any knight that ever I found, for much beholden
am I unto him ; would God he would abide with me. Sir, said
Merlin, look ye keep well the scabbard of Excalibur, for ye
shall lose no blood while ye have the scabbard upon you,
though ye have as many wounds upon you as ye may have.
So after, for great trust, Arthur betook the scabbard to
Morgan le Fay his sister, and she loved another knight
better than her husband King Uriens or King Arthur, and
she would have had Arthur her brother slain, and therefore
she let make another scabbard like it by enchantment, and
gave the scabbard Excalibur to her love ; and the knight's
name was called Accolon, that after had near slain King
Arthur. After this Merlin told unto King Arthur of the

prophecy that there should be a great battle beside Salisbury, and Mordred his own son should be against him. Also he told him that Basdemegus was his cousin, and germain unto King Uriens.

CHAPTER XII

WITHIN a day or two King Arthur was somewhat sick, and he let pitch his pavilion in a meadow, and there he laid him down on a pallet to sleep, but he might have no rest. Right so he heard a great noise of an horse, and therewith the king looked out at the porch of the pavilion, and saw a knight coming even by him and making great dole. Abide, fair sir, said Arthur, and tell me wherefore thou makest this sorrow. Ye may little amend me, said the knight, and so passed forth to the castle of Meliot. Anon after there came Balin, and when he saw King Arthur he alit off his horse, and came to the king on foot, and saluted him. By my head, said Arthur, ye be welcome. Sir, right now came riding this way a knight making great mourn, for what cause I cannot tell; wherefore I would desire of you of your courtesy and of your gentleness to fetch again that knight either by force or else by his good will. I will do more for your lordship than that, said Balin; and so he rode more than a pace, and found the knight with a damosel in a forest, and said, Sir knight, ye must come with me unto King Arthur, for to tell him of your sorrow. That will I not, said the knight, for it will scathe me greatly, and do you none avail. Sir, said Balin, I pray you make you ready, for ye must go with me, or else I must fight with you and bring you by force, and that were me loath to do. Will ye be my warrant, said the knight, an I go with you? Yea, said Balin, or else I will die therefor. And so he made him ready to go with Balin, and left the damosel still. And as they were even afore King Arthur's pavilion, there came one invisible, and smote this knight that went with Balin throughout the body with a spear. Alas, said the knight, I am slain under your conduct with a knight called Garlon; therefore take my horse that is better than yours, and ride to the damosel, and follow the quest that I was in as she will lead you, and revenge my death when ye may. That shall I do, said Balin, and that I make a vow unto knighthood; and so he departed from this knight with great sorrow. So King Arthur let bury this knight richly, and made a mention on his tomb, how there was slain Herlews le Berbeus, and by whom the treachery was done, the knight Garlon. But ever the damosel bare the truncheon of the spear with her that Sir Herlews was slain withal.

CHAPTER XIII

HOW BALIN AND THE DAMOSEL MET WITH A KNIGHT WHICH WAS
IN LIKEWISE SLAIN, AND HOW THE DAMOSEL BLED FOR THE
CUSTOM OF A CASTLE

So Balin and the damosel rode into a forest, and there met with a knight that had been a-hunting, and that knight asked Balin for what cause he made so great sorrow. Me list not to tell you, said Balin. Now, said the knight, an I were armed as ye be I would fight with you. That should little need, said Balin, I am not afeard to tell you, and told him all the cause how it was. Ah, said the knight, is this all? here I ensure you by the faith of my body never to depart from you while my life lasteth. And so they went to the hostelry and armed them, and so rode forth with Balin. And as they came by an hermitage even by a churchyard, there came the knight Garlon invisible, and smote this knight, Perin de Mountbeliard, through the body with a spear. Alas, said the knight, I am slain by this traitor knight that rideth invisible. Alas, said Balin, it is not the first despite he hath done me; and there the hermit and Balin buried the knight under a rich stone and a tomb royal. And on the morn they found letters of gold written, how Sir Gawaine shall revenge his father's death, King Lot, on the King Pellinore. Anon after this Balin and the damosel rode till they came to a castle, and there Balin alit, and he and the damosel went to go into the castle, and anon as Balin came within the castle's gate the portcullis fell down at his back, and there fell many men about the damosel, and would have slain her. When Balin saw that, he was sore aggrieved, for he might not help the damosel; and then he went up into the tower, and leapt over the walls into the ditch, and hurt him not ; and anon he pulled out his sword and would have foughten with them. And they all said nay, they would not fight with him, for they did nothing but the old custom of the castle, and told him how their lady was sick, and had lain many years, and she might not be whole but if she had a dish of silver full of blood of a clean maid and a king's daughter ; and therefore the custom of this castle is, there shall no damosel pass this way but she shall bleed of her blood in a silver dish full. Well, said Balin, she shall bleed as much as she may bleed, but I will not lose the life of her whiles my life lasteth. And so Balin made her to bleed by her good will, but her blood helped not the lady. And so he and she rested there all night, and had there right good cheer, and on the morn they passed on their ways. And as it telleth after in the Sangreal, that Sir Percivale's sister helped that lady with her blood, whereof she was dead.

CHAPTER XIV

HOW BALIN MET WITH THAT KNIGHT NAMED GARLON AT A
FEAST, AND THERE HE SLEW HIM TO HAVE HIS BLOOD TO
HEAL THEREWITH THE SON OF HIS HOST

THEN they rode three or four days and never met with adventure, and by hap they were lodged with a gentle man that was a rich man and well at ease. And as they sat at their supper Balin overheard one complain grievously by him in a chair. What is this noise? said Balin. Forsooth, said his host, I will tell you. I was but late at a jousting, and there I jousted with a knight that is brother unto King Pellam, and twice smote I him down, and then he promised to requite me on my best friend ; and so he wounded my son, that cannot be whole till I have of that knight's blood, and he rideth always invisible, but I know not his name. Ah ! said Balin, I know that knight, his name is Garlon, he hath slain two knights of mine in the same manner, therefore I had lever meet with that knight than all the gold in this realm, for the despite he hath done me. Well, said his host, I shall tell you, King Pellam of Listeneise hath made do cry in all this country a great feast that shall be within these twenty days, and no knight may come there but if he bring his wife with him, or his paramour; and that knight, your enemy and mine, ye shall see that day. Then I behote you, said Balin, part of his blood to heal your son withal. We will be forward to-morn, said his host. So on the morn they rode all three toward Pellam, and they had fifteen days' journey or they came thither; and that same day began the great feast. And so they alit and stabled their horses, and went into the castle; but Balin's host might not be let in by cause he had no lady. Then Balin was well received and brought unto a chamber and unarmed him, and there were brought him robes to his pleasure, and would have had Balin leave his sword behind him. Nay, said Balin, that do I not, for it is the custom of my country a knight always to keep his weapon with him, and that custom will I keep, or else I will depart as I came. Then they gave him leave to wear his sword, and so he went unto the castle, and was set among knights of worship, and his lady afore him. Soon Balin asked a knight, Is there not a knight in this court whose name is Garlon? Yonder he goeth, said a knight, he with the black face; he is the marvellest knight that is now living, for he destroyeth many good knights, for he goeth invisible. Ah well, said Balin, is that he? Then Balin advised him long: If I slay him here I shall not escape, and if I leave him now, peradventure I shall never meet with him again at such a steven, and much harm he will do an he live. Therewith this Garlon espied that this Balin beheld him, and then he came and smote Balin on the face with the back of his hand, and said, Knight, why beholdest me so? for shame therefor, eat thy meat and do that thou came for. Thou sayest sooth, said Balin, this is not the first despite that thou hast done me, and therefore I will do what I came for, and rose up fiercely and clave his head to the shoulders. Give me the truncheon, said Balin to his lady, wherewith he slew your knight. Anon she gave it him, for always she bare the truncheon with her. And therewith Balin smote him through the body, and said openly, With that truncheon thou has slain a good knight, and now it sticketh in thy body. And then Balin called unto him his host, saying, Now may ye fetch blood enough to heal your son withal.

CHAPTER XV

ANON all the knights arose from the table for to set on Balin, and King Pellam himself arose up fiercely, and said, Knight, hast thou slain my brother? thou shalt die therefor or thou depart. Well, said Balin, do it yourself. Yes, said King Pellam, there shall no man have ado with thee but myself, for the love of my brother. Then King Pellam caught in his hand a grim weapon and smote eagerly at Balin; but Balin put the sword betwixt his head and the stroke, and therewith his sword burst in sunder. And when Balin was weaponless he ran into a chamber for to seek some weapon, and so from chamber to chamber, and no weapon he could find, and always King Pellam after him. And at the last he entered into a chamber that was marvellously well dight and richly, and a bed arrayed with cloth of gold the richest that might be thought, and one lying therein, and thereby stood a table of clene gold with four pillars of silver that bare up the table, and upon the table stood a marvellous spear strangely wrought. And when Balin saw that spear, he gat it in his hand and turned him to King Pellam, and smote him passingly sore with that spear, that King Pellam fell down in a swoon, and therewith the castle roof and walls brake and fell to the earth, and Balin fell down so that he might not stir foot nor hand. And so the most part of the castle, that was fallen down through that dolorous stroke, lay upon Pellam and Balin three days.

CHAPTER XVI

THEN Merlin came thither and took up Balin, and gat him a good horse, for his was dead, and bad him ride out of that country. I would have my damosel, said Balin. Lo, said Merlin, where she lieth dead. And King Pellam lay so, many years sore wounded, and might never be whole till Galahad the haughty prince healed him in the quest of the Sangreal, for in that place was part of the blood of our Lord Jesus Christ, that Joseph of Arimathea brought into this land, and there himself lay in that rich bed. And that was the same spear that Longius smote our Lord to the heart; and King Pellam was nigh of Joseph's kin, and that was the most worshipful man that lived in those days, and great pity it was of his hurt, for through that stroke, turned to great dole, tray and tene. Then departed Balin from Merlin, and said, In this world we meet never no more. So he rode forth through the fair countries and cities, and found the people dead, slain on every side. And all that were alive cried, O Balin, thou hast caused great damage in these countries; for the dolorous stroke thou gavest unto King Pellam, three countries are destroyed, and doubt not but the vengeance will fall on thee at the last. When Balin was past those countries he was passing fayne. So he rode eight days or he met with adventure. And at the last he came into a fair forest in a valley, and was ware of a tower, and there beside he saw a great horse of war, tied to a tree, and there beside sat a fair knight on the ground and made great mourning, and he was a likely man, and a well made. Balin said, God save you, why be ye so heavy? tell me and I will amend it, an I may to my power. Sir knight, said he again, thou doest me great grief, for I was in merry thoughts, and now thou puttest me to more pain. Balin went a little from him, and looked on his horse; then heard Balin him say thus: Ah, fair lady, why have ye broken my promise, for thou promisest me to meet me here by noon, and I may curse thee that ever ye gave me this sword, for with this sword I slay myself, and pulled it out. And therewith Balin sterte unto him and took him by the hand. Let go my hand, said the knight, or else I shall slay thee. That shall not need, said Balin, for I shall promise you my help to get you your lady, an ye will tell me where she is. What is your name? said the knight. My name is Balin le Savage. Ah, sir, I know you well enough, ye are the knight with the two swords, and the man of most prowess of your hands living. What is your name? said Balin. My name is Garnish of the Mount, a poor man's son, but by my prowess and hardiness a duke hath made me knight, and gave me lands; his name is Duke Hermel, and his daughter is she that I love, and she me as I deemed. How far is she hence? said Balin. But six mile, said the knight. Now ride we hence, said these two knights. So they rode more than a pace, till that they came to a fair castle well walled and ditched. I will into the castle, said Balin, and look if she be there. So he went in and searched from chamber to chamber, and found her bed, but she was not there. Then Balin looked into a fair little garden, and under a laurel tree he saw her lie upon a quilt of green samite and a knight in her arms, fast halsynge either other, and under their heads grass and herbs. When Balin saw her lie so with the foulest knight that ever he saw, and she a fair lady, then Balin went through all the chambers again, and told the knight how he found her as she had slept fast, and so brought him in the place where she lay fast sleeping.

CHAPTER XVII

HOW THAT KNIGHT SLEW HIS LOVE AND A KNIGHT LYING BY HER, AND AFTER, HOW HE SLEW HIMSELF WITH HIS OWN SWORD, AND HOW BALIN RODE TOWARD A CASTLE WHERE HE LOST HIS LIFE

AND when Garnish beheld her so lying, for pure sorrow his mouth and nose burst out on bleeding, and with his sword he smote off both their heads, and then he made sorrow out of measure, and said, O Balin, much sorrow hast thou brought unto me, for haddest thou not shewed me that sight I should have passed my sorrow. Forsooth, said Balin, I did it to this intent that it should better thy courage, and that ye might see and know her falsehood, and to cause you to leave love of such a lady; God knoweth I did none other but as I would ye did to me. Alas, said Garnish, now is my sorrow double that I may not endure, now have I slain that I most loved in all my life; and therewith suddenly he rove himself on his own sword unto the hilts. When Balin saw that, he dressed him thenceward, lest folk would say he had slain them; and so he rode forth, and within three days he came by a cross, and thereon were letters of gold written, that said, It is not for no knight alone to ride toward this castle. Then saw he an old hoar gentleman coming toward him, that said, Balin le Savage, thou passest thy bounds to come this way, therefore turn again and it will avail thee.

And he vanished away anon ; and so he heard an horn blow as it had been the death of a beast. That blast, said Balin, is blown for me, for I am the prize and yet am I not dead. Anon withal he saw an hundred ladies and many knights, that welcomed him with fair semblance, and made him passing good cheer unto his sight, and led him into the castle, and there was dancing and minstrelsy and all manner of joy. Then the chief lady of the castle said, Knight with the two swords, ye must have ado and joust with a knight hereby that keepeth an island, for there may no man pass this way but he must joust or he pass. That is an unhappy custom, said Balin, that a knight may not pass this way but if he joust. Ye shall not have ado but with one knight, said the lady. Well, said Balin, syne I shall thereto I am ready, but travelling men are oft weary and their horses too ; but though my horse be weary my heart is not weary, I would be fain there my death should be. Sir, said a knight to Balin, methinketh your shield is not good, I will lend you a bigger, thereof I pray you. And so he took the shield that was unknown and left his own, and so rode unto the island, and put him and his horse in a great boat ; and when he came on the other side he met with a damosel, and she said, O knight Balin, why have ye left your own shield? alas ye have put yourself in great danger, for by your shield ye should have been known ; it is great pity of you as ever was of knight, for of thy prowess and hardiness thou hast no fellow living. Me repenteth, said Balin, that ever I came within this country, but I may not turn now again for shame, and what adventure shall fall to me, be it life or death, I will take the adventure that shall come to me   And then he looked on his armour, and understood he was well armed, and therewith blessed him and mounted upon his horse.

CHAPTER XVIII

HOW BALIN MET WITH HIS BROTHER BALAN, AND HOW EACH OF THEM SLEW OTHER UNKNOWN, TILL THEY WERE WOUNDED TO DEATH

THEN afore him he saw come riding out of a castle a knight; and his horse trapped all red, and himself in the same colour. When this knight in the red beheld Balin, him thought it should be his brother Balin by cause of his two swords, but by cause he knew not his shield he deemed it was not he.　And so they aventryd their spears and came marvellously fast together, and they smote each other in the shields, but their spears and their course were so big that it bare down horse and man that they lay both in a swoon. But Balin was bruised sore with the fall of his horse, for he was weary of travel.　And Balan was the first that rose on foot and drew his sword, and went toward Balin, and he arose and went against him ; but Balan smote Balin first, and he put up his shield and smote him through the shield and tamyd his helm.　Then Balin smote him again with that unhappy sword, and well nigh had felled his brother Balan, and so they fought there together till their breaths failed.　Then Balin looked up to the castle and saw the towers stand full of ladies.　So they went unto battle again, and wounded every each other dolefully, and then they breathed ofttimes, and so went unto battle that all the place there as they fought was blood red.　And at that time there was none of them both but they had either smitten other seven great wounds, so that the least of them might have been the death of the mightiest giant in this world.　Then they went to battle again so marvellously that doubte it was to hear of that battle for the great blood-shedding, and their hauberks unnailed that naked they were on every side.　At last Balan the younger brother withdrew him a little and laid him down.　Then said Balin le Savage, What knight art thou ? for or now I found never no knight that matched me.　My name is, said he, Balan, brother unto the good knight, Balin.　Alas, said Balin, that ever I should see this day, and therewith he fell backward in a swoon.　Then Balan yede on all four feet and hands, and put off the helm of his brother, and might not know him by the visage it was so ful hewen and bledde ; but when he awoke he said, O Balan, my brother, thou hast slain me and I thee, wherefore all the wide world shall speak of us both.　Alas, said Balan, that ever I saw this day, that through mishap I might not know you, for I espied well your two swords, but by cause ye had another shield I deemed ye had been another knight. Alas, said Balin, all that made an unhappy knight in the castle, for he caused me to leave my own shield to our both's destruction, and if I might live I would destroy that castle for ill customs.　That were well done, said Balan, for I had never grace to depart from them syne that I came hither, for here it happed me to slay a knight that kept this island, and syne might I never depart, and no more should ye, brother, an ye might have slain me as ye have, and escaped yourself with the life. Right so came the lady of the tower with four knights and six ladies and six yeomen unto them, and there she heard how they made their moan either to other, and said, We came both out of one tomb, that is to say one mother's belly, and so shall we lie both in one pit. So Balan prayed the lady of her gentleness, for his true service, that she would bury them both in that same place where the battle was done. And she granted them with weeping it should be done richly in the best manner. Now, will ye send for a priest, that we may receive our sacrament, and receive the blessed body of our Lord Jesus Christ? Yea, said the lady, it shall be done; and so she sent for a priest and gave them their rites. Now, said Balin, when we are buried in one tomb, and the mention made over us how two brethren slew each other, there will never good knight nor good man see our tomb but they will pray for our souls. And so all the ladies and gentlewomen wept for pity. Then anon Balan died, but Balin died not till the midnight after, and so were they buried both, and the lady let make a mention of Balan how he was there slain by his brother's hands, but she knew not Balin's name.

CHAPTER XIX

HOW MERLIN BURIED THEM BOTH IN ONE TOMB, AND OF BALIN'S SWORD

IN the morning came Merlin and let write Balin's name on the tomb with letters of gold, that here lieth Balin le Savage that was the knight with the two swords, and he that smote the dolorous stroke. Also Merlin let make there a bed, that there should never man lie therein but he went out of his wit, yet Launcelot de Lake fordyd that bed through his noblesse. And anon after Balin was dead, Merlin took his sword, and took off the pommel and set on another pommel. So Merlin bad a knight that stood afore him handle that sword, and he assayed, and he might not handle it. Then Merlin laughed. Why laugh ye? said the knight. This is the cause, said Merlin: there shall never man handle this sword but the best knight of the world, and that shall be Sir Launcelot or else Galahad his son, and Launcelot with this sword shall slay the man that in the world he loved best, that shall be Sir Gawaine. All this he let write in the pommel of the sword. Then Merlin let make a bridge of iron and of steel into that island, and it was but half a foot broad, and there shall never man pass that bridge, nor have hardiness to go over, but if he were a passing good man and a good knight without treachery or villainy. Also the scabbard of Balin's sword Merlin left it on this side the island, that Galahad should find it. Also Merlin let make by his subtilty that Balin's sword was put in a marble stone standing upright as great as a mill stone, and the stone hoved always above the water and did many years, and so by adventure it swam down the stream to the City of Camelot, that is in English Winchester. And that same day Galahad the haughty prince came with King Arthur, and so Galahad brought with him the scabbard and achieved the sword that was there in the marble stone hoving upon the water. And on Whitsunday he achieved the sword as it is rehearsed in the book of Sangreal. Soon after this was done Merlin came to King Arthur and told him of the dolorous stroke that Balin gave to King Pellam, and how Balin and Balan fought together the marvellest battle that ever was heard of, and how they were buried both in one tomb. Alas, said King Arthur, this is the greatest pity that ever I heard tell of two knights, for in the world I know not such two knights. Thus endeth the tale of Balin and of Balan, two brethren born in Northumberland, good knights.

Sequitur iit. liber

BOOK III

CHAPTER I

HOW KING ARTHUR TOOK A WIFE, AND WEDDED GUENEVER, DAUGHTER TO LEODEGRANCE, KING OF THE LAND OF CAMELIARD, WITH WHOM HE HAD THE ROUND TABLE

In the beginning of Arthur, after he was chosen king by adventure and by grace; for the most part of the barons knew not that he was Uther Pendragon's son, but as Merlin made it openly known. But yet many kings and lords held great war against him for that cause, but well Arthur overcame them all, for the most part the days of his life he was ruled much by the counsel of Merlin. So it fell on a time King Arthur said unto Merlin, My barons will let me have no rest, but needs I must take a wife, and I will none take but by thy counsel and by thine advice. It is well done, said Merlin, that ye take a wife, for a man of your bounty and noblesse should not be without a wife. Now is there any that ye love more than another? Yea, said King Arthur, I love Guenever the king's daughter, Leodegrance of the land of Cameliard, the which holdeth in his house the Table Round that ye told he had of my father Uther. And this damosel is the most valiant and fairest lady that I know living, or yet that ever I could find. Sir, said Merlin, as of her beauty and fairness she is one of the fairest on live, but, an ye loved her not so well as ye do, I should find you a damosel of beauty and of goodness that should like you and please you, an your heart were not set; but there as a man's heart is set, he will be loth to return. That is truth, said King Arthur. But Merlin warned the king covertly that Guenever was not wholesome for him to take to wife, for he warned him that Launcelot should love her, and she him again; and so he turned his tale to the adventures of Sangreal. Then Merlin desired of the king for to have men with him that should enquire of Guenever, and so the king granted him, and Merlin went forth unto King Leodegrance of Cameliard, and told him of the desire of the king that he would have unto his wife Guenever his daughter. That is to me, said King Leodegrance, the best tidings that ever I heard, that so worthy a king of prowess and noblesse will wed my daughter. And as for my lands, I will give him, wist I it might please him, but he hath lands enow, him needeth none, but I shall send him a gift shall please him much more, for I shall give him the Table Round, the which Uther Pendragon gave me, and when it is full complete, there is an hundred knights and fifty. And as for an hundred good knights I have myself, but I fawte fifty, for so many have been slain in my days. And so Leodegrance delivered his daughter Guenever unto Merlin, and the Table Round with the hundred knights, and so they rode freshly, with great royalty, what by water and what by land, till that they came nigh unto London.

CHAPTER II

HOW THE KNIGHTS OF THE ROUND TABLE WERE ORDAINED AND THEIR SIEGES BLESSED BY THE BISHOP OF CANTERBURY

WHEN King Arthur heard of the coming of Guenever and the hundred knights with the Table Round, then King Arthur made great joy for her coming, and that rich present, and said openly, This fair lady is passing welcome unto me, for I have loved her long, and therefore there is nothing so lief to me. And these knights with the Round Table please me more than right great riches. And in all haste the king let ordain for the marriage and the coronation in the most honourable wise that could be devised. Now, Merlin, said King Arthur, go thou and espy me in all this land fifty knights which be of most prowess and worship. Within short time Merlin had found such knights that should fulfil twenty and eight knights, but no more he could find. Then the Bishop of Canterbury was fetched, and he blessed the sieges with great royalty and devotion, and there set the eight and twenty knights in their sieges. And when this was done Merlin said, Fair sirs, you must all arise and come to King Arthur for to do him homage; he will have the better will to maintain you. And so they arose and did their homage, and when they were gone Merlin found in every sieges letters of gold that told the knights' names that had sitten therein. But two sieges were void. And so anon came young Gawaine and asked the king a gift. Ask, said the king, and I shall grant it you. Sir, I ask that ye will make me knight that same day ye shall wed fair Guenever. I will do it with a good will, said King Arthur, and do unto you all the worship that I may, for I must by reason ye are my nephew, my sister's son.

CHAPTER III

HOW A POOR MAN RIDING UPON A LEAN MARE DESIRED KING ARTHUR TO MAKE HIS SON KNIGHT

FORTHWITHAL there came a poor man into the court, and brought with him a fair young man of eighteen years of age riding upon a lean mare; and the poor man asked all men that he met, Where shall I find King Arthur? Yonder he is, said the knights, wilt thou anything with him? Yea, said the poor man, therefore I came hither. Anon as he came before the king, he saluted him and said: O King Arthur, the flower of all knights and kings, I beseech Jesu save thee. Sir, it was told me that at this time of your marriage ye would give any man the gift that he would ask, out except that were unreasonable. That is truth, said the king, such cries I let make, and that will I hold, so it impair not my realm nor mine estate. Ye say well and graciously, said the poor man; Sir, I ask nothing else but that ye will make my son here a knight. It is a great thing thou askest of me said the king. What is thy name? said the king to the poor man. Sir, my name is Aries the cowherd. Whether cometh this of thee or of thy son? said the king. Nay, sir, said Aries, this desire cometh of my son and not of me, for I shall tell you I have thirteen sons, and all they will fall to what labour I put them, and will be right glad to do labour, but this child will not labour for me, for anything that my wife or I may do, but always he will be shooting or casting darts, and glad for to see battles and to behold knights, and always day and night he desireth of me to be made a knight. What is thy name? said the king unto the young man. Sir, my name is Tor. The king beheld him fast, and saw he was passingly well-visaged and passingly well made of his years. Well, said King Arthur unto Aries the cowherd, fetch all thy sons afore me that I may see them. And so the poor man did, and all were shaped much like the poor man. But Tor was not like none of them all in shape nor in countenance, for he was much more than any of them. Now, said King Arthur unto the cowherd, where is the sword he shall he made knight withal? It is here, said Tor. Take it out of the sheath, said the king, and require me to make you a knight. Then Tor alit off his mare and pulled out his sword, kneeling, and requiring the king that he would make him knight, and that he might be a knight of the Table Round. As for a knight I will make you, and therewith smote him in the neck with the sword, saying, Be ye a good knight, and so I pray to God so ye may be, and if ye be of prowess and of worthiness ye shall be a knight of the Table Round. Now Merlin, said Arthur, say whether this Tor shall be a good knight or no. Yea, sir, he ought to be a good knight, for he is come of as good a man as any is alive, and of kings' blood. How so, sir? said the king. I shall tell you, said Merlin: This poor man, Aries the cowherd, is not his father, he is nothing syb to him, for King Pellinore is his father. I suppose nay, said the cowherd. Fetch thy wife afore me, said Merlin, and she shall not say nay. Anon the wife was fetched, which was a fair housewife, and there she answered Merlin full womanly, and there she told the king and Merlin that when she was a maid, and went to milk kine, there met with her a stern knight, and half by force he had my maidenhead, and at that time he begat my son Tor, and he took away from me my greyhound that I had that time with me, and said that he would keep the greyhound for my love. Ah, said the cowherd, I weened not this, but I may believe it well, for he had never no tatches of me. Sir, said Tor unto Merlin, dishonour not my mother. Sir, said Merlin, it is more for your worship than hurt, for your father is a good man and a king, and he may right well advance you and your mother, for ye were begotten or ever she was wedded. That is truth, said the wife. It is the less grief unto me. said the cowherd.

CHAPTER IV

HOW SIR TOR WAS KNOWN FOR SON OF KING PELLINORE, AND
HOW GAWAINE WAS MADE KNIGHT

So on the morn King Pellinore came to the court of King Arthur, which had great joy of him, and told him of Tor, how he was his son, and how he had made him knight at the request of the cowherd. When Pellinore beheld Tor, he pleased him much. So the king made Gawaine knight, but Tor was the first he made at the feast. What is the cause, said King Arthur, that there be two places void in the sieges? Sir, said Merlin, there shall no man sit in those places but they that shall be of most worship. But in the Siege Perilous there shall no man sit therein but one, and if there be any so hardy to do it he shall be destroyed, and he that shall sit there shall have no fellow. And therewith Merlin took King Pellinore by the hand, and in the one hand next the two sieges and the Siege Perilous he said, in open audience, This is your place and best ye are worthy to sit therein of any that is here. Thereat sat Sir Gawaine in great envy and told Gaheris his brother, yonder knight is put to great worship, the which grieveth me sore, for he slew our father King Lot, therefore I will slay him, said Gawaine, with a sword that was sent me that is passing trenchant. Ye shall not so, said Gaheris, at this time, for at this time I am but a squire, and when I am made knight I would be avenged on him, and therefore, brother, it is best ye suffer till another time, that we may have him out of the court, for an we did so we should trouble this high feast. I will well, said Gawaine, as ye will.

CHAPTER V

HOW AT FEAST OF THE WEDDING OF KING ARTHUR TO GUENEVER,
A WHITE HART CAME INTO THE HALL, AND THIRTY COUPLE
HOUNDS, AND HOW A BRACHET PINCHED THE HART WHICH
WAS TAKEN AWAY

THEN was the high feast made ready, and the king was wedded at Camelot unto Dame Guenever in the church of Saint Stephen's, with great solemnity. And as every man was set after his degree, Merlin went to all the knights of the Round Table, and bad them sit still, that none of them remove. For ye shall see a strange and a marvellous adventure. Right so as they sat there came running in a white hart into the hall, and a white brachet next him, and thirty couple of black running hounds came after with a great cry, and the hart went about the Table Round as he went by other boards, the white brachet bit him by the buttock and puiled out a piece, wherethrough the hart leapt a great leap and overthrew a knight that sat at the board side, and therewith the knight arose and took up the brachet, and so went forth out of the hall, and took his horse and rode his way with the brachet. Right so anon came in a lady on a white palfrey, and cried aloud to King Arthur, Sir, suffer me not to have this despite, for the brachet was mine that the knight led away. I may not do therewith, said the king. With this there came a knight riding all armed on a great horse, and took the lady away with him with force, and ever she cried and made great dole. When she was gone the king was glad, for she made such a noise. Nay, said Merlin, ye may not leave these adventures so lightly, for these adventures must be brought again or else it would be disworship to you and to your feast. I will, said the king, that all be done by your advice. Then, said Merlin, let call Sir Gawaine, for he must bring again the white hart. Also, sir, ye must let call Sir Tor, for he must bring again the brachet and the knight, or else slay him. Also let call King Pellinore, for he must bring again the lady and the knight, or else slay him. And these three knights shall do marvellous adventures or they come again. Then were they called all three as it rehearseth afore, and every each of them took his charge, and armed them surely. But Sir Gawaine had the first request, and therefore we will begin at him.

CHAPTER VI

HOW SIR GAWAINE RODE FOR TO FETCH AGAIN THE HART, AND HOW TWO BRETHREN FOUGHT EACH AGAINST OTHER FOR THE HART

SIR GAWAINE rode more than a pace, and Gaheris his brother that rode with him instead of a squire to do him service. So as they rode they saw two knights fight on horseback passing sore, so Sir Gawaine and his brother rode betwixt them, and asked them for what cause they fought so. The one knight answered and said, We fight for a simple matter, for we two be two brethren born and begotten of one man and of one woman. Alas, said Sir Gawaine, why do ye so? Sir, said the elder, there came a white hart this way this day, and many hounds chased him, and a white brachet was always next him, and we understood it was adventure made for the high feast of King Arthur, and therefore I would have gone after to have won me worship; and here my younger brother said he would go after the hart, for he was better knight than I: and for this cause we fell at debate, and so we thought to prove which of us both was better knight. This is a simple cause, said Sir Gawaine; uncouth men ye should debate withal, and not brother with brother; therefore but if you will do by my counsel I will have ado with you, that is ye shall yield you unto me, and that ye go unto King Arthur and yield you unto his grace. Sir knight, said the two brethren, we are forfoughten and much blood have we lost through our wilfulness, and therefore we would be loth to have ado with you. Then do as I will have you, said Sir Gawaine. We will agree to fulfil your will; but by whom shall we say that we be thither sent? Ye may say, By the knight that followeth the quest of the hart that was white. Now what is your name? said Gawaine. Sorlouse of the Forest, said the elder. And my name is, said the younger, Brian of the Forest. And so they departed and went to the king's court, and Sir Gawaine on his quest. And as Gawaine followed the hart by the cry of the hounds, even afore him there was a great river, and the hart swam over; and as Sir Gawaine would follow after, there stood a knight over the other side, and said, Sir knight, come not over after this hart but if thou wilt joust with me. I will not fail as for that, said Sir Gawaine, to follow the quest that I am in, and so made his horse to swim over the water. And anon they gat their spears and ran together full hard; but Sir Gawaine smote him off his horse, and then he turned his horse and bade him yield him. Nay, said the knight, not so, though thou have the better of me on horseback. I pray thee, valiant knight, alight afoot, and match we together with swords. What is your name? said Sir Gawaine. Allardin of the Isles, said the other. Then either dressed their shields and smote together, but Sir Gawaine smote him so hard through the helm that it went to the brains, and the knight fell down dead. Ah! said Gaheris, that was a mighty stroke of a young knight.

CHAPTER VII

HOW THE HART WAS CHASED INTO A CASTLE AND THERE SLAIN, AND HOW SIR GAWAINE SLEW A LADY

THEN Gawaine and Gaheris rode more than a pace after the white hart, and let slip at the hart three couple of greyhounds, and so they chased the hart into a castle, and in the chief place of the castle they slew the hart; Sir Gawaine and Gaheris followed after. Right so there came a knight out of a chamber with a sword drawn in his hand and slew two of the greyhounds, even in the sight of Sir Gawaine, and the remnant he chased them with his sword out of the castle. And when he came again, he said, O my white hart, me repenteth that thou art dead, for my sovereign lady gave thee to me, and evil have I kept thee, and thy death shall be dear bought an I live. And anon he went into his chamber and armed him, and came out fiercely, and there met he with Sir Gawaine. Why have ye slain my hounds? said Sir Gawaine, for they did but their kind, and lever I had ye had wroken your anger upon me than upon a dumb beast. Thou sayest truth, said the knight, I have avenged me on thy hounds, and so I will on thee or thou go. Then Sir Gawaine alit afoot and dressed his shield, and they struck together mightily, and clave their shields, and stoned their helms, and brake their hauberks that the blood ran down to their feet. At last Sir Gawaine smote the knight so hard that he fell to the earth, and then he cried mercy, and yielded him, and besought him as he was a knight and gentleman, to save his life. Thou shalt die, said Sir Gawaine, for slaying of my hounds. I will make amends, said the knight, unto my power. Sir Gawaine would no mercy have but unlaced his helm to have stricken off his head. Right so came his lady out of a chamber and fell over him, and so he smote off her head by misadventure. Alas, said Gaheris, that is foully and shamefully done, that shame shall never from you; also ye should give mercy unto them that ask mercy, for a knight without mercy is without worship. Sir Gawaine was so stonyed of the death of this fair lady that he wist not what he did, and said unto the knight, Arise, I will give thee mercy. Nay, nay, said the knight, I take no force of mercy now, for thou hast slain my love and my lady that I loved best of all earthly things. Me sore repenteth it, said Sir Gawaine, for I thought to strike unto thee; but now thou shalt go unto King Arthur and tell him of thine adventures, and how thou art overcome by the knight that went in the quest of the white hart. I take no force, said the knight, whether I live or I die; but so for dread of death he swore to go unto King Arthur, and he made him to bear one greyhound before him on his horse, and another behind him. What is your name? said Sir Gawaine, or we depart. My name is, said the knight, Ablamar of the Marsh. So he departed toward Camelot.

CHAPTER VIII

HOW FOUR KNIGHTS FOUGHT AGAINST GAWAINE AND GAHERIS, AND HOW THEY WERE OVERCOME, AND THEIR LIVES SAVED AT REQUEST OF FOUR LADIES

AND Sir Gawaine went into the castle, and made him ready to lie there all night, and would have unarmed him. What will ye do, said Gaheris, will ye unarm you in this country? Ye may think ye have many enemies here. They had not sooner said that word but there came four knights well armed, and assailed Sir Gawaine hard, and said unto him, Thou new-made knight, thou hast shamed thy knighthood, for a knight without mercy is dishonoured. Also thou hast slain a fair lady to thy great shame to the world's end, and doubt thou not thou shalt have great need of mercy or thou depart from us. And therewith one of them smote Sir Gawaine a great stroke that nigh he fell to the earth, and Gaheris smote him again sore, and so they were on the one side and on the other, that Sir Gawaine and Gaheris were in jeopardy of their lives; and one with a bow, an archer, smote Sir Gawaine through the arm that it grieved him wonderly sore. And as they should have been slain, there came four fair ladies, and besought the knights of grace for Sir Gawaine; and goodly at request of the ladies they gave Sir Gawaine and Gaheris their lives, and made them to yield them as prisoners. Then Gawaine and Gaheris made great dole. Alas! said Sir Gawaine, mine arm grieveth me sore, I am like to be maimed; and so made his complaint piteously. Early on the morrow there came to Sir Gawaine one of the four ladies that had heard all his complaint, and said, Sir knight, what cheer? Not good, said he. It is your own default, said the lady, for ye have done a passing foul deed in the slaying of the lady, the which will be great villainy unto you. But be ye not of King Arthur's kin? said the lady. Yes truly, said Sir Gawaine. What is your name? said the lady, ye must tell it me or ye pass. My name is Gawaine, the King Lot of Orkney's son, and my mother is King Arthur's sister. Ah! then are ye nephew unto King Arthur, said the lady, and I shall so speak for you that ye shall have conduct to go to King Arthur for his love. And so she departed and told the four knights how their prisoner was King Arthur's nephew, and his name is Sir Gawaine, King Lot's son of Orkney. And they gave him the hart's head because it was in his quest. Then anon they delivered Sir Gawaine under this promise, that he should bear the dead lady with him in this manner; the head of her was hanged about his neck, and the whole body of her lay before him on his horse's mane. Right so rode he forth unto Camelot. And anon as he was come, Merlin desired of King Arthur that Sir Gawaine should be sworn to tell of all his adventures, and how he slew the lady, and how he would give no mercy unto the knight, wherethrough the lady was slain. Then the king and the queen were greatly displeased with Sir Gawaine for the slaying of the lady. And there by ordinance of the queen there was set a quest of ladies on Sir Gawaine, and they judged him for ever while he lived to be with all ladies, and to fight for their quarrels; and that ever he should be courteous, and never to refuse mercy to him that asketh mercy. Thus was Gawaine sworn upon the four Evangelists that he should never be against lady nor gentlewoman, but if he fought for a lady and his adversary fought for another. And thus endeth the adventure of Sir Gawaine that he did at the marriage of King Arthur. Amen.

CHAPTER IX

HOW SIR TOR RODE AFTER THE KNIGHT WITH THE BRACHET,
AND OF HIS ADVENTURE BY THE WAY

WHEN Sir Tor was ready, he mounted upon his horseback, and rode after the knight with the brachet. So as he rode he met with a dwarf suddenly that smote his horse on the head with a staff, that he went backward his spear length. Why dost thou so ? said Sir Tor. For thou shalt not pass this way, but if thou joust with yonder knights of the pavilions. Then was Tor ware where two pavilions were, and great spears stood out, and two shields hung on trees by the pavilions. I may not tarry, said Sir Tor, for I am in a quest that I must needs follow. Thou shalt not pass, said the dwarf, and therewithal he blew his horn. Then there came one armed on horseback, and dressed his shield, and came fast toward Tor, and he dressed him against him, and so ran together that Tor bare him from his horse. And anon the knight yielded him to his mercy. But, sir, I have a fellow in yonder pavilion that will have ado with you anon. He shall be welcome, said Sir Tor. Then was he ware of another knight coming with great raundon, and each of them dressed to other, that marvel it was to see ; but the knight smote Sir Tor a great stroke in midst of the shield that his spear all to-shivered. And Sir Tor smote him through the shield below of the shield that it went through the coost of the knight, but the stroke slew him not. And therewith Sir Tor alit and smote him on the helm a great stroke, and therewith the knight yielded him and besought him of mercy. I will well, said Sir Tor, but thou and thy fellow must go unto King Arthur, and yield you prisoners unto him. By whom shall we say are we thither sent ? Ye shall say by the knight that went in the quest of the knight that went with the brachet. Now, what be your two names ? said Sir Tor. My name is, said the one, Sir Felot of Langduk ; and my name is, said the other, Sir Petipase of Winchelsea. Now go ye forth, said Sir Tor, and God speed you and me. Then came the dwarf and said unto Sir Tor, I pray you give me a gift. I will well, said Sir Tor, ask. I ask no more, said the dwarf, but that ye will suffer me to do you service, for I will serve no more recreant

knights. Take an horse, said Sir Tor, and ride on with me.
I wot ye ride after the knight with the white brachet, and I
shall bring you where he is, said the dwarf. And so they
rode throughout a forest, and at the last they were ware of
two pavilions even by a priory with two shields, and the one
shield was enewed with white, and the other shield was red.

CHAPTER X

HOW SIR TOR FOUND THE BRACHET WITH A LADY, AND HOW A KNIGHT ASSAILED HIM FOR THE SAID BRACHET

THEREWITH Sir Tor alit and took the dwarf his glaive,
and so he came to the white pavilion, and saw three
damosels lie in it, on one pallet sleeping, and so he went to
the other pavilion, and found a lady lying sleeping therein,
but there was the white brachet that bayed at her fast, and
therewith the lady yede out of the pavilion and all her
damosels. But anon as Sir Tor espied the white brachet,
he took her by force and took her to the dwarf. What,
will ye so, said the lady, take my brachet from me? Yea,
said Sir Tor, this brachet have I sought from King Arthur's
court hither. Well, said the lady, knight, ye shall not go
far with her, but that ye shall be met and grieved. I shall
abide what adventure that cometh by the grace of God, and
so mounted upon his horse, and passed on his way toward
Camelot; but it was so near night he might not pass but
little further. Know ye any lodging? said Tor. I know
none, said the dwarf, but here beside is an hermitage, and
here ye must take lodging as ye find. And within a while
they came to the hermitage and took lodging; and was
there grass, oats and bread for their horses; soon it was
sped, and full hard was their supper; but there they rested
them all night till on the morn, and heard a mass devoutly,
and took their leave of the hermit, and Sir Tor prayed the
hermit to pray for him. He said he would, and betook him
to God. And so he mounted upon horseback and rode
towards Camelot a long while. With that they heard a
knight call loud that came after them, and he said, Knight,
abide and yield my brachet that thou took from my lady.
Sir Tor returned again, and beheld him how he was a
seemly knight and well horsed, and well armed at all points;

then Sir Tor dressed his shield, and took his spear in his hands, and the other came fiercely upon him, and smote both horse and man to the earth. Anon they arose lightly and drew their swords as eagerly as lions, and put their shields afore them, and smote through the shields, that the cantels fell off both parties. Also they tamyd their helms that the hot blood ran out, and the thick mails of their hauberks they carved and rove in sunder that the hot blood ran to the earth, and both they had many wounds and were passing weary. But Sir Tor espied that the other knight fainted, and then he sewed fast upon him, and doubled his strokes, and garte him go to the earth on the one side. Then Sir Tor bad him yield him. That will I not, said Abelleus, while my life lasteth and the soul is within my body, unless that thou wilt give me the brachet. That will I not do, said Sir Tor, for it was my quest to bring again thy brachet, thee, or both.

CHAPTER XI

HOW SIR TOR OVERCAME THE KNIGHT, AND HOW HE LOST HIS HEAD AT THE REQUEST OF A LADY

WITH that came a damosel riding on a palfrey as fast as she might drive, and cried with a loud voice unto Sir Tor. What will ye with me? said Sir Tor. I beseech thee, said the damosel, for King Arthur's love, give me a gift; I require thee gentle knight, as thou art a gentleman. Now, said Tor, ask a gift and I will give it you. Gramercy, said the damosel; now I ask the head of the false knight Abelleus, for he is the most outrageous knight that liveth, and the greatest murderer. I am loth, said Sir Tor, of that gift I have given you; let him make amends in that he hath trespassed unto you. Now, said the damosel, he may not, for he slew mine own brother afore mine own eyes, that was a better knight than he, an he had had grace; and I kneeled half an hour afore him in the mire for to save my brother's life, that had done him no damage, but fought with him by adventure of arms, and so for all that I could do he struck off his head; wherefore I require thee, as thou art a true knight, to give me my gift, or else I shall shame thee in all the court of King Arthur; for he is the falsest knight living, and a great destroyer of good knights. Then when Abelleus heard this, he was more afeard, and yielded him and asked mercy. I may not now, said Sir Tor, but if I should be found false of my promise; for while I would have taken you to mercy ye would none ask but if ye had the brachet again that was my quest. And therewith he took off his helm, and he arose and fled, and Sir Tor after him, and smote off his head quite. Now sir, said the damosel, it is near night; I pray you come and lodge with me here at my place, it is here fast by. I will well, said Sir Tor, for his horse and he had fared evil syne they departed from Camelot, and so he rode with her, and had passing good cheer with her; and she had a passing fair old knight to her husband that made him passing good cheer, and well eased both his horse and him. And on the morn he heard his mass, and brake his fast, and took his leave of the knight and of the lady, that besought him to tell them his name. Truly, he said, my name is Sir Tor that was late made knight, and this was the first quest of arms that ever I did, to bring again that this knight Abelleus took away from King Arthur's court. O fair knight, said the lady and her husband, an ye come here in our marches, come and see our poor lodging, and it shall be always at your commandment. So Sir Tor departed and came to Camelot on the third day by noon, and the king and the queen and all the court was passing fain of his coming, and made great joy that he was come again; for he went from the court with little succour, but as King Pellinore his father gave him an old courser, and King Arthur gave him armour and a sword, and else had he none other succour, but rode so forth himself alone. And then the king and the queen by Merlin's advice made him to swear to tell of his adventures, and so he told and made proofs of his deeds as it is afore rehearsed, wherefore the king and the queen made great joy. Nay, nay, said Merlin, these be but japes to that he shall do; for he shall prove a noble knight of prowess, as good as any is living, and gentle and courteous, and of good tatches, and passing true of his promise, and never shall outrage. Wherethrough Merlin's words King Arthur gave him an earldom of lands that fell unto him. And here endeth the quest of Sir Tor, King Pellinore's son.

CHAPTER XII

HOW KING PELLINORE RODE AFTER THE LADY AND THE KNIGHT THAT LED HER AWAY, AND HOW A LADY DESIRED HELP OF HIM, AND HOW HE FOUGHT WITH TWO KNIGHTS FOR THAT LADY, OF WHOM HE SLEW THE ONE AT THE FIRST STROKE

THEN King Pellinore armed him and mounted upon his horse, and rode more than a paas after the lady that the knight led away. And as he rode in a forest, he saw in a valley a damosel sit by a well, and a wounded knight in her arms, and Pellinore saluted her. And when she was ware of him, she cried overloud, Help me, knight, for Christ's sake, King Pellinore. And he would not tarry, he was so eager in his quest, and ever she cried an hundred times after help. When she saw he would not abide, she prayed unto God to send him as much need of help as she had, and that he might feel it or he died. So, as the book telleth, the knight there died that there was wounded, wherefore the lady for pure sorrow slew herself with his sword. As King Pellinore rode in that valley he met with a poor man, a labourer. Sawest thou not, said Pellinore, a knight riding and leading away a lady? Yea, said the man, I saw that knight, and the lady that made great dole; and yonder beneath in a valley there shall ye see two pavilions, and one of the knights of the pavilions challenged that lady of that knight, and said she was his cousin near, wherefore he should lead her no farther. And so they waged battle in that quarrel, the one said he would have her by force, and the other said he would have the rule of her, by cause he was her kinsman, and would lead her to her kin. For this quarrel he left them fighting. And if ye will ride a pace ye shall find them fighting, and the lady was beleft with the two squires in the pavilions. God thank thee, said King Pellinore. Then he rode a wallop till he had a sight of the two pavilions, and the two knights fighting. Anon he rode unto the pavilions, and saw the lady that was his quest, and said, Fair lady, ye must go with me unto the court of King Arthur. Sir knight, said the two squires that were with her, yonder are two knights that fight for this lady, go thither and depart them, and be agreed with them, and then may ye have her at your pleasure. Ye say well, said King Pellinore. And anon he rode betwixt them, and departed them, and asked them the causes why that they fought? Sir knight, said the one, I shall tell you, this lady is my kinswoman nigh, mine aunt's daughter, and when I heard her complain that she was with him maugre her head, I waged battle to fight with him. Sir knight, said the other, whose name was Hontzlake of Wentland, and this lady I gat by my prowess of arms this day at Arthur's court. That is untruly said, said King Pellinore, for ye came in suddenly there as we were at the high feast, and took away this lady or any man might make him ready, and therefore it was my quest to bring her again and you both, or else the one of us to abide in the field; therefore the lady shall go with me, or I will die for it, for I have promised it King Arthur. And therefore fight ye no more, for none of you shall have no part of her at this time, and if ye list to fight for her, fight with me, and I will defend her. Well, said the knights, make you ready, and we shall assail you with all our power, And as King Pellinore would have put his horse from them, Sir Hontzlake rove his horse through with a sword, and said: Now art thou on foot as well as we are. When King Pellinore espied that his horse was slain, lightly he leapt from his horse and pulled out his sword, and put his shield afore him, and said, Knight, keep well thy head, for thou shalt have a buffet for the slaying of my horse. So King Pellinore gave him such a stroke upon the helm that he clave the head down to the chin, that he fell to the earth dead.

CHAPTER XIII

HOW KING PELLINORE GAT THE LADY AND BROUGHT HER TO CAMELOT TO THE COURT OF KING ARTHUR

AND then he turned him to the other knight that was sore wounded. But when he saw the other's buffet, he would not fight, but kneeled down and said, Take my cousin the lady with you at your request, and I require you, as ye be a true knight, put her to no shame nor villainy. What, said King Pellinore, will ye not fight for her? No, sir, said the knight, I will not fight with such a knight of prowess as ye be. Well, said Pellinore, ye say well; I promise you she shall have no villainy by me, as I am true knight; but now me lacketh an horse, said Pellinore, but I will have Hontzlake's horse. Ye shall not need, said the knight, for I shall give you such an horse as shall please you, so that you will lodge with me, for it is near night. I will well, said King Pellinore, abide with you all night. And there he had with him right good cheer, and fared of the best with passing good wine, and had merry rest that night. And on the morn he heard a mass and dined; and then was brought him a fair bay courser, and King Pellinore's saddle set upon him. Now, what shall I call you? said the knight, inasmuch as ye have my cousin at your desire of your quest. Sir, I shall tell you, my name is King Pellinore of the Isles and knight of the Table Round. Now I am glad, said the knight, that such a noble man shall have the rule of my cousin. Now, what is your name? said Pellinore, I pray you tell me. Sir, my name is Sir Meliot of Logurs, and this lady my cousin hight Nimue, and the knight that was in the other pavilion is my sworn brother, a passing good knight, and his name is Brian of the Isles, and he is full loth to do wrong, and full loth to fight with any man, but if he be sore sought on, so that for shame he may not leave it. It is marvel, said Pellinore, that he will not have ado with me. Sir, he will not have ado with no man but if it be at his request. Bring him to the court, said Pellinore, one of these days. Sir, we will come together. And ye shall be welcome, said Pellinore, to the court of King Arthur, and greatly allowed for your coming. And so he departed with the lady, and brought her to Camelot. So as they rode in a valley it was full of stones, and there the lady's horse stumbled and threw her down, that her arm was sore bruised and near she swooned for pain. Alas! sir, said the lady, mine arm is out of lythe, wherethrough I must needs rest me. Ye shall well, said King Pellinore. And so he alit under a fair tree where was fair grass, and he put his horse thereto, and so laid him under the tree and slept till it was nigh night. And when he awoke he would have ridden. Sir, said the lady, it is so dark that ye may as well ride backward as forward. So they abode still and made there their lodging. Then Sir Pellinore put off his armour; then a little afore midnight they heard the trotting of an horse. Be ye still, said King Pellinore, for we shall hear of some adventure.

CHAPTER XIV

AND therewith he armed him. So right even afore him there met two knights, the one came froward Camelot, and the other from the north, and either saluted other. What tidings at Camelot? said the one. By my head, said the other, there have I been and espied the court of King Arthur, and there is such a fellowship they may never be broken, and well-nigh all the world holdeth with Arthur, for there is the flower of chivalry. Now for this cause I am riding into the north, to tell our chieftains of the fellowship that is withholden with King Arthur. As for that, said the other knight, I have brought a remedy with me, that is the greatest poison that ever ye heard speak of, and to Camelot will I with it, for we have a friend right nigh King Arthur, and well cherished, that shall poison King Arthur; for so he hath promised our chieftains, and received great gifts for to do it. Beware, said the other knight, of Merlin, for he knoweth all things by the devil's craft. Therefore will I not let it, said the knight. And so they departed asunder. Anon after Pellinore made him ready, and his lady, and rode toward Camelot; and as they came by the well there as the wounded knight was and the lady, there he found the knight, and the lady eaten with lions or wild beasts, all save the head, wherefore he made great sorrow, and wept passing sore, and said, Alas! her life might I have saved, but I was so fierce in my quest therefore I would not abide. Wherefore make ye such dole? said the lady. I wot not, said Pellinore, but my heart mourneth sore of the death of her, for she was a passing fair lady and a young. Now, will ye do by mine advice? said the lady, take this knight and let him be buried in an hermitage, and then take the lady's head and bear it with you unto Arthur. So King Pellinore took this dead knight on his shoulders, and brought him to the hermitage, and charged the hermit with the corpse, that service should be done for the soul; and take his harness for your pain. It shall be done, said the hermit, as I will answer unto God.

CHAPTER XV

HOW WHEN HE WAS COME TO CAMELOT HE WAS SWORN UPON
A BOOK TO TELL THE TRUTH OF HIS QUEST

AND therewith they departed, and came there as the head of the lady lay with a fair yellow hair, that grieved King Pellinore passingly sore when he looked on it, for much he cast his heart on the visage. And so by noon they came to Camelot; and the king and the queen were passing fain of his coming to the court. And there he was made to swear upon the four Evangelists, to tell the truth of his quest from the one to the other. Ah! Sir Pellinore, said Queen Guenever, ye were greatly to blame that ye saved not this lady's life. Madam, said Pellinore, ye were greatly to blame an ye would not save your own life an ye might, but, save your pleasure, I was so furious in my quest that I would not abide, and that repenteth me, and shall the days of my life. Truly, said Merlin, ye ought sore to repent it, for that lady was your own daughter begotten on the lady of the Rule, and that knight that was dead was her love, and should have wedded her, and he was a right good knight of a young man, and would have proved a good man, and to this court was he coming, and his name was Sir Miles of the Launds, and a knight came behind him and slew him with a spear, and his name is Loraine le Savage, a false knight and a coward; and she for great sorrow and dole slew herself with his sword, and her name was Eleine. And because ye would not abide and help her, ye shall see your best friend fail you when ye be in the greatest distress that ever ye were or shall be. And that penance God hath ordained you for that deed, that he that ye shall most trust to of any man alive, he shall leave you where ye shall be slain. Me forthynketh, said King Pellinore, that this shall me betide, but God may fordo well destiny. Thus, when the quest was done of the white hart, the which followed Sir Gawaine; and the quest of the brachet, followed of Sir Tor, Pellinore's son; and the quest of the lady that the knight took away, the which King Pellinore at that time followed; then the king stablished all his knights, and gave them that were of lands not rich, he gave them lands, and charged them never to do outrageousity nor murder, and always to flee treason; also, by no means to be cruel, but to give mercy unto him that asketh mercy, upon pain of forfeiture of their worship and lordship of King Arthur for evermore; and always to do ladies, damosels, and gentlewomen succour, upon pain of death. Also, that no man take no battles in a wrongful quarrel for no law, nor for no world's goods. Unto this were all the knights sworn of the Table Round, both old and young. And every year were they sworn at the high feast of Pentecost.

Explicit the Wedding of King Arthur.

Sequitur quartus liber.

BOOK IV

CHAPTER I

HOW MERLIN WAS ASSOTTED AND DOATED ON ONE OF THE LADIES OF THE LAKE, AND HOW HE WAS SHUT IN A ROCK UNDER A STONE AND THERE DIED

So after these quests of Sir Gawaine, Sir Tor, and King Pellinore, it fell so that Merlin fell in a dotage on the damosel that King Pellinore brought to court, and she was one of the damosels of the lake, that hight Nimue. But Merlin would let have her no rest, but always he would be with her. And ever she made Merlin good cheer till she had learned of him all manner thing that she desired; and he was assotted upon her, that he might not be from her. So on a time he told King Arthur that he should not dure long, but for all his crafts he should be put in the earth quick, and so he told the king many things that should befall, but always he warned the king to keep well his sword and the scabbard, for he told him how the sword and the scabbard should be stolen by a woman from him that he most trusted. Also he told King Arthur that he should miss him,—Yet had ye lever than all your lands to have me again. Ah, said the king, since ye know of your adventure, purvey for it, and put away by your crafts that misadventure. Nay, said Merlin, it will not be; so he departed from the king. And within a while the damosel of the lake departed, and Merlin went with her evermore wheresomever she went. And ofttimes Merlin would have had her privily away by his subtle crafts; then she made him to swear that he should never do none enchantment upon her if he would have his will. And so he sware; so she and Merlin went over the sea unto the land of Benwick, whereas King Ban was king that had great war against King Claudas, and there Merlin spake with King Ban's wife, a fair lady and a good, and her name was Elaine, and there he saw young Launcelot. There the queen made great sorrow for the mortal war that King Claudas made on her lord and on her lands. Take none heaviness, said Merlin, for this same child within this twenty year shall revenge you on King Claudas, that all Christendom shall speak of it; and this same child shall be the most man of worship of the world, and his first name is Galahad, that know I well, said Merlin, and syne ye have confirmed him Launcelot. That is truth, said the queen, his first name was Galahad. O Merlin, said the queen, shall I live to see my son such a man of prowess? Yea, lady, on my peril ye shall see it, and live many winters after. And so soon after the lady and Merlin departed, and by the way Merlin showed her many wonders, and came into Cornwall. And always Merlin lay about the lady to have her maidenhood, and she was ever passing weary of him, and fain would have been delivered of him, for she was afeared of him because he was a devil's son, and she could not beskyfte him by no mean. And so on a time it happed that Merlin showed to her in a rock whereas was a great wonder, and wrought by enchantment, that went under a great stone. So by her subtle working she made Merlin to go under that stone to let her wit of the marvels there, but she wrought so there for him that he came never out for all the craft he could do. And so she departed and left Merlin.

CHAPTER II

HOW FIVE KINGS CAME INTO THIS LAND TO WAR AGAINST KING ARTHUR, AND WHAT COUNSEL ARTHUR HAD AGAINST THEM

AND as King Arthur rode to Camelot, and held there a great feast with mirth and joy, so soon after he returned unto Cardoile, and there came unto Arthur new tidings that the king of Denmark, and the king of Ireland that was his brother, and the king of the Vale, and the king of Soleise, and the king of the Isle of Longtains, all these five kings with a great host were entered into the land of King Arthur, and burnt and slew clean afore them, both cities and castles, that it was pity to hear. Alas, said Arthur, yet had I never rest one month syne I was crowned king of this land. Now shall I never rest till I meet with those kings in a fair field, that I make mine avow; for my true liege people shall not be destroyed in my default, go with me who will, and abide who that will. Then the king let write unto King Pellinore, and prayed him in all haste to make him ready with such people as he might lightliest rear and hie him after in all haste. All the barons were privily wroth that the king would depart so suddenly; but the king by no mean would abide, but made writing unto them that were not there, and bade them hie after him, such as were not at that time in the court. Then the king came to Queen Guenever, and said, Lady, make you ready, for ye shall go with me, for I may not long miss you, ye shall cause me to be the more hardy, what adventure so befall me; I will not wit my lady to be in no jeopardy. Sir, said she, I am at your commandment, and shall be ready what time so ye be ready. So on the morn the king and the queen departed with such fellowship as they had, and came into the north, into a forest beside Humber, and there lodged them. When the word and tiding came unto the five kings above said, that Arthur was beside Humber in a forest, there was a knight, brother unto one of the five kings, that gave them this counsel: Ye know well that Sir Arthur hath the flower of chivalry of the world with him, as it is proved by the great battle he did with the eleven kings; and therefore hie unto him night and day till that we be nigh him, for the longer he tarrieth the bigger he is, and we ever the weaker; and he is so courageous of himself that he is come to the field with little people, and therefore let us set upon him or day and we shall slay down; of his knights there shall none escape.

CHAPTER III

HOW KING ARTHUR HAD ADO WITH THEM AND OVERTHREW THEM, AND SLEW THE FIVE KINGS AND MADE THE REMNANT TO FLEE

UNTO this counsel these five kings assented, and so they passed forth with their host through North Wales, and came upon Arthur by night, and set upon his host as the king and his knights were in their pavilions. King Arthur was unarmed, and had lain him to rest with his Queen Guenever. Sir, said Sir Kay, it is not good we be unarmed. We shall have no need, said Sir Gawaine and Sir Griflet, that lay in a little pavilion by the king. With that they heard a great noise, and many cried, Treason, treason! Alas, said King Arthur, we be betrayed! Unto arms, fellows, then he cried. So they were armed anon at all points. Then came there a wounded knight unto the king, and said, Sir, save yourself and my lady the queen, for our host is destroyed, and much people of ours slain. So anon the king and the queen and the three knights took their horses, and rode toward Humber to pass over it, and the water was so rough that they were afraid to pass over. Now may ye choose, said King Arthur, whether ye will abide and take the adventure on this side, for an ye be taken they will slay you. It were me lever, said the queen, to die in the water than to fall in your enemies' hands and there be slain. And as they stood so talking, Sir Kay saw the five kings coming on horseback by themself alone, with their spears in their hands even toward them. Lo, said Sir Kay, yonder be the five kings; let us go to them and match them. That were folly, said Sir Gawaine, for we are but three and they be five. That is truth, said Sir Griflet. No force, said Sir Kay, I will undertake for two of them, and then may ye three undertake for the other three. And therewithal, Sir Kay let his horse run as fast as he might, and struck one of them through the shield and the body a fathom, that the king fell to the earth stark dead. That saw Sir Gawaine, and ran unto another king so hard that he smote him through the body. And therewithal King Arthur ran to another, and smote him through the body with a spear, that he fell to the earth dead. Then Sir Griflet ran unto the fourth king, and gave him such a fall that his neck brake. Anon Sir Kay ran unto the fifth king, and smote him so hard on the helm that the stroke clave the helm and the head to the earth. That was well stricken, said King Arthur, and worshipfully hast thou holden thy promise, therefore I shall honour thee while that I live, and therewithal they set the queen in a barge into Humber; but always Queen Guenever praised Sir Kay for his deeds, and said, What lady that ye love, and she love you not again she were greatly to blame; and among ladies, said the queen, I shall bear your noble fame, for ye spake a great word, and fulfilled it worshipfully. And therewith the queen departed. Then the king and the three knights rode into the forest, for there they supposed to hear of them that were escaped; and there he found the most part of his people, and told them all how the five kings were dead. And therefore let us hold us together till it be day, and when their host have espied that their chieftains be slain, they will make such dole that they shall no more help themselves. And right so as the king said, so it was; for when they found the five kings dead, they made such dole that they fell from their horses. Therewithal came King Arthur but with a few people, and slew on the left hand and on the right hand, that well-nigh there escaped no man, but all were slain to the number thirty thousand. And when the battle was all ended, the king kneeled down and thanked God meekly. And then he sent for the queen, and soon she was come, and she made great joy of the overcoming of that battle.

CHAPTER IV

HOW THE BATTLE WAS FINISHED OR HE CAME, AND HOW KING ARTHUR FOUNDED AN ABBEY WHERE THE BATTLE WAS

THEREWITHAL came one to King Arthur, and told him that King Pellinore was within three mile with a great host; and he said, Go unto him, and let him understand how we have sped. So within a while King Pellinore came with a great host, and saluted the people and the king, and there was great joy made on every side. Then the king let search how much people of his party there was slain; and there were found but little past two hundred men slain and eight knights of the Table Round in their pavilions. Then the king let rear and devise in the same place whereat the battle was done a fair abbey, and endowed it with great livelihood, and let it call the Abbey of La Beale Adventure. But when some of them came into their countries, whereof the five kings were kings, and told them how they were slain, there was made great dole. And when all King Arthur's enemies, as the King of North Wales, and the kings of the North, wist of the battle, they were passing heavy. And so the king returned unto Camelot in haste. And when he was come to Camelot he called King Pellinore unto him, and said, Ye understand well that we have lost eight knights of the best of the Table Round, and by your advice we will choose eight again of the best we may find in this court. Sir, said Pellinore, I shall counsel you after my conceit the best: there are in your court full noble knights both of old and young; and therefore by mine advice ye shall choose half of the old and half of the young. Which be the old? said King Arthur. Sir, said King Pellinore, meseemeth that King Uriens that hath wedded your sister Morgan le Fay, and the King of the Lake, and Sir Hervise de Revel, a noble knight, and Sir Galagars, the fourth. This is well devised, said King Arthur, and right so shall it be. Now, which are the four young knights? said Arthur. Sir, said Pellinore, the first is Sir Gawaine, your nephew, that is as good a knight of his time as any is in this land; and the second as meseemeth best is Sir Griflet le Fise de Dieu, that is a good knight and full desirous in arms, and who may see him live he shall prove a good knight; and the third as meseemeth is well to be one of the knights of the Round Table, Sir Kay the Seneschal, for many times he hath done full worshipfully, and now at your last battle he did full honourably for to undertake to slay two kings. By my head, said Arthur, he is best worth to be a knight of the Round Table of any that ye have rehearsed, an he had done no more prowess in his life days.

CHAPTER V

HOW SIR TOR WAS MADE KNIGHT OF THE ROUND TABLE, AND HOW BAGDEMAGUS WAS DISPLEASED

Now, said King Pellinore, I shall put to you two knights, and ye shall choose which is most worthy, that is Sir Bagdemagus, and Sir Tor, my son. But because Sir Tor is my son I may not praise him, but else, an he were not my son, I durst say that of his age there is not in this land a better knight than he is, nor of better conditions and loth to do any wrong, and loth to take any wrong. By my head, said Arthur, he is a passing good knight as any ye spake of this day, that wot I well, said the king; for I have seen him proved, but he sayeth little and he doth more, for I know none in all this court an he were as well born on his mother's side as he is on your side, that is like him of prowess and of might: and therefore I will have him at this time, and leave Sir Bagdemagus till another time. So when they were so chosen by the assent of all the barons, so were there found in their sieges every knights' names that here are rehearsed; and so were they set in their sieges, whereof Sir Bagdemagus was wonderly wroth, that Sir Tor was advanced afore him, and therefore suddenly he departed from the court, and took his squire with him, and rode long in a forest till they came to a cross, and there alit and said his prayers devoutly. The meanwhile his squire found written upon the cross, that Bagdemagus should never return unto the court again, till he had won a knight's body of the Round Table, body for body. So, sir, said the squire, here I find writing of you, therefore I rede you return again to the court. That shall I never, said Bagdemagus, till men speak of me great worship, and that I be worthy to be a knight of the Round Table. And so he rode forth, and there by the way he found a branch of an holy herb that was the sign of the Sangreal, and no knight found such tokens but he were a good liver. So, as Sir Bagdemagus rode to see many adventures, it happed him to come to the rock whereas the Lady of the Lake had put Merlin under the stone, and there he heard him make great dole; whereof Sir Bagdemagus would have holpen him, and went unto the great stone, and it was so heavy that an hundred men might not lift it up. When Merlin wist he was there, he bad leave his labour, for all was in vain, for he might never be holpen but by her that put him there. And so Bagdemagus departed and did many adventures, and proved after a full good knight, and came again to the court and was made knight of the Round Table. So on the morn there fell new tidings and other adventures.

CHAPTER VI

HOW KING ARTHUR, KING URIENS, AND SIR ACCOLON OF GAUL, CHASED AN HART, AND OF THEIR MARVELLOUS ADVENTURES

THEN it befell that Arthur and many of his knights rode a-hunting into a great forest, and it happed King Arthur, King Uriens, and Sir Accolon of Gaul, followed a great hart, for they three were well horsed, and so they chased so fast that within a while they three were then ten mile from their fellowship. And at the last they chased so sore that they slew their horses underneath them. Then were they all three on foot, and ever they saw the hart afore them passing weary and embushed. What will we do? said King Arthur, we are hard bestad. Let us go on foot, said King Uriens, till we may meet with some lodging. Then were they ware of the hart that lay on a great water bank, and a brachet biting on his throat, and more other hounds came after. Then King Arthur blew the prise and dight the hart. Then the king looked about the world, and saw afore him in a great water a little ship, all apparelled with silk down to the water, and the ship came right unto them and landed on the sands. Then Arthur went to the bank and looked in, and saw none earthly creature therein. Sirs, said the king, come thence, and let us see what is in this ship. So they went in all three, and found it richly behanged with cloth of silk. By then it was dark night, and there suddenly were about them an hundred torches set upon all the sides of the ship boards, and it gave great light; and therewithal there came out twelve fair damosels and saluted King Arthur on their knees, and called him by his name, and said he was right welcome, and such cheer as they had he should have of the best. The king thanked them fair. Therewithal they led the king and his two fellows into a fair chamber, and there was a cloth laid richly bisene of all that longed unto a table, and there were they served of all wines and meats that they could think; of that the king had great marvel, for he fared never better in his life as for one supper. And so when they had supped at their leisure, King Arthur was led into a chamber, a richer bisene chamber saw he never none, and so was King Uriens served, and led into such another chamber, and Sir Accolon was led into the third chamber passing richly

and well bisene ; and so they were laid in their beds easily.
And anon they fell a-sleep, and slept marvellously sore all
the night. And on the morrow King Uriens was in Camelot abed in his wife's arms, Morgan le Fay. And when he
awoke he had great marvel, how he came there, for on the
even afore he was two days' journey from Camelot. And
when King Arthur awoke he found himself in a dark prison,
hearing about him many complaints of woful knights.

CHAPTER VII

HOW ARTHUR TOOK UPON HIM TO FIGHT TO BE DELIVERED OUT OF PRISON, AND ALSO FOR TO DELIVER TWENTY KNIGHTS THAT WERE IN PRISON

WHAT are ye that so complain ? said King Arthur. We
be here twenty knights, prisoners, said they, and some of us
have lain here seven year, and some more and some less.
For what cause ? said Arthur. We shall tell you, said the
knights ; this lord of this castle, his name is Sir Damas, and
he is the falsest knight that liveth, and full of treason, and a
very coward as any liveth, and he hath a younger brother, a
good knight of prowess, his name is Sir Ontzlake, and
this traitor Damas, the elder brother will give him no part
of his livelihood, but as Sir Ontzlake keepeth thorough
prowess of his hands, and so he keepeth from him
a full fair manor and a rich, and therein Sir Ontzlake
dwelleth worshipfully, and is well beloved of all people. And
this Sir Damas, our master is as evil beloved, for he is
without mercy, and he is a coward, and great war hath been
betwixt them both, but Ontzlake hath ever the better, and
ever he proffereth Sir Damas to fight for the livelihood,
body for body, but he will not do ; other els to find a
knight to fight for him. Unto that Sir Damas had granted
to find a knight, but he is so evil beloved and hated, that
there is never a knight will fight for him. And when Damas
saw this, that there was never a knight would fight for him,
he hath daily lain await with many knights with him, and
taken all the knights in this country to see and espy their
adventures, he hath taken them by force and brought them
to his prison. And so he took us separately as we rode on
our adventures, and many good knights have died in this

prison for hunger, to the number of eighteen knights ; and if any of us all that here is, or hath been, would have foughten with his brother Ontzlake, he would have delivered us, but for because this Damas is so false and so full of treason we would never fight for him to die for it. And we be so lean for hunger that unnethe we may stand on our feet. God deliver you, for his mercy, said Arthur. Anon, therewithal there came a damosel unto Arthur, and asked him, What cheer? I cannot say, said he. Sir, said she, an ye will fight for my lord, ye shall be delivered out of prison, and else ye escape never the life. Now, said Arthur, that is hard, yet had I lever to fight with a knight than to die in prison ; with this, said Arthur, I may be delivered and all these prisoners, I will do the battle. Yes, said the damosel. I am ready, said Arthur, an I had horse and armour. Ye shall lack none, said the damosel. Meseemeth, damosel, I should have seen you in the court of Arthur. Nay, said the damosel, I came never there, I am the lord's daughter of this castle. Yet was she false, for she was one of the damosels of Morgan le Fay. Anon she went unto Sir Damas, and told him how he would do battle for him, and so he sent for Arthur. And when he came he was well coloured, and well made of his limbs, that all knights that saw him said it were pity that such a knight should die in prison. So Sir Damas and he were agreed that he should fight for him upon this covenant, that all other knights should be delivered ; and unto that was Sir Damas sworn unto Arthur, and also to do the battle to the uttermost. And with that all the twenty knights were brought out of the dark prison into the hall, and delivered, and so they all abode to see the battle.

CHAPTER VIII

HOW ACCOLON FOUND HIMSELF BY A WELL, AND HE TOOK UPON HIM TO DO BATTLE AGAINST ARTHUR

Now turn we unto Accolon of Gaul, that when he awoke he found himself by a deep well-side, within half a foot, in great peril of death. And there came out of that fountain a pipe of silver, and out of that pipe ran water all on high in a stone of marble. When Sir Accolon saw this, he blessed him and said, Jesus save my lord King Arthur, and King Uriens, for these damosels in this ship have betrayed us, they were devils and no women; and if I may escape this misadventure, I shall destroy all where I may find these false damosels that use enchantments. Right with that there came a dwarf with a great mouth and a flat nose, and saluted Sir Accolon, and said how he came from Queen Morgan le Fay, and she greeteth you well, and biddeth you be of strong heart, for ye shall fight to-morrow with a knight at the hour of prime, and therefore she hath sent you here Excalibur Arthur's sword, and the scabbard, and she biddeth you as ye love her, that ye do the battle to the uttermost, without any mercy, like as ye had promised her when ye spake together in private; and what damosel that bringeth her the knight's head, which ye shall fight withal, she will make her a queen. Now I understand you well, said Accolon, I shall hold that I have promised her now I have the sword: when saw ye my lady Queen Morgan le Fay? Right late, said the dwarf. Then Accolon took him in his arms and said, Recommend me unto my lady queen, and tell her all shall be done that I have promised her, and else I will die for it. Now I suppose, said Accolon, she hath made all these crafts and enchantments for this battle. Ye may well believe it, said the dwarf. Right so there came a knight and a lady with six squires, and saluted Accolon, and prayed him for to arise, and come and rest him at his manor. And so Accolon mounted upon a void horse, and went with the knight unto a fair manor by a priory, and there he had passing good cheer. Then Sir Damas sent unto his brother Sir Ontzlake, and bade make him ready by to-morn at the hour of prime, and to be in the field to fight with a good knight, for he had found a good knight that was ready to do battle at all points. When this word came unto Sir Ontzlake he was passing heavy, for he was wounded a little tofore through both his thighs with a spear, and made great dole; but as he was wounded he would have taken the battle on hand. So it happed at that time, by the means of Morgan le Fay, Accolon was with Sir Ontzlake lodged; and when he heard of that battle, and how Ontzlake was wounded, he said that he would fight for him, because Morgan le Fay had sent him Excalibur and the sheath for to fight with the knight on the morn: this was the cause Sir Accolon took the battle on hand. Then Sir

Ontzlake was passing glad, and thanked Sir Accolon with all his heart that he would do so much for him. And therewithal Sir Ontzlake sent word unto his brother Sir Damas, that he had a knight that for him should be ready in the field by the hour of prime. So on the morn Sir Arthur was armed and well horsed, and asked Sir Damas, When shall we to the field? Sir, said Sir Damas, ye shall hear mass. And so Arthur heard a mass, and when mass was done there came a squire on a great horse, and asked Sir Damas if his knight were ready, for our knight is ready in the field. Then Sir Arthur mounted upon horseback, and there were all the knights and commons of that country; and so by all advices there were chosen twelve good men of the country for to wait upon the two knights. And right as Arthur was on horseback there came a damosel from Morgan le Fay, and brought unto Sir Arthur a sword like unto Excalibur, and the scabbard, and said unto Arthur, Morgan le Fay sendeth here your sword for great love. And he thanked her, and weened it had been so, but she was false, for the sword and the scabbard were counterfeit, and brittle, and false.

CHAPTER IX

OF THE BATTLE BETWEEN KING ARTHUR AND ACCOLON

AND then they dressed them on both parties of the field, and let their horses run so fast that either smote other in the middes of the shield with their spear-heads, that both horse and man went to the earth; and then they started up both, and pulled out their swords. The meanwhile that they were thus at the battle, came the damosel of the lake into the field, that put Merlin under the stone; and she came thither for love of King Arthur, for she knew how Morgan le Fay had so ordained that King Arthur should have been slain that day, and therefore she came to save his life. And so they went eagerly to the battle, and gave many great strokes, but always Arthur's sword bit not like Accolon's sword; but for the most part, every stroke that Accolon gave he wounded sore Arthur, that it was marvellous he stood, and always his blood fell from him fast. When Arthur beheld the ground so sore be-bled he was dismayed, and then he deemed treason that his sword was changed; for his sword bit not steel as it was wont to do, therefore he dread him sore to be dead, for ever him seemed that the sword in Accolon's hand was Excalibur, for at every stroke that Accolon struck he drew blood on Arthur. Now, knight, said Accolon unto Arthur, keep thee well from me; but Arthur answered not again, and gave him such a buffet on the helm that it made him to stoop, nigh falling down to the earth. Then Sir Accolon withdrew him a little, and came on with Excalibur on high, and smote Sir Arthur such a buffet that he fell nigh to the earth. Then were they wroth both, and gave each other many sore strokes, but always Sir Arthur lost so much blood that it was marvel he stood on his feet, but he was so full of knighthood that knightly he endured the pain. And Sir Accolon lost not a dele of blood, therefore he waxed passing light, and Sir Arthur was passing feeble, and weened verily to have died; but for all that he made countenance as though he might endure, and held Accolon as short as he might. But Accolon was so bold because of Excalibur that he waxed passing hardy. But all men that beheld him said they saw never knight fight so well as Arthur did considering the blood that he bled. So was all the people sorry for him, but the two brethren would not accord; then always they fought together as fierce knights, and Sir Arthur withdrew him a little for to rest him, and Sir Accolon called him to battle and said, It is no time for me to suffer thee to rest. And therewith he came fiercely upon Arthur, and Sir Arthur was wroth for the blood that he had lost, and smote Accolon on high upon the helm, so mightily, that he made him nigh to fall to the earth; and therewith Arthur's sword brast at the cross, and fell in the grass among the blood, and the pommel and the sure handles he held in his hands. When Sir Arthur saw that, he was in great fear to die, but always he held up his shield and lost no ground, nor bated no cheer.

CHAPTER X

HOW KING ARTHUR'S SWORD THAT HE FOUGHT WITH BRAKE, AND
HOW HE RECOVERED OF ACCOLON HIS OWN SWORD EXCALIBUR,
AND OVERCAME HIS ENEMY

THEN Sir Accolon began with words of treason, and said, Knight, thou art overcome, and mayst not endure, and also thou art weaponless, and thou hast lost much of thy blood, and I am full loath to slay thee, therefore yield thee to me as recreant. Nay, said Sir Arthur, I may not so, for I have promised to do the battle to the uttermost, by the faith of my body, while me lasteth the life, and therefore I had lever to die with honour than to live with shame; and if it were possible for me to die an hundred times, I had lever to die so oft than yield me to thee; for though I lack weapon, I shall lack no worship, and if thou slay me weaponless that shall be thy shame. Well, said Accolon, as for the shame I will not spare, now keep thee from me, for thou art but a dead man. And therewith Accolon gave him such a stroke that he fell nigh to the earth, and would have had Arthur to have cried him mercy. But Sir Arthur pressed unto Accolon with his shield, and gave him with the pommel in his hand such a buffet that he went three strides aback. When the damosel of the lake beheld Arthur, how full of prowess his body was, and the false treason that was wrought for him to have had him slain; she had great pity that so good a knight and such a man of worship should so be destroyed. And at the next stroke Sir Accolon struck him such a stroke that by the damosel's enchantment the sword Excalibur fell out of Accolon's hand to the earth. And therewithal Sir Arthur lightly leapt to it, and gat it in his hand, and forthwithal he knew that it was his sword Excalibur, and said, Thou hast been from me all too long, and much damage hast thou done me; and therewith he espied the scabbard hanging by his side, and suddenly he sterte to him and pulled the scabbard from him, and threw it from him as far as he might throw it. O knight, said Arthur, this day hast thou done me great damage with this sword; now are ye come unto your death, for I shall not warrant you but ye shall as well be rewarded with this sword or ever we depart as thou hast rewarded me, for much pain have ye made me to endure, and much blood have I lost. And therewith Sir Arthur rushed on him with all his might and pulled him to the earth, and then rushed off his helm, and gave him such a buffet on the head that the blood came out at his ears, his nose, and his mouth. Now will I slay thee, said Arthur. Slay me ye may well, said Accolon, an it please you, for ye are the best knight that ever I found, and I see well that God is with you. But for I promised to do this battle, said Accolon, to the uttermost, and never to be recreant while I lived, therefore shall I never yield me with my mouth, but God do with my body what he will. Then Sir Arthur remembered him, and thought he should have seen this knight. Now tell me, said Arthur, or I will slay thee, of what country art thou, and of what court? Sir knight, said Sir Accolon, I am of the court of King Arthur, and my name is Accolon of Gaul. Then was Arthur more dismayed than he was beforehand; for then he remembered him of his sister Morgan le Fay, and of the enchantment of the ship. O sir knight, said he, I pray you tell me who gave you this sword, and by whom ye had it.

CHAPTER XI

HOW ACCOLON CONFESSED THE TREASON OF MORGAN LE FAY, KING ARTHUR'S SISTER, AND HOW SHE WOULD HAVE DONE SLAY HIM

THEN Sir Accolon bethought him, and said, Woe worth this sword, for by it have I gotten my death. It may well be, said the king. Now, sir, said Accolon, I will tell you; this sword hath been in my keeping the most part of this twelvemonth; and Morgan le Fay, King Uriens' wife, sent it me yesterday by a dwarf, to this intent, that I should slay King Arthur, her brother. For ye shall understand King Arthur is the man in the world that she most hateth, because he is most of worship and of prowess of any of her blood; also she loveth me out of measure as paramour, and I her again; and if she might bring about to slay Arthur by her crafts, she would slay her husband King Uriens lightly, and then had she me devised to be king in this land, and so to reign, and she to be my queen; but that is now done, said Accolon, for I am sure of my death. Well, said Sir Arthur, I feel by you ye would have been king in this land. It had been great damage to have destroyed your lord, said Arthur. It is truth, said Accolon, but now I have told you truth, wherefore I pray you tell me of whence ye are, and of what court? O Accolon, said King Arthur, now I let thee wit that I am King Arthur, to whom thou hast done great damage. When Accolon heard that he cried aloud, Fair, sweet lord, have mercy on me, for I knew not you. O Sir Accolon, said King Arthur, mercy shalt thou have, because I feel by thy words at this time thou knewest not my person; but I understand well by thy words that thou hast agreed to the death of my person, and therefore thou art a traitor; but I wyte thee the less, for my sister Morgan le Fay by her false crafts made thee to agree and consent to her false lusts, but I shall be sore avenged upon her an I live, that all Christendom shall speak of it; God knoweth I have honoured her and worshipped her more than all my kin, and more have I trusted her than mine own wife and all my kin after. Then Sir Arthur called the keepers of the field, and said, Sirs, come hither, for here are we two knights that have fought unto a great damage unto us both, and like each one of us to have slain other, if it had happed so; and had any of us known other, here had been no battle, nor stroke stricken. Then all aloud cried Accolon unto all the knights and men that were then there gathered together, and said to them in this manner, O lords, this noble knight that I have fought withal, the which me sore repenteth, is the most man of prowess, of manhood, and of worship in the world, for it is himself King Arthur, our alther liege lord, and with mishap and with misadventure have I done this battle with the king and lord that I am holden withall.

CHAPTER XII

HOW ARTHUR ACCORDED THE TWO BRETHREN, AND DELIVERED THE TWENTY KNIGHTS, AND HOW SIR ACCOLON DIED

THEN all the people fell down on their knees and cried King Arthur mercy. Mercy shall ye have, said Arthur: here may ye see what adventures befall ofttime of errant knights, how that I have fought with a knight of mine own unto my great damage and his both. But, sirs, because I am sore hurt, and he both, and I had great need of a little rest, ye shall understand the opinion betwixt you two brethren: As to thee, Sir Damas, for whom I have been champion and won the field of this knight, yet will I judge because ye, Sir Damas, are called an orgulous knight, and full of villainy, and not worth of prowess your deeds, therefore I will that ye give unto your brother all the whole manor with the appurtenance, under this form, that Sir Ontzlake hold the manor of you, and yearly to give you a palfrey to ride upon, for that will become you better to

ride on than upon a courser. Also I charge thee, Sir Damas.
upon pain of death, that thou never distress no knights
errant that ride on their adventure. And also that thou
restore these twenty knights that thou hast long kept
prisoners, of all their harness, that they be content for; and
if any of them come to my court and complain of thee, by
my head thou shalt die therefor. Also, Sir Ontzlake, as
to you, because ye are named a good knight, and full of
prowess, and true and gentle in all your deeds, this shall be
your charge. I will give you that in all goodly haste ye
come unto me and my court, and ye shall be a knight of
mine, and if your deeds be thereafter I shall so prefer you,
by the grace of God, that ye shall in short time be in ease
for to live as worshipfully as your brother Sir Damas. God
thank your largeness of your goodness and of your bounty, I
shall be from henceforward at all times at your commandment; for, sir, said Sir Ontzlake, as God would, as I was
hurt but late with an adventurous knight through both my
thighs, that grieved me sore, and else had I done this battle
with you. God would, said Arthur, it had been so, for then
had not I been hurt as I am. I shall tell you the cause why:
for I had not been hurt as I am, had it not been mine own
sword, that was stolen from me by treason; and this battle
was ordained aforehand to have slain me, and so it was
brought to the purpose by false treason, and by false enchantment. Alas, said Sir Ontzlake, that is great pity that ever so
noble a man as ye are of your deeds and prowess, that any man
or woman might find in their hearts to work any treason
against you. I shall reward them, said Arthur, in short
time, by the grace of God. Now, tell me, said Arthur, how
far am I from Camelot? Sir, ye are two days' journey
therefrom. I would fain be at some place of worship, said
Sir Arthur, that I might rest me. Sir, said Sir Ontzlake,
hereby is a rich abbey of your elders' foundation, of nuns,
but three miles hence. So the king took his leave of all the
people, and mounted upon horseback, and Sir Accolon
with him. And when they were come to the abbey, he let
fetch leeches and search his wounds and Accolon's both;
but Sir Accolon died within four days, for he had bled so
much blood that he might not live, but King Arthur was
well recovered. So when Accolon was dead he let send
him on an horse-bier with six knights unto Camelot, and
said: Bear him to my sister Morgan le Fay, and say that I

send her him to a present, and tell her I have my sword Excalibur and the scabbard; so they departed with the body.

CHAPTER XIII

HOW MORGAN WOULD HAVE SLAIN SIR URIENS HER HUSBAND, AND HOW SIR UWAINE HER SON SAVED HIM

THE meanwhile Morgan le Fay had weened King Arthur had been dead. So on a day she espied King Uriens lay in his bed sleeping. Then she called unto her a maiden of her counsel, and said, Go fetch me my lord's sword, for I saw never better time to slay him than now. O madam, said the damosel, an ye slay my lord ye can never escape. Care not you, said Morgan le Fay, for now I see my time in the which it is best to do it, and therefore hie thee fast and fetch me the sword. Then the damosel departed, and found Sir Uwaine sleeping upon a bed in another chamber, so she went unto Sir Uwaine, and awaked him, and bad him, Arise, and waite on my lady your mother, for she will slay the king your father sleeping in his bed, for I go to fetch his sword. Well, said Sir Uwaine, go on your way, and let me deal. Anon the damosel brought Morgan the sword with quaking hands, and she lightly took the sword, and pulled it out, and went boldly unto the bed's side, and awaited how and where she might slay him best. And as she lifted up the sword to smite, Sir Uwaine leapt unto his mother, and caught her by the hand, and said, Ah, fiend, what wilt thou do? An thou wert not my mother, with this sword I should smite off thy head. Ah, said Sir Uwaine, men saith that Merlin was begotten of a devil, but I may say an earthly devil bare me. O fair son, Uwaine, have mercy upon me, I was tempted with a devil, wherefore I cry thee mercy; I will never more do so; and save my worship and discover me not. On this covenant, said Sir Uwaine, I will forgive it you, so ye will never be about to do such deeds. Nay, son, said she, and that I make you assurance.

CHAPTER XIV

HOW QUEEN MORGAN LE FAY MADE GREAT SORROW FOR THE DEATH
OF ACCOLON, AND HOW SHE STOLE AWAY THE SCABBARD FROM
ARTHUR

THEN came tidings unto Morgan le Fay that Accolon was dead, and his body brought unto the church, and how King Arthur had his sword again. But when Queen Morgan wist that Accolon was dead, she was so sorrowful that near her heart to-brast. But because she would not it were known, outward she kept her countenance, and made no semblance of sorrow. But well she wist an she abode till her brother Arthur came thither, there should no gold go for her life. Then she went unto Queen Guenever, and asked her leave to ride into the country. Ye may abide, said Queen Guenever, till your brother the king come home. I may not, said Morgan le Fay, for I have such hasty tidings, that I may not tarry. Well, said Guenever, ye may depart when ye will. So early on the morn, or it was day, she took her horse and rode all that day and most part of the night, and on the morn by noon she came to the same abbey of nuns whereat lay King Arthur; and she knowing he was there, she asked where he was. And they answered how he had laid him in his bed to sleep, for he had had but little rest these three nights. Well, said she, I charge you that none of you awake him till I do, and then she alit off her horse, and thought for to steal away Excalibur his sword, and so she went straight unto his chamber, and no man durst disobey her commandment, and there she found Arthur asleep in his bed, and Excalibur in his right hand naked. When she saw that she was passing heavy that she might not come by the sword without she had awaked him, and then she wist well she had been dead. Then she took the scabbard and went her way on horseback. When the king awoke and missed his scabbard, he was wroth, and he asked who had been there, and they said his sister, Queen Morgan had been there, and had put the scabbard under her mantle and was gone. Alas, said Arthur, falsely ye have watched me. Sir, said they all, we durst not disobey your sister's commandment. Ah, said the king, let fetch the best horse may be found, and bid Sir Ontzlake arm him in all haste, and take another good horse and ride with me. So anon the king and Ontzlake were well armed, and rode after this lady, and so they came by a cross and found a cowherd, and they asked the poor man if there came any lady late riding that way. Sir, said this poor man, right late came a lady riding with a forty horses, and to yonder forest she rode. Then they spurred their horses, and followed fast, and within a while Arthur had a sight of Morgan le Fay, then he chased as fast as he might. When she espied him following her, she rode a greater pace through the forest till she came to a plain, and when she saw she might not escape, she rode unto a lake thereby, and said, Whatsoever come of me, my brother shall not have this scabbard. And then she let throw the scabbard in the deepest of the water so it sank, for it was heavy of gold and precious stones. Then she rode into a valley where many great stones were, and when she saw she must be overtaken, she shaped herself, horse and man, by enchantment unto a great marble stone. Anon withal came Sir Arthur and Sir Ontzlake whereas the king might know his sister and her men, and one knight from another. Ah, said the king, here may ye see the vengeance of God, and now am I sorry that this misadventure is befallen. And then he looked for the scabbard, but it would not be found, so he returned to the abbey where he came from. So when Arthur was gone she turned all into the likeliness as she and they were before, and said, Sirs, now may we go where we will.

CHAPTER XV

HOW MORGAN LE FAY SAVED A KNIGHT THAT SHOULD HAVE BEEN DROWNED, AND HOW KING ARTHUR RETURNED HOME AGAIN

THEN said Morgan, Saw ye Arthur, my brother? Yea, said her knights, right well, and that ye should have found an we might have stered from one stede, for by his army-vestal countenance he would have caused us to have fled. I believe you, said Morgan. Anon after as she rode she met a knight leading another knight on his horse before him, bound hand and foot, blindfold, to have drowned him in a fountain. When she saw this knight so bound, she asked him, What will ye do with that knight? Lady, said he, I will drown him. For what cause? she asked. For I found him with my wife, and she shall have the same death anon. That were pity, said Morgan le Fay! Now, what say ye, knight, is it truth that he saith of you? she said to the knight that should be drowned. Nay truly, madam, he saith not right on me. Of whence be ye, said Morgan le Fay, and of what country? I am of the court of King Arthur, and my name is Manassen, cousin unto Accolon of Gaul. Ye say well, said she, and for the love of him ye shall be delivered, and ye shall have your adversary in the same case ye be in. So Manassen was loosed and the other knight bound. And anon Manassen unarmed him, and armed himself in his harness, and so mounted on horseback, and the knight afore him, and so threw him into the fountain and drowned him. And then he rode unto Morgan again, and asked if she would anything unto King Arthur. Tell him that I rescued thee, not for the love of him but for the love of Accolon, and tell him I fear him not while I can make me and them that be with me in likeness of stones; and let him wit I can do much more when I see my time. And so she departed into the country of Gore, and there was she richly received, and made her castles and towns passing strong, for always she dread much King Arthur. When the king had well rested him at the abbey, he rode unto Camelot, and found his queen and his barons right glad of his coming. And when they heard of his strange adventures as is afore rehearsed, then all had marvel of the falsehood of Morgan le Fay; many knights wished her burnt. Then came Manassen to court and told the king of his adventure. Well, said the king, she is a kind sister; I shall so be avenged on her an I live, that all Christendom shall speak of it. So on the morn there came a damosel from Morgan to the king, and she brought with her the richest mantle that ever was seen in that court, for it was set as full of precious stones as one might stand by another, and there were the richest stones that ever the king saw. And the damosel said, Your sister sendeth you this mantle, and desireth that ye should take this gift of her; and in what thing she hath offended you, she will amend it at your own pleasure. When the king beheld this mantle it pleased him much, but he said but little.

CHAPTER XVI

HOW THE DAMOSEL OF THE LAKE SAVED KING ARTHUR FROM A MANTLE THAT SHOULD HAVE BURNT HIM

WITH that came the damosel of the lake unto the king, and said, Sir, I must speak with you in private. Say on, said the king, what ye will. Sir, said the damosel, put not on you this mantle till ye have seen more, and in no wise let it not come on you nor on no knight of yours till ye command the bringer thereof to put it upon her. Well, said King Arthur, it shall be done as ye counsel me. And then he said unto the damosel that came from his sister, Damosel, this mantle that ye have brought me, I will see it upon you. Sir, she said, It will not beseem me to wear a king's garment. By my head, said Arthur, ye shall wear it or it come on my back, or any man's that here is. And so the king made it to be put upon her, and forthwithal she fell down dead, and never more spake word after and burnt to coals. Then was the king wonderly wroth, more than he was toforehand, and said unto King Uriens, My sister, your wife, is alway about to betray me, and well I wot either ye, or my nephew, your son, is of counsel with her to have me destroyed; but as for you, said the king to King Uriens, I deem not greatly that ye be of her counsel, for Accolon confessed to me by his own mouth, that he would have destroyed you as well as me, therefore I hold you excused; but as for your son, Sir Uwaine, I hold him suspect, therefore I charge you put him out of my court. So Sir Uwaine was discharged. And when Sir Gawaine wist that, he made him ready to go with him; and said, Whoso banisheth my cousin-germain shall banish me. So they two departed, and rode into a great forest, and so they came to an abbey of monks, and there were well lodged. But when the king wist that Sir Gawaine was departed from the court, there was made great sorrow among all the estates. Now, said Gaheris, Gawaine's brother, we have lost two good knights for the love of one. So on the morn they heard their masses in the abbey, and so they rode forth till that they came to a great forest. Then was Sir Gawaine ware in a valley by a turret, twelve fair damosels, and two knights armed on great horses, and the damosels went to and fro by a tree. And then was Sir Gawaine ware how there hung a white shield on that tree, and ever as the damosels came by it they spit upon it, and some threw mire upon the shield.

CHAPTER XVII

HOW SIR GAWAINE AND SIR UWAINE MET WITH TWELVE FAIR DAMOSELS, AND HOW THEY COMPLAINED ON SIR MARHAUS

THEN Sir Gawaine and Sir Uwaine went and saluted them, and asked why they did that despite to the shield. Sirs, said the damosels, we shall tell you. There is a knight in this country that owneth this white shield, and he is a passing good man of his hands, but he hateth all ladies and gentlewomen, and therefore we do all this despite to the shield. I shall say you, said Sir Gawaine, it beseemeth evil a good knight to despise all ladies and gentlewomen, and peradventure though he hate you he hath some certain cause, and peradventure he loveth in some other places ladies and gentlewomen, and to be loved again, an he be such a man of prowess as ye speak of. Now, what is his name? Sir, said they, his name is Marhaus, the king's son of Ireland. I know him well, said Sir Uwaine, he is a passing good knight as any is a-live, for I saw him once proved at a jousts where many knights were gathered, and that time there might no man withstand him. Ah! said Sir Gawaine, damosels, methinketh ye are to blame, for it is to suppose, he that hung that shield there, he will not be long therefrom, and then may those knights match him on horse-back, and that is more your worship than thus; for I will abide no longer to see a knight's shield dishonoured. And therewith Sir Uwaine and Gawaine departed a little from them, and then were they ware where Sir Marhaus came riding on a great horse straight towards them. And when the twelve damosels saw Sir Marhaus they fled into the turret as they were wild, so that some of them fell by the way. Then the one of the knights of the tower dressed his shield, and said on high, Sir Marhaus, defend thee. And so they ran together that the knight brake his spear on Marhaus, and Marhaus smote him so hard that he brake his neck and the horse's back. That saw the other knight of the turret, and dressed him toward Marhaus, and they met so eagerly together that the knight of the turret was soon smitten down, horse and man, stark dead.

CHAPTER XVIII

HOW SIR MARHAUS JOUSTED WITH SIR GAWAINE AND SIR UWAINE, AND OVERTHREW THEM BOTH

AND then Sir Marhaus rode unto his shield, and saw how it was defouled, and said, Of this despite I am a part avenged, but for her love that gave me this white shield I shall wear thee, and hang mine where thou wast; and so he hanged it about his neck. Then he rode straight unto Sir Gawaine and to Sir Uwaine, and ask them what they did there? They answered him that they came from King Arthur's court to see adventures. Well, said Sir Marhaus, here am I ready, an adventurous knight that will fulfil any adventure that ye will desire; and so departed from them, to fetch his range. Let him go, said Sir Uwaine unto Sir Gawaine, for he is a passing good knight as any is living; I would not by my will that any of us were matched with him. Nay, said Sir Gawaine, not so, it were shame to us were he not assayed, were he never so good a knight. Well, said Sir Uwaine, I will assay him afore you, for I am more weaker than ye, and if he smite me down then may ye revenge me. So these two knights came together with great raundon, that Sir Uwaine smote Sir Marhaus that his spear brast in pieces on the shield, and Sir Marhaus smote him so sore that horse and man he bare to the earth, and hurt Sir Uwaine on the left side. Then Sir Marhaus turned his horse and rode toward Gawaine with his spear, and when Sir Gawaine saw that he dressed his shield, and they aventred their spears, and they came together with all the might of their horses, that either knight smote other so hard in middes of their shields, but Sir Gawaine's spear brake, but Sir Marhaus's spear held; and therewith Sir Gawaine and his horse rushed down to the earth. And lightly Sir Gawaine rose on his feet, and pulled out his sword, and dressed him toward Sir Marhaus on foot, and Sir Marhaus saw that, and pulled out his sword and began to come to Sir Gawaine on horseback. Sir knight, said Sir Gawaine, alight on foot, or else I will slay thy horse. Gramercy, said Sir Marhaus, of your gentleness ye teach me courtesy, for it is not for one knight to be on foot, and the other on horseback. And therewith Sir Marhaus set his spear against a tree and alit and tied his horse to a tree, and dressed his shield, and either came unto other eagerly, and smote together with their swords that their shields flew in cantels, and they bruised their helms and their hauberks, and wounded either other. But Sir Gawaine from it passed nine of the clock waxed ever stronger and stronger, for then it came to the hour of noon, and thrice his might was increased. All this espied Sir Marhaus and had great wonder how his might increased, and so they wounded other passing sore. And then when it was past noon, and when it drew toward evensong, Sir Gawaine's strength feebled, and waxed passing faint that unnethes he might dure any longer, and Sir Marhaus was then bigger and bigger. Sir knight, said Sir Marhaus, I have well felt that ye are a passing good knight and a marvellous man of might as ever I felt any, while it lasteth, and our quarrels are not great, and therefore it were pity to do you hurt, for I feel ye are passing feeble. Ah, said Sir Gawaine, gentle knight, ye say the word that I should say. And therewith they took off their helms, and either kissed other, and there they swore together either to love other as brethren. And Sir Marhaus prayed Sir Gawaine to lodge with him that night. And so they took their horses, and rode toward Sir Marhaus's house. And as they rode by the way, Sir knight, said Sir Gawaine, I have marvel that so valiant a man as ye be love no ladies nor damosels. Sir, said Sir Marhaus, they name me wrongfully those that give me that name, but well I wot it be the damosels of the turret that so name me, and other such as they be; now shall I tell you for what cause I hate them: for they be sorceresses and enchanters many of them, and be a knight never so good of his body and full of prowess as man may be, they will make him a stark coward to have the better of him, and this is the principal cause that I hate them; and to all good ladies and gentlewomen I owe my service as a knight ought to do. As the book rehearseth in French, there were many knights that overmatched Sir Gawaine, for all the thrice might that he had: Sir Launcelot de Lake, Sir Tristram, Sir Bors de Ganis, Sir Percivale, Sir Pelleas, and Sir Marhaus, these six knights had the better of Sir Gawaine. Then within a little while they came to Sir Marhaus's place, which was in a little priory, and there they alit, and ladies and damosels unarmed them, and hastily looked to their hurts, for they were all three hurt. And so they had all three good lodging with Sir Marhaus, and good cheer; for when he wist that they were King Arthur's sisters' sons he made them all the cheer that lay in his power, and so they sojourned there a se'nnight, and were well eased of their wounds, and at the last departed. Now, said Sir Marhaus, we will not depart so lightly, for I will bring you through the forest; and rode day by day well a seven days or they found any adventure. At the last they came into a great forest, that was named the country and forest of Arroy, and the country of strange adventures. In this country, said Sir Marhaus, came never knight syne it was christened, but he found strange adventures, and so they rode, and came into a deep valley full of stones, and thereby they saw a fair stream of water; above thereby was the head of the stream a fair fountain, and three damosels sitting thereby. And then they rode to them, and either saluted other, and the eldest had a garland of gold about her head, and she was three score winter of age or more, and her hair was white under the garland. The second damosel was of thirty winter of age, with a circlet of gold about her head. The third damosel was but fifteen year of age, and a garland of flowers about her head. When these knights had so beheld them, they asked them the cause why they sat at that fountain? We be here, said the damosels, for this cause: if we may see any errant knights, to teach them unto strange adventures; and ye be three knights that seeken adventures, and we be three damosels, and therefore each one of you must choose one of us; and when ye have done so we will lead you unto three highways, and there each of you shall choose a way and his damosel with him. And this day twelvemonth ye must meet here again, and God send you your lives, and thereto ye must plight your troth. This is well said, said Sir Marhaus.

CHAPTER XIX

HOW SIR MARHAUS, SIR GAWAINE, AND SIR UWAINE MET THREE DAMOSELS, AND EACH OF THEM TOOK ONE

Now shall every each of us choose a damosel. I shall tell you, said Sir Uwaine, I am the youngest and most weakest of you both, therefore I will have the eldest damosel, for she hath seen much, and can best help me when I have need, for I have most need of help of you both. Now, said Sir Marhaus, I will have the damosel of thirty winter age, for she falleth best to me. Well, said Sir Gawaine, I thank you, for ye have left me the youngest and the fairest, and she is most liefest to me. Then every damosel took her knight by the reins of his bridle, and brought him to the three ways, and there was their oath made to meet at the fountain that day twelvemonth an they were living, and so they kissed and departed, and every each knight set his lady behind him. And Sir Uwaine took the way that lay west, and Sir Marhaus took the way that lay south, and Sir Gawaine took the way that lay north. Now will we begin at Sir Gawaine, that held that way till that he came unto a fair manor, where dwelled an old knight and a good householder, and there Sir Gawaine asked the knight if he knew any adventures in that country. I shall show you some to-morn, said the old knight, and that marvellous. So, on the morn they rode into the forest of adventures to a launde, and thereby they found a cross, and as they stood and hoved, there came by them the fairest knight and the seemliest man that ever they saw, making the greatest dole that ever man made. And then he was ware of Sir Gawaine, and saluted him, and prayed God to send him much worship. As to that, said Sir Gawaine, gramercy; also I pray to God that he send you honour and worship. Ah, said the knight, I may lay that a-side, for sorrow and shame cometh to me after worship.

CHAPTER XX

HOW A KNIGHT AND A DWARF STROVE FOR A LADY

And therewith he passed unto the one side of the launde; and on the other side saw Sir Gawaine ten knights that hoved still and made them ready with their shields and spears against that one knight that came by Sir Gawaine. Then this one knight aventred a great spear, and one of the ten knights encountered with him, but this woful knight smote him so hard that he fell over his horse's tail. So this same dolorous knight served them all, that at the leastway he smote down horse and man, and all he did with one spear; and so when they were all ten on foot, they went to that one knight, and he stood stone still, and suffered them to pull him down off his horse, and bound him hand and

foot, and tied him under the horse's belly, and so led him
with them. O Jesu! said Sir Gawaine, this is a doleful
sight, to see the yonder knight so to be entreated, and it
seemeth by the knight that he suffereth them to bind him
so, for he maketh no resistance. No, said his host, that is
truth, for an he would they all were too weak so to do him.
Sir, said the damosel unto Sir Gawaine, meseemeth it were
your worship to help that dolorous knight, for methinketh
he is one of the best knights that ever I saw. I would do
for him, said Sir Gawaine, but it seemeth he will have no
help. Then, said the damosel, methinketh ye have no lust
to help him. Thus as they talked they saw a knight on the
other side of the launde all armed save the head. And on the
other side there came a dwarf on horseback all armed save the
head, with a great mouth and a short nose; and when the
dwarf came nigh he said, Where is the lady should meet us
here? and therewithal she came forth out of the wood. And
then they began to strive for the lady; for the knight said
he would have her, and the dwarf said he would have her.
Will we do well? said the dwarf; yonder is a knight at the
cross, let us put it both upon him, and as he deemeth so
shall it be. I will well, said the knight, and so they went all
three unto Sir Gawaine and told him wherefore they strove.
Well, sirs, said he, will ye put the matter in my hand? Yea,
they said both. Now damosel, said Sir Gawaine, ye shall
stand betwixt them both, and whether ye list better to go
to, he shall have you. And when she was set between
them both, she left the knight and went to the dwarf, and
the dwarf took her and went his way singing, and the knight
went his way with great mourning. Then came there two
knights all armed, and cried on high, Sir Gawaine! knight
of King Arthur's make thee ready in all haste and joust with
me. So they ran together, that either fell down, and then
on foot they drew their swords, and did full actually. The
meanwhile the other knight went to the damosel, and asked
her why she abode with that knight, and if ye would abide
with me, I will be your faithful knight. And with you will
I be, said the damosel, for with Sir Gawaine I may not find
in mine heart to be with him; for now here was one knight
discomfited ten knights, and at the last he was cowardly led
away; and therefore let us two go whilst they fight. And
Sir Gawaine fought with that other knight long, but at the
last they accorded both. And then the knight prayed Sir

Gawaine to lodge with him that night. So as Sir Gawaine
went with this knight he asked him, What knight is he in this
country that smote down the ten knights? For when he
had done so manfully he suffered them to bind him hand
and foot, and so led him away. Ah, said the knight, that is
the best knight I trow in the world, and the most man of
prowess, and he hath been served so as he was even more
than ten times, and his name hight Sir Pelleas, and he
loveth a great lady in this country and her name is Ettard.
And so when he loved her there was cried in this country a
great jousts three days, and all the knights of this country
were there and gentlewomen, and who that proved him the
best knight should have a passing good sword and a circlet
of gold, and the circlet the knight should give it to the
fairest lady that was at the jousts. And this knight Sir
Pelleas was the best knight that was there, and there were
five hundred knights, but there was never man that ever Sir
Pelleas met withal but he struck him down, or else from his
horse; and every day of three days he struck down twenty
knights, therefore they gave him the prize, and forthwithal
he went thereas the lady Ettard was, and gave her the
circlet, and said openly she was the fairest lady that there
was, and that would he prove upon any knight that would
say nay.

CHAPTER XXI

HOW KING PELLEAS SUFFERED HIMSELF TO BE TAKEN PRISONER
    BECAUSE HE WOULD HAVE A SIGHT OF HIS LADY, AND HOW
    SIR GAWAINE PROMISED HIM TO GET TO HIM THE LOVE OF
    HIS LADY

AND so he chose her for his sovran lady, and never to
love other but her, but she was so proud that she had scorn
of him, and said that she would never love him though he
would die for her. Wherefore all ladies and gentlewomen had
scorn of her that she was so proud, for there were fairer than
she, and there was none that was there but an Sir Pelleas
would have proffered them love, they would have loved him
for his noble prowess. And so this knight promised the
lady Ettard to follow her into this country, and never to
leave her till she loved him. And thus he is here the most
part nigh her, and lodged by a priory, and every week she
sendeth knights to fight with him. And when he hath put
them to the worse, then will he suffer them wilfully to take

him prisoner, by cause he would have a sight of this lady. And always she doth him great despite, for sometime she maketh her knights to tie him to his horse's tail, and some to bind him under the horse's belly; thus in the most shamefullest ways that she can think he is brought to her; and all she doth it for to cause him to leave this country, and to leave his loving; but all this cannot make him to leave, for an he would have fought on foot he might have had the better of the ten knights as well on foot as on horseback. Alas, said Sir Gawaine, it is great pity of him; and after this night I will seek him to-morrow, in this forest, to do him all the help I can. So on the morn Sir Gawaine took his leave of his host Sir Carados, and rode into the forest; and at the last he met with Sir Pelleas, making great moan out of measure, so each of them saluted other, and asked him why he made such sorrow. And as it is above rehearsed, Sir Pelleas told Sir Gawaine: But always I suffer her knights to fare so with me as ye saw yesterday, in trust at the last to win her love, for she knoweth well all her knights should not lightly win me, an me list to fight with them to the uttermost. Wherefore an I loved her not so sore, I had lever die an hundred times, an I might die so oft, rather than I would suffer that despite; but I trust she will have pity upon me at the last, for love causeth many a good knight to suffer to have his entent, but alas I am unfortunate. And therewith he made so great dole and sorrow that unnethe he might hold him on horseback. Now, said Sir Gawaine, leave your mourning and I shall promise you by the faith of my body to do all that lieth in my power to get you the love of your lady, and thereto I will plight you my troth. Ah, said Sir Pelleas, of what court are ye? tell me, I pray you, my good friend. And then Sir Gawaine said, I am of the court of King Arthur, and his sister's son, and King Lot of Orkney was my father, and my name is Sir Gawaine. And then he said, My name is Sir Pelleas, born in the Isles, and of many isles I am lord, and never have I loved lady nor damosel till now in an unhappy time; and, sir knight, syne ye are so nigh cousin unto King Arthur, and a king's son, therefore betray me not but help me, for I may never come by her but by some good knight, for she is in a strong castle here, fast by within this four mile, and over all this country she is lady of. And so I may never come to her presence, but as I suffer her knights to take me, and but if I did so that I might have a sight of her, I had been dead long or this time ; and yet fair word had I never of her, but when I am brought tofore her she rebuketh me in the foulest manner, and then they take my horse and harness and putten me out of the gates, and she will not suffer me to eat nor drink ; and always I offer me to be her prisoner, but that she will not suffer me, for I would desire no more, what pains so ever I had, so that I might have a sight of her daily. Well, said Sir Gawaine, all this shall I amend an ye will do as I shall devise : I will have your horse and your armour, and so will I ride unto her castle and tell her that I have slain you, and so shall I come within her to cause her to cherish me, and then shall I do my true part that ye shall not fail to have the love of her.

CHAPTER XXII

HOW SIR GAWAINE CAME TO THE LADY ETTARD, AND HOW SIR PELLEAS FOUND THEM SLEEPING

AND therewith Sir Gawaine plight his troth unto Sir Pelleas to be true and faithful unto him ; so each one plight their troth to other, and so they changed horses and harness, and Sir Gawaine departed, and came to the castle whereas stood the pavilions of this lady without the gate. And as soon as Ettard had espied Sir Gawaine she fled in toward the castle. Sir Gawaine spake on high, and bade her abide, for he was not Sir Pelleas ; I am another knight that have slain Sir Pelleas. Do off your helm, said the Lady Ettard, that I may see your visage. And so when she saw that it was not Sir Pelleas, she bade him alight and led him unto her castle, and asked him faithfully whether he had slain Sir Pelleas. And he said her yea, and told her his name was Sir Gawaine of the court of King Arthur, and his sister's son. Truly, said she, that is great pity, for he was a passing good knight of his body, but of all men a-live I hated him most, for I could never be quit of him ; and for ye have slain him I shall be your woman, and to do anything that might please you. So she made Sir Gawaine good cheer. Then Sir Gawaine said that he loved a lady and by no means she would love him. She is to blame, said Ettard, an she will not love you, for ye that be so well born a man, and such a man of prowess, there is no lady in the world too good for you. Will ye, said Sir Gawaine, promise me to do all that ye may, by the faith of your body, to get me the love of my lady? Yea, sir, said she, and that I promise you by the faith of my body. Now, said Sir Gawaine, it is yourself that I love so well, therefore I pray you hold your promise. I may not choose, said the Lady Ettard, but if I should be forsworn; and so she granted him to fulfil all his desire. So it was then in the month of May that she and Sir Gawaine went out of the castle and supped in a pavilion, and there was made a bed, and there Sir Gawaine and the Lady Ettard went to bed together, and in another pavilion she laid her damosels, and in the third pavilion she laid part of her knights, for then she had no dread of Sir Pelleas. And there Sir Gawaine lay with her in that pavilion two days and two nights. And on the third day, in the morning early, Sir Pelleas armed him, for he had never slept syne Sir Gawaine departed from him; for Sir Gawaine had promised him by the faith of his body, to come to him unto his pavilion by that priory within the space of a day and a night. Then Sir Pelleas mounted upon horseback, and came to the pavilions that stood without the castle, and found in the first pavilion three knights in three beds, and three squires lying at their feet. Then went he to the second pavilion and found four gentlewomen lying in four beds. And then he yede to the third pavilion and found Sir Gawaine lying in bed with his Lady Ettard, and either clipping other in arms, and when he saw that his heart wellnigh brast for sorrow, and said: Alas! that ever a knight should be found so false; and then he took his horse and might not abide no longer for pure sorrow. And when he had ridden nigh half a mile he turned again and thought to slay them both; and when he saw them both so lie sleeping fast, unnethe he might hold him on horseback for sorrow, and said thus to himself, Though this knight be never so false, I will never slay him sleeping, for I will never destroy the high order of knighthood; and therewith he departed again. And or he had ridden half a mile he returned again, and thought then to slay them both, making the greatest sorrow that ever man made. And when he came to the pavilions he tied his horse unto a tree, and pulled out his sword naked in his hand, and went to them thereas they lay, and yet he thought it were shame to slay them sleeping, and laid the naked sword overthwart both their throats, and so took his horse and rode his way. And when Sir Pelleas came to his pavilions he told his knights and his squires how he had sped, and said thus to them, For your true and good service ye have done me I shall give you all my goods, for I will go unto my bed and never arise until I am dead. And when that I am dead I charge you that ye take the heart out of my body and bear it her betwixt two silver dishes, and tell her how I saw her lie with the false knight Sir Gawaine. Right so Sir Pelleas unarmed himself, and went unto his bed making marvellous dole and sorrow. When Sir Gawaine and Ettard awoke of their sleep, and found the naked sword overthwart their throats, then she knew well it was Sir Pelleas' sword. Alas! said she to Sir Gawaine, ye have betrayed me and Sir Pelleas both, for ye told me ye had slain him, and now I know well it is not so, he is on live. And if Sir Pelleas had been as uncourteous to you as ye have been to him ye had been a dead knight; but ye have deceived me and betrayed me falsely, that all ladies and damosels may beware by you and me. And therewith Sir Gawaine made him ready, and went into the forest. So it happed then that the damosel of the lake Nimue met with a knight of Sir Pelleas, that went on his foot in the forest making great dole, and she asked him the cause. And so the woful knight told her how his master and lord was betrayed through a knight and lady, and how he will never arise out of his bed till he be dead. Bring me to him, said she anon, and I will warrant his life he shall not die for love, and she that hath caused him so to love, she shall be in as evil plight as he is or it be long to, for it is no joy of such a proud lady that will have no mercy of such a valiant knight. Anon that knight brought her unto him, and when she saw him lie in his bed, she thought she saw never so likely a knight; and therewith she threw an enchantment upon him, and he fell on sleep. And therewhile she rode unto the Lady Ettard, and charged no man to awake him till she came again. So within two hours she brought the Lady Ettard thither, and both ladies found him on sleep: Lo, said the damosel of the lake, ye ought to be ashamed for to murder such a knight. And therewith she threw such an enchantment upon her that she loved him sore, that well nigh she was out of her mind. O Lord Jesu, said the Lady Ettard, how is it befallen unto me that I love now him that I have most hated of any man alive? That is the righteous judgment of God, said the damosel. And then anon Sir Pelleas awaked and looked upon Ettard; and when he saw her he knew her, and then he hated her more than any woman alive, and said: Away, traitress, come never in my sight. And when she heard him say so, she wept and made great sorrow out of measure.

CHAPTER XXIII

HOW SIR PELLEAS LOVED NO MORE ETTARD BY MEANS OF THE DAMOSEL OF THE LAKE, WHOM HE LOVED EVER AFTER

Sir knight Pelleas, said the damosel of the lake, take your horse and come forth with me out of this country, and ye shall love a lady that shall love you. I will well, said Sir Pelleas, for this lady Ettard hath done me great despite and shame, and there he told her the beginning and ending, and how he had purposed never to have arisen till that he had been dead.—And now such grace God hath sent me, that I hate her as much as ever I loved her, thanked be our Lord Jesus! Thank me, said the damosel of the lake. Anon Sir Pelleas armed him, and took his horse, and commanded his men to bring after his pavilions and his stuff where the damosel of the lake would assign. So the Lady Ettard died for sorrow, and the damosel of the lake rejoiced Sir Pelleas, and loved together during their life days.

CHAPTER XXIV

HOW SIR MARHAUS RODE WITH THE DAMOSEL, AND HOW HE CAME TO THE DUKE OF THE SOUTH MARCHES

Now turn we unto Sir Marhaus, that rode with the damosel of thirty winter of age, southward. And so they came into a deep forest, and by fortune they were nighted, and rode long in a deep way, and at the last they came unto a courtelage, and there they asked harbour. But the man of the courtelage would not lodge them for no treaty that they could treat, but thus much the good man said, An ye will take the adventure of your lodging, I shall bring you where ye shall be lodged. What adventure is that that I shall have for my lodging? said Sir Marhaus. Ye shall wit when ye come there, said the good man. Sir, what adventure so it be, bring me thither I pray thee, said Sir Marhaus; for I am weary, my damosel, and my horse. So the good man went and opened the gate, and within an hour he brought him unto a fair castle, and then the poor man called the porter, and anon he was let into the castle, and so he told the lord how he brought him a knight errant and a damosel that would be lodged with him. Let him in, said the lord, it may happen he shall repent that they took their lodging here. So Sir Marhaus was let in with torchlight, and there was a goodly sight of young men that welcomed him. And then his horse was led into the stable, and he and the damosel were brought into the hall, and there stood a mighty duke and many goodly men about him. Then this lord asked him what he hyghte, and from whence he came, and with whom he dwelt. Sir, he said, I am a knight of King Arthur's and knight of the Table Round, and my name is Sir Marhaus, and born I am in Ireland. And then said the duke to him, That me sore repenteth: the cause is this, for I love not thy lord nor none of thy fellows of the Table Round; and therefore ease thyself this night as well as thou mayest, for as to-morn I and my six sons shall match with you. Is there no remedy but that I must have ado with you and your six sons at once? said Sir Marhaus. No, said the duke, for this cause I made mine avow, for Sir Gawaine slew my seven sons in a recounter, therefore I made mine avow, there should never knight of King Arthur's court lodge with me, or come there as I might have ado with him, but that I would have a revenging of my sons' death. What is your name? said Sir Marhaus; I require you tell me, an it please you. Wit thou well I am the Duke of South Marches. Ah, said Sir Marhaus, I have heard say that ye have been long time a great foe unto my lord Arthur and to his knights. That shall ye feel to-morn, said the duke. Shall I have ado with you? said Sir Marhaus. Yea, said the duke, thereof shalt thou not choose, and therefore take you to your chamber, and ye shall have all that to you longeth. So Sir Marhaus departed and was led to a chamber, and his damosel was led unto her chamber. And on the morn the duke sent unto Sir Marhaus and bad make him ready. And so Sir Marhaus arose and armed him, and then there was a mass sung afore him, and brake his fast, and so mounted on horseback in the court of the castle where they should do the battle. So there was the duke all ready on horseback, clene armed, and his six sons by him, and every each had a spear in his hand, and so they encountered, whereas the duke and his two sons brake their spears upon him, but Sir Marhaus held up his spear and touched none of them.

CHAPTER XXV

HOW SIR MARHAUS FOUGHT WITH THE DUKE AND HIS FOUR SONS AND MADE THEM TO YIELD THEM

THEN came the four sons by couple, and two of them brake their spears, and so did the other two. And all this while Sir Marhaus touched them not. Then Sir Marhaus ran to the duke, and smote him with his spear that horse and man fell to the earth, and so he served his sons; and then Sir Marhaus alit down and bad the duke yield him or else he would slay him. And then some of his sons recovered, and would have set upon Sir Marhaus; then Sir Marhaus said to the duke, Cease thy sons, or else I will do the uttermost to you all. When the duke saw he might not escape the death, he cried to his sons, and charged them to yield them to Sir Marhaus; and they kneeled all down and put the pommels of their swords to the knight, and so he received them. And then they helped up their father, and so by their comynal assent promised to Sir Marhaus never to be foes unto King Arthur, and thereupon at Whitsuntide after, to come he and his sons, and put them in the king's grace. Then Sir Marhaus departed, and within two days his damosel brought him whereas was a great tournament that the Lady de Vawse had cried. And who that did best should have a rich circlet of gold worth a thousand besauntes. And there Sir Marhaus did so nobly that he was renowned, and had sometime down forty knights, and so the circlet of gold was rewarded him. Then he departed from thence with great worship; and so within seven nights his damosel brought him to an earl's place, his name was the Earl Fergus, that after was Sir Tristram's knight; and this earl was but a young man, and late come into his lands, and there was a giant fast by him that hight Taulurd, and he had another brother in Cornwall that hight Taulas, that Sir Tristram slew when he was out of his mind. So this earl made his complaint unto Sir Marhaus, that there was a giant by him that destroyed all his lands, and how he durst nowhere ride nor go for him. Sir, said the knight, whether useth he to fight, on horseback or on foot? Nay, said the earl, there may no horse bare him. Well, said Sir Marhaus, then will I fight with him on foot; so on the morn Sir Marhaus prayed the earl that one of his men might bring him whereas the giant was; and so he was, for he saw him sit under a tree of holly, and many clubs of iron and gysarms about him. So this knight dressed him to the giant, putting his shield afore him, and the giant took an iron club in his hand, and at the first stroke he clave Sir Marhaus' shield in two pieces. And there he was in great peril, for the giant was a wily fighter, but at last Sir Marhaus smote off his right arm above the elbow. Then the giant fled and the knight after him, and so he drove him into a water, but the giant was so high that he might not wade after him. And then Sir Marhaus made the Earl Fergus' man to fetch him stones, and with those stones the knight gave the giant many sore knocks, till at the last he made him fall down into the water, and so was he there dead. Then Sir Marhaus went unto the giant's castle, and there he delivered twenty-four ladies and twelve knights out of the giant's prison, and there he had great riches without number, so that the days of his life he was never poor man. Then he returned to the Earl Fergus, the which thanked him greatly, and would have given him half his lands, but he would none take. So Sir Marhaus dwelled with the earl nigh half a year, for he was sore bruised with the giant, and at the last he took his leave. And as he rode by the way, he met with Sir Gawaine and Sir Uwaine, and so by adventure he met with four knights of Arthur's court, the first was Sir Sagramore le Desirous, Sir Osanna, Sir Dodinas le Savage, and Sir Felot of Listinoise; and there Sir Marhaus with one spear smote down these four knights, and hurt them sore. So he departed to meet at his day aforeset.

CHAPTER XXVI

HOW SIR UWAINE RODE WITH THE DAMOSEL OF SIXTY YEAR OF AGE,
AND HOW HE GAT THE PRIZE AT TOURNEYING

Now turn we unto Sir Uwaine, that rode westward with his damosel of three score winter of age, and she brought him there as was a tournament nigh the march of Wales. And at that tournament Sir Uwaine smote down thirty knights, therefore was given him the prize, and that was a gerfalcon, and a white steed trapped with cloth of gold. So then Sir Uwaine did many strange adventures by the means of the old damosel, and so she brought him to a lady that was called the Lady of the Rock, the which was much courteous. So there were in the country two knights that were brethren, and they were called two perilous knights, the one knight hight Sir Edward of the Red Castle, and the other Sir Hue of the Red Castle; and these two brethren had disherited the Lady of the Rock of a barony of lands by their extortion. And as this knight was lodged with this lady she made her complaint to him of these two knights. Madam, said Sir Uwaine, they are to blame, for they do against the high order of knighthood, and the oath that they made; and if it like you I will speak with them, by cause I am a knight of King Arthur's, and I will entreat them with fairness; and if they will not, I shall do battle with them, and in the defence of your right. Gramercy, said the lady, and thereas I may not acquit you, God shall. So on the morn the two knights were sent for, that they should come thither to speak with the Lady of the Rock, and wit ye well they failed not, for they came with an hundred horse. But when this lady saw them in this manner so big, she would not suffer Sir Uwaine to go out to them upon no surety nor for no fair language, but she made him speak with them over a tower, but finally these two brethren would not be entreated, and answered that they would keep that they had. Well, said Sir Uwaine, then will I fight with one of you, and prove that ye do this lady wrong. That will we not, said they, for an we do battle, we two will fight with one knight at once, and therefore if ye will fight so, we will be ready at what hour ye will assign. And if ye win us in battle the lady shall have her lands again. Ye say well, said Sir Uwaine, therefore make you ready so that ye be here to-morn in the defence of the lady's right.

CHAPTER XXVII

HOW SIR UWAINE FOUGHT WITH TWO KNIGHTS AND OVERCAME THEM

So was there sykernesse made on both parties that no treason should be wrought on neither party; so then the knights departed and made them ready, and that night Sir Uwaine had great cheer. And on the morn he arose early and heard mass, and brake his fast, and so he rode unto the plain without the gates, where hoved the two brethren abiding him. So they rode together passing sore, that Sir Edward and Sir Hue brake their spears upon Sir Uwaine. And Sir Uwaine smote Sir Edward that he fell over his horse and yet his spear brast not. And then he spurred his horse and came upon Sir Hue and overthrew him, but they soon recovered and dressed their shields and drew their swords and bad Sir Uwaine alight and do his battle to the uttermost. Then Sir Uwaine devoided his horse suddenly, and put his shield afore him and drew his sword, and so they dressed together, and either gave other such strokes, and there these two brethren wounded Sir Uwaine passing grievously that the Lady of the Rock weened he should have died. And thus they fought together five hours as men raged out of reason. And at the last Sir Uwaine smote Sir Edward upon the helm such a stroke that his sword carved unto his canel bone, and then Sir Hue abated his courage, but Sir Uwaine pressed fast to have slain him. That saw Sir Hue: he kneeled down and yielded him to Sir Uwaine. And he of his gentleness received his sword, and took him by the hand, and went into the castle together, Then the Lady of the Rock was passing glad, and the other brother made great sorrow for his brother's death. Then the lady was restored of all her lands, and Sir Hue was commanded to be at the court of King Arthur at the next feast of Pentecost. So Sir Uwaine dwelt with the lady nigh half a year, for it was long or he might be whole of his great hurts. And so when it drew nigh the term-day that Sir Gawaine, Sir Marhaus, and Sir Uwaine should meet at the cross-way, then every knight drew him thither to hold his promise that they had made; and Sir Marhaus and Sir Uwaine brought their damosels with them, but Sir Gawaine had lost his damosel as it is afore rehearsed

CHAPTER XXVIII

HOW AT THE YEAR'S END ALL THREE KNIGHTS WITH THEIR THREE
DAMOSELS MET AT THE FOUNTAIN

RIGHT so at the twelvemonths' end they met all three knights at the fountain and their damosels, but the damosel that Sir Gawaine had could say but little worship of him; so they departed from the damosels and rode through a great forest, and there they met with a messenger that came from King Arthur, that had sought them well nigh a twelvemonth throughout all England, Wales, and Scotland, and charged if ever he might find Sir Gawaine and Sir Uwaine to bring them to the court again. And then were they all glad, and so prayed they Sir Marhaus to ride with them to the king's court. And so within twelve days they came to Camelot, and the king was passing glad of their coming, and so was all the court. Then the king made them to swear upon a book to tell him all their adventures that had befallen them that twelvemonth, and so they did. And there was Sir Marhaus well-known, for there were knights that he had matched aforetime, and he was named one of the best knights living. Against the feast of Pentecost came the damosel of the Lake and brought with her Sir Pelleas; and at that high feast there was great jousting of knights, and of all knights that were at that jousts, Sir Pelleas had the prize, and Sir Marhaus was named the next; but Sir Pelleas was so strong there might but few knights sit him a buffet with a spear. And at that next feast Sir Pelleas and Sir Marhaus were made knights of the Table Round, for there were two sieges void, for two knights were slain that twelvemonth, and great joy had King Arthur of Sir Pelleas and of Sir Marhaus. But Pelleas loved never after Sir Gawaine, but as he spared him for the love of King Arthur; but ofttimes at jousts and tournaments Sir Pelleas quyte Sir Gawaine, for so it rehearseth in the book of French. So Sir Tristram many days after fought with Sir Marhaus in an island, and there they did a great battle, but at the last Sir Tristram slew him, so Sir Tristram was wounded that unnethe he might recover, and lay at a nunnery half a year. And Sir Pelleas was a worshipful knight, and was one of the four that achieved the Sangreal, and the damosel of the Lake made by her means that never he had ado with Sir Launcelot de Lake, for where Sir Launcelot was at any jousts or any tournament, she would not suffer him be there that day, but if it were on the side of Sir Launcelot.

Explicit Liber Quartus.

Incipit Liber Quintus.

BOOK V

CHAPTER I

HOW TWELVE AGED AMBASSADORS OF ROME CAME TO KING ARTHUR TO DEMAND TRUAGE FOR BRITAIN

WHEN King Arthur had after long war rested, and held a royal feast and Table Round with his allies of kings, princes, and noble knights all of the Round Table, there came into his hall, he sitting in his throne royal, twelve ancient men, bearing each of them a branch of olive, in token that they came as ambassadors and messengers from the Emperor Lucius, which was called at that time, Dictator or Procuror of the Public Weal of Rome ; which said messengers, after their entering and coming into the presence of King Arthur, did to him their obeisance in making to him reverence, and said to him in this wise : The high and mighty Emperor Lucius sendeth to the King of Britain greeting, commanding thee to acknowledge him for thy lord, and to send him the truage due of this realm unto the Empire, which thy father and other tofore thy precessors have paid as is of record, and thou as rebel not knowing him as thy sovereign, withholdest and retainest contrary to the statutes and decrees made by the noble and worthy Julius Cesar, conqueror of this realm, and first Emperor of Rome. And if thou refuse his demand and commandment, know thou for certain that he shall make strong war against thee, thy realms and lands, and shall chastise thee and thy subjects, that it shall be ensample perpetual unto all kings and princes, for to deny their truage unto that noble empire which domineth upon the universal world. Then when they had showed the effect of their message, the king commanded them to withdraw them, and said he should take advice of council and give to them an answer. Then some of the young knights, hearing this their message, would have run on them to have slain them, saying that it was a rebuke to all the knights there being present to suffer them to say so to the king. And anon the king commanded that none of them, upon pain of death, to myssaye them nor do them any harm, and commanded a knight to bring them to their lodging, and see that they have all that is necessary and requisite for them, with the best cheer, and that no dainty be spared, for the Romans be great lords, and though their message please me not nor my court, yet I must remember mine honour. After this the king let call all his lords and knights of the Round Table to counsel upon this matter, and desired them to say their advice. Then Sir Cador of Cornwall spake first and said, Sir, this message liketh me well, for we have many days rested us and have been idle, and now I hope ye shall make sharp war on the Romans, where I doubt not we shall get honour. I believe well, said Arthur, that this matter pleaseth thee well, but these answers may not be answered, for the demand grieveth me sore, for truly I will never pay truage to Rome, wherefore I pray you to counsel me. I have understood that Belinus and Brenius, kings of Britain, have had the empire in their hands many days, and also Constantine the son of Heleine, which is an open evidence that we owe no tribute to Rome, but of right we that be descended of them have right to claim the title of the empire.

CHAPTER II

HOW THE KINGS AND LORDS PROMISED TO KING ARTHUR AID AND HELP AGAINST THE ROMANS

THEN answered King Anguish of Scotland, Sir, ye ought of right to be above all other kings, for unto you is none like nor pareylle in Christendom, of knighthood nor of dignity, and I counsel you never to obey the Romans, for when they reigned on us they distressed our elders, and put this land to great extortions and taylles, wherefore I make here mine avow to avenge me on them; and for to strengthen your quarrel I shall furnish twenty thousand good men of war, and wage them on my costs, which shall await on you with myself when it shall please you. And the king of Little Britain granted him to the same thirty thousand; wherefore King Arthur thanked them. And then every man agreed to make war, and to aid after their power; that is to wit, the lord of West Wales promised to bring thirty thousand men, and Sir Uwaine, Sir Ider his son, with their cousins, promised to bring thirty thousand. Then Sir Launcelot with all other promised in likewise every man a great multitude. And when King Arthur understood their courages and good wills he thanked them heartily, and after let call the ambassadors to hear their answer. And in presence of all his lords and knights he said to them in this wise: I will that ye return unto your lord and Procuror of the Common Weal for the Romans, and say ye to him, Of his demand and commandment I set nothing, and that I know of no truage nor tribute that I owe to him, nor to none earthly prince, Christian nor heathen; but I pretend to have and occupy the sovereignty of the empire, wherein I am entitled by the right of my predecessors, sometime kings of this land; and say to him that I am delibered and fully concluded, to go with mine army with strength and power unto Rome, by the grace of God, to take possession in the empire and subdue them that be rebel. Wherefore I command him and all them of Rome, that incontinent they make to me their homage, and to acknowledge me for their Emperor and Governor, upon pain that shall ensue. And then he commanded his treasurer to give to them great and large gifts, and to pay all their dispenses, and assigned Sir Cador to convey them out of the land. And so they took their leave and departed, and took their shipping at Sandwich, and passed forth by Flanders, Almaine, the mountains, and all Italy, until they came unto Lucius. And after the reverence made, they made relation of their answer, like as ye tofore have heard. When the Emperor Lucius had well understood their credence, he was sore moved as he had been all araged, and said, I had supposed that Arthur would have obeyed to my commandment, and have served you himself, as him well beseemed or any other king to do. O Sir, said one of the senators, let be such vain words, for we let you wit that I and my fellows were full sore afeared to behold his countenance; I fear me ye have made a rod for yourself, for he intendeth to be lord of this empire, which sore is to be doubted if he come, for he is all another man than ye ween, and holdeth the most noble court of the world, all other kings nor princes may not compare unto his noble maintenance. On New Year's Day we saw him in his estate, which was the royalest that ever we saw, for he was served at his table with nine kings, and the noblest fellowship of other princes, lords, and knights that be in the world, and every knight approved and like a lord, and holdeth Table Round: and in his person the most manly man that liveth, and is like to conquer all the world, for unto his courage it is too little: wherefore I advise you to keep well your marches and straits in the mountains; for certainly he is a lord to be doubted. Well, said Lucius, before Easter I suppose to pass the mountains, and so forth into France, and there bereave him his lands with Genoese and other mighty warriors of Tuscany and Lombardy. And I shall send for them all that be subjects and allied to the empire of Rome to come to mine aid. And forthwith sent old wise knights unto these countries following: first to Ambage and Arrage, to Alexandria, to India, to Armenia, whereas the river of Euphrates runneth into Asia, to Africa, and Europe the Large, to Ertayne and Elamye, to Araby, Egypt, and to Damascus, to Damietta and Cayer, to Cappadocia, to Tarsus, Turkey, Pontus and Pamphylia, to Syria and Galatia. And all these were subject to Rome and many more, as Greece, Cyprus, Macedonia, Calabria, Cateland, Portugal, with many thousands of Spaniards. Thus all these kings, dukes, and admirals, assembled about Rome, with sixteen kings at once, with great multitude of people. When the emperor understood their coming he made ready his Romans and all the people between him and Flanders. Also he had gotten with him fifty giants which had been engendered of fiends; and they were ordained to guard his person, and to break the front of the battle of King Arthur. And thus departed from Rome, and came down the mountains for to destroy the lands that Arthur had conquered, and came unto Cologne, and besieged a castle thereby, and won it soon, and stuffed it with two hundred Saracens or Infidels, and after destroyed many fair countries which Arthur had won of King Claudas. And thus Lucius came with all his host which were disperplyd sixty mile in breadth, and commanded them to meet with him in Burgoyne, for he purposed to destroy the realm of Little Britain.

CHAPTER III

HOW KING ARTHUR HELD A PARLIAMENT AT YORK, AND HOW HE ORDAINED THE REALM SHOULD BE GOVERNED IN HIS ABSENCE

Now leave we of Lucius the Emperor and speak we of King Arthur, that commanded all them of his retinue to be ready at the utas of Hilary for to hold a Parliament at York. And at that Parliament was concluded to arrest all the navy of the land, and to be ready within fifteen days at Sandwich, and there he showed to his army how he purposed to conquer the empire which he ought to have of right. And there he ordained two governors of this realm, that is to say, Sir Bawdwin of Britain, for to counsel to the best, and Sir Constantine, son to Sir Cador of Cornwall, which after the death of Arthur was king of this realm. And in the presence of all his lords he resigned the rule of the realm and Gwenever his queen to them, wherefore Sir Launcelot was wroth, for he left Sir Tristram with King Mark for the love of Beale Isoud. Then the Queen Gwenever made great sorrow for the departing of her lord and other, and swooned in such wise that the ladies bare her into her chamber. Thus the king with his great army departed, leaving the queen and realm in the governance of Sir Bawdwin and Constantine. And when he was on his horse he said with an high voice, If I die in this journey I will that Sir Constantine be mine heir and king crowned of this realm as next of my blood. And after departed and entered into the sea at Sandwich with all his army, with a great multitude of ships, galleys, cogges, and dromoundes, sailing on the sea.

CHAPTER IV

HOW KING ARTHUR BEING SHIPPED AND LYING IN HIS CABIN HAD A MARVELLOUS DREAM AND OF THE EXPOSITION THEREOF

AND as the king lay in his cabin in the ship, he fell in a slumbering and dreamed a marvellous dream: him seemed that a dreadful dragon did drown much of his people, and he came flying out of the west, and his head was enamelled

with azure, and his shoulders shone as gold, his belly like
mails of a marvellous hue, his tail full of tatters, his feet full
of fine sable, and his claws like fine gold; and an hideous
flame of fire flew out of his mouth, like as the land and
water had flamed all of fire. After, him seemed there
came out of the orient, a grimly boar all black in a cloud,
and his paws as big as a post; he was rugged looking
roughly, he was the foulest beast that ever man saw, he
roared and romed so hideously that it were marvel to hear.
Then the dreadful dragon advanced him and came in the
wind like a falcon giving great strokes on the boar, and the
boar hit him again with his grizzly tusks that his breast was
all bloody, and that the hot blood made all the sea red of
his blood. Then the dragon flew away all on an hight, and
came down with such a swough, and smote the boar on the
ridge, which was ten foot large from the head to the tail,
and smote the boar all to powder both flesh and bones, that
it flittered all abroad on the sea. And therewith the king
awoke anon, and was sore abashed of this dream, and sent
anon for a wise philosopher, commanding to tell him the
signification of his dream. Sir, said the philosopher, the
dragon that thou dreamedst of betokeneth thine own person
that sailest here, and the colours of his wings be thy realms
that thou hast won, and his tail which is all to-tattered
signifieth the noble knights of the Round Table; and the
boar that the dragon slew coming from the clouds betokeneth
some tyrant that tormenteth the people, or else thou art like
to fight with some giant thyself, being horrible and abomin-
able, whose peer ye saw never in your days, wherefore of this
dreadful dream doubt thee nothing, but as a conqueror
come forth thyself. Then after this soon they had sight of
land. and sailed till they arrived at Barflete in Flanders, and
when they were there he found many of his great lords
ready, as they had been commanded to wait upon him.

CHAPTER V

HOW A MAN OF THE COUNTRY TOLD TO HIM OF A MARVELLOUS GIANT, AND HOW HE FOUGHT AND CONQUERED HIM

THEN came to him an husbandman of the country, and
told him how there was in the country of Constantine,
beside Brittany, a great giant which had slain, murdered

and devoured much people of the country, and had been sustained seven year with the children of the commons of that land, insomuch that all the children be all slain and destroyed; and now late he hath taken the Duchess of Brittany as she rode with her meyne, and hath led her to his lodging which is in a mountain, for to ravish and lie by her to her life's end, and many people followed her, more than five hundred, but all they might not rescue her, but they left her shrieking and crying lamentably, wherefore I suppose that he hath slain her in fulfilling his foul lust of lechery. She was wife unto thy cousin Sir Howell, whom we call full nigh of thy blood. Now, as thou art a rightful king, have pity on this lady, and revenge us all as thou art a noble conqueror. Alas, said King Arthur, this is a great mischief, I had lever than the best realm that I have that I had been a furlong way tofore him for to have rescued that lady. Now, fellow, said King Arthur, canst thou bring me thereas this giant haunteth? Yea, Sir, said the good man, look yonder whereas thou seest those two great fires, there shalt thou find him, and more treasure than I suppose is in all France. When the king had understood this piteous case, he returned into his tent. Then he called to him Sir Kay and Sir Bedivere, and commanded them secretly to make ready horse and harness for himself and them twain; for after evensong he would ride on pilgrimage with them two only unto Saint Michael's mount. And then anon he made him ready, and armed him at all points, and took his horse and his shield. And so they three departed thence and rode forth as fast as ever they might till that they came to the forbond of that mount. And there they alighted, and the king commanded them to tarry there, for he would himself go up into that mount. And so he ascended up into that hill till he came to a great fire, and there he found a careful widow wringing her hands and making great sorrow, sitting by a grave new made. And then King Arthur saluted her, and demanded of her wherefore she made such lamentation, to whom she answered and said, Sir knight, speak soft, for yonder is a devil, if he hear thee speak he will come and destroy thee; I hold thee unhappy; what dost thou here in this mountain? for if ye were such fifty as ye be, ye were not able to make resistance against this devil: here lieth a duchess dead, the which was the fairest of all the world, wife to Sir Howell, Duke of Brittany, he hath murdered her in forcing her, and hath slit her unto the navel. Dame, said the king, I come from the noble conqueror King Arthur, for to treat with that tyrant for his liege people. Fie on such treaties, said she, he setteth not by the king nor by no man else; but an if thou have brought Arthur's wife, dame Gwenever, he shall be gladder than thou hadst given to him half France. Beware, approach him not too nigh, for he hath vanquished fifteen kings, and hath made him a coat full of precious stones enbroidered with their beards, which they sent him to have his love for salvation of their people at this last Christmas. And if thou wilt, speak with him at yonder great fire at supper. Well, said Arthur, I will accomplish my message for all your fearful words; and went forth by the crest of that hill, and saw where he sat at supper gnawing on a limb of a man, baking his broad limbs by the fire, and breechless, and three fair damosels turning three broaches whereon were broached twelve young children late born, like young birds. When King Arthur beheld that piteous sight he had great compassion on them, so that his heart bled for sorrow, and hailed him saying in this wise: He that all the world wieldeth give thee short life and shameful death; and the devil have thy soul; why hast thou murdered these young innocent children, and murdered this duchess? Therefore, arise and dress thee, thou glutton, for this day shalt thou die of my hand. Then the glutton anon started up, and took a great club in his hand, and smote at the king that his coronal fell to the earth. And the king hit him again that he carve his belly and cut off his genytours, that his guts and his entrails fell down to the ground. Then the giant threw away his club, and caught the king in his arms that he crushed his ribs. Then the three maidens kneeled down and called to Christ for help and comfort of Arthur. And then Arthur weltered and wrung, that he was other while under and another time above. And so weltering and wallowing they rolled down the hill till they came to the sea mark, and ever as they so weltered Arthur smote him with his dagger. And it fortuned they came to the place whereas the two knights were and kept Arthur's horse; then when they saw the king fast in the giant's arms they came and loosed him. And then the king commanded Sir Kay to smite off the giant's head, and to set it upon a truncheon of a spear, and bear it to Sir Howell, and tell him that his

enemy was slain; and after let this head be bounden to a
barbican that all the people may see and behold it; and go
ye two up to the mountain, and fetch me my shield, my
sword, and the club of iron; and as for the treasure, take ye
it, for ye shall find there goods out of number; so I have
the kirtle and the club I desire no more. This was the
fiercest giant that ever I met with, save one in the mount
of Araby, which I overcame, but this was greater and fiercer.
Then the knights fetched the club and the kirtle, and some
of the treasure they took to themselves, and returned again
to the host. And anon this was known through all the
country, wherefore the people came and thanked the king.
And he said again, Give the thanks to God, and depart the
goods among you. And after that King Arthur said and
commanded his cousin Howell, that he should ordain for a
church to be builded on the same hill in the worship of
Saint Michael. And on the morn the king removed with
his great battle, and came into Champayne and in a valley,
and there they pyght their tents; and the king being set at
his dinner, there came in two messengers, of whom that one
was Marshal of France, and said to the king that the
emperor was entered into France, and had destroyed a great
part, and was in Burgoyne, and had destroyed and made
great slaughter of people, and burnt towns and boroughs;
wherefore, if thou come not hastily, they must yield up their
bodies and goods.

CHAPTER VI

HOW KING ARTHUR SENT SIR GAWAINE AND OTHER TO LUCIUS, AND HOW THEY WERE ASSAILED AND ESCAPED WITH WORSHIP

THEN the king did do call Sir Gawaine, Sir Bors, Sir Lionel,
and Sir Bedivere, and commanded them to go straight to Sir
Lucius, and say ye to him that hastily he remove out of my
land; and if he will not, bid him make him ready to battle
and not distress the poor people. Then anon these noble
knights dressed themselves to horseback, and when they
came to the green wood, they saw many pavilions set in a
meadow, of silk of divers colours, beside a river, and the
emperor's pavilion was in the middle with an eagle displayed above. To the which tent our knights rode toward,
and ordained Sir Gawaine and Sir Bors to do the message,

and left in a bushment Sir Lionel and Sir Bedivere. And then Sir Gawaine and Sir Bors did their message, and commanded Lucius, in Arthur's name to avoid his land, or shortly to address him to battle. To whom Lucius answered and said, Ye shall return to your lord, and say ye to him that I shall subdue him and all his lands. Then Sir Gawaine was wroth and said, I had lever than all France fight against thee; and so had I, said Sir Bors, lever than all Brittany or Burgoyne. Then a knight named Sir Gainus, nigh cousin to the emperor, said, Lo, how these Britons be full of pride and boast, and they brag as though they bare up all the world. Then Sir Gawaine was sore grieved with these words, and pulled out his sword and smote off his head. And therewith turned their horses and rode over waters and through woods till they came to their bushment, whereas Sir Lionel and Sir Bedivere were hovyng. The Romans followed fast after, on horseback and on foot, over a champaign unto a wood; then Sir Bors turned his horse and saw a knight come fast on, whom he smote through the body with a spear that he fell dead down to the earth; then came Caliburn one of the strongest of Pavie, and smote down many of Arthur's knights. And when Sir Bors saw him do so much harm, he addressed toward him, and smote him through the breast, that he fell down dead to the earth. Then Sir Feldenak thought to revenge the death of Gainus upon Sir Gawaine, but Sir Gawaine was ware thereof, and smote him on the head, which stroke stinted not till it came to his breast. And then he returned and came to his fellows in the bushment. And there was a recounter, for the bushment brake on the Romans, and slew and hew down the Romans, and forced the Romans to flee and return, whom the noble knights chased unto their tents. Then the Romans gathered more people, and also foot-men came on, and there was a new battle, and so much people that Sir Bors and Sir Berel were taken. But when Sir Gawaine saw that, he took with him Sir Idrus the good knight, and said he would never see King Arthur but if he rescued them, and pulled out Galatine his good sword, and followed them that led those two knights away; and he smote him that led Sir Bors, and took Sir Bors from him and delivered him to his fellows. And Sir Idrus in likewise rescued Sir Berel. Then began the battle to be great, that our knights were in great jeopardy, wherefore Sir Gawaine sent to King Arthur for succour, and that he hie him, for I am sore wounded, and that our prisoners may pay goods out of number. And the messenger came to the king and told him his message. And anon the king did do assemble his army, but anon, or he departed the prisoners were come, and Sir Gawaine and his fellows gat the field and put the Romans to flight, and after returned and came with their fellowship in such wise that no man of worship was lost of them, save that Sir Gawaine was sore hurt. Then the king did do ransake his wounds and comforted him. And thus was the beginning of the first journey of the Britons and Romans, and there were slain of the Romans more than ten thousand, and great joy and mirth was made that night in the host of King Arthur. And on the morn he sent all the prisoners into Paris under the guard of Sir Launcelot. with many knights, and of Sir Cador.

CHAPTER VII

HOW LUCIUS SENT CERTAIN SPIES IN A BUSHMENT FOR TO HAVE TAKEN HIS KNIGHTS BEING PRISONERS, AND HOW THEY WERE LETTED

Now turn we to the Emperor of Rome, which espied that these prisoners should be sent to Paris, and anon he sent to lie in a bushment certain knights and princes with sixty thousand men, for to rescue his knights and lords that were prisoners. And so on the morn as Launcelot and Sir Cador, chieftains and governors of all them that conveyed the prisoners, as they should pass through a wood, Sir Launcelot sent certain knights to espy if any were in the woods to let them. And when the said knights came into the wood, anon they espied and saw the great embushment, and returned and told Sir Launcelot that there lay in await for them three score thousand Romans. And then Sir Launcelot with such knights as he had, and men of war to the number of ten thousand, put them in array, and met with them and fought with them manly, and slew and dretenchid many of the Romans, and slew many knights and admirals of the party of the Romans and Saracens ; there was slain the king of Lyly and three great lords, Aladuke, Herawd, and Heringdale. But Sir Launcelot fought so nobly that no man might endure a stroke of his hand, but where he came he shewed his prowess and might, for he slew down right on every side; and the Romans and Saracens fled from him as the sheep from the wolf or from the lion, and put them all that abode alive to flight. And so long they fought that tidings came to King Arthur, and anon he graythed him and came to the battle, and saw his knights how they had vanquished the battle, he embraced them knight by knight in his arms, and said, Ye be worthy to wield all your honour and worship; there was never king save myself that had so noble knights. Sir, said Cador, there was none of us failed other, but of the prowess and manhood of Sir Launcelot were more than wonder to tell, and also of his cousins which did that day many noble feats of war. And also Sir Cador told who of his knights were slain, as Sir Beriel, and other Sir Moris and Sir Maurel, two good knights. Then the king wept, and dried his eyes with a kerchef, and said, Your courage had near hand destroyed you, for though ye had returned again, ye had lost no worship; for I call it folly, knights to abide when they be overmatched. Nay, said Launcelot and the other, for once shamed may never be recovered.

CHAPTER VIII

HOW A SENATOR TOLD TO LUCIUS OF THEIR DISCOMFITURE, AND ALSO OF THE GREAT BATTLE BETWEEN ARTHUR AND LUCIUS

Now leave we King Arthur and his noble knights which had won the field, and had brought their prisoners to Paris, and speak we of a senator which escaped from the battle, and came to Lucius the emperor, and said to him, Sir emperor, I advise thee for to withdraw thee; what dost thou here? thou shalt win nothing in these marches but great strokes out of all measure, for this day one of Arthur's knights was worth in the battle an hundred of ours. Fie on thee, said Lucius, thou speakest cowardly; for thy words grieve me more than all the loss that I had this day. And anon he sent forth a king, which hight Sir Leomie, with a great army, and bad him hie him fast tofore, and he would follow hastily after. King Arthur was warned privily, and sent his people to Sessoine, and took up the towns and castles from the Romans. Then the king commanded Sir

Cador to take the rearward, and to take with him certain knights of the Round Table,—And Sir Launcelot, Sir Bors, Sir Kay, Sir Marrok, with Sir Marhaus, shall await on our person. Thus the King Arthur disperplyd his host in divers parties, to the end that his enemies should not escape. When the emperor was entered into the vale of Sessoine, he might see where King Arthur was embattled and his banner displayed ; and he was beset round about with his enemies, that needs he must fight or yield him, for he might not flee, but said openly unto the Romans, Sirs, I admonish you that this day ye fight and acquit you as men, and remember how Rome domineth and is chief and head over all the earth and universal world, and suffer not these Britons this day to abide against us ; and therewith he did command his trumpets to blow the bloody sounds, in such wise that the ground trembled and dyndled. Then the battles approached and shove and shouted on both sides, and great strokes were smitten on both sides, many men overthrown, hurt, and slain ; and great valiances, prowesses and appertyces of war were that day showed, which were over long to recount the noble feats of every man, for they should contain an whole volume. But in especial, King Arthur rode in the battle exhorting his knights to do well, and himself did as nobly with his hands as was possible a man to do ; he drew out Excalibur his sword, and awaited ever whereas the Romans were thickest and most grieved his people, and anon he addressed him on that part, and hew and slew down right, and rescued his people ; and he slew a great giant named Galapas, which was a man of an huge quantity and height, he shorted him and smote off both his legs by the knees, saying, Now art thou better of a size to deal with than thou were, and after smote off his head. There Sir Gawaine fought nobly and slew three admirals in that battle. And so did all the knights of the Round Table. Thus the battle between King Arthur and Lucius the Emperor endured long. Lucius had on his side many Saracens which were slain. And thus the battle was great, and oftsydes that one party was at a fordele and anon at an afterdele, which endured so long till at the last King Arthur espied where Lucius the Emperor fought, and did wonder with his own hands. And anon he rode to him. And either smote other fiercely, and at last Lucius smote Arthur thwart the visage, and gave him a large wound. And when King

Arthur felt himself hurt, anon he smote him again with Excalibur that it cleft his head, from the summit of his head, and stinted not till it came to his breast. And then the emperor fell down dead and there ended his life. And when it was known that the emperor was slain, anon all the Romans with all their host put them to flight, and King Arthur with all his knights followed the chase, and slew down right all them that they might attain. And thus was the victory given to King Arthur, and the triumph; and there were slain on the part of Lucius more than an hundred thousand. And after King Arthur did do ransack the dead bodies, and did do bury them that were slain of his retinue, every man according to the estate and degree that he was of. And them that were hurt he let the surgeons do search their hurts and wounds, and commanded to spare no salves nor medicines till they were whole. Then the king rode straight to the place where the Emperor Lucius lay dead, and with him he found slain the Sultan of Syria, the King of Egypt and of Ethiopia, which were two noble kings, with seventeen other kings of divers regions, and also sixty senators of Rome, all noble men, whom the king did do bawme and gum with many good gums aromatic, and after did do cere them in sixty fold of cered cloth of Sendal, and laid them in chests of lead, by cause they should not chafe nor savour, and upon all these bodies their shields with their arms and banners were set, to the end they should be known of what country they were. And after he found three senators which were on live, to whom he said, For to save your lives I will that ye take these dead bodies, and carry them with you unto great Rome, and present them to the Potestate on my behalf, shewing him my letters, and tell them that I in my person shall hastily be at Rome. And I suppose the Romans shall beware how they shall demand any tribute of me. And I command you to say when ye shall come to Rome, to the Potestate and all the Council and Senate, that I send to them these dead bodies for the tribute that they have demanded. And if they be not content with these, I shall pay more at my coming, for other tribute owe I none, nor none other will I pay. And methinketh this sufficeth for Britain, Ireland and all Almaine with Germany. And furthermore, I charge you to say to them, that I command them upon pain of their heads never to demand tribute nor tax of me nor of my lands.

Then with this charge and commandment, the three senators aforesaid departed with all the said dead bodies, laying the body of Lucius in a car covered with the arms of the Empire all alone; and after alway two bodies of kings in a chariot, and then the bodies of the senators after them, and so went toward Rome, and showed their legation and message to the Potestate and Senate, recounting the battle done in France, and how the field was lost and much people and innumerable slain. Wherefore they advised them in no wise to move no more war against that noble conqueror Arthur, for his might and prowess is most to be doubted, seeing the noble kings and great multitude of knights of the Round Table, to whom none earthly prince may compare.

CHAPTER IX

HOW ARTHUR, AFTER HE HAD ACHIEVED THE BATTLE AGAINST THE ROMANS, ENTERED INTO ALMAINE, AND SO INTO ITALY

Now turn we unto King Arthur and his noble knights, which, after the great battle achieved against the Romans, entered into Loraine, Brabant and Flanders, and sythen returned into Haut Almaine, and so over the mountains into Lombardy, and after, into Tuscany wherein was a city which in no wise would yield themself nor obey, wherefore King Arthur besieged it, and lay long about it, and gave many assaults to the city; and they within defended them valiantly. Then, on a time, the king called Sir Florence, a knight, and said to him they lacked victual, And not far from hence be great forests and woods, wherein be many of mine enemies with much bestyayl: I will that thou make thee ready and go thither in foraging, and take with thee Sir Gawaine my nephew, Sir Wisshard, Sir Clegis, Sir Cleremond, and the Captain of Cardiff with other, and bring with you all the beasts that ye there can get. And anon these knights made them ready, and rode over holts and hills, through forests and woods, till they came into a fair meadow full of fair flowers and grass; and there they rested them and their horses all that night. And in the springing of the day in the next morn, Sir Gawaine took his horse and stole away from his fellowship, to seek some adventures. And anon he was ware of a man armed, walking his horse easily by a wood side, and his shield laced to his shoulder, sitting on a strong courser, without any man saving a page bearing a mighty spear. The knight bare in his shield three griffins of gold, in sable carbuncle, the chief of silver. When Sir Gawaine espied this gay knight, he fewtryd his spear, and rode straight to him, and demanded of him from whence that he was. That other answered and said he was of Tuscany, and demanded of Sir Gawaine, What, profferest thou, proud knight, thee so boldly? here gettest thou no prey, thou mayest prove what thou wilt, for thou shalt be my prisoner or thou depart. Then said Gawaine, thou avauntest thee greatly and speakest proud words, I counsel thee for all thy boast that thou make thee ready, and take thy gear to thee, tofore greater grame fall to thee.

CHAPTER X

OF A BATTLE DONE BY SIR GAWAINE AGAINST A SARACEN, WHICH AFTER WAS YIELDEN AND BECAME CHRISTIAN

THEN they took their spears and ran each at other with all the might they had, and smote each other through their shields into their shoulders, wherefore anon they pulled out their swords, and smote great strokes that the fire sprang out of their helms. Then Sir Gawaine was all abashed, and with Galatine his good sword he smote through shield and thick hauberk made of thick mails, and all to-rushed and break the precious stones, and made him a large wound, that men might see both liver and lung. Then groaned that knight, and addressed him to Sir Gawaine, and with an awke stroke gave him a great wound and cut a vein, which grieved Gawaine sore, and he bled sore. Then the knight said to Sir Gawaine, bind thy wound or thy bleeding change, for thou be-bleedest all thy horse and thy fair arms, for all the barbers of Brittany shall not conne staunch thy blood, for whosomever is hurt with this blade he shall never be staunched of bleeding. Then answered Gawaine, it grieveth me but little, thy great words shall not fear me nor lessen my courage, but thou shalt suffer tene and sorrow or we depart, but tell me in haste who may staunch my bleeding. That may I do, said the knight, if I will, and so will I if thou wilt succour and aid me, that I may be christened and believe on God, and thereof I require thee of thy manhood, and it shall be great merit for thy soul. I grant, said Gawaine, so God help me, to accomplish all thy desire, but first tell me what thou soughtest here thus alone, and of what land and liegiance thou art of. Sir, he said, my name is Priamus, and a great prince is my father, and he hath been rebel unto Rome and overridden many of their lands. My father is lineally descended of Alexander and of Hector by right line. And Duke Joshua and Maccabæus were of our lineage. I am right inheritor of Alexandria and Africa, and all the out isles, yet will I believe on thy Lord that thou believest on; and for thy labour I shall give thee treasure enough. I was so elate and haughty in my heart that I thought no man my peer, nor to me semblable. I was sent into this war with seven score knights, and now I have encountered with thee, which hast given to me of fighting my fill, wherefore sir knight, I pray thee to tell me what thou art. I am no knight, said Gawayn, I have been brought up in the guardrobe with the noble King Arthur many years, for to take heed to his armour and his other array, and to poynt his paltockes that long to himself. At yule last he made me yeoman, and gave to me horse and harness, and an hundred pound in money; and if fortune be my friend, I doubt not but to be well advanced and holpen by my liege lord. Ah, said Priamus, if his knaves be so keen and fierce, his knights be passing good: now for the King's love of Heaven, whether thou be a knave or a knight, tell thou me thy name. By God, said Sir Gawaine, now I will say thee sooth, my name is Sir Gawaine, and known I am in his court and in his chamber, and one of the knights of the Round Table, he dubbed me a duke with his own hand. Therefore grudge not if this grace is to me fortuned, it is the goodness of God that lent to me my strength. Now am I better pleased, said Priamus, than thou hadst given to me all the Provence and Paris the rich. I had liever to have been torn with wild horses, than any varlet had won such loos, or any page or pryker should have had prize on me. But now sir knight I warn thee that hereby is a Duke of Lorraine with his army, and the noblest men of Dolphiny, and lords of Lombardy, with the garrison of Godard, and Saracens of Southland, that numbered sixty-thousand of good men of arms; wherefore but if we hie us hence, it will harm us both, for we be sore hurt, never like to recover; but take heed to my page, that he no horn blow, for if he do, there be hoving here fast by an hundred knights awaiting on my person, and if they take thee, there shall no ransom of gold nor silver acquit thee. Then Sir Gawaine rode over a water for to save him, and the knight followed him, and so rode forth till they came to his fellows which were in the meadow, where they had been all the night. Anon as Sir Wisshard was ware of Sir Gawaine and saw that he was hurt, he ran to him sorrowfully weeping, and demanded of him who had so hurt him; and Gawaine told how he had foughten with that man, and each of them had hurt other, and how he had salves to heal them; but I can tell you other tidings, that soon we shall have ado with many enemies. Then Sir Priamus and Sir Gawaine alighted, and let their horses graze in the meadow, and unarmed them, and then the blood ran freshly from their wounds. And Priamus took from his page a phial full of the four waters that came out of paradise, and with certain balm anointed their wounds, and washed them with that water, and within an hour after they were both as whole as ever they were. And then with a trumpet were they all assembled to council, and there Priamus told unto them what lords and knights had sworn to rescue him, and that without fail they should be assailed with many thousands, wherefore he counselled them to withdraw them. Then Sir Gawaine said, it were great shame to them to avoid without any strokes; Wherefore I advise to take our arms and to make us ready to meet with these Saracens and misbelieving men, and with the help of God we shall overthrow them and have a fair day on them. And Sir Florence shall abide still in this field to keep the stale as a noble knight, and we shall not forsake yonder fellows. Now, said Priamus, cease your words, for I warn you ye shall find in yonder woods many perilous knights; they will put forth beasts to call you on, they be out of number, and ye are not past seven hundred, which be over few to fight with so many. Nevertheless said Sir Gawaine we shall once encounter them, and see what they can do, and the best shall have the victory.

CHAPTER XI

HOW THE SARACENS CAME OUT OF A WOOD FOR TO RESCUE THEIR BEASTS, AND OF A GREAT BATTLE

THEN Sir Florence called to him Sir Floridas, with an hundred knights, and drove forth the herd of beasts. Then followed him seven hundred men of arms; and Sir Ferant of Spain on a fair steed came springing out of the woods, and came to Sir Florence and asked him why he fled. Then Sir Florence took his spear and rode against him, and smote him in the forehead and brake his neck bone. Then all the other were moved, and thought to avenge the death of Sir Ferant, and smote in among them, and there was great fight, and many slain and laid down to ground, and Sir Florence with his hundred knights alway kept the stale, and fought manly. Then when Priamus the good knight perceived the great fight, he went to Sir Gawaine, and bad him that he should go and succour his fellowship, which were sore bystad with their enemies. Sir, grieve you not, said Sir Gawaine, for their gree shall be theirs. I shall not once move my horse to them ward, but if I see more than there be; for they be strong enough to match them. And with that he saw an earl called Sir Ethelwold, and the duke of Dutchmen come leaping out of a wood with many thousands, and Priamus' knights, and come straight unto the battle. Then Sir Gawaine comforted his knights, and bade them not to be abashed, for all shall be ours. Then they began to wallop and met with their enemies, there were men slain and overthrown on every side. Then thrust in among them the knights of the Table Round, and smote down to the earth all them that withstood them, in so much that they made them to recoil and flee. By God, said Sir Gawaine, this gladdeth my heart, for now be they less in number by twenty thousand. Then entered into the battle Jubance a giant, and fought and slew downright, and distressed many of our knights, among whom was slain Sir Gherard, a knight of Wales. Then our knights took heart to them, and slew many Saracens. And then came in Sir Priamus with his pennon, and rode with the knights of the Round Table, and fought so manfully that many of their enemies lost their lives. And there Sir Priamus slew the

Marquis of Moises land, and Sir Gawaine with his fellows so quit them that they had the field, but in that stour was Sir Chestelaine, a child and ward of Sir Gawaine slain, wherefor was much sorrow made, and his death was soon avenged. Thus was the battle ended, and many lords of Lombardy and Saracens left dead in the field. Then Sir Florence and Sir Gawaine harboured surely their people, and took great plenty of bestial, of gold and silver, and great treasure and riches, and returned unto King Arthur, which lay still at the siege. And when they came to the king they presented their prisoners and recounted their adventures, and how they had vanquished their enemies.

CHAPTER XII

HOW SIR GAWAINE RETURNED TO KING ARTHUR WITH HIS PRISONERS, AND HOW THE KING WON A CITY, AND HOW HE WAS CROWNED EMPEROR

Now thanked be God, said the noble King Arthur. But what manner man is he that standeth by himself, him seemeth no prisoner. Sir, said Gawaine, this is a good man of arms, he hath matched me, but he is yielden unto God, and to me, for to become Christian ; had not he have been we should never have returned, wherefore I pray you that he may be baptised, for there liveth not a nobler man nor better knight of his hands. Then the king let him anon be christened, and did do call his first name Priamus, and made him a duke and knight of the Table Round. And then anon the king let do cry assault to the city, and there was rearing of ladders, breaking of walls, and the ditch filled, that men with little pain might enter into the city. Then came out a duchess, and Clarisin the countess, with many ladies and damosels, and kneeling before King Arthur, required him for the love of God to receive the city, and not to take it by assault, for then should many guiltless be slain. Then the king avalyd his visor with a meek and noble countenance, and said, Madam, there shall none of my subjects misdo you nor your maidens, nor to none that to you belong, but the duke shall abide my judgment. Then anon the king commanded to leave the assault, and anon the duke's oldest son brought out the keys, and kneeling delivered them to the king, and besought him of grace; and the king seized the town by assent of his lords, and took the duke and sent him to Dover, there for to abide prisoner term of his life, and assigned certain rents for the dower of the duchess and for her children. Then he made lords to rule those lands, and laws as a lord ought to do in his own country; and after he took his journey toward Rome, and sent Sir Floris and Sir Floridas tofore, with five hundred men of arms, and they came to the city of Urbino and laid there a bushment, thereas them seemed most best for them, and rode tofore the town, where anon issued out much people and skirmished with the fore-riders. Then brake out the bushment and won the bridge, and after the town, and set upon the walls the king's banner. Then came the king upon an hill, and saw the city and his banner on the walls, by which he knew that the city was won. And anon he sent and commanded that none of his liege men should defoul nor lie by no lady, wife, nor maiden; and when he came into the city, he passed to the castle, and comforted them that were in sorrow, and ordained there a captain, a knight of his own country. And when they of Milan heard that thilk city was won, they sent to King Arthur great sums of money, and besought him as their lord to have pity on them, promising to be his subjects for ever, and yield to him homage and fealty for the lands of Pleasance and Pavia, Petersaint, and the Port of Tremble, and to give him yearly a million of gold all his lifetime. Then he rideth into Tuscany, and winneth towns and castles, and wasted all in his way that to him will not obey, and so to Spolute and Viterbe, and from thence he rode into the Vale of Vicecount among the vines. And from thence he sent to the senators, to wit whether they would know him for their lord. But soon after on a Saturday came unto King Arthur all the senators that were left on live, and the noblest cardinals that then dwelt in Rome, and prayed him of peace, and proferred him full large, and besought him as governor to give licence for six weeks for to assemble all the Romans, and then to crown him emperor with chrism as it belongeth to so high estate. I assent, said the king, like as ye have devised, and at Christmas there to be crowned, and to hold my Round Table with my knights as me liketh. And then the senators made ready for his enthronization. And at the day appointed, as the romance telleth, he came into Rome, and was crowned emperor by the pope's hand, with all the royalty that could be made, and sojourned there a time, and established all his lands from Rome into France, and gave lands and realms unto his servants and knights, to every each after his desert, in such wise that none complained, rich nor poor. And he gave to Sir Priamus the duchy of Lorraine; and he thanked him, and said he would serve him the days of his life; and after made dukes and earls, and made every man rich. Then after this all his knights and lords assembled them afore him, and said: Blessed be God, your war is finished and your conquest achieved, in so much that we know none so great nor mighty that dare make war against you: wherefore we beseech you to return homeward, and give us licence to go home to our wives, from whom we have been long, and to rest us, for your journey is finished with honour and worship. Then said the king, Ye say truth, and for to tempt God it is no wisdom, and therefore make you ready and return we into England. Then there was trussing of harness and baggage and great carriage. And after licence given, he returned and commanded that no man in pain of death should not rob nor take victual, nor other thing by the way but that he should pay therefor. And thus he came over the sea and landed at Sandwich, against whom Queen Gwenever his wife came and met him, and he was nobly received of all his commons in every city and burgh, and great gifts presented to him at his home-coming to welcome him with.

*Thus endeth the fifth book of the conquest that King Arthur
had against Lucius the Emperor of Rome, and here
followeth the sixth book, which is of Sir
Launcelot du Lake.*

BOOK VI

CHAPTER I

HOW SIR LAUNCELOT AND SIR LIONEL DEPARTED FROM THE COURT,
AND HOW SIR LIONEL LEFT HIM SLEEPING AND WAS TAKEN

SOON after that King Arthur was come from Rome into England, then all the knights of the Table Round resorted unto the king, and made many jousts and tournaments, and some there were that were but knights, which increased so in arms and worship that they passed all their fellows in prowess and noble deeds, and that was well proved on many; but in especial it was proved on Sir Launcelot du Lake, for in all tournaments and jousts and deeds of arms, both for life and death, he passed all other knights, and at no time he was never overcome but if it were by treason or enchantment, so Sir Launcelot increased so marvellously in worship, and in honour, therefore is he the first knight that the French book maketh mention of after King Arthur came from Rome. Wherefore Queen Guenever had him in great favour above all other knights, and in certain he loved the queen again above all other ladies and damosels of his life, and for her he did many deeds of arms, and saved her from the fire through his noble chivalry. Thus Sir Launcelot rested him long with play and game. And then he thought himself to prove himself in strange adventures, then he bade his nephew, Sir Lionel, for to make him ready; for we too will seek adventures. So they mounted on their horses, armed at all rights, and rode into a deep forest and so into a deep plain. And then the weather was hot about noon, and Sir Launcelot had great lust to sleep. Then Sir Lionel espied a great apple tree that stood by an hedge, and said, Brother, yonder is a fair shadow, there may we rest us on our horses. It is well said, fair brother, said Sir Launcelot, for this seven year I was not so sleepy as I am now; and so they there alighted and tied their horses unto sundry trees, and so Sir Launcelot laid him down under an apple tree, and his helm he laid under his head. And Sir Lionel waked while he slept. So Sir Launcelot was asleep passing fast. And in the meanwhile there came three knights riding, as fast fleeing as ever they might ride. And there followed them three but one knight. And when Sir Lionel saw him, him thought he saw never so great a knight, nor so well faring a man, neither so well apparelled unto all rights. So within a while this strong knight had overtaken one of these knights, and there he smote him to the cold earth that he lay still. And then he rode unto the second knight, and smote him so that man and horse fell down. And then straight to the third knight he rode, and smote him behind his horse arse a spear length. And then he alit down and reined his horse on the bridle, and bound all the three knights fast with the reins of their own bridles. When Sir Lionel saw him do thus, he thought to assay him, and made him ready, and stilly and privily he took his horse, and thought not for to awake Sir Launcelot. And when he was mounted upon his horse, he overtook this strong knight, and bade him turn, and the other smote Sir Lionel so hard that horse and man he bare to the earth, and so he alit down and bound him fast, and threw him overthwart his own horse, and so he served them all four, and rode with them away to his own castle. And when he came there he garte unarm them, and beat them with thorns all naked, and after put them in a deep prison where were many more knights that made great dolour.

CHAPTER II

HOW SIR ECTOR FOLLOWED FOR TO SEEK SIR LAUNCELOT, AND HOW HE WAS TAKEN BY SIR TURQUINE

WHEN Sir Ector de Maris wist that Sir Launcelot was passed out of the court to seek adventures, he was wroth with himself, and made him ready to seek Sir Launcelot, and as he had ridden long in a great forest he met with a man was like a forester. Fair fellow, said Sir Ector, knowest thou in this country any adventures that be here nigh hand? Sir, said the forester, this country know I well, and hereby, within this mile, is a strong manor, and well dyked, and by that manor, on the left hand, there is a fair ford for horses to drink of, and over that ford there groweth a fair tree, and thereon hang many fair shields that wielded sometime good knights, and at the hole of the tree hangeth a basin of copper and laton, and strike upon that basin with the butt of thy spear thrice, and soon after thou shalt hear new tidings, and else hast thou the fairest grace that many a year had ever knight that passed through this forest. Gramercy, said Sir Ector, and departed and came to the tree, and saw many fair shields. And among them he saw his brother's shield, Sir Lionel, and many more that he knew that were his fellows of the Round Table, the which grieved his heart, and he promised to revenge his brother. Then anon Sir Ector beat on the basin as he were wood, and then he gave his horse drink at the ford, and there came a knight behind him and bade him come out of the water and make him ready; and Sir Ector anon turned him shortly, and in fewter cast his spear, and smote the other knight a great buffet that his horse turned twice about. This was well done, said the strong knight, and knightly thou hast stricken me; and therewith he rushed his horse on Sir Ector, and cleyghte him under his right arm, and bare him clean out of the saddle, and rode with him away into his own hall, and threw him down in myddes of the floor. The name of this knight was Sir Turquine. Then he said unto Sir Ector, For thou hast done this day more unto me than any knight did these twelve years, now will I grant thee thy life, so thou wilt be sworn to be my prisoner all thy life days. Nay, said Sir Ector, that will I never promise thee, but that I will do mine advantage. That me repenteth, said Sir Turquine. And then he garte to unarm him, and beat him with thorns all naked, and sythen put him down in a deep dungeon, where he knew many of his fellows. But when Sir Ector saw Sir Lionel, then made he great sorrow. Alas, brother, said Sir Ector, where is my brother, Sir Launcelot? Fair brother, I left him on sleep when that I from him yode, under an apple tree; and what is become of him I cannot tell you. Alas, said the knights, but Sir Launcelot help us we may never be delivered, for we know now no knight that is able to match our master Turquine.

CHAPTER III

HOW FOUR QUEENS FOUND LAUNCELOT SLEEPING, AND HOW BY EN-
CHANTMENT HE WAS TAKEN AND LED INTO A CASTLE

Now leave we these knights prisoners, and speak we of Sir Launcelot du Lake that lieth under the Apple Tree sleeping. Even about the noon there come by him four queens of great estate; and, for the heat should not annoy them, there rode four knights about them, and bare a cloth of green silk on four spears, betwixt them and the sun, and the queens rode on four white mules. Thus as they rode they heard by them a great horse grimly neigh, then were they ware of a sleeping knight, that lay all armed under an apple tree; anon as these queens looked on his face, they knew it was Sir Launcelot. Then they began for to strive for that knight, every each one said they would have him to her love. We shall not strive, said Morgan le Fay, that was King Arthur's sister, I shall put an enchantment upon him that he shall not awake in six hours, and then I will lead him away unto my castle, and when he is surely within my hold, I shall take the enchantment from him, and then let him choose which of us he will have unto paramour. So this enchantment was cast upon Sir Launcelot, and then they laid him upon his shield, and bare him so on horseback betwixt two knights, and brought him unto the castle Chariot, and there they laid him in a chamber cold, and at night they sent unto him a fair damosel with his supper ready dight. By that the enchantment was past, and when she came she saluted him, and asked him what cheer. I cannot say, fair damosel, said Sir Launcelot, for I wot not how I came into this castle but it be by an enchantment. Sir, said she, ye must make good cheer, and if ye be such a knight as it is said ye be, I shall tell you more to-morn by prime of the day. Gramercy, fair damosel, said Sir Launcelot, of your good will I require you. And so she departed. And there he lay all on that night without comfort of anybody. And on the morn early came these four queens, passingly well bysene, all they bidding him good morn, and he them again. Sir knight, the four queens said, thou must understand thou art our prisoner, and we here know thee well that thou art Sir Launcelot du Lake, King Ban's son, and by cause we understand your worthiness, that thou art the noblest knight living, and as we know well there can no lady have thy love but one, and that is Queen Guenever, and now thou shalt lose her for ever, and she thee, and therefore thee behoveth now to choose one of us four. I am the Queen Morgan le Fay, queen of the land of Gore, and here is the queen of Northgalis, and the queen of Eastland, and the queen of the Out Isles; now choose one of us which thou wilt have to thy paramour, for thou mayest not choose or else in this prison to die. This is an hard case, said Sir Launcelot, that either I must die or else chose one of you, yet had I lever to die in this prison with worship, than to have one of you to my paramour maugre my head. And therefore ye be answered, I will none of you, for ye be false enchantresses, and as for my lady, Dame Guenever, were I at my liberty as I was, I would prove it on you or on yours, that she is the truest lady unto her lord living. Well, said the queens, is this your answer, that ye will refuse us. Yea, on my life, said Sir Launcelot, refused ye be of me. So they departed and left him there alone and made great sorrow.

CHAPTER IV

HOW SIR LAUNCELOT WAS DELIVERED BY THE MEAN OF A DAMOSEL

Right so at the noon came the damosel unto him with his dinner, and asked him what cheer. Truly, fair damosel, said Sir Launcelot, in my life days never so ill. Sir, she said, that me repentest, but an ye will be ruled by me, I shall help you out of this distress, and ye shall have no shame nor villainy, so that ye hold me a promise. Fair damosel, I will grant you, and sore I am of these queen-sorceresses afeard, for they have destroyed many a good knight. Sir, said she, that is sooth, and for the renown and bounte that they hear of you they would have your love, and Sir, they say, your name is Sir Launcelot du Lake, the flower of knights, and they be passing wroth with you that ye have refused them. But Sir, an ye would promise me to help my father on Tuesday next coming, that hath made a tournament betwixt him and the king of Northgalis; for the last Tuesday past my father lost the field through three knights of Arthur's court; an ye will be there on Tuesday next coming, and help my father, to-morn or prime, by the grace of God, I shall deliver you clene. Fair maiden, said Sir Launcelot, tell me what is your father's name, and then shall I give you an answer. Sir knight, she said, my father is King Bagdemagus, that was foul rebuked at the last tournament. I know your father well, said Sir Launcelot, for a noble king and a good knight, and by the faith of my body, ye shall have my body ready to do your father and

you service at that day. Sir, she said, gramercy, and
to-morn await ye be ready betimes, and I shall be she that
shall deliver you, and take you your armour and your horse,
shield and spear, and hereby, within this ten mile, is an
abbey of white monks, there I pray you that ye me abide,
and thither shall I bring my father unto you. All this shall
be done, said Sir Launcelot, as I am true knight. And so
she departed, and came on the morn early, and found him
ready; then she brought him out of twelve locks, and
brought him unto his armour, and when he was clene
armed, she brought him until his own horse, and lightly he
saddled him and took a great spear in his hand, and so rode
forth, and said, Fair damosel, I shall not fail you by the
grace of God. And so he rode into a great forest all that
day, and never could find no highway, and so the night fell
on him, and then was he ware in a slade, of a pavilion of red
sendal. By my faith, said Sir Launcelot, in that pavilion
will I lodge all this night, and so there he alit down, and
tied his horse to the pavilion, and there he unarmed him,
and there he found a bed, and laid him therein and fell on
sleep sadly.

CHAPTER V

HOW A KNIGHT FOUND SIR LAUNCELOT LYING IN HIS LEMAN'S
BED, AND HOW SIR LAUNCELOT FOUGHT WITH THE KNIGHT

THEN within an hour there came the knight to whom the
pavilion ought, and he weened that his leman had lain in
that bed, and so he laid him down beside Sir Launcelot,
and took him in his arms and began to kiss him. And
when Sir Launcelot felt a rough beard kissing him, he
started out of the bed lightly, and the other knight after
him, and either of them gat their swords in their hands, and
out at the pavilion door went the knight of the pavilion, and
Sir Launcelot followed him, and there by a little slake
Sir Launcelot wounded him sore, nigh unto the death. And then
he yielded him unto Sir Launcelot, and so he granted him,
sc that he would tell him why he came in to the bed. Sir,
said the knight, the pavilion is mine own, and there this
night I had assigned my lady to have slept with me, and now
I am likely to die of this wound. That me repenteth, said
Launcelot, of your hurt, but I was adread of treason, for I

was late beguiled, and therefore come on your way into your pavilion and take your rest, and as I suppose I shall staunch your blood. And so they went both into the pavilion, and anon Sir Launcelot staunched his blood. Therewithal came the knight's lady, that was a passing fair lady, and when she espied that her Lord Belleus was sore wounded, she cried out on Sir Launcelot, and made great dole out of measure. Peace, my lady and my love, said Belleus, for this knight is a good man, and a knight adventurous, and there he told her all the cause how he was wounded; And when that I yielded me unto him, he left me goodly and hath staunched my blood. Sir, said the lady, I require thee tell me what knight ye be, and what is your name? Fair lady, he said, my name is Sir Launcelot du Lake. So me thought ever by your speech, said the lady, for I have seen you oft or this, and I know you better than ye ween. But now an ye would promise me of your courtesy, for the harms that ye have done to me and my Lord Belleus, that when he cometh unto Arthur's court for to cause him to be made knight of the Round Table, for he is a passing good man of arms, and a mighty lord of lands of many out isles. Fair lady, said Sir Launcelot, let him come unto the court the next high feast, and look that ye come with him, and I shall do my power, an ye prove you doughty of your hands, that ye shall have your desire. So thus within a while as they thus talked the night passed, and the day shone, and then Sir Launcelot armed him, and took his horse, and they taught him to the Abbey, and thither he rode within the space of two hours.

CHAPTER VI

HOW SIR LAUNCELOT WAS RECEIVED OF KING BAGDEMAGUS' DAUGHTER, AND HOW HE MADE HIS COMPLAINT TO HER FATHER

AND soon as Sir Launcelot came within the abbey yard, the daughter of King Bagdemagus heard a great horse go on the pavement. And she then arose and yede unto a window, and there she saw Sir Launcelot, and anon she made men fast to take his horse from him and let lead him into a stable, and himself was led into a fair chamber, and unarmed him, and the lady sent him a long gown, and anon she came herself. And then she made Launcelot passing good cheer, and she said he was the knight in the world was most welcome to her. Then in all haste she sent for her father Bagdemagus that was within twelve mile of that Abbey, and afore even he came with a fair fellowship of knights with him. And when the king was alit off his horse he yode straight unto Sir Launcelot's chamber and there he found his daughter, and then the king embraced Sir Launcelot in his arms, and either made other good cheer. Anon Sir Launcelot made his complaint unto the king how he was betrayed, and how his brother Sir Lionel was departed from him he wist not where, and how his daughter had delivered him out of prison; Therefore while I live I shall do her service and all her kindred. Then am I sure of your help, said the king, on Tuesday next coming? Yea, sir, said Sir Launcelot, I shall not fail you, for so I have promised my lady your daughter. But, sir, what knights be they of my lord Arthur's that were with the King of Northgalis? And the king said it was Sir Mador de la Porte, and Sir Mordred and Sir Gahalantine that all for-fared my knights, for against them three I nor my knights might bear no strength. Sir, said Sir Launcelot, as I hear say that the tournament shall be here within this three mile of this abbey, ye shall send unto me three knights of yours, such as ye trust, and look that the three knights have all white shields, and I also, and no painture on the shields, and we four will come out of a little wood in middes of both parties, and we shall fall in the front of our enemies and grieve them that we may; and thus shall I not be known what knight I am. So they took their rest that night, and this was on the Sunday, and so the king departed, and sent unto Sir Launcelot three knights with the four white shields. And on the Tuesday they lodged them in a little leaved wood beside where the tournament should be. And there were scaffolds and holes that lords and ladies might behold and to give the prize. Then came into the field the King of Northgalis with eight score helms. And then the three knights of Arthur's stood by themself. Then came into the field King Bagdemagus with four score of helms. And then they fewtryd their spears, and came together with a great dash, and there were slain of knights at the first recounter twelve of King Bagdemagus' party, and six of the King of Northgalis' party, and King Bagdemagus' party was far set aback.

CHAPTER VII

HOW SIR LAUNCELOT BEHAVED HIM IN A TOURNAMENT, AND HOW HE MET WITH SIR TURQUINE LEADING SIR GAHERIS

WITH that came Sir Launcelot du Lake, and he thrust in with his spear in the thickest of the press, and there he smote down with one spear five knights, and of four of them he brake their backs. And in that throng he smote down the King of Northgalis, and brake his thigh in that fall. All this doing of Sir Launcelot saw the three knights of Arthur's. Yonder is a shrewd guest, said Sir Mador de la Porte, therefore have here once at him. So they encountered, and Sir Launcelot bare him down horse and man, so that his shoulder went out of lyth. Now befalleth it to me to joust, said Mordred, for Sir Mador hath a sore fall. Sir Launcelot was ware of him, and gat a great spear in his hand, and met him, and Sir Mordred brake a spear upon him, and Sir Launcelot gave him such a buffet that the arsson of his saddle brake, and so he flew over his horse's tail, that nigh his helm butted into the earth a foot and more, that nigh his neck was broken, and there he lay long in a swoon. Then came in Sir Gahalantine with a great spear and Launcelot against him, with all their strength that they might drive, that both their spears to-brast even to their hands, and then they flang out with their swords and gave many a grim stroke. Then was Sir Launcelot wroth out of measure, and then he smote Sir Gahalantine on the helm that his nose brast out on blood, and ears and mouth both, and therewith his head hung low. And therewith his horse ran away with him, and he fell down to the earth. Anon therewithal Sir Launcelot gat a great spear in his hand, and or ever that great spear brake, he bare down to the earth sixteen knights, some horse and man, and some the man and not the horse, and there was none but that he hit surely, he bare none arms that day. And then he gat another great spear, and smote down twelve knights, and the most part of them never throve after. And then the knights of the King of Northgalis would joust no more. And there the gree was given to King Bagdemagus. So either party departed unto his own place, and Sir Launcelot rode forth with King Bagdemagus unto his castle, and there he had passing good cheer both with the king and with his daughter, and they proffered him great gifts. And on the morn he took his leave, and told the king that he would go and seek his brother Sir Lionel, that went from him when that he slept, so he took his horse, and betaught them all to God. And there he said unto the king's daughter, If ye have need any time of my service I pray you let me have knowledge, and I shall not fail you as I am true knight. And so Sir Launcelot departed, and by adventure he came into the same forest where he was taken sleeping. And in the midst of a highway he met a damosel riding on a white palfrey, and there either saluted other. Fair damosel, said Sir Launcelot, know ye in this country any adventures? Sir knight, said that damosel, here are adventures near hand, an thou durst prove them. Why should I not prove adventures? said Sir Launcelot, for that cause come I hither. Well, said she, thou seemest well to be a good knight, and if thou dare meet with a good knight, I shall bring thee where is the best knight, and the mightiest that ever thou found, so thou wilt tell me what is thy name, and what knight thou art. Damosel, as for to tell thee my name I take no great force, truly my name is Sir Launcelot du Lake. Sir, thou beseemest well, here be adventures by that fall for thee, for hereby dwelleth a knight that will not be overmatched for no man I know but ye overmatch him, and his name is Sir Turquine. And, as I understand, he hath in his prison, of Arthur's court, good knights three score and four, that he hath won with his own hands. But when ye have done that journey ye shall promise me as ye are a true knight for to go with me, and to help me and other damosels that are distressed daily with a false knight. All your intent, damosel, and desire I will fulfil, so ye will bring me unto this knight. Now, fair knight, come on your way; and so she brought him unto the ford and the tree where hung the basin. So Sir Launcelot let his horse drink, and then he beat on the basin with the butt of his spear so hard with all his might till the bottom fell out, and long he did so but he saw nothing. Then he rode endlong the gates of that manor nigh half-an-hour. And then was he ware of a great knight that drove an horse afore him, and overthwart the horse there lay an armed knight bound. And ever as they came near and near, Sir Launcelot thought he should know him. Then Sir Launcelot was ware that it was Sir Gaheris,

Gawaine's brother, a knight of the Table Round. Now, fair damosel, said Sir Launcelot, I see yonder cometh a knight fast bounden that is a fellow of mine, and brother he is unto Sir Gawaine. And at the first beginning I promise you, by the love of God, to rescue that knight; but if his master sit better in the saddle I shall deliver all the prisoners that he hath out of danger, for I am sure he hath two brethren of mine prisoners with him. By that time that either had seen other, they gripped their spears unto them. Now, fair knight, said Sir Launcelot, put that wounded knight off the horse, and let him rest awhile, and let us two prove our strengths; for as it is informed me, thou doest and hast done great despite and shame unto knights of the Round Table, and therefore now defend thee. An thou be of the Table Round, said Turquine, I defy thee and all thy fellowship. That is overmuch said, said Sir Launcelot.

CHAPTER VIII

HOW SIR LAUNCELOT AND SIR TURQUINE FOUGHT TOGETHER

AND then they put their spears in the rests, and came together with their horses as fast as they might run, and either smote other in middes of their shields, that both their horses' backs brast under them, and the knights were both stonied, and as soon as they might avoid their horses, they took their shields afore them, and drew out their swords, and came together eagerly, and either gave other many strong strokes, for there might neither shields nor harness hold their strokes. And so within a while they had both grimly wounds, and bled passing grievously. Thus they fared two hours or more trasyng and rasyng either other where they might hit any bare place. Then at the last they were breathless both, and stood leaning on their swords. Now fellow, said Sir Turquine, hold thy hand a while, and tell me what I shall ask thee. Say on. Then Turquine said, Thou art the biggest man that ever I met withal, and the best breathed, and like one knight that I hate above all other knights; so be it that thou be not he I will lightly accord with thee, and for thy love I will deliver all the prisoners that I have, that is three score and four, so thou wilt tell me thy name. And thou and I we will be fellows together, and never to fail the while that I live. It is well said, said Sir Launcelot, but sithen it is so that I may have thy friendship, what knight is he that thou so hatest above all other? Faithfully, said Sir Turquine, his name is Sir Launcelot du Lake, for he slew my brother, Sir Carados, at the dolorous tower, that was one of the best knights on live; and therefore him I expect of all knights, for may I once meet with him, the one of us shall make an end of other, I make mine avow. And for Sir Launcelot's sake I have slain an hundred good knights, and as many I have maimed all utterly that they might never after help themself, and many have died in prison, and yet have I three score and four, and all shall be delivered so thou wilt tell me thy name, so be it that thou be not Sir Launcelot. Now, see I well, said Sir Launcelot, that such a man I might be, I might have peace, and such a man I might be, that there should be war mortal betwixt us. And now, sir knight, at thy request I will that thou wit and know that I am Launcelot du Lake, King Ban's son of Benwick, and very knight of the Table Round. And now I defy thee, and do thy best. Ah, said Turquine, Launcelot, thou art unto me most welcome that ever was knight, for we shall never depart till the one of us be dead. Then they hurtled together as two wild bulls rashing and lashing with their shields and swords, that sometime they fell both over their noses. Thus they fought still two hours and more, and never would have rest, and Sir Turquine gave Sir Launcelot many wounds that all the ground thereas they fought was all bespeckled with blood.

CHAPTER IX

HOW SIR TURQUINE WAS SLAIN, AND HOW SIR LAUNCELOT BADE SIR GAHERIS DELIVER ALL THE PRISONERS

THEN at the last Sir Turquine waxed faint, and gave somewhat aback, and bare his shield low for weariness. That espied Sir Launcelot, and leapt upon him fiercely and gat him by the beaver of his helmet, and plucked him down on his knees, and anon he rased off his helm, and smote his neck in sunder. And when Sir Launcelot had done this, he yode unto the damosel and said, Damosel, I am ready to go with you where ye will have me, but I have no horse. Fair sir, said she, take this wounded knight's horse and send him into this manor, and command him to deliver all the prisoners. So Sir Launcelot went unto Gaheris, and prayed him not to be aggrieved for to lend him his horse. Nay, fair lord, said Gaheris, I will that ye take my horse at your own commandment, for ye have both saved me and my horse, and this day I say ye are the best knight in the world, for ye have slain this day in my sight the mightiest man and the best knight except you that ever I saw, and, fair sir, said Gaheris, I pray you tell me your name. Sir, my name is Sir Launcelot du Lake, that ought to help you of right for King Arthur's sake, and in especial for my lord Sir Gawaine's sake, your own dear brother; and when that ye come within yonder manor, I am sure ye shall find there many knights of the Round Table, for I have seen many of their shields that I know on yonder tree. There is Kay's shield, and Sir Brandel's shield, and Sir Marhaus' shield, and Sir Galind's shield, and Sir Brian de Listonois's shield, and Sir Aliduke's shield, with many more that I am not now advised of, and also my two brethren's shields, Sir Ector de Maris and Sir Lionel; wherefore I pray you greet them all from me, and say that I bid them take such stuff there as they find, and that in any wise my brethren go unto the court and abide me there till that I come, for by the feast of Pentecost I cast me to be there, for as at this time I must ride with this damosel for to save my promise. And so he departed from Gaheris, and Gaheris yede in to the manor, and there he found a yeoman porter keeping there many keys. Anon withal Sir Gaheris threw the porter unto the ground and took the keys from him, and hastily he opened the prison door, and there he let out all the prisoners, and every man loosed other of their bonds. And when they saw Sir Gaheris, all they thanked him, for they weened that he was wounded. Not so, said Gaheris, it was Launcelot that slew him worshipfully with his own hands. I saw it with mine own eyes. And he greeteth you all well, and prayeth you to haste you to the court; and as unto Sir Lionel and Ector de Maris he prayeth you to abide him at the court. That shall we not do, says his brethren, we will find him an we may live. So shall I, said Sir Kay, find him or I come at the court as I am true knight. Then all those knights sought the house where as the armour was, and then they armed them, and every knight found his own horse, and all that ever longed unto him.

And when this was done, there came a forester with four horses laden with fat venison. Anon, Sir Kay said, Here is good meat for us for one meal, for we had not many a day no good repast. And so that venison was roasted, baken, and sodden, and so after supper some abode there all night, but Sir Lionel and Ector de Maris and Sir Kay rode after Sir Launcelot for to find him if they might.

CHAPTER X

HOW SIR LAUNCELOT RODE WITH A DAMOSEL AND SLEW A KNIGHT THAT DISTRESSED ALL LADIES AND ALSO A VILLAIN THAT KEPT A BRIDGE

Now turn we unto Sir Launcelot, that rode with the damosel in a fair highway. Sir, said the damosel, here by this way haunteth a knight that distressed all ladies and gentle-women, and at the least he robbeth them or lieth by them. What, said Sir Launcelot, is he a thief and a knight and a ravisher of women? he doth shame unto the order of knighthood, and contrary unto his oath; it is pity that he liveth. But, fair damosel, ye shall ride on afore, yourself, and I will keep myself in covert, and if that he trouble you or distress you I shall be your rescue and learn him to be ruled as a knight. So the maid rode on by the way a soft ambling pace. And within a while came out that knight on horseback out of the wood, and his page with him, and there he put the damosel from her horse, and then she cried. With that came Launcelot as fast as he might till he came to that knight, saying, O thou false knight and traitor unto knighthood, who did learn thee to distress ladies and gentlewomen? When the knight saw Sir Launcelot thus rebuking him he answered not, but drew his sword and rode unto Sir Launcelot, and Sir Launcelot threw his spear from him, and drew out his sword, and struck him such a buffet on the helmet that he clave his head and neck unto the throat. Now hast thou thy payment that long thou hast deserved, that is truth, said the damosel. For like as Sir Turquine watched to destroy knights, so did this knight attend to destroy and distress ladies, damosels, and gentlewomen, and his name was Sir Peris de Forest Savage. Now, damosel, said Sir Launcelot, will ye any more service of me? Nay, sir, she said, at this time, but almighty Jesu preserve you wheresomever ye ride or go, for the curtiest knight thou art, and meekest, unto all ladies and gentlewomen that now liveth. But one thing, sir knight, methinketh ye lack, ye that are a knight wifeless, that ye will not love some maiden or gentlewoman, for I could never hear say that ever ye loved any of no manner degree, and that is great pity; but it is noised that ye love Queen Gwenever, and that she hath ordained by enchantment that ye shall never love none other but her, nor none other damosel nor lady shall rejoice you; wherefore many in this land of high estate and low make great sorrow. Fair damosel, said Sir Launcelot, I may not warne people to speak of me what it pleaseth them; but for to be a wedded man, I think it not; for then I must couch with her, and leave arms and tournaments, battles, and adventures; and as for to say for to take my pleasaunce with paramours, that will I refuse in principle for dread of God; for knights that be adventurous or lecherous shall not be happy nor fortunate unto the wars, for either they shall be overcome with a simpler knight than they be themself, other else they shall by unhap and their cursedness slay better men than they be themself. And so who that useth paramours shall be unhappy, and all thing is unhappy that is about them. And so Sir Launcelot and she departed. And then he rode in a deep forest two days and more, and had strait lodging. So on the third day he rode over a long bridge, and there started upon him suddenly a passing foul churl, and he smote his horse on the nose that he turned about, and asked him why he rode over that bridge without his licence. Why should I not ride this way? said Sir Launcelot, I may not ride beside. Thou shalt not choose, said the churl, and lashed at him with a great club shod with iron. Then Sir Launcelot drew his sword and put the stroke aback, and clave his head unto the paps. At the end of the bridge was a fair village, and all the people, men and women, cried on Sir Launcelot, and said, A worse deed didst thou never for thyself, for thou hast slain the chief porter of our castle. Sir Launcelot let them say what they would, and straight he went into the castle; and when he came into the castle he alit, and tied his horse to a ring on the wall, and there he saw a fair green court, and thither he dressed him, for there him thought was a fair place to fight in. So he looked about, and saw much people in doors and windows that said, Fair knight, thou art unhappy.

CHAPTER XI

HOW SIR LAUNCELOT SLEW TWO GIANTS, AND MADE A CASTLE FREE

ANON withal came there upon him two great giants, well armed all save the heads, with two horrible clubs in their hands. Sir Launcelot put his shield afore him and put the stroke away of the one giant, and with his sword he clave his head asunder. When his fellow saw that he ran away as he were wood, for fear of the horrible strokes, and Launcelot after him with all his might, and smote him on the shoulder, and clave him to the navel. Then Sir Launcelot went into the hall, and there came afore him three score ladies and damosels, and all kneeled unto him, and thanked God and him of their deliverance; For sir, said they, the most part of us have been here this seven year their prisoners, and we have worked all manner of silk works for our meat, and we are all great gentlewomen born, and blessed be the time, knight, that ever thou be born; for thou hast done the most worship that ever did knight in this world, that will we bear record, and we all pray you to tell us your name, that we may tell our friends who delivered us out of prison. Fair damosel, he said, my name is Sir Launcelot du Lake. Ah, sir, said they all, well mayest thou be he, for else save yourself, as we deemed, there might never knight have the better of these two giants; for many fair knights have assayed it, and here have ended, and many times have we wished after you, and these two giants dread never knight but you. Now may ye say, said Sir Launcelot, unto your friends how and who hath delivered you, and greet them all from me, and if that I come in any of your marches, show me such cheer as ye have cause, and what treasure that there in this castle is I give it you for a reward for your grievance. And the lord that is owner of this castle I would he received it as is right. Fair sir, said they, the name of this castle is Tintagil, and a duke ought it sometime that had wedded fair Igraine. and after wedded her Uther Pendragon, and gat on her Arthur. Well, said Sir Launcelot, I understand to whom this castle longeth; and so he departed from them, and by-taughte them unto God. And then he mounted upon his horse, and rode into many strange and wild countries, and through many waters and valleys, and evil was he lodged.

And at the last by fortune him happened, against a night to come to a fair courtelage, and therein he found an old gentlewoman that lodged him with good will, and there he had good cheer for him and his horse. And when time was, his host brought him into a fair garret, over the gate, to his bed. There Sir Launcelot unarmed him, and set his harness by him, and went to bed, and anon he fell on sleep. So, soon after, there came one on horseback, and knocked at the gate in great haste, and when Sir Launcelot heard this, he arose up and looked out at the window, and saw by the moonlight three knights came riding after that one man, and all three lashed on him at once with swords, and that one knight turned on them knightly again, and defended him. Truly, said Sir Launcelot, yonder one knight shall I help, for it were shame for me to see three knights on one. And if he be slain I am partner of his death, and therewith he took his harness, and went out at a window by a sheet down to the four knights, and then Sir Launcelot said on high, Turn you knights unto me, and leave your fighting with that knight. And then they all three left Sir Kay, and turned unto Sir Launcelot, and there began great battle, for they alit all three, and struck many great strokes at Sir Launcelot, and assailed him on every side. Then Sir Kay dressed him for to have holpen Sir Launcelot. Nay, sir, said he, I will none of your help; therefore as ye will have my help, let me alone with them. Sir Kay, for the pleasure of the knight, suffered him for to do his will, and so stood on side. And then anon within six strokes, Sir Launcelot had stricken them to the earth. And then they all three cried : Sir knight, we yield us unto you as a man of might, makeless. As to that, said Sir Launcelot, I will not take your yielding unto me. But so that ye will yield you unto Sir Kay the Seneschal, on that covenant I will save your lives, and else not. Fair knight, said they, that were we loth to do ; for as for Sir Kay, we chased him hither, and had overcome him had not ye been, therefore to yield us unto him it were no reason. Well, as to that, said Launcelot, advise you well, for ye may choose whether ye will die or live, for an ye be yolden it shall be unto Sir Kay. Fair knight, then they said, in saving of our lives we will do as thou commandest us. Then shall ye, said Sir Launcelot, on Whitsunday next coming, go unto the court of King Arthur and there shall ye yield you unto Queen

Gwenever, and put you all three in her grace and mercy, and say that Sir Kay sent you thither to be her prisoners. Sir, they said, it shall be done by the faith of our bodies, an we be living, and there they swore every knight upon his sword. And so Sir Launcelot suffered them so to depart. And then Sir Launcelot knocked at the gate with the pommel of his sword, and with that came his host, and in they entered Sir Kay and he. Sir, said his host, I weened ye had been in your bed. So I was, said Sir Launcelot, but I rose and leapt out at my window for to help an old fellow of mine. And so when they came nigh the light, Sir Kay knew well that it was Sir Launcelot, and therewith he kneeled down and thanked him of all his kindness that he had holpen him twice from the death. Sir, he said, I have nothing done but that me ought for to do, and ye are welcome, and here shall ye repose you and take your rest. So when Sir Kay was unarmed, he asked after meat; so there was meat fetched him, and he ate strongly. And when he had supped they went to their beds and were lodged together in one bed. On the morn Sir Launcelot arose early, and left Sir Kay sleeping, and Sir Launcelot took Sir Kay's armour and his shield, and armed him, and so he went to the stable, and took his horse, and took his leave of his host, and so he departed. Then soon after arose Sir Kay and missed Sir Launcelot. And then he espied that he had his armour and his horse. Now by my faith I know well that he will grieve some of the court of King Arthur; for on him knights will be bold, and deem that it is I, and that will beguile them. And bycause of his armour and shield I am sure I shall ride in peace. And then soon after departed Sir Kay and thanked his host.

CHAPTER XII

HOW SIR LAUNCELOT RODE DISGUISED IN SIR KAY'S HARNESS, AND HOW HE SMOTE DOWN A KNIGHT

Now turn we unto Sir Launcelot that had ridden long in a great forest, and at the last he came into a low country, full of fair rivers and meadows. And afore him he saw a long bridge, and three pavilions stood thereon, of silk and sendal of divers hue. And without the pavilions hung three white shields on truncheons of spears, and great long spears stood upright by the pavilions, and at every pavilion's door stood three fresh squires, and so Sir Launcelot passed by them and spake no word. When he was passed the three knights saiden him that it was the proud Kay; He weeneth no knight so good as he, and the contrary is ofttime proved. By my faith, said one of the knights, his name was Sir Gaunter, I will ride after him and assay him for all his pride, and ye may behold how that I speed. So this knight, Sir Gaunter, armed him, and hung his shield upon his shoulder, and mounted upon a great horse, and gat his spear in his hand, and walloped after Sir Launcelot. And when he came nigh him, he cried, Abide, thou proud knight Sir Kay, for thou shalt not pass quit. So Sir Launcelot turned him, and either feutryd their spears, and came together with all their mights, and Sir Gaunter's spear brake, but Sir Launcelot smote him down horse and man. And when Sir Gaunter was at the earth his brethren said each one to other, Yonder knight is not Sir Kay, for he is bigger than he. I dare lay my head, said Sir Gilmere, yonder knight hath slain Sir Kay and hath taken his horse and his harness. Whether it be so or no, said Sir Raynold, the third brother, let us now go mount upon our horses and rescue our brother Sir Gaunter, upon pain of death. We all shall have work enough to match that knight, for ever meseemeth by his person it is Sir Launcelot, or Sir Tristram, or Sir Pelleas, the good knight. Then anon they took their horses and overtook Sir Launcelot, and Sir Gilmere put forth his spear, and ran to Sir Launcelot, and Sir Launcelot smote him down that he lay in a swoon. Sir knight, said Sir Raynold, thou art a strong man, and as I suppose thou hast slain my two brethren, for the which rasyth my heart sore against thee, and if I might with my worship I would not have ado with you, but needs I must take part as they do, and therefore, knight, he said, keep thyself. And so they hurtled together with all their mights, and all to-shivered both their spears. And then they drew their swords and lashed together eagerly. Anon therewith arose Sir Gaunter, and came unto his brother Sir Gilmere, and bade him, Arise, and help we our brother Sir Raynold, that yonder marvellously matched yonder good knight. Therewithal, they leapt on their horses and hurtled unto Sir Launcelot. And when he saw them come he smote a sore stroke unto Sir Raynold, that he fell off his horse to the ground, and then he struck to the other two brethren, and at two strokes he strake them down to the earth. With that Sir Raynold began to start up with his head all bloody, and came straight unto Sir Launcelot. Now let be, said Sir Launcelot, I was not far from thee when thou wert made knight, Sir Raynold, and also I know thou art a good knight, and loth I were to slay thee. Gramercy, said Sir Raynold, as for your goodness; and I dare say as for me and my brethren, we will not be loth to yield us unto you, with that we knew your name, for well we know ye are not Sir Kay. As for that be it as it be may, for ye shall yield you unto dame Gwenever, and look that ye be with her on Whitsunday, and yield you unto her as prisoners, and say that Sir Kay sent you unto her. Then they swore it should be done, and so passed forth Sir Launcelot, and each one of the brethren help other as well as they might.

CHAPTER XIII

HOW SIR LAUNCELOT JOUSTED AGAINST FOUR KNIGHTS OF THE ROUND TABLE AND OVERTHREW THEM

So Sir Launcelot rode into a deep forest, and thereby in a slade, he saw four knights hoving under an oak, and they were of Arthur's court, one was Sir Sagramour le Desirous, and Ector de Maris, and Sir Gawaine, and Sir Uwaine. Anon as these four knights had espied Sir Launcelot, they weened by his arms it had been Sir Kay. Now by my faith, said Sir Sagramour, I will prove Sir Kay's might, and gat his spear in his hand, and came toward Sir Launcelot. Therewith Sir Launcelot was ware and knew him well, and feutryd his spear against him, and smote Sir Sagramour so sore that horse and man fell both to the earth. Lo, my fellows, said he, yonder ye may see what a buffet he hath; that knight is much bigger than ever was Sir Kay. Now shall ye see what I may do to him. So Sir Ector gat his spear in his hand and walloped toward Sir Launcelot, and Sir Launcelot smote him through the shield and shoulder, that man and horse went to the earth, and ever his spear held. By my faith, said Sir Uwaine, yonder is a strong knight, and I am sure he hath slain Sir Kay; and I see by his great strength it will be hard to match him. And therewithal, Sir Uwaine gat his spear in his hand and rode toward Sir Launcelot, and Sir Launcelot knew him well, and so he met him on the plain, and gave him such a buffet that he was astonied, that long he wist not where he was. Now see I well, said Sir Gawaine, I must encounter with that knight. Then he dressed his shield and gat a good spear in his hand, and Sir Launcelot knew him well; and then they let run their horses with all their mights, and either knight smote other in middes of the shield. But Sir Gawaine's spear to-brast, and Sir Launcelot charged so sore upon him that his horse reversed up-so-down. And much sorrow had Sir Gawaine to avoid his horse, and so Sir Launcelot passed on a pace and smiled, and said, God give him joy that this spear made, for there came never a better in my hand. Then the four knights went each one to other and comforted each other. What say ye by this guest? said Sir Gawaine, that one spear hath felled us all four. We commend him unto the devil, they said all, for he is a man of great might. Ye may well say it, said Sir Gawaine, that he is a man of might, for I dare lay my head it is Sir Launcelot, I know it by his riding. Let him go, said Sir Gawaine, for when we come to the court then shall we wit; and then had they much sorrow to get their horses again.

CHAPTER XIV

HOW SIR LAUNCELOT FOLLOWED A BRACHET INTO A CASTLE, WHERE HE FOUND A DEAD KNIGHT, AND HOW HE AFTER WAS REQUIRED OF A DAMOSEL TO HEAL HER BROTHER

Now leave we there and speak of Sir Launcelot that rode a great while in a deep forest, where he saw a black brachet, seeking in manner as it had been in the feute of an hurt deer. And therewith he rode after the brachet, and he saw lie on the ground a large feute of blood. And then Sir Launcelot rode after. And ever the brachet looked behind her, and so she went through a great marsh, and ever Sir Launcelot followed. And then was he ware of an old manor, and thither ran the brachet, and so over the bridge. So Sir Launcelot rode over that bridge that was old and feeble; and when he came in middes of a great hall, there he saw lie a dead knight that was a seemly man, and that brachet licked his wounds. And therewithal came out a lady weeping and wringing her hands; and then she said, O knight, too much sorrow hast thou brought me. Why say ye so? said Sir Launcelot, I did never this knight no harm, for hither by feute of blood this brachet brought me; and therefore, fair lady, be not displeased with me, for I am full sore aggrieved of your grievance. Truly, sir, she said, I trow it be not ye that hath slain my husband, for he that did that deed is sore wounded, and he is never likely to recover, that shall I ensure him. What was your husband's name? said Sir Launcelot. Sir, said she, his name was called Sir Gilbert the Bastard, one of the best knights of the world, and he that hath slain him I know not his name. Now God send you better comfort, said Sir Launcelot; and so he departed and went into the forest again, and there he met with a damosel, the which knew him well, and she said on loud, Well be ye found, my lord; and now I require thee, on thy knighthood, help my brother that is sore wounded, and never stinteth bleeding; for this day he fought with Sir Gilbert the Bastard and slew him in plain battle, and there was my brother sore wounded, and there is a lady a sorceress that dwelleth in a castle here beside, and this day she told me my brother's wounds should never be whole till I could find a knight that would go into the Chapel Perilous, and there he should find a sword and a bloody cloth that the wounded knight was lapped in, and a piece of that cloth and sword should heal my brother's wounds, so that his wounds were searched with the sword and the cloth. This is a marvellous thing, said Sir Launcelot, but what is your brother's name? Sir, she said, his name was Sir Meliot de Logres. That me repenteth, said Sir Launcelot, for he is a fellow of the Table Round, and to his help I will do my power. Then, sir, said she, follow even this highway, and it will bring you unto the Chapel Perilous; and here I shall abide till God send you here again, and, but you speed, I know no knight living that may achieve that adventure.

CHAPTER XV

HOW SIR LAUNCELOT CAME INTO THE CHAPEL PERILOUS AND
GAT THERE OF A DEAD CORPSE A PIECE OF THE CLOTH AND
A SWORD

RIGHT so Sir Launcelot departed, and when he came
unto the Chapel Perilous he alit down, and tied his horse
unto a little gate. And as soon as he was within the
churchyard he saw on the front of the chapel many fair
rich shields turned up so down, and many of the shields
Sir Launcelot had seen knights bear beforehand. With
that he saw by him there stand thirty great knights, more
by a yard than any man that ever he had seen, and all
those grinned and gnashed at Sir Launcelot. And when he
saw their countenance he dread him sore, and so put his
shield afore him, and took his sword ready in his hand
ready unto battle, and they were all armed in black
harness ready with their shields and their swords drawn.
And when Sir Launcelot would have gone throughout
them, they scattered on every side of him, and gave
him the way, and therewith he waxed all bold, and
entered into the chapel, and then he saw no light but
a dim lamp burning, and then was he ware of a corpse
hylled with a cloth of silk. Then Sir Launcelot stooped
down, and cut a piece away of that cloth, and then it fared
under him as the earth had quaked a little; therewithal he
feared. And then he saw a fair sword lie by the dead
knight, and that he gat in his hand and hied him out of
the chapel. Anon as ever he was in the chapel yard all
the knights spake to him with a grimly voice, and said,
Knight Sir Launcelot, lay that sword from thee or else thou
shalt die. Whether that I live or die, said Sir Launcelot,
with no great word get ye it again, therefore fight for it an
ye list. Then right so he passed throughout them, and
beyond the chapel yard there met him a fair damosel, and
said, Sir Launcelot, leave that sword behind thee, or thou
wilt die for it. I leave it not, said Sir Launcelot, for no
entreaties. No, said she, an thou didst leave that sword,
Queen Guenever should thou never see. Then were I a
fool an I would leave this sword, said Launcelot. Now,
gentle knight, said the damosel, I require thee to kiss me
but once. Nay, said Sir Launcelot, that God me forbid.

Well, sir, said she, an thou hadst kissed me thy life days had been done, but now, alas, she said, I have lost all my labour, for I ordained this chapel for thy sake, and for Sir Gawaine. And once I had Sir Gawaine within me, and at that time he fought with that knight that lieth there dead in yonder chapel, Sir Gilbert the Bastard; and at that time he smote the left hand off of Sir Gilbert the Bastard. And, Sir Launcelot, now I tell thee, I have loved thee this seven year, but there may no woman have thy love but Queen Guenever. But sythen I may not rejoice thee to have thy body on live, I had kept no more joy in this world but to have thy body dead. Then would I have balmed it and served it, and so have kept it my life days, and daily I should have clipped thee, and kissed thee, in despite of Queen Guenever. Ye say well, said Sir Launcelot, Jesu preserve me from your subtle crafts. And therewithal he took his horse and so departed from her. And as the book saith, when Sir Launcelot was departed she took such sorrow that she died within a fourteen night, and her name was Hellawes the sorceress, Lady of the Castle Nigramous. Anon Sir Launcelot met with the damosel, Sir Meliot's sister. And when she saw him she clapped her hands, and wept for joy. And then they rode unto a castle thereby where lay Sir Meliot. And anon as Sir Launcelot saw him he knew him, but he was passing pale as the earth for bleeding. When Sir Meliot saw Sir Launcelot he kneeled upon his knees and cried on high: O lord Sir Launcelot, help me! Anon Sir Launcelot leapt unto him and touched his wounds with Sir Gilbert's sword. And then he wiped his wounds with a part of the bloody cloth that Sir Gilbert was wrapped in, and anon an wholer man in his life was he never. And then there was great joy between them, and they made Sir Launcelot all the cheer that they might, and so on the morn Sir Launcelot took his leave, and bade Sir Meliot hie him to the court of my lord Arthur, for it draweth nigh to the Feast of Pentecost, and there by the grace of God ye shall find me. And therewith they departed.

CHAPTER XVI

HOW SIR LAUNCELOT AT THE REQUEST OF A LADY RECOVERED A FALCON, BY WHICH HE WAS DECEIVED

AND so Sir Launcelot rode through many strange countries, over marshes and valleys, till by fortune he came to a fair castle, and as he passed beyond the castle him thought he heard two bells ring. And then was he ware of a falcon came flying over his head toward an high elm, and long lines about her feet, and as she flew unto the elm to take her perch the lines over-cast about a bough. And when she would have taken her flight she hung by the legs fast; and Sir Launcelot saw how she hung, and beheld the fair falcon perigot, and he was sorry for her. The meanwhile came a lady out of the castle and cried on high: O Launcelot, Launcelot, as thou art flower of all knights, help me to get my hawk, for an my hawk be lost my lord will destroy me; for I kept the hawk and she slipped from me, and if my lord my husband wit it he is so hasty that he will slay me. What is your lord's name? said Sir Launcelot. Sir, she said, his name is Sir Phelot, a knight that longeth unto the King of Northgalis. Well, fair lady, syne that ye know my name, and require me of knighthood to help you, I will do what I may to get your hawk, and yet God knoweth I am an ill climber, and the tree is passing high, and few boughs to help me withal. And therewith Sir Launcelot alit, and tied his horse to the same tree, and prayed the lady to unarm him. And so when he was unarmed, he put off all his clothes unto his shirt and breech, and with might and force he clomb up to the falcon, and tied the lines to a great rotten boyshe, and threw the hawk down and it withal. Anon the lady gat the hawk in her hand; and therewithal came out Sir Phelot out of the groves suddenly, that was her husband, all armed and with his naked sword in his hand, and said: O knight Launcelot, now have I found thee as I would, and stood at the bole of the tree to slay him. Ah, lady, said Sir Launcelot, why have ye betrayed me? She hath done, said Sir Phelot, but as I commanded her, and therefore there nys none other boote but thine hour is come that thou must die. That were shame unto thee, said Sir Launcelot, thou an armed knight to slay a naked man by treason. Thou gettest none other grace, said Sir Phelot, and therefore help thyself an thou canst. Truly, said Sir Launcelot, that shall be thy shame, but syne thou wilt do none other, take mine harness with thee, and hang my sword upon a bough that I may get it, and then do thy best to slay me an thou canst. Nay, nay, said Sir Phelot, for I know thee better than thou weenest, therefore thou gettest no weapon an I may keep you therefrom. Alas, said Sir Launcelot, that ever a knight should die weaponless. And therewith he wayted above him and under him, and over his head he saw a rownsepyk, a big bough leafless, and therewith he brake it off by the body. And then he came lower and awaited how his own horse stood, and suddenly he leapt on the further side of the horse, froward the knight. And then Sir Phelot lashed at him eagerly, weening to have slain him. But Sir Launcelot put away the stroke with the rownsepyk, and therewith he smote him on the one side of the head, that he fell down in a swoon to the ground. So then Sir Launcelot took his sword out of his hand, and struck his neck from the body. Then cried the lady, Alas! why hast thou slain my husband? I am not causer, said Sir Launcelot, for with falsehood ye would have had slain me with treason, and now it is fallen on you both. And then she swooned as though she would die. And therewithal Sir Launcelot gat all his armour as well as he might, and put it upon him for dread of more resort, for he dread that the knight's castle was so nigh. And so as soon as he might he took his horse and departed, and thanked God that he had escaped that adventure.

CHAPTER XVII

HOW SIR LAUNCELOT OVERTOOK A KNIGHT WHICH CHASED HIS WIFE TO HAVE SLAIN HER, AND HOW HE SAID TO HIM

So Sir Launcelot rode many wild ways, throughout marches and many wild ways. And as he rode in a valley he saw a knight chasing a lady, with a naked sword, to have slain her. And by fortune as this knight should have slain this lady, she cried on Sir Launcelot and prayed him to rescue her. When Sir Launcelot saw that mischief, he took his horse and rode between them, saying, Knight, fie for shame, why wilt thou slay this lady? thou dost shame unto thee and all knights. What hast thou to do betwixt me and my wife? said the knight. I will slay her maugre thy head. That shall ye not, said Sir Launcelot, for rather we two will have ado together. Sir Launcelot, said the knight, thou dost not thy part, for this lady hath betrayed me. It is not so, said the lady, truly he saith wrong on me. And for because I love and cherish my cousin germain, he is jealous betwixt him and me; and as I shall answer to God there was never sin betwixt us. But, sir, said the lady, as thou art called the worshipfullest knight of the world, I require thee of true knighthood, keep me and save me. For whatsomever ye say he will slay me, for he is without mercy. Have ye no doubt, said Launcelot, it shall not lie in his power. Sir, said the knight, in your sight I will be ruled as ye will have me. And so Sir Launcelot rode on the one side and she on the other: he had not ridden but a while, but the knight bade Sir Launcelot turn him and look behind him, and said, Sir, yonder come men of arms after us riding. And so Sir Launcelot turned him and thought no treason, and therewith was the knight and the lady on one side, and suddenly he swapped off his lady's head. And when Sir Launcelot had espied him what he had done, he said, and called him, Traitor, thou hast shamed me for ever. And suddenly Sir Launcelot alit off his horse, and pulled out his sword to slay him, and therewithal he fell flat to the earth, and gripped Sir Launcelot by the thighs, and cried mercy. Fie on thee, said Sir Launcelot, thou shameful knight, thou mayest have no mercy, and therefore arise and fight with me. Nay, said the knight, I will never arise till ye grant me mercy. Now will I proffer thee fair, said Launcelot, I will unarm me unto my shirt, and I will have nothing upon me but my shirt, and my sword in my hand. And if thou canst slay me, quit be thou for ever. Nay, sir, said Pedivere, that will I never. Well, said Sir Launcelot, take this lady and the head, and bear it upon thee, and here shalt thou swear upon my sword, to bear it always upon thy back, and never to rest till thou come to Queen Guenever. Sir, said he, that will I do, by the faith of my body. Now, said Launcelot, tell me what is your name? Sir, my name is Pedivere. In a shameful hour wert thou born, said Launcelot. So Pedivere departed with the dead lady and the head, and found the queen with King Arthur at Winchester, and there he told all the truth. Sir knight, said the queen, this is an horrible deed and a shameful, and a great rebuke unto Sir Launcelot; but notwithstanding his worship is not known in many divers countries; but this shall I give you in penance, make ye as good shift as ye can, ye shall bear this lady with you on horseback unto the Pope of Rome, and of him receive your penance for your foul deeds; and ye shall never rest one night whereas ye do another, an ye go to any bed the dead body shall lie with you. This oath there he made, and so departed. And as it telleth in the French book, when he came to Rome, the Pope bad him go again unto Queen Guenever, and in Rome was his lady buried by the Pope's commandment. And after this Sir Pedivere fell to great goodness, and was an holy man and an hermit.

CHAPTER XVIII

HOW SIR LAUNCELOT CAME TO KING ARTHUR'S COURT, AND HOW THERE WERE RECOUNTED ALL HIS NOBLE FEATS AND ACTS

Now turn we unto Sir Launcelot du Lake, that came home two days afore the Feast of Pentecost; and the king and all the court were passing fain of his coming. And when Sir Gawaine, Sir Uwaine, Sir Sagramore, Sir Ector de Maris, saw Sir Launcelot in Kay's armour, then they wist well it was he that smote them down all with one spear. Then there was laughing and smiling among them. And ever now and now came all the knights home that Sir Turquine had prisoners, and they all honoured and worshipped Sir Launcelot. When Sir Gaheris heard them speak, he said, I saw all the battle from the beginning to the ending, and there he told King Arthur all how it was, and how Sir Turquine was the strongest knight that ever he saw except Sir Launcelot: there were many knights bare him record, nigh three score. Then Sir Kay told the king how Sir Launcelot had rescued him when he should have been slain, and how he made the knights yield them to me, and not to him. And there they were all three, and bare record. And by Jesu, said Sir Kay, because Sir Launcelot took my harness and left me his I rode in good peace, and no man would have ado with me. Anon therewithal there came the three knights that fought with Sir Launcelot at the long bridge. And there they yielded them unto Sir Kay, and Sir Kay forsook them and said he fought never with them. But I shall ease your heart, said Sir Kay, yonder is Sir Launcelot that overcame you. When they wist that they were glad. And then Sir Meliot de Logres came home, and told the king how Sir Launcelot had saved him from the death. And all his deeds were known, how four queens, sorceresses, had him in prison, and how he was delivered by King Bagdemagus's daughter. Also there were told all the great deeds of arms that Sir Launcelot did betwixt the two kings, that is for to say the King of Northgalis and King Bagdemagus. All the truth Sir Gahalantine did tell, and Sir Mador de la Porte and Sir Mordred, for they were at that same tournament. Then came in the lady that knew Sir Launcelot when that he wounded Sir Belleus at the pavilion. And there, at request of Sir Launcelot, Sir Belleus was made knight of the Round Table. And so at that time Sir Launcelot had the greatest name of any knight of the world, and most he was honoured of high and low.

Explicit the noble tale of Sir Launcelot du Lake, which is the vi. book. Here followeth the tale of Sir Gareth of Orkney that was called Beaumains by Sir Kay, and is the seventh book.

BOOK VII

CHAPTER I

HOW BEAUMAINS CAME TO KING ARTHUR'S COURT AND DEMANDED THREE PETITIONS OF KING ARTHUR

WHEN Arthur held his Round Table most plenour, it fortuned that he commanded that the high feast of Pentecost should be holden at a site and a castle, the which in those days was called Kynke Kenadonne, upon the sands that marched nigh Wales. So ever the king had a custom that at the feast of Pentecost in especial, afore other feasts in the year, he would not go that day to meat until he had heard or seen of a great marvel. And for that custom all manner of strange adventures came before Arthur as at that feast before all other feasts. And so Sir Gawaine, a little tofore noon of the day of Pentecost, espied at a window three men upon horseback, and a dwarf on foot, and so the three men alit, and the dwarf kept their horses, and one of the three men was higher than the other twain by a foot and an half. Then Sir Gawaine went unto the king and said, Sir, go to your meat, for here at the hand come strange adventures. So Arthur went unto his meat with many other kings. And there were all the knights of the Round Table only those that were prisoners or slain at a recounter. Then at the high feast evermore they should be fulfilled the whole number of an hundred and fifty, for then was the Round Table fully complished. Right so came into the hall two men well bisene and richly, and upon their shoulders there leaned the goodliest young man and the fairest that ever they all saw, and he was large and long and broad in the shoulders, and well visaged, and the fairest and the largest handed that ever man saw, but he fared as though he might not go nor bear himself but if he leaned upon their shoulders. Anon as Arthur saw him there was made peace and room, and right so they yede with him unto the high dais, without saying of any words. Then this much young man pulled him aback, and easily stretched up straight, saying, King Arthur, God you bless and all your fair fellowship, and in especial the fellowship of the Table Round. And for this cause I am come hither, to pray you and require you to give me three gifts, and they shall not be unreasonably asked, but that ye may worshipfully and honourably grant them me, and to you no great hurt nor loss. And the first done and gift I will ask now, and the other two gifts I will ask this day twelvemonth, wheresomever ye hold your high feast. Now ask, said Arthur, and ye shall have your asking. Now, sir, this is my petition for this feast, that ye will give me meat and drink sufficiently for this twelvemonth, and at that day I will ask mine other two gifts. My fair son, said Arthur, ask better, I counsel thee, for this is but a simple asking; for my heart giveth me to thee greatly, that thou art come of men of worship, and greatly my conceit faileth me but thou shalt prove a man of right great worship. Sir, he said, thereof be as it be may, I have asked that I will ask. Well, said the king, ye shall have meat and drink enough ; I never defended

that none, neither my friend nor my foe. But what is thy
name I would wit? I cannot tell you, said he. That is
marvel, said the king, that thou knowest not thy name, and
thou art the goodliest young man one that ever I saw.
Then the king betook him to Sir Kay the steward, and
charged him that he should give him of all manner of
meats and drinks of the best, and also that he had all
manner of finding as though he were a lord's son. That
shall little need, said Sir Kay, to do such cost upon him;
for I dare undertake he is a villain born, and never will
make man, for an he had come of gentlemen he would
have asked of you horse and armour, but such as he is, so
he asketh. And sythen he hath no name, I shall give him
a name that shall be Beaumains, that is Fair-hands, and
into the kitchen I shall bring him, and there he shall have
fat brose every day, that he shall be as fat by the twelvemonths' end as a pork hog. Right so the two men departed
and beleft him to Sir Kay, that scorned him and mocked
him.

CHAPTER II

HOW SIR LAUNCELOT AND SIR GAWAINE WERE WROTH BY CAUSE SIR KAY MOCKED BEAUMAINS, AND OF A DAMOSEL WHICH DESIRED A KNIGHT TO FIGHT FOR A LADY

THEREAT was Sir Gawaine wroth, and in especial Sir
Launcelot bade Sir Kay leave his mocking, for I dare lay
my head he shall prove a man of great worship. Let be,
said Sir Kay, it may not be by no reason, for as he is, so he
hath asked. Beware, said Sir Launcelot, so ye gave the
good knight Brewnor, Sir Dinadan's brother, a name, and
ye called him La Cote Male Taile, and that turned you to
anger afterward. As for that, said Sir Kay, this shall never
prove none such. For Sir Brewnor desired ever worship,
and this desireth bread and drink and broth; upon pain of
my life he was fostered up in some abbey, and, howsomever
it was, they failed meat and drink, and so hither he is come
for his sustenance. And so Sir Kay bad get him a place,
and sit down to meat; so Beaumains went to the hall door,
and set him down among boys and lads, and there he ate
sadly. And then Sir Launcelot after meat bad him come

to his chamber, and there he should have meat and drink enough. And so did Sir Gawaine: but he refused them all; he would do none other but as Sir Kay commanded him, for no proffer. But as touching Sir Gawaine, he had reason to proffer him lodging, meat, and drink, for that proffer came of his blood, for he was nearer kin to him than he wist. But that as Sir Launcelot did was of his great gentleness and courtesy. So thus he was put into the kitchen, and lay nightly as the boys of the kitchen did. And so he endured all that twelvemonth, and never displeased man nor child, but always he was meek and mild. But ever when that he was any jousting of knights, that would he see an he might. And ever Sir Launcelot would give him gold to spend, and clothes, and so did Sir Gawaine, and where there were any masteries done, thereat would he be, and there might none cast bar nor stone to him by two yards. Then would Sir Kay say, How liketh you my boy of the kitchen? So it passed on till the feast of Whitsuntide. And at that time the king held it at Carlion in the most royallest wise that might be, like as he did yearly. But the king would no meat eat upon the Whitsunday, until he heard some adventures. Then came there a squire to the king and said, Sir, ye may go to your meat, for here cometh a damosel with some strange adventures. Then was the king glad and sat him down. Right so there came a damosel into the hall and saluted the king, and prayed him of succour. For whom? said the king, what is the adventure? Sir, she said, I have a lady of great worship and renown, and she is besieged with a tyrant, so that she may not out of her castle; and by cause here are called the noblest knights of the world, I come to you to pray you of succour. What hight your lady, and where dwelleth she, and who is she, and what is his name that hath besieged her? Sir King, she said, as for my lady's name that shall not ye know for me as at this time, but I let you wit she is a lady of great worship and of great lands; and as for the tyrant that besiegeth her and destroyeth her lands, he is called the Red Knight of the Red Laundes. I know him not, said the king. Sir, said Sir Gawaine, I know him well, for he is one of the perilloust knights of the world; men say that he hath seven men's strength, and from him I escaped once full hard with my life. Fair damosel, said the king, there be knights here would do their power for to rescue your lady, but by cause you will not tell her name, nor where she dwelleth, therefore none of my knights that here be now shall go with you by my will. Then must I speak further, said the damosel.

CHAPTER III

HOW BEAUMAINS DESIRED THE BATTLE, AND HOW IT WAS GRANTED TO HIM, AND HOW HE DESIRED TO BE MADE KNIGHT OF SIR LAUNCELOT

WITH these words came before the king Beaumains, while the damosel was there, and thus he said, Sir king, God thank you I have been this twelvemonth in your kitchen, and have had my full sustenance, and now I will ask my two gifts that be behind. Ask, upon my peril, said the king. Sir, this shall be my two gifts, first that ye will grant me to have this adventure of the damosel, for it belongeth unto me. Thou shalt have it, said the king, I grant it thee. Then, sir, this is the other gift, that ye shall bid Launcelot du Lake to make me knight, for of him I will be made knight and else of none. And when I am passed I pray you let him ride after me, and make me knight when I require him. All this shall be done, said the king. Fie on thee, said the damosel, shall I have none but one that is your kitchen page? Then was she wroth, and took her horse and departed. And with that there came one to Beaumains and told him his horse and armour was come for him ; and there was the dwarf come with all thing that him needed, in the richest manner ; thereat all the court had much marvel from whence came all that gear. So when he was armed there was none but few so goodly a man as he was ; and right so as he came into the hall and took his leave of King Arthur, and Sir Gawaine, and Sir Launcelot, and prayed that he would hie after him, and so departed and rode after the damosel.

CHAPTER IV

HOW BEAUMAINS DEPARTED, AND HOW HE GAT OF SIR KAY A SPEAR AND A SHIELD, AND HOW HE JOUSTED WITH SIR LAUNCELOT

BUT there went many after to behold how well he was horsed and trapped in cloth of gold, but he had neither shield nor spear. Then Sir Kay said all open in the hall, I will ride after my boy in the kitchen, to wit whether he will know me for his better. Said Sir Launcelot and Sir Gawaine, Yet abide at home. So Sir Kay made him ready and took his horse and his spear, and rode after him. And right as Beaumains overtook the damosel, right so came Sir Kay and said, Beaumains, what, sir, know ye not me? Then he turned his horse, and knew it was Sir Kay, that had done him all the despite as ye have heard afore. Yea, said Beaumains, I know you for an ungentle knight of the court, and therefore beware of me. Therewith Sir Kay put his spear in the rest, and ran straight upon him; and Beaumains came as fast upon him with his sword in his hand, and so he put away his spear with his sword, and with a foyne thrust him through the side, that Sir Kay fell down as he had been dead; and he alit down and took Sir Kay's shield and his spear, and start upon his own horse and rode his way. All that saw Sir Launcelot, and so did the damosel. And then he bad his dwarf start upon Sir Kay's horse, and so he did. By that Sir Launcelot was come, then he proffered Sir Launcelot to joust; and either made them ready, and they came together so fiercely that either bare down other to the earth, and sore were they bruised. Then Sir Launcelot arose and helped him from his horse. And then Beaumains threw his shield from him, and proffered to fight with Sir Launcelot on foot; and so they rushed together like boars, tracynge, racynge, and foyning to the mountenance of an hour; and Sir Launcelot felt him so big that he marvelled of his strength, for he fought more liker a giant than a knight, and that his fighting was durable and passing perilous. For Sir Launcelot had so much ado with him that he dread himself to be shamed, and said, Beaumains, fight not so sore, your quarrel and mine is not so great but we may leave off. Truly that is truth, said Beaumains, but it doth me good to feel your might, and yet, my lord, I showed not the utteraunce.

CHAPTER V

HOW BEAUMAINS TOLD TO SIR LAUNCELOT HIS NAME, AND HOW
HE WAS DUBBED KNIGHT OF SIR LAUNCELOT, AND AFTER
OVERTOOK THE DAMOSEL

IN God's name, said Sir Launcelot, for I promise you,
by the faith of my body, I had as much to do as I might
to save myself from you unshamed, and therefore have ye
no doubt of none earthly knight. Hope ye so that I may
any while stand a proved knight? said Beaumains. Yea,
said Launcelot, do as ye have done, and I shall be your
warrant. Then, I pray you, said Beaumains, give me the
order of knighthood. Then must ye tell me your name,
said Launcelot, and of what kin ye be born. Sir, so that
ye will not discover me I shall, said Beaumains. Nay,
said Sir Launcelot, and that I promise you by the faith of
my body until it be openly known. Then, sir, he said, my
name is Gareth, and brother unto Sir Gawaine of father
and mother. Ah, sir, said Sir Launcelot, I am more gladder
of you than I was; for ever me thought ye should be of
great blood, and that ye came not to the court neither for
meat nor for drink. And then Sir Launcelot gave him the
order of knighthood, and then Sir Gareth prayed him for
to depart and let him go. So Sir Launcelot departed from
him and came to Sir Kay, and made him to be borne home
upon his shield, and so he was healed hard with the life;
and all men scorned Sir Kay, and in especial Sir Gawaine
and Sir Launcelot said it was not his part to rebuke no
young man, for full little knew he of what birth he is come,
and for what cause he came to this court; and so we leave
Sir Kay and turn we unto Beaumains. When he had overtaken the damosel, anon she said, What dost thou here?
thou stinkest all of the kitchen, thy clothes be bawdy of
the grease and tallow that thou gainest in King Arthur's
kitchen; weenest thou, said she, that I allow thee, for
yonder knight that thou killest. Nay truly, for thou slewest
him unhappily and cowardly; therefore turn again, bawdy
kitchen page, I know thee well, for Sir Kay named thee
Beaumains. What art thou but a luske and a turner of
broches and a ladle-washer? Damosel, said Beaumains,
say to me what ye will, I will not go from you whatsomever
ye say, for I have undertaken to King Arthur for to achieve

your adventure, and so shall I finish it to the end, either I shall die therefor. Fie on thee, kitchen knave, wilt thou finish mine adventure? thou shalt anon be met withal, that thou wouldest not for all the broth that ever thou suppest once look him in the face. I shall essay, said Beaumains. So thus as they rode in the wood, there came a man flying all that ever he might. Whither wilt thou? said Beaumains. O lord, he said, help me, for here by in a slade are six thieves that have taken my lord and bound him, so I am afeard lest they will slay him. Bring me thither, said Beaumains. And so they rode together until they came thereas was the knight bounden; and then he rode unto them, and struck one unto the death, and then another, and at the third stroke he slew the third thief, and then the other three fled. And he rode after them, and he overtook them; and then those three thieves turned again and assailed Beaumains hard, but at the last he slew them, and returned and unbound the knight. And the knight thanked him, and prayed him to ride with him to his castle there a little beside, and he should worshipfully reward him for his good deeds. Sir, said Beaumains, I will no reward have: I was this day made knight of noble Sir Launcelot, and therefore I will no reward have, but God reward me. And also I must follow this damosel. And when he came nigh her she bad him ride from her, For thou smellest all of the kitchen: weenest thou that I have joy of thee, for all this deed that thou hast done is but mishapped thee: but thou shalt see a sight shall make thee turn again, and that lightly. Then the same knight which was rescued of the thieves rode after that damosel, and prayed her to lodge with him all that night. And because it was near night the damosel rode with him to his castle, and there they had great cheer, and at supper the knight sat Sir Beaumains afore the damosel. Fie, fie, said she, Sir knight, ye are uncourteous to set a kitchen page afore me; him beseemeth better to stick a swine than to sit afore a damosel of high parage. Then the knight was ashamed at her words, and took him up, and set him at a sideboard, and set himself afore him, and so all that night they had good cheer and merry rest.

CHAPTER VI

HOW BEAUMAINS FOUGHT AND SLEW TWO KNIGHTS AT A PASSAGE

AND on the morn the damosel and he took their leave and thanked the knight, and so departed, and rode on their way until they came to a great forest. And there was a great river and but one passage, and there were ready two knights on the farther side to let them the passage. What sayest thou, said the damosel, wilt thou match yonder knights or turn again? Nay, said Sir Beaumains, I will not turn again an they were six more. And therewithal he rushed into the water, and in middes of the water either brake their spears upon other to their hands, and then they drew their swords, and smote eagerly at other. And at the last Sir Beaumains smote the other upon the helm that his head stonied, and therewithal he fell down in the water, and there was he drowned. And then he spurred his horse upon the land, where the other knight fell upon him, and brake his spear, and so they drew their swords and fought long together. At the last Sir Beaumains clave his helm and his head down to the shoulders; and so he rode unto the damosel and bad her ride forth on her way. Alas, she said, that ever a kitchen page should have that fortune to destroy such two doughty knights: thou weenest thou hast done doughtily, that is not so; for the first knight his horse stumbled, and there he was drowned in the water, and never it was by thy force, nor by thy might. And the last knight by mishap thou camest behind him and mishappily thou slew him. Damosel, said Beaumains, ye may say what ye will, but with whomsomever I have ado withal, I trust to God to serve him or he depart. And therefore I reck not what ye say, so that I may win your lady. Fie, fie, foul kitchen knave, thou shalt see knights that shall abate thy boast. Fair damosel, give me goodly language, and then my care is past, for what knights somever they be, I care not, nor I doubt them not. Also, said she, I say it for thine avail, yet mayest thou turn again with thy worship; for an thou follow me, thou art but slain, for I see all that ever thou dost is but by misadventure, and not by prowess of thy hands. Well, damosel, ye may say what ye will, but wheresomever ye go I will follow you. So this Beaumains rode with that lady till evensong time, and ever she chid him, and would not rest. And they came to a black launde; and there was a black hawthorn, and thereon hung a black banner, and on the other side there hung a black shield, and by it stood a black spear great and long, and a great black horse covered with silk, and a black stone fast by.

CHAPTER VII

HOW BEAUMAINS FOUGHT WITH THE KNIGHT OF THE BLACK LAUNDES, AND FOUGHT WITH HIM TILL HE FELL DOWN AND DIED

THERE sat a knight all armed in black harness, and his name was the knight of the black land. Then the damosel, when she saw that knight, she bad him flee down that valley, for his horse was not saddled. Gramercy, said Beaumains, for always ye would have me a coward. With that the black knight, when she came nigh him, spake and said, Damosel, have ye brought this knight of King Arthur to be your champion? Nay, fair knight, said she, this is but a kitchen knave that was fed in King Arthur's kitchen for alms. Why cometh he, said the knight, in such array? it is shame that he beareth you company. Sir, I cannot be delivered of him, said she, for with me he rideth maugre mine head: God would that ye should put him from me, outher to slay him an ye may, for he is an unhappy knave, and unhappily he hath done this day: through mishap I saw him slay two knights at the passage of the water; and other deeds he did before right marvellous and through unhappiness. That marvelleth me, said the black knight, that any man that is of worship will have ado with him. They know him not, said the damosel, and for because he rideth with me, they ween that he be some man of worship born. That may be, said the black knight; howbeit as ye say that he be no man of worship, he is a full likely person, and full like to be a strong man: but thus much shall I grant you, said the black knight; I shall put him down upon one foot, and his horse and his harness he shall leave with me, for it were shame to me to do him any more harm. When Sir Beaumains heard him say thus, he said, Sir knight, thou art full large of my horse and my harness; I let thee wit it cost thee nought, and whether it liketh thee or not, this launde will I pass maugre thine head. And horse nor harness gettest thou none of mine, but if thou win them with thy hands; and therefore let see what thou canst do. Sayest thou that? said the black knight, now yield thy lady from thee, for it beseemeth never a kitchen page to ride with such a lady. Thou liest, said Beaumains, I am a gentleman born, and of more high lineage than thou, and that will I prove on thy body. Then in great wrath they departed with their horses, and came together as it had been the thunder, and the black knight's spear brake, and Beaumains thrust him through both his sides, and therewith his spear brake, and the truncheon left still in his side. But nevertheless the black knight drew his sword, and smote many eager strokes, and of great might, and hurt Beaumains full sore. But at the last the black knight, within an hour and an half, he fell down off his horse in swoon, and there he died. And when Beaumains saw him so well horsed and armed, then he alit down and armed him in his armour, and so took his horse and rode after the damosel. When she saw him come nigh, she said, Away, kitchen knave, out of the wind, for the smell of thy bawdy clothes grieveth me. Alas, she said, that ever such a knave should by mishap slay so good a knight as thou hast done, but all this is thine unhappiness. But here by is one shall pay thee all thy payment, and therfore yet I counsel thee, flee. It may happen me, said Beaumains, to be beaten or slain, but I warn you, fair damosel, I will not flee away, nor leave your company, for all that ye can say; for ever ye say that they will kill me or beat me, but howsomever it happeneth I escape, and they lie on the ground. And therefore it were as good for you to hold you still thus all day rebuking me, for away will I not till I see the uttermost of this journey, or else I will be slain, outher truly beaten; therefore ride on your way, for follow you I will whatsomever happen.

CHAPTER VIII

HOW THE BROTHER OF THE KNIGHT THAT WAS SLAIN MET WITH
BEAUMAINS, AND FOUGHT WITH BEAUMAINS TILL HE WAS
YIELDEN

THUS as they rode together, they saw a knight come driving by them all in green, both his horse and his harness; and when he came nigh the damosel, he asked her, Is that my brother the black knight that ye have brought with you? Nay, nay, she said, this unhappy kitchen knave hath slain your brother through unhappiness. Alas, said the green knight, that is great pity, that so noble a knight as he was should so unhaply be slain, and namely of a knave's hand, as ye say that he is. Ah! traitor, said the green knight, thou shalt die for slaying of my brother; he was a full noble knight, and his name was Sir Percard. I defy thee, said Beaumains, for I let thee wit I slew him knightly and not shamefully. Therewithal the green knight rode unto an horn that was green, and it hung upon a thorn, and there be blew three deadly motys, and there came two damosels and armed him lightly. And then he took a great horse, and a green shield and a green spear. And then they ran together with all their mights, and brake their spears unto their hands. And then they drew their swords, and gave many sad strokes, and either of them wounded other full ill. And at the last at an overthwart Beaumains with his horse struck the green knight's horse upon the side, that he fell to the earth. And then the green knight avoided his horse lightly, and dressed him upon foot. That saw Beaumains, and therewithal he alit, and they rushed together like two mighty kempys a long while, and sore they bled both. With that came the damosel, and said, My lord the green knight, why for shame stand ye so long fighting with the kitchen knave? Alas, it is shame that ever ye were made knight, to see such a lad to match such a knight, as the weed overgrew the corn. Therewith the green knight was ashamed, and therewithal he gave a great stroke of might, and clave his shield through. When Beaumains saw his shield cloven asunder he was a little ashamed of that stroke and of her language; and then he gave him such a buffet upon the helm that he fell on his knees. And so suddenly Beaumains pulled him upon the ground grovelling.

And then the green knight cried him mercy, and yielded him unto Sir Beaumains, and prayed him to slay him not. All is in vain, said Beaumains, for thou shalt die but if this damosel that came with me pray me to save thy life. And therewithal he unlaced his helm like as he would slay him. Fie upon thee, false kitchen page, I will never pray thee to save his life, for I will never be so much in thy danger. Then shall he die, said Beaumains. Not so hardy, thou bawdy knave, said the damosel, that thou slay him. Alas, said the green knight, suffer me not to die for a fair word may save me. Fair knight, said the green knight, save my life, and I will forgive thee the death of my brother, and for ever to become thy man, and thirty knights that hold of me for ever shall do you service. In the devil's name, said the damosel, that such a bawdy kitchen knave should have thee and thirty knights' service. Sir knight, said Beaumains, all this availeth thee not, but if my damosel speak with me for thy life. And therewithal he made a semblaunt to slay him. Let be, said the damosel, thou bawdy knave; slay him not, for an thou do thou shalt repent it. Damosel, said Beaumains, your charge is to me a pleasure, and at your commandment his life shall be saved, and else not. Then he said, Sir knight with the green arms, I release thee quit at this damosel's request, for I will not make her wroth, I will fulfil all that she chargeth me. And then the green knight kneeled down, and did him homage with his sword. Then said the damosel, Me repenteth, green knight, of your dommage, and of your brother's death, the black knight, for of your help I had great myster, for I dread me sore to pass this forest. Nay, dread you not, said the green knight, for ye shall lodge with me this night, and to-morn I shall help you through this forest. So they took their horses and rode to his manor, which was fast there beside.

CHAPTER IX

HOW THE DAMOSEL AGAIN REBUKED BEAUMAINS, AND WOULD NOT SUFFER HIM TO SIT AT HER TABLE, BUT CALLED HIM KITCHEN BOY

AND ever she rebuked Beaumains, and would not suffer him to sit at her table, but as the green knight took him and sat him at a side table. Marvel methinketh, said the green knight to the damosel, why ye rebuke this noble knight as ye do, for I warn you, damosel, he is a full noble knight, and I know no knight is able to match him; therefore ye do great wrong to rebuke him, for he shall do you right good service, for whatsomever he maketh himself, ye shall prove at the end that he is come of a noble blood and of king's lineage. Fie, fie, said the damosel, it is shame for you to say of him such worship. Truly, said the green knight, it were shame for me to say of him any disworship, for he hath proved himself a better knight than I am, yet have I met with many knights in my days, and never or this time have I found no knight his match. And so that night they yede unto rest, and all that night the green knight commanded thirty knights privily to watch Beaumains, for to keep him from all treason. And so on the morn they all arose, and heard their mass and brake their fast; and then they took their horses and rode on their way, and the green knight conveyed them through the forest; and there the green knight said, My lord Beaumains, I and these thirty knights shall be always at your summons, both early and late, at your calling and whither that ever ye will send us. It is well said, said Beaumains; when that I call upon you ye must yield you unto King Arthur, and all your knights. If that ye so command us, we shall be ready at all times, said the green knight. Fie, fie upon thee, in the devil's name, said the damosel, that any good knights should be obedient unto a kitchen knave. So then departed the green knight and the damosel. And then she said unto Beaumains, Why followest thou me, thou kitchen boy? Cast away thy shield and thy spear, and flee away; yet I counsel thee betimes or thou shalt say right soon, alas; for wert thou as wight as ever was Wade or Launcelot, Tristram, or the good knight Sir Lamorak, thou shalt not pass a pass here that is called the Pass Perilous. Damosel, said Beaumains, who is afeared let him flee, for it were shame to turn again sythen I have ridden so long with you. Well, said the damosel, ye shall soon, whether ye will or not.

CHAPTER X

So within a while they saw a tower as white as any snow, well matchecold all about, and double dyked. And over the tower gate there hung a fifty shields of divers colours, and under that tower there was a fair meadow. And therein were many knights and squires to behold, scaffolds and pavilions; for there upon the morn should be a great tournament: and the lord of the tower was in his castle and looked out at a window, and saw a damosel, a dwarf, and a knight armed at all points. So God me help, said the lord, with that knight will I joust, for I see that he is a knight-errant. And so he armed him and horsed him hastily. And when he was on horseback with his shield and his spear, it was all red both his horse and his harness, and all that to him longeth. And when that he came nigh him he weened it had been his brother the black knight; and then he cried aloud, Brother, what do ye in these marches? Nay, nay, said the damosel, it is not he; this is but a kitchen knave that was brought up for alms in King Arthur's court. Nevertheless, said the Red Knight, I will speak with him or he depart. Ah, said the damosel, this knave hath killed thy brother, and Sir Kay named him Beaumains, and this horse and this harness was thy brother's, the black knight. Also I saw thy brother the green knight overcome of his hands. Now may ye be revenged upon him, for I may never be quit of him. With this either knights departed in sunder, and they came together with all their might, and either of their horses fell to the earth, and they avoided their horses, and put their shields afore them and drew their swords, and either gave other sad strokes, now here, now there, racynge, tracynge, foining, and hurling like two boars, the space of two hours. And then she cried on high to the red knight, Alas, thou noble red knight, think what worship hath followed thee, let never a kitchen knave endure thee so long as he doth. Then the red knight waxed wroth and doubled his strokes, and hurt Beaumains wonderly sore, that the blood ran down to the ground, that it was wonder to see that strong battle. Yet at the last Sir Beaumains struck him to the earth, and as he would have slain the red knight, he cried mercy, saying, Noble knight, slay me not, and I shall yield me to thee with fifty knights with me that be at my commandment. And I forgive thee all the despite that thou hast done to me, and the death of my brother the black knight. All this availeth not, said Beaumains, but if my damosel pray me to save thy life. And therewith he made semblaunt to strike off his head. Let be, thou Beaumains, slay him not, for he is a noble knight, and not so hardy upon thine head but thou save him. Then Beaumains bad the red knight, Stand up, and thank the damosel now of thy life. Then the red knight prayed him to see his castle, and to be there all night. So the damosel then granted him, and there they had merry cheer. But always the damosel spake many foul words unto Beaumains, whereof the red knight had great marvel; and all that night the red knight made three score knights to watch Beaumains, that he should have no shame nor villainy. And upon the morn they heard mass and dined, and the red knight came before Beaumains with his three score knights, and there he proffered him his homage and fealty at all times, he and his knights to do him service. I thank you, said Beaumains, but this ye shall grant me : when I call upon you, to come afore my lord King Arthur, and yield you unto him to be his knights. Sir, said the red knight, I will be ready and my fellowship at your summons. So Sir Beaumains departed and the damosel, and ever she rode chiding him in the foulest manner.

CHAPTER XI

HOW SIR BEAUMAINS SUFFERED GREAT REBUKES OF THE DAMOSEL, AND HE SUFFERED IT PATIENTLY

DAMOSEL, said Beaumains, ye are uncourteous so to rebuke me as ye do, for meseemeth I have done you good service, and ever ye threaten me I shall be beaten with knights that we meet, but ever for all your boast they lie in the dust or in the mire, and therefore I pray you rebuke me no more ; and when ye see me beaten or yielden as recreant, then may ye bid me go from you shamefully ; but first I let you wit I will not depart from you, for I were worse than a fool an I would depart from you all the while that I win worship. Well, said she, right soon there shall meet a knight shall pay thee all thy wages, for he is the most man of worship of the world, except King Arthur. I will well, said Beaumains, the more he is of worship, the more shall be my worship to have ado with him. Then anon they were ware where was afore them a city rich and fair. And betwixt them and the city a mile and an half there was a fair meadow that seemed new mown, and therein were many pavilions fair to behold. Lo, said the damosel, yonder is a lord that owneth yonder city, and his custom is when the weather is fair to lie in this meadow to joust and tourney. And ever there be about him five hundred knights and gentlemen of arms, and there be all manner of games that any gentleman can devise. That goodly lord, said Beaumains, would I fain see. Thou shalt see him time enough, said the damosel, and so as she rode near she espied the pavilion where he was. Lo, said she, seest thou yonder pavilion that is all of the colour of Inde, and all manner of thing that there is about, men and women, and horses trapped, shields and spears were all of the colour of Inde, and his name is Sir Persant of Inde, the most lordliest knight that ever thou lookedst on. It may well be, said Beaumains, but be he never so stout a knight, in this field I shall abide till that I see him under his shield. Ah, fool, said she, thou wert better flee betimes. Why, said Beaumains, an he be such a knight as ye make him, he will not set upon me with all his men, or with his five hundred knights. For an there come no more but one at once, I shall him not fail whilst my life lasteth. Fie, fie, said the damosel, that ever such a stinking knave should blow such a boast. Damosel, he said, ye are to blame so to rebuke me, for I had lever do five battles than so to be rebuked, let him come and then let him do his worst. Sir, she said, I marvel what thou art and of what kin thou art come ; boldly thou speakest, and boldly thou hast done, that have I seen ; therefore I pray thee save thyself an thou mayest, for thy horse and thou have had great travail, and I dread we dwell over long from the siege, for it is but hence seven mile, and all perilous passages we are passed save all only this passage ; and here I dread me sore lest ye shall catch some hurt, therefore I would ye were hence, that ye were not bruised nor hurt with this strong knight. But I let you wit that Sir Persant of Inde is nothing of might nor strength unto the knight that laid the siege about my lady. As for that, said Sir Beaumains, be it as it be may. For sythen I am come so nigh this knight I will prove his might or I depart from him, and else I shall be shamed an I now withdraw me from him. And therefore, damosel, have ye no doubt by the grace of God I shall so deal with this knight that within two hours after noon I shall deliver him. And then shall we come to the siege by daylight. O Jesu, marvel have I, said the damosel, what manner a man ye be, for it may never be otherwise but that ye be come of a noble blood, for so foul nor shamefully did never woman rule a knight as I have done you, and ever courteously ye have suffered me, and that came never but of a gentle blood. Damosel, said Beaumains, a knight may little do that may not suffer a damosel, for whatsomever ye said unto me I took none heed to your words, for the more ye said the more ye angered me, and my wrath I wreaked upon them that I had ado withal. And therefore all the missaying that ye missaid me furthered me in my battle, and caused me to think to show and prove myself at the end what I was; for peradventure though I had meat in King Arthur's kitchen, yet I might have had meat enough in other places, but all that I did it for to prove and assay my friends, and that shall be known another day; and whether that I be a gentleman born or none, I let you wit, fair damosel, I have done you gentleman's service, and peradventure better service yet will I do or I depart from you. Alas, she said, fair Beaumains, forgive me all that I have missaid or done against thee. With all my heart, said he, I forgive it you, for ye did nothing but as ye should do, for all your evil words pleased me; and damosel, said Beaumains, syne it liketh you to say thus fair unto me, wit ye well it gladdeth my heart greatly, and now meseemeth there is no knight living but I am able enough for him.

CHAPTER XII

HOW BEAUMAINS FOUGHT WITH SIR PERSANT OF INDE, AND MADE HIM TO BE YIELDEN

WITH this Sir Persant of Inde had espied them as they hoved in the field, and knightly he sent to them whether he came in war or in peace. Say to thy lord, said Beaumains,

I take no force, but whether as him list himself. So the messenger went again unto Sir Persant and told him all his answer. Well then will I have ado with him to the utterance, and so he purveyed him and rode against him. And Beaumains saw him and made him ready, and there they met with all that ever their horses might run, and brast their spears either in three pieces, and their horses rushed so together that both their horses fell dead to the earth; and lightly they avoided their horses and put their shields afore them, and drew their swords, and gave many great strokes that sometime they hurtled together that they fell grovelling on the ground. Thus they fought two hours and more, that their shields and their hauberks were all forhewen, and in many stedys they were wounded. So at the last Sir Beaumains smote him through the cost of the body, and then he retrayed him here and there, and knightly maintained his battle long time. And at the last, though him loath were, Beaumains smote Sir Persant above upon the helm, that he fell grovelling to the earth; and then he leapt upon him overthwart and unlaced his helm to have slain him. Then Sir Persant yielded him and asked him mercy. With that came the damosel and prayed to save his life. I will well, for it were pity this noble knight should die. Gramercy, said Persant, gentle knight and damosel. For certainly now I wot well it was ye that slew my brother the black knight at the black thorn; he was a full noble knight, his name was Sir Percard. Also I am sure that ye are he that won mine other brother the green knight, his name was Sir Pertolepe. Also ye won my brother the red knight, Sir Perimones. And now syne ye have won these, this shall I do for to please you: ye shall have homage and fealty of me, and an hundred knights to be always at your commandment, to go and ride where ye will command us. And so they went unto Sir Persant's pavilion and drank the wine, and ate spices, and afterward Sir Persant made him to rest upon a bed until supper time, and after supper to bed again. When Beaumains was abed, Sir Persant had a lady, a fair daughter of eighteen year of age, and there he called her unto him, and charged her and commanded her upon his blessing to go unto the knight's bed, and lie down by his side, and make him no strange cheer, but good cheer, and take him in thine arms and kiss him, and look that this be done, I charge you, as ye will have my love and my good will. So Sir Persant's daughter did as her father bad her, and so she went unto Sir Beaumains' bed, and privily she dispoiled her, and laid her down by him, and then he awoke and saw her, and asked her what she was. Sir, she said, I am Sir Persant's daughter, that by the commandment of my father am come hither. Be ye a maid or a wife? said he. Sir, she said, I am a clene maiden. God defend, said he, that I should defoil you to do Sir Persant such a shame; therefore, fair damosel, arise out of this bed or else I will. Sir, she said, I came not to you by mine own will, but as I was commanded. Alas, said Sir Beaumains, I were a shameful knight an I would do your father any disworship; and so he kissed her, and so she departed and came unto Sir Persant her father, and told him all how she had sped. Truly, said Sir Persant, whatsomever he be, he is come of a noble blood. And so we leave them there till on the morn.

CHAPTER XIII

OF THE GOODLY COMMUNICATION BETWEEN SIR PERSANT AND BEAUMAINS, AND HOW HE TOLD HIM THAT HIS NAME WAS SIR GARETH

AND SO on the morn the damosel and Sir Beaumains heard mass and brake their fast, and so took their leave. Fair damosel, said Persant, whitherward are ye way-leading this knight? Sir, she said, this knight is going to the siege that besiegeth my sister in the Castle Dangerous. Ah, ah, said Persant, that is the Knight of the Red Launde, the which is the most perilous knight that I know now living, and a man that is without mercy, and men say that he hath seven men's strength. God save you, said he to Beaumains, from that knight, for he doth great wrong to that lady, and that is great pity, for she is one of the fairest ladies of the world, and meseemeth that your damosel is her sister: is not your name Linet? said he. Yea, sir, said she, and my lady my sister's name is Dame Lionesse. Now shall I tell you, said Sir Persant, this Red Knight of the Red Launde hath lain long at the siege, well-nigh this two years, and many times he might have had her an he had would, but he pro-longeth the time to this intent, for to have Sir Launcelot du Lake to do battle with him, or Sir Tristram, or Sir Lamorak de Galis, or Sir Gawaine, and this is his tarrying so long at the siege. Now my lord Sir Persant of Inde, said the damosel Linet, I require you that ye will make this gentleman knight or ever he fight with the red knight. I will with all my heart, said Sir Persant, an it please him to take the order of knighthood of so simple a man as I am. Sir, said Beaumains, I thank you for your good will, for I am better sped, for certainly the noble knight Sir Launcelot made me knight. Ah, said Sir Persant, of a more renowned knight might ye not be made knight; for of all knights he may be called chief of knighthood; and so all the world saith, that betwixt three knights is departed clearly knighthood, that is Launcelot du Lake, Sir Tristram de Liones, and Sir Lamorak de Galis : these bear now the renown. There be many other knights, as Sir Palamides the Saracen and Sir Sasere his brother; also Sir Bleoberis and Sir Blamore de Ganis his brother ; also Sir Bors de Ganis and Sir Ector de Maris and Sir Percivale de Galis ; these and many more be noble knights, but there be none that pass that four above said ; therefore God speed you well, said Sir Persant, for an ye may match the red knight ye shall be called the fourth of the world. Sir, said Beaumains, I would fain be of good fame and of knighthood. And I let you wit I came of good men, for I dare say my father was a noble man, and so that ye will keep it in close, and this damosel, I will tell you of what kin I am. We will not discover you, said they both, till ye command us, by the faith we owe unto God. Truly then, said he, my name is Gareth of Orkney, and King Lot was my father, and my mother is King Arthur's sister, her name is Dame Morgawse, and Sir Gawaine is my brother, and Sir Agravaine and Sir Gaheris, and I am the youngest of them all. And yet wot not King Arthur nor Sir Gawaine what I am.

CHAPTER XIV

HOW THE LADY THAT WAS BESIEGED HAD WORD FROM HER SISTER HOW SHE HAD BROUGHT A KNIGHT TO FIGHT FOR HER, AND WHAT BATTLES HE HAD ACHIEVED

So the book saith that the lady that was besieged had word of her sister's coming by the dwarf, and a knight with her, and how he had passed all the perilous passages. What manner a man is he ? said the lady. He is a noble knight truly, madam, said the dwarf, and but a young man, but he is as likely a man as ever ye saw any. What is he? said the damosel, and of what kin is he come, and of whom was he made knight? Madam, said the dwarf, he is the king's son of Orkney, but his name I will not tell you as at this time; but wit ye well, of Sir Launcelot was he made knight, for of none other would he be made knight, and Sir Kay named him Beaumains. How escaped he, said the lady, from the brethren of Persant? Madam, he said, as a noble knight should. First, he slew two brethren at a passage of a water. Ah! said she, they were good knights, but they were murderers, the one hight Gherard de Breuse, and the other knight hight Sir Arnold de Breuse. Then, madam, he recountered with the black knight, and slew him in plain battle, and so he took his horse and his armour and fought with the green knight and won him in plain battle, and in like wise he served the red knight, and after in the same wise he served the blue knight and won him in plain battle. Then, said the lady, he hath overcome Sir Persant of Inde, one of the noblest knights of the world, and the dwarf said, He hath won all the four brethren and slain the black knight, and yet he did more tofore: he overthrew Sir Kay and left him nigh dead upon the ground; also he did a great battle with Sir Launcelot, and there they departed on even hands: and then Sir Launcelot made him knight. Dwarf, said the lady, I am glad of these tidings, therefore go thou in an hermitage of mine hereby, and there shalt thou bear with thee of my wine in two flagons of silver, they are of two gallons, and also two cast of bread with fat venison baked, and dainty fowls; and a cup of gold here I deliver thee, that is rich and precious; and bear all this to mine hermitage, and put it in the hermit's hands. And sythen go thou unto my sister and greet her well, and commend me unto that gentle knight, and pray him to eat and to drink and make him strong, and say ye him I thank him of his courtesy and goodness, that he would take upon him such labour for me that never did him bounte nor courtesy. Also pray him that he be of good heart and courage, for he shall meet with a full noble knight, but he is neither of bounte, courtesy, nor gentleness; for he attendeth unto nothing but to murder, and that is the cause I cannot praise him nor love him. So this dwarf departed, and came to Sir Persant, where he found the damosel Linet and Sir Beaumains, and there he told them all as ye have heard ; and then they took their leave, but Sir Persant took an ambling hackney and conveyed them on their ways, and then beleft them to God ; and so within a little while they came to that hermitage, and there they drank the wine, and ate the venison and the fowls baken. And so when they had repasted them well, the dwarf returned again with his vessel unto the castle again ; and there met with him the red knight of the red launstes, and asked him from whence that he came, and where he had been. Sir, said the dwarf, I have been with my lady's sister of this castle, and she hath been at King Arthur's court, and brought a knight with her. Then I account her travail but lost ; for though she had brought with her Sir Launcelot, Sir Tristram, Sir Lamorak, or Sir Gawaine, I would think myself good enough for them all. It may well be, said the dwarf, but this knight hath passed all the perilous passages, and slain the black knight and other two more, and won the green knight, the red knight, and the blue knight. Then is he one of these four that I have afore rehearsed. He is none of those, said the dwarf, but he is a king's son. What is his name ? said the red knight of the red launstes. That will I not tell you, said the dwarf, but Sir Kay upon scorn named him Beaumains. I care not, said the knight, what knight so ever he be, for I shall soon deliver him. And if I ever match him he shall have a shameful death as many other have had. That were pity, said the dwarf, and it is marvel that ye make such shameful war upon noble knights.

CHAPTER XV

Now leave we the knight and the dwarf, and speak we of Beaumains, that all night lay in the hermitage ; and upon the morn he and the damosel Linet heard their mass and brake their fast. And then they took their horses and rode throughout a fair forest ; and then they came to a plain, and saw where were many pavilions and tents, and a fair castle, and there was much smoke and great noise ; and when they

came near the siege Sir Beaumains espied upon great trees,
as he rode, how there hung full goodly armed knights by the
neck, and their shields about their necks with their swords,
and gilt spurs upon their heels, and so there hung nigh a forty
knights shamefully with full rich arms. Then Sir Beaumains
abated his countenance and said, What meaneth this? Fair
sir, said the damosel, abate not your cheer for all this sight,
for ye must courage yourself, or else ye be all shente, for all
these knights came hither to this siege to rescue my sister
Dame Liones, and when the red knight of the red laundes
had overcome them, he put them to this shameful death
without mercy and pity. And in the same wise he will serve
you but if you quit you the better. Now Jesu defend me,
said Beaumains, from such a villainous death and shenship
of arms. For rather than I should so be faren withal, I
would rather be slain manly in plain battle. So were ye
better, said the damosel; for trust not, in him is no courtesy,
but all goeth to the death or shameful murder, and that is
pity, for he is a full likely man, well made of body, and a full
noble knight of prowess, and a lord of great lands and posses-
sions. Truly, said Beaumains, he may well be a good knight,
but he useth shameful customs, and it is marvel that he
endureth so long that none of the noble knights of my lord
Arthur's have not dealt with him. And then they rode to the
dykes, and saw them double dyked with full warlike walls;
and there were lodged many great lords nigh the walls; and
there was great noise of minstrelsy; and the sea beat upon
the one side of the walls, where were many ships and mariners'
noise with 'hale and how.' And also there was fast by a
sycamore tree, and there hung an horn, the greatest that ever
they saw, of an elephant's bone; and this Knight of the Red
Laundes had hanged it up there, that if there came any
errant-knight, he must blow that horn, and then will he make
him ready and come to him to do battle. But, sir, I pray
you, said the damosel Linet, blow ye not the horn till it be
high noon, for now it is about prime, and now increaseth his
might, that as men say he hath seven men's strength. Ah,
fie for shame, fair damosel, say ye never so more to me; for,
an he were as good a knight as ever was, I shall never fail
him in his most might, for either I will win worship worshipfully, or die knightly in the field. And therewith he spurred
his horse straight to the sycamore tree, and blew so the horn
eagerly that all the siege and the castle rang thereof. And

then there leapt out knights out of their tents and pavilions, and they within the castle looked over the walls and out at windows. Then the red knight of the red laundes armed him hastily, and two barons set on his spurs upon his heels, and all was blood red, his armour, spear and shield. And an earl buckled his helm upon his head, and then they brought him a red spear and a red steed, and so he rode into a little vale under the castle, that all that were in the castle and at the siege might behold the battle.

CHAPTER XVI

HOW THE TWO KNIGHTS MET TOGETHER, AND OF THEIR TALKING, AND HOW THEY BEGAN THEIR BATTLE

Sir, said the damosel Linet unto Sir Beaumains, look ye be glad and light, for yonder is your deadly enemy, and at yonder window is my lady, my sister, Dame Liones. Where? said Beaumains. Yonder, said the damosel, and pointed with her finger. That is truth, said Beaumains. She beseemeth afar the fairest lady that ever I looked upon ; and truly, he said, I ask no better quarrel than now for to do battle, for truly she shall be my lady, and for her I will fight. And ever he looked up to the window with glad countenance. And the Lady Liones made curtsey to him down to the earth, with holding up both [their] hands. With that the red knight of the red laundes called to Sir Beaumains, Leave, sir knight, thy looking, and behold me, I counsel thee ; for I warn thee well she is my lady, and for her I have done many strong battles. If thou have so done, said Beaumains, meseemeth it was but waste labour, for she loveth none of thy fellowship, and thou to love that loveth not thee is but great folly. For an I understood that she were not glad of my coming, I would be advised or I did battle for her. But I understand by the besieging of this castle she may forbear thy fellowship. And therefore wit thou well, thou red knight of the red laundes, I love her, and will rescue her, or else to die. Sayest thou that? said the red knight, meseemeth thou ought of reason to be ware by yonder knights that thou sawest hang upon yonder trees. Fie for shame, said Beaumains, that ever thou shouldest say or do so evil, for in that thou shamest thyself and knight-

hood, and thou mayest be sure there will no lady love thee
that knoweth thy wicked customs. And now thou weenest
that the sight of these hanged knights should fear me. Nay
truly, not so; that shameful sight causeth me to have
courage and hardiness against thee, more than I would have
had against thee an thou wert a well-ruled knight. Make
thee ready, said the red knight of the red laundes, and talk
no longer with me. Then Sir Beaumains bade the damosel
go from him; and then they put their spears in their rests,
and came together with all their might that they had both,
and either smote other in middes of their shields that the
paytrellys, surcingles, and cruppers brast, and fell to the
earth both, and the reins of their bridles in their hands;
and so they lay a great while sore astoned, that all that were
in the castle and in the siege weened their necks had been
broken; and then many a stranger and other said the
strange knight was a big man, and a noble jouster, for or
now we saw never no knight match the red knight of the
red laundes: thus they said both within the castle and
without. Then lightly they avoided their horses and put
their shields afore them, and drew their swords and ran
together like two fierce lions, and either gave other such
buffets upon their helms that they reeled backward both
two strides; and then they recovered both, and hewed great
pieces off their harness and their shields that a great part
fell into the fields.

CHAPTER XVII

HOW AFTER LONG FIGHTING BEAUMAINS OVERCAME THE KNIGHT
AND WOULD HAVE SLAIN HIM, BUT AT THE REQUEST OF THE
LORDS HE SAVED HIS LIFE, AND MADE HIM TO YIELD HIM TO
THE LADY

AND then thus they fought till it was past noon, and
never would stint, till at the last they lacked wind both;
and then they stood wagging and scattering, panting, blowing
and bleeding, that all that beheld them for the most part
wept for pity. So when they had rested them a while they
yede to battle again, tracyng, racyng, foynyng as two boars.
And at some time they took their run as it had been two
rams, and hurtled together that sometime they fell grovelling

to the earth : and at sometime they were so amazed that either took other's sword instead of his own. Thus they endured till evensong time, that there was none that beheld them might know whether was like to win the battle ; and their armour was so forhewen that men might see their naked sides ; and in other places they were naked, but ever the naked places they did defend. And the red knight was a wily knight of war, and his wily fighting taught Sir Beaumains to be wise ; but he abought it full sore or he did espy his fighting. And thus by assent of them both they granted either other to rest ; and so they set them down upon two mole-hills there beside the fighting place, and either of them unlaced his helm, and took the cold wind ; for either of their pages was fast by them, to come when they called to unlace their harness and to set them on again at their commandment. And then when Sir Beaumains' helm was off, he looked up to the window, and there he saw the fair lady Dame Liones, and she made him such countenance that his heart waxed light and jolly ; and therewith he bad the red knight of the red laundes make him ready, and let us do the battle to the utterance. I will well, said the knight, and then they laced up their helms, and their pages avoided, and they stepped together and fought freshly ; but the red knight of the red laundes awaited him, and at an overthwart smote him within the hand, that his sword fell out of his hand ; and yet he gave him another buffet upon the helm that he fell grovelling to the earth, and the red knight fell over him, for to hold him down. Then cried the maiden Linet on high : O Sir Beaumains, where is thy courage become ? Alas, my lady my sister beholdeth thee, and she sobbeth and weepeth, that maketh mine heart heavy. When Sir Beaumains heard her say so, he abrayed up with a great might and gat him upon his feet, and lightly he leapt to his sword and gripped it in his hand, and doubled his pace unto the red knight, and there they fought a new battle together. But Sir Beaumains then doubled his strokes, and smote so thick that he smote the sword out of his hand, and then he smote him upon the helm that he fell to the earth, and Sir Beaumains fell upon him, and unlaced his helm to have slain him ; and then he yielded him and asked mercy, and said with a loud voice : O noble knight, I yield me to thy mercy. Then Sir Beaumains bethought him upon the knights that he had made to be hanged shamefully, and then he said : I may not with my worship save thy life, for the shameful deaths that thou hast caused many full good knights to die. Sir, said the red knight of the red laundes, hold your hand and ye shall know the causes why I put them to so shameful a death. Say on, said Sir Beaumains. Sir, I loved once a lady, a fair damosel, and she had her brother slain ; and she said it was Sir Launcelot du Lake, or else Sir Gawaine ; and she prayed me as that I loved her heartily, that I would make her a promise by the faith of my knighthood, for to labour daily in arms unto I met with one of them ; and all that I might overcome I should put them unto a villainous death ; and this is the cause that I have put all these knights to death, and so I ensured her to do all the villainy unto King Arthur's knights, and that I should take vengeance upon all these knights. And, sir, now I will thee tell that every day my strength increaseth till noon, and all this time have I seven men's strength.

CHAPTER XVIII

HOW THE KNIGHT YIELDED HIM, AND HOW BEAUMAINS MADE HIM TO GO UNTO KING ARTHUR'S COURT, AND TO CRY SIR LAUNCELOT MERCY

THEN came there many earls, and barons, and noble knights, and prayed that knight to save his life, and take him to your prisoner. And all they fell upon their knees, and prayed him of mercy, and that he would save his life ; and, Sir, they all said, it were fairer of him to take homage and fealty, and let him hold his lands of you than for to slay him ; by his death ye shall have none advantage, and his misdeeds that be done may not be undone ; and therefore he shall make amends to all parties, and we all will become your men and do you homage and fealty. Fair lords, said Beaumains, wit you well I am full loath to slay this knight, nevertheless he hath done passing ill and shamefully ; but insomuch all that he did was at a lady's request I blame him the less ; and so for your sake I will release him that he shall have his life upon this covenant, that he go within the castle, and yield him there to the lady, and if she will forgive and quit him, I will well ; with this he make her amends of

all the trespass he hath done against her and her lands.
And also, when that is done, that ye go unto the court of
King Arthur, and there that ye ask Sir Launcelot mercy,
and Sir Gawaine, for the evil will ye have had against them.
Sir, said the red knight of the red laundes, all this will I do
as ye command, and syker assurance and borowes ye shall
have. And so then when the assurance was made, he made
his homage and fealty, and all those earls and barons with
him. And then the maiden Linet came to Sir Beaumains,
and unarmed him and searched his wounds, and stinted his
blood, and in likewise she did to the red knight of the red
laundes. And there they sojourned ten days in their tents;
and the red knight made his lords and servants to do all the
pleasure that they might unto Sir Beaumains. And so
within a while the red knight of the red laundes yede unto
the castle, and put him in her grace. And so she received
him upon sufficient surety, so all her hurts were well restored
of all that she could complain. And then he departed unto
the court of King Arthur, and there openly the red knight
of the red laundes put him in the mercy of Sir Launcelot
and Sir Gawaine, and there he told openly how he was overcome and by whom, and also he told all the battles from
the beginning unto the ending. Jesu mercy, said King
Arthur and Sir Gawaine, we marvel much of what blood he
is come, for he is a noble knight. Have ye no marvel, said
Sir Launcelot, for ye shall right well wit that he is come of a
full noble blood; and as for his might and hardiness, there
be but few now living that is so mighty as he is, and so
noble of prowess. It seemeth by you, said King Arthur,
that ye know his name, and from whence he is come, and of
what blood he is. I suppose I do so, said Launcelot, or
else I would not have given him the order of knighthood;
but he gave me such charge at that time that I should never
discover him until he required me, or else it be known
openly by some other.

CHAPTER XIX

Now turn we unto Sir Beaumains that desired of Linet that he might see her sister, his lady. Sir, she said, I would fain ye saw her. Then Sir Beaumains all armed him, and took his horse and his spear, and rode straight unto the castle. And when he came to the gate he found there many men armed, and pulled up the drawbridge and drew the port close. Then marvelled he why they would not suffer him to enter. And then he looked up to the window; and there he saw the fair Liones that said on high: Go thy way, Sir Beaumains, for as yet thou shalt not have wholly my love, unto the time that thou be called one of the number of the worthy knights. And therefore go labour in worship this twelvemonth, and then thou shalt hear new tidings. Alas, fair lady, said Beaumains, I have not deserved that ye should show me this strangeness, and I had weened that I should have right good cheer with you, and unto my power I have deserved thank, and well I am sure I have bought your love with part of the best blood within my body. Fair courteous knight, said Dame Liones, be not displeased nor over-hasty; for wit you well your great travail nor good love shall not be lost, for I consider your great travail and labour, your bounty and your goodness as me ought to do. And therefore go on your way, and look that ye be of good comfort, for all shall be for your worship and for the best, and perdy a twelvemonth will soon be done, and trust me, fair knight, I shall be true to you, and never to betray you, but to my death I shall love you and none other. And therewithal she turned her from the window, and Sir Beaumains rode awayward from the castle, making great dole, and so he rode here and there and wist not where he rode, till it was dark night. And then it happened him to come to a poor man's house, and there he was harboured all that night. But Sir Beaumains had no rest, but wallowed and writhed for the love of the lady of the castle. And so upon the morrow he took his horse and rode until underne, and then he came to a broad water, and thereby was a great lodge, and there he alit to sleep and laid his head upon the shield, and betook his horse to the dwarf, and commanded him to watch all night. Now turn we to the lady of the same castle, that thought much upon Beaumains, and then she called unto her Sir Gringamore her brother, and prayed him in all manner, as he loved her heartily, that he would ride after Sir Beaumains: And ever have ye wayte upon him till ye may find him sleeping, for I am sure in his heaviness he will alight down in some place, and lie him down to sleep; and therefore have ye your wayte upon him, and in the priviest manner ye can, take his dwarf, and go ye your way with him as fast as ever ye may or Sir Beaumains awake. For my sister Linet telleth me that he can tell of what kindred he is come, and what is his right name. And the meanwhile I and my sister will ride unto your castle to await when ye bring with you the dwarf. And then when ye have brought him unto your castle, I will have him in examination myself: unto the time that I know what is his right name, and of what kindred he is come, shall I never be merry at my heart. Sister, said Sir Gringamore, all this shall be done after your intent. And so he rode all the other day and the night till that he found Sir Beaumains lying by a water, and his head upon his shield, for to sleep. And then when he saw Sir Beaumains fast on sleep, he came stilly stalking behind the dwarf, and plucked him fast under his arm, and so he rode away with him as fast as ever he might unto his own castle. And this Sir Gringamore's arms were all black, and that to him longeth. But ever as he rode with the dwarf toward his castle, he cried unto his lord and prayed him of help. And therewith awoke Sir Beaumains, and up he leapt lightly, and saw where Sir Gringamore rode his way with the dwarf, and so Sir Gringamore rode out of his sight.

CHAPTER XX

HOW SIR BEAUMAINS RODE AFTER TO RESCUE HIS DWARF, AND CAME INTO THE CASTLE WHERE HE WAS

THEN Sir Beaumains put on his helm anon, and buckled his shield, and took his horse, and rode after him all that ever he might ride through marshes, and fields, and great dales, that many times his horse and he plunged over the head in deep mires, for he knew not the way, but took the gainest way in that woodness, that many times he was like to perish. And at the last him happened to come to a fair green way, and there he met with a poor man of the country, whom he saluted and asked him whether he met not with a knight upon a black horse and all black harness, a little dwarf sitting behind him with heavy cheer. Sir, said the poor man, here by me came Sir Gringamore the knight, with such a dwarf mourning as ye say ; and therefore I rede you not follow him, for he is one of the periloust knights of the world, and his castle is here nigh hand but two mile ; therefore we advise you ride not after Sir Gringamore, but if ye owe him good will. So leave we Sir Beaumains riding toward the castle, and speak we of Sir Gringamore and the dwarf. Anon as the dwarf was come to the castle, Dame Liones and Dame Linet her sister, asked the dwarf where was his master born, and of what lineage he was come. And but if thou tell me, said Dame Liones, thou shalt never escape this castle, but ever here to be prisoner. As for that, said the dwarf, I fear not greatly to tell his name and of what kin he is come. Wit you well he is a king's son, and his mother is sister to King Arthur, and he is brother to the good knight Sir Gawaine, and his name is Sir Gareth of Orkney. And now I have told you his right name, I pray you, fair lady, let me go to my lord again, for he will never out of this country until that he have me again. And if he be angry he will do much harm or that he be stint, and work you wrack in this country. As for that threatening, said Sir Gringamore, be it as it be may, we will go to dinner. And so they washed and went to meat, and made them merry and well at ease, and because the Lady Liones of the castle was there, they made great joy. Truly, madam, said Linet unto her sister, well may he be a king's son, for he hath many good tatches on him, for he is courteous and mild, and the most suffering man that ever I met withal. For I dare say there was never gentlewoman reviled man in so foul a manner as I have rebuked him ; and at all times he gave me goodly and meek answers again. And as they sat thus talking, there came Sir Gareth in at the gate with an angry countenance, and his sword drawn in his hand, and cried aloud that all the castle might hear it, saying : Thou traitor, Sir Gringamore, deliver me my dwarf again, or by the faith that I owe to the order of knighthood,

I shall do thee all the harm that I can. Then Sir Gringamore looked out at a window and said, Sir Gareth of Orkney, leave thy boasting words, for thou gettest not thy dwarf again. Thou coward knight, said Sir Gareth, bring him with thee, and come and do battle with me, and win him and take him. So will I do, said Sir Gringamore, an me list, but for all thy great words thou gettest him not. Ah! fair brother, said Dame Liones, I would he had his dwarf again, for I would he were not wroth, for now he hath told me all my desire I keep no more of the dwarf. And also, brother, he hath done much for me, and delivered me from the red knight of the red laundes, and therefore, brother, I owe him my service afore all knights living. And wit ye well that I love him before all other, and full fain I would speak with him. But in nowise I would that he wist what I were, but that I were another strange lady. Well, said Sir Gringamore, sythen I know now your will, I will obey now unto him. And right therewithal he went down unto Sir Gareth, and said : Sir, I cry you mercy, and all that I have misdone I will amend it at your will. And therefore I pray you that ye would alight, and take such cheer as I can make you in this castle. Shall I have my dwarf? said Sir Gareth. Yea, sir, and all the pleasaunce that I can make you, for as soon as your dwarf told me what ye were and of what blood ye are come, and what noble deeds ye have done in these marches, then I repented of my deeds. And then Sir Gareth alit, and there came his dwarf and took his horse. O my fellow, said Sir Gareth, I have had many adventures for thy sake. And so Sir Gringamore took him by the hand and led him into the hall where his own wife was.

CHAPTER XXI

HOW SIR GARETH, OTHERWISE CALLED BEAUMAINS, CAME TO THE PRESENCE OF HIS LADY, AND HOW THEY TOOK ACQUAINTANCE, AND OF THEIR LOVE

AND then came forth Dame Liones arrayed like a princess, and there she made him passing good cheer, and he her again; and they had goodly language and lovely countenance together. And Sir Gareth thought many times, Jesu, would that the lady of the Castle Perilous were so fair as she was. There were all manner of games and plays, of dancing and singing. And ever the more Sir Gareth beheld that lady, the more he loved her; and so he burned in love that he was past himself in his reason; and forth toward night they yede unto supper, and Sir Gareth might not eat, for his love was so hot that he wist not where he was. All these looks espied Sir Gringamore, and then at after-supper he called his sister Dame Liones into a chamber, and said: Fair sister, I have well espied your countenance betwixt you and this knight, and I will, sister, that ye wit he is a full noble knight, and if ye can make him to abide here I will do him all the pleasure that I can, for an ye were better than ye are, ye were well bywaryd upon him. Fair brother, said Dame Liones, I understand well that the knight is good, and come he is of a noble house. Notwithstanding, I will assay him better, howbeit I am most beholden to him of any earthly man; for he hath had great labour for my love, and passed many a dangerous passage. Right so Sir Gringamore went unto Sir Gareth, and said, Sir, make ye good cheer, for ye shall have none other cause, for this lady, my sister, is yours at all times, her worship saved, for wit ye well she loveth you as well as ye do her, and better if better may be. An I wist that, said Sir Gareth, there lived not a gladder man than I would be. Upon my worship, said Sir Gringamore, trust unto my promise; and as long as it liketh you ye shall sojourn with me, and this lady shall be with us daily and nightly to make you all the cheer that she can. I will well, said Sir Gareth, for I have promised to be nigh this country this twelvemonth. And well I am sure King Arthur and other noble knights will find me where that I am within this twelvemonth. For I shall be sought and found, if that I be on live. And then the noble knight Sir Gareth went unto the Dame Liones, which he then much loved, and kissed her many times, and either made great joy of other. And there she promised him her love certainly, to love him and none other the days of her life. Then this lady, Dame Liones, by the assent of her brother, told Sir Gareth all the truth what she was, and how she was the same lady that he did battle for, and how she was lady of the Castle Perilous, and there she told him how she caused her brother to take away his dwarf.

CHAPTER XXII

HOW AT NIGHT CAME AN ARMED KNIGHT, AND FOUGHT WITH SIR
GARETH, AND HE, SORE HURT IN THE THIGH, SMOTE OFF THE
KNIGHT'S HEAD

FOR this cause, to know the certainty what was your name, and of what kin ye were come. And then she let fetch tofore him Linet, the damosel that had ridden with him many wildsome ways. Then was Sir Gareth more gladder than he was tofore. And then they troth-plight each other to love, and never to fail whiles their life lasteth. And so they burnt both in love, that they were accorded to abate their lusts secretly. And there Dame Liones counselled Sir Gareth to sleep in none other place but in the hall. And there she promised him to come to his bed a little afore midnight. This counsel was not so privily kept but it was understood ; for they were but young both, and tender of age, and had not used none such crafts tofore. Wherefore the damosel Linet was a little displeased, and she thought her sister Dame Liones was a little over-hasty, that she might not abide the time of her marriage ; and for saving their worship, she thought to abate their hot lusts. And so she let ordain by her subtle crafts that they had not their intents neither with other, as in their delights, until they were married. And so it passed on. At after-supper was made clean avoidance, that every lord and lady should go unto his rest. But Sir Gareth said plainly he would go no farther than the hall, for in such places, he said, was convenient for an errant-knight to take his rest in ; and so there were ordained great couches, and thereon feather beds, and there laid him down to sleep ; and within a while came Dame Liones, wrapped in a mantle furred with ermine, and laid her down beside Sir Gareth. And therewithal he began to kiss her. And then he looked afore him, and there he perceived and saw come an armed knight, with many lights about him ; and this knight had a long gysarme in his hand, and made grim countenance to smite him. When Sir Gareth saw him come in that wise, he leapt out of his bed, and gat in his hand his sword, and leapt straight toward that knight. And when the knight saw Sir Gareth come so fiercely upon him, he smote him with a foyne through the thick of the thigh that the wound

was a shaftmon broad and had cut a-two many veins and
sinews. And therewithal Sir Gareth smote him upon the
helm such a buffet that he fell grovelling; and then he leapt
over him and unlaced his helm, and smote off his head from
the body. And then he bled so fast that he might not stand,
but so he laid him down upon his bed, and there he swooned
and lay as he had been dead. Then Dame Liones cried aloud,
that her brother Sir Gringamore heard, and came down.
And when he saw Sir Gareth so shamefully wounded he was sore
displeased, and said: I am shamed that this noble knight is
thus honoured. Sir, said Sir Gringamore, how may this be,
that ye be here, and this noble knight wounded? Brother,
she said, I can not tell you, for it was not done by me, nor
by mine assent. For he is my lord and I am his, and he
must be mine husband; therefore, my brother, I will that
ye wit I shame me not to be with him, nor to do him all the
pleasure that I can. Sister, said Sir Gringamore, and I will
that ye wit it, and Sir Gareth both, that it was never done by
me, nor by my assent that this unhappy deed was done. And
there they staunched his bleeding as well as they might, and
great sorrow made Sir Gringamore and Dame Liones. And
forthwithal came Dame Linet, and took up the head in the
sight of them all, and anointed it with an ointment thereas
it was smitten off; and in the same wise she did to the other
part thereas the head stuck, and then she set it together, and
it stuck as fast as ever it did. And the knight arose lightly
up, and the damosel Linet put him in her chamber. All this
saw Sir Gringamore and Dame Liones, and so did Sir Gareth;
and well he espied that it was the damosel Linet, that rode
with him through the perilous passages. Ah well, damosel,
said Sir Gareth, I weened ye would not have done as ye
have done. My lord Gareth, said Linet, all that I have
done I will avow, and all that I have done shall be for your
honour and worship, and to us all. And so within a while
Sir Gareth was nigh whole, and waxed light and jocund, and
sang, danced, and gamed; and he and Dame Liones were
so hot in burning love that they made their covenant at the
tenth night after, that she should come to his bed. And
by cause he was wounded afore, he laid his armour and his
sword nigh his bed's side.

CHAPTER XXIII

HOW THE SAID KNIGHT CAME AGAIN THE NEXT NIGHT AND WAS
BEHEADED AGAIN, AND HOW AT THE FEAST OF PENTECOST ALL
THE KNIGHTS THAT SIR GARETH HAD OVERCOME CAME AND
YIELDED THEM TO KING ARTHUR

RIGHT as she promised she came; and she was not so soon in his bed but she espied an armed knight coming toward the bed: therewithal she warned Sir Gareth, and lightly through the good help of Dame Liones he was armed; and they hurtled together with great ire and malice all about the hall; and there was great light as it had been the number of twenty torches both before and behind, so that Sir Gareth strained him, so that his old wound brast again on bleeding; but he was hot and courageous and took no keep, but with his great force he struck down that knight, and voided his helm, and struck off his head. Then he hewed the head in an hundred pieces. And when he had done so he took up all those pieces, and threw them out at a window into the ditches of the castle; and by this done he was so faint that unnethes he might stand for bleeding. And by when he was almost unarmed he fell in a deadly swoon on the floor; and then Dame Liones cried so that Sir Gringamore heard; and when he came and found Sir Gareth in that plight he made great sorrow; and there he awaked Sir Gareth, and gave him a drink that relieved him wonderly well; but the sorrow that Dame Liones made there may no tongue tell, for she so fared with herself as she would have died. Right so came this damosel Linet before them all, and she had fetched all the gobbets of the head that Sir Gareth had thrown out at a window, and there she anointed them as she had done tofore, and set them together again. Well, damosel Linet, said Sir Gareth, I have not deserved all this despite that ye do unto me. Sir knight, she said, I have nothing done but I will avow, and all that I have done shall be to your worship, and to us all. And then was Sir Gareth staunched of his bleeding. But the leeches said that there was no man that bare the life should heal him throughout of his wound but if they healed him that caused that stroke by enchantment. So leave we Sir Gareth there with Sir Gringamore and his sisters, and turn we unto King Arthur, that at the next feast of Pentecost held his feast;

and there came the Green Knight with fifty knights, and yielded them all unto King Arthur. And so there came the Red Knight his brother, and yielded him to King Arthur, and three score knights with him. Also there came the Blue Knight, brother to them, with an hundred knights, and yielded them unto King Arthur; and the Green Knight's name was Pertolepe, and the Red Knight's name was Perimones, and the Blue Knight's name was Sir Persant of Inde. These three brethren told King Arthur how they were overcome by a knight that a damosel had with her, and called him Beaumains. Jesu, said the king, I marvel what knight he is, and of what lineage he is come. He was with me a twelvemonth, and poorly and shamefully he was fostered, and Sir Kay in scorn named him Beaumains. So right as the king stood so talking with these three brethren, there came Sir Launcelot du Lake, and told the king that there was come a goodly lord with six hundred knights with him. Then the king went out of Carlion, for there was the feast, and there came to him this lord, and saluted the king in a goodly manner. What will ye, said King Arthur, and what is your errand? Sir, he said, my name is the red knight of the red laundes, but my name is Sir Ironside; and sir, wit ye well, here I am sent to you of a knight that is called Beaumains, for he won me in plain battle hand for hand, and so did never no knight but he, that ever had the better of me this thirty winter; the which commanded to yield me to you at your will. Ye are welcome, said the king, for ye have been long a great foe to me and my court, and now I trust to God I shall so entreat you that ye shall be my friend. Sir, both I and these five hundred knights shall always be at your summons to do you service as may lie in our powers. Jesu mercy, said King Arthur, I am much beholden unto that knight that hath put so his body in devoir to worship me and my court. And as to thee, Ironside, that are called the red knight of the red laundes, thou art called a perilous knight; and if thou wilt hold of me I shall worship thee and make thee knight of the Table Round; but then thou must be no more a murderer. Sir, as to that, I have promised unto Sir Beaumains never more to use such customs, for all the shameful customs that I used I did at the request of a lady that I loved; and therefore I must go unto Sir Launcelot, and unto Sir Gawaine, and ask them forgiveness of the evil will I had unto them; for all that I put to death was all only for the love of Sir Launcelot and of Sir Gawaine. They be here now, said the king, afore thee, now may ye say to them what ye will. And then he kneeled down unto Sir Launcelot, and to Sir Gawaine, and prayed them of forgiveness of his enmity that ever he had against them.

CHAPTER XXIV

HOW KING ARTHUR PARDONED THEM, AND DEMANDED OF THEM WHERE SIR GARETH WAS

THEN goodly they said all at once, God forgive you, and we do, and pray you that ye will tell us where we may find Sir Beaumains. Fair lords, said Sir Ironside, I cannot tell you, for it is full hard to find him; for such young knights as he is one, when they be in their adventures be never abiding in no place. But to say the worship that the red knight of the red laundes, and Sir Persant and his brother said of Beaumains, it was marvel to hear. Well, my fair lords, said King Arthur, wit you well I shall do you honour for the love of Sir Beaumains, and as soon as ever I meet with him I shall make you all upon one day knights of the Table Round. And as to thee, Sir Persant of Inde, thou hast been ever called a full noble knight, and so have ever been thy three brethren called. But I marvel, said the king, that I hear not of the Black Knight your brother, he was a full noble knight. Sir, said Pertolepe, the Green Knight, Sir Beaumains slew him in a recounter with his spear, his name was Sir Percard. That was great pity, said the king, and so said many knights. For these four brethren were full well known in the court of King Arthur for noble knights, for long time they had holden war against the knights of the Round Table. Then said Pertolepe, the Green Knight, to the king: At a passage of the water of Mortaise there encountered Sir Beaumains with two brethren that ever for the most part kept that passage, and they were two deadly knights, and there he slew the eldest brother in the water, and smote him upon the head such a buffet that he fell down in the water, and there he was drowned, and his name was Sir Gherard le Breusse; and after he slew the other brother upon the land, his name was Sir Arnold le Breusse.

CHAPTER XXV

HOW THE QUEEN OF ORKNEY CAME TO THIS FEAST OF PENTECOST, AND SIR GAWAINE AND HIS BRETHREN CAME TO ASK HER BLESSING

So then the king and they went to meat, and were served in the best manner. And as they sat at the meat, there came in the queen of Orkney, with ladies and knights a great number. And then Sir Gawaine, Sir Agravaine, and Gaheris arose, and went to her and saluted her upon their knees, and asked her blessing; for in fifteen year they had not seen her. Then she spake on high to her brother King Arthur: Where have ye done my young son Sir Gareth? He was here amongst you a twelvemonth, and ye made a kitchen knave of him, the which is shame to you all. Alas, where have ye done my dear son that was my joy and bliss? O dear mother, said Sir Gawaine, I knew him not. Nor I, said the king, that now me repenteth, but thanked be God he is proved a worshipful knight as any is now living of his years, and I shall never be glad till I may find him. Ah, brother, said the queen unto King Arthur, and unto Sir Gawaine, and to all her sons, ye did yourself great shame when ye amongst you kept my son in the kitchen and fed him like a poor hog. Fair sister, said King Arthur, ye shall right well wit I knew him not, nor no more did Sir Gawaine, nor his brethren; but sythen it is so, said the king, that he is thus gone from us all, we must shape a remedy to find him. Also, sister, meseemeth ye might have done me to wit of his coming, and then an I had not done well to him ye might have blamed me. For when he came to this court he came leaning upon two men's shoulders, as though he might not have gone. And then he asked me three gifts; and one he asked the same day, that was that I would give him meat enough that twelvemonth; and the other two gifts he asked that day a twelvemonth, and that was that he might have the adventure of the damosel Linet, and the third was that Sir Launcelot should make him knight when he desired him. And so I granted him all his desire, and many in this court marvelled that he desired his sustenance for a twelvemonth. And thereby, we deemed, many of us, that he was not come of a noble house. Sir, said the queen of Orkney unto King Arthur her brother, wit ye well that

I sent him unto you right well armed and horsed, and worshipfully bisene of his body, and gold and silver plenty to spend. It may be, said the King, but thereof saw we none, save that same day as he departed from us, knights told me that there came a dwarf hither suddenly, and brought him armour and a good horse full well and richly bisene ; and thereat we all had marvel from whence that riches came, that we deemed all that he was come of men of worship. Brother, said the queen, all that ye say I believe, for ever sithin he was grown he was marvellously witted, and ever he was faithful and true of his promise. But I marvel, said she, that Sir Kay did mock him and scorn him, and gave him that name Beaumains ; yet, Sir Kay, said the queen, named him more righteously than he weened ; for I dare say an he be on live, he is as fair an handed man and well disposed as any is living. Sir, said Arthur, let this language be still, and by the grace of God he shall be found an he be within this seven realms, and let all this pass and be merry, for he is proved to be a man of worship, and that is my joy.

CHAPTER XXVI

HOW KING ARTHUR SENT FOR THE LADY LIONES, AND HOW SHE LET CRY A TOURNEY AT HER CASTLE, WHEREAS CAME MANY KNIGHTS

THEN said Sir Gawaine and his brethren unto Arthur, Sir, an ye will give us leave, we will go and seek our brother. Nay, said Sir Launcelot, that shall ye not need ; and so said Sir Baudwin of Britain : for as by our advice the king shall send unto Dame Liones a messenger, and pray her that she will come to the court in all the haste that she may, and doubt ye not she will come ; and then she may give you best counsel where ye shall find him. This is well said of you, said the king. So then goodly letters were made, and the messenger sent forth, that night and day he went till he came unto the Castle Perilous. And then the lady Dame Liones was sent for thereas she was with Sir Gringamore her brother and Sir Gareth. And when she understood this message, she bad him ride on his way unto King Arthur, and she would come after in all goodly haste.

Then when she came to Sir Gringamore and to Sir Gareth, she told them all how King Arthur had sent for her. That is by cause of me, said Sir Gareth. Now advise me, said Dame Liones, what shall I say, and in what manner I shall rule me. My lady and my love, said Sir Gareth, I pray you in no wise be ye aknowen where I am; but well I wot my mother is there and all my brethren, and they will take upon them to seek me, I wot well that they do. But this, madam, I would ye said and advised the king when he questioned with you of me. Then may ye say, this is your advice that, an it like his good grace, ye will do make a cry against the feast of the Assumption of our Lady, that what knight there proveth him best he shall welde you and all your land. And if so be that he be a wedded man, that his wife shall have the degree, and a coronal of gold beset with stones of virtue to the value of a thousand pound, and a white gerfalcon. So Dame Liones departed and came to King Arthur, where she was nobly received, and there she was sore questioned of the king and of the Queen of Orkney. And she answered, where Sir Gareth was she could not tell. But thus much she said unto Arthur: Sir, I will let cry a tournament that shall be done before my castle at the Assumption of our Lady, and the cry shall be this: that you, my lord Arthur, shall be there, and your knights, and I will purvey that my knights shall be against yours; and then I am sure ye shall hear of Sir Gareth. This is well advised, said King Arthur; and so she departed. And the King and she made great provision to that tournament. When Dame Liones was come to the Isle of Avilion, that was the same isle thereas her brother Sir Gringamore dwelt, then she told them all how she had done, and what promise she had made to King Arthur. Alas, said Sir Gareth, I have been so wounded with unhappiness sythen I came into this castle that I shall not be able to do at that tournament like a knight; for I was never thoroughly whole syne I was hurt. Be ye of good cheer, said the damosel Linet, for I undertake within these fifteen days to make ye whole, and as lusty as ever ye were. And then she laid an ointment and a salve to him as it pleased to her, that he was never so fresh nor so lusty. Then said the damosel Linet: Send you unto Sir Persant of Inde, and summon him and his knights to be here with you as they have promised. Also, that ye send unto Sir Ironside, that is the red

knight of the red laundes, and charge him that he be ready
with you with his whole sum of knights, and then shall ye
be able to match with King Arthur and his knights. So this
was done, and all knights were sent for unto the Castle
Perilous; and then the Red Knight answered and said unto
Dame Liones, and to Sir Gareth, Madam, and my lord Sir
Gareth, ye shall understand that I have been at the court of
King Arthur, and Sir Persant of Inde and his brethren, and
there we have done our homage as ye commanded us. Also
Sir Ironside said, I have taken upon me with Sir Persant of
Inde and his brethren to hold part against my lord Sir
Launcelot and the knights of that court. And this have I
done for the love of my lady Dame Liones, and you my
lord Sir Gareth. Ye have well done, said Sir Gareth; but
wit you well ye shall be full sore matched with the most
noble knights of the world; therefore we must purvey us of
good knights, where we may get them. That is well said,
said Sir Persant, and worshipfully. And so the cry was
made in England, Wales, and Scotland, Ireland, Cornwall,
and in all the Out Isles, and in Brittany and in many
countries; that at the feast of our Lady the Assumption
next coming, men should come to the Castle Perilous beside
the Isle of Avilion; and there all the knights that there
came should have the choice whether them list to be on the
one party with the knights of the castle, or on the other
party with King Arthur. And two months was to the
day that the tournament should be. And so there came
many good knights that were at their large, and held them
for the most part against King Arthur and his knights of the
Round Table, and came in the side of them of the castle.
For Sir Epinogrus was the first, and he was the king's son of
Northumberland, and Sir Palamides the Saracen was another,
and Sir Safere his brother, and Sir Segwarides his brother,
but they were christened, and Sir Malegrine another, and Sir
Brian de les Isles, a noble knight, and Sir Grummore Grummursum, a good knight of Scotland, and Sir Carados of the
dolorous tower, a noble knight, and Sir Turquine his
brother, and Sir Arnold and Sir Gauter, two brethren, good
knights of Cornwall, there came Sir Tristram de Liones, and
with him Sir Dinadan, the Seneschal, and Sir Sadok; but
this Sir Tristram was not at that time knight of the Table
Round, but he was one of the best knights of the world.
And so all these noble knights accompanied them with the

lady of the castle, and with the red knight of the red laundes ; but as for Sir Gareth, he would not take upon him more but as other mean knights.

CHAPTER XXVII

HOW KING ARTHUR WENT TO THE TOURNAMENT WITH HIS
KNIGHTS, AND HOW THE LADY RECEIVED HIM WORSHIPFULLY,
AND HOW THE KNIGHTS ENCOUNTERED

AND then there came with King Arthur Sir Gawaine, Agravaine, Gaheris, his brethren. And then his nephews Sir Uwaine le Blanchemains, and Sir Aglovale, Sir Tor, Sir Percivale de Galis, and Sir Lamorak de Galis. Then came Sir Launcelot du Lake with his brethren, nephews, and cousins, as Sir Lionel, Sir Ector de Maris, Sir Bors de Ganis, and Sir Galihodin, Sir Galihud, and many more of Sir Launcelot's blood, and Sir Dinadan, Sir La Cote Male Taile, his brother, a good knight, and Sir Sagramore, a good knight ; and all the most part of the Round Table. Also there came with King Arthur these knights, the King of Ireland, King Agwisance, and the King of Scotland, King Carados and King Uriens of the land of Gore, and King Bagdemagus and his son Sir Meliaganus, and Sir Galahault the noble prince. All these kings, princes, and earls, barons, and other noble knights, as Sir Brandiles, Sir Uwaine les Avoutres, and Sir Kay, Sir Bedevere, Sir Meliot de Logres, Sir Petipase of Winchelsea, Sir Godelake : all these came with King Arthur, and more that cannot be rehearsed. Now leave we of these kings and knights, and let us speak of the great array that was made within the castle and about the castle for both parties. The Lady Dame Liones ordained great array upon her part for her noble knights, for all manner of lodging and victual that came by land and by water, that there lacked nothing for her party, nor for the other, but there was plenty to be had for gold and silver for King Arthur and his knights. And then there came the harbingers from King Arthur for to harbour him, and his kings, dukes, earls, barons, and knights. And then Sir Gareth prayed Dame Liones and the red knight of the red laundes, and Sir Persant and his brother, and Sir Gringamore, that in no wise there should none of them tell

not his name, and make no more of him than of the least
knight that there was, for, he said, I will not be known of
neither more nor less, neither at the beginning neither at
the ending. Then Dame Liones said unto Sir Gareth:
Sir, I will lend you a ring, but I would pray you as you love
me heartily let me have it again when the tournament is
done, for that ring increaseth my beauty much more than it
is of himself. And the virtue of my ring is that, that is
green it will turn to red, and that is red it will turn in likeness to green, and that is blue it will turn to likeness of white,
and that is white it will turn in likeness to blue, and so it
will do of all manner of colours. Also who that beareth my
ring shall lose no blood, and for great love I will give you
this ring. Gramercy, said Sir Gareth, mine own lady, for
this ring is passing meet for me, for it will turn all manner
of likeness that I am in, and that shall cause me that I shall
not be known. Then Sir Gringamore gave Sir Gareth a bay
courser that was a passing good horse; also he gave him
good armour and sure, and a noble sword that sometime
Sir Gringamore's father won upon an heathen tyrant. And
so thus every knight made him ready to that tournament.
And King Arthur was come two days tofore the Assumption
of our Lady. And there was all manner of royalty of all
minstrelsy that might be found. Also there came Queen
Gwenever and the Queen of Orkney, Sir Gareth's mother.
And upon the Assumption Day, when mass and matins
were done, there were heralds with trumpets commanded to
blow to the field. And so there came out Sir Epinogrus, the
king's son of Northumberland, from the castle, and there
encountered with him Sir Sagramore le Desirous, and either
of them brake their spears to their hands. And then came
in Sir Palamides out of the castle, and there encountered
with him Gawaine, and either of them smote other so hard
that both the good knights and their horses fell to the earth.
And then knights of either party rescued their knights.
And then came in Sir Safere and Sir Segwarides, brethren
to Sir Palamides; and there encountered Sir Agravaine with
Sir Safere and Sir Gaheris encountered with Sir Segwarides.
So Sir Safere smote down Agravaine, Sir Gawaine's brother;
and Sir Segwarides, Sir Safere's brother. And Sir Malgrine,
a knight of the castle, encountered with Sir Uwaine le
Blanchemains, and there Sir Uwaine gave Sir Malgrine a
fall, that he had almost broke his neck

CHAPTER XXVIII

HOW THE KNIGHTS BARE THEM IN THE BATTLE

THEN Sir Brian de les Isles and Grummore Grummursum, knights of the castle, encountered with Sir Aglovale, and Sir Tor smote down Sir Grummore Grummursum to the earth. Then came in Sir Carados of the dolorous tower, and Sir Turquine, knights of the castle; and there encountered with them Sir Percivale de Galis and Sir Lamorak de Galis, that were two brethren. And there encountered Sir Percivale with Sir Carados, and either brake their spears unto their hands, and then Sir Turquine with Sir Lamorak, and either of them smote down other's horse and all to the earth, and either parties rescued other, and horsed them again. And Sir Arnold and Sir Gauter, knights of the castle, encountered with Sir Brandiles and Sir Kay, and these four knights encountered mightily, and brake their spears to their hands. Then came in Sir Tristram, Sir Sadok, and Sir Dinas, knights of the castle, and there encountered Sir Tristram with Sir Bedivere, and there Sir Bedivere was smitten to the earth both horse and man. And Sir Sadok encountered with Sir Petipase, and there Sir Sadok was overthrown. And there Uwaine les Avoutres smote down Sir Dinas, the Seneschal. Then came in Sir Persant of Inde, a knight of the castle, and there encountered with him Sir Launcelot du Lake, and there he smote Sir Persant, horse and man, to the earth. Then came Sir Pertolepe from the castle, and there encountered with him Sir Lionel, and there Sir Pertolepe, the Green Knight, smote down Sir Lionel, brother to Sir Launcelot. All this was marked by noble heralds, who bare him best, and their names. And then came into the field Sir Perimones, the Red Knight, Sir Persant's brother, that was a knight of the castle, and he encountered with Sir Ector de Maris, and either smote other so hard that both their horses and they fell to the earth. And then came in the red knight of the red laundes, and Sir Gareth, from the castle, and there encountered with them Sir Bors de Ganis and Sir Bleoberis, and there the Red Knight and Sir Bors smote other so hard that their spears brast, and their horses fell grovelling to the earth. Then Sir Bleoberis brake his spear upon Sir Gareth, but of that stroke Sir Bleoberis fell to the earth. When Sir Galihodin saw that he bade Sir Gareth keep him, and Sir Gareth smote him to the earth. Then Sir Galihud gat a spear to avenge his brother, and in the same wise Sir Gareth served him, and Sir Dinadan and his brother, La Cote Male Taile, and Sir Sagramore le Desirous, and Sir Dodinas le Savage. All these he bare down with one spear. When King Agwisance of Ireland saw Sir Gareth fare so, he marvelled what he might be that one time seemed green, and another time, at his again coming, he seemed blue. And thus at every course that he rode to and fro he changed his colour, so that there might neither king nor knight have ready cognisance of him. Then Sir Agwisance, the King of Ireland, encountered with Sir Gareth, and there Sir Gareth smote him from his horse, saddle and all. And then came King Carados of Scotland, and Sir Gareth smote him down horse and man. And in the same wise he served King Uriens of the land of Gore. And then came in Sir Bagdemagus, and Sir Gareth smote him down, horse and man, to the earth. And Bagdemagus' son, Meliganus, brake a spear upon Sir Gareth mightily and knightly. And then Sir Galahault, the noble prince, cried on high: Knight with the many colours, well hast thou jousted; now make thee ready that I may joust with thee. Sir Gareth heard him, and he gat a great spear, and so they encountered together, and there the prince brake his spear; but Sir Gareth smote him upon the left side of the helm that he reeled here and there, and he had fallen down had not his men recovered him. So God me help, said King Arthur, that same knight with the many colours is a good knight. Wherefore the king called unto him Sir Launcelot, and prayed him to encounter with that knight. Sir, said Launcelot, I may well find in my heart for to forbear him as at this time, for he hath had travail enough this day; and when a good knight doth so well upon some day, it is no good knight's part to let him of his worship, and namely, when he seeth a knight hath done so great labour; for peradventure, said Sir Launcelot, his quarrel is here this day, and peradventure he is best beloved with this lady of all that be here; for I see well he paineth him and enforceth him to do great deeds, and therefore, said Sir Launcelot, as for me, this day he shall have the honour; though it lay in my power to put him from it I would not.

CHAPTER XXIX

YET OF THE SAID TOURNAMENT

THEN when this was done there was drawing of swords, and then there began a sore tournament. And there did Sir Lamorak marvellous deeds of arms; and betwixt Sir Lamorak and Sir Ironside, that was the red knight of the red laundes, there was strong battle; and betwixt Sir Palamides and Bleoberis there was a strong battle; and Sir Gawaine and Sir Tristram met, and there Sir Gawaine had the worse, for he pulled Sir Gawaine from his horse, and there he was long upon foot, and defouled. Then came in Sir Launcelot, and he smote Sir Turquine, and he him; and then came Sir Carados his brother, and both at once they assailed him, and he as the most noblest knight of the world worshipfully fought with them both, that all men wondered of the noblesse of Sir Launcelot. And then came in Sir Gareth, and knew that it was Sir Launcelot that fought with the two perilous knights. And then Sir Gareth came with his good horse and hurtled them in-sunder, and no stroke would he smite to Sir Launcelot. That espied Sir Launcelot, and deemed it should be the good knight Sir Gareth: and then Sir Gareth rode here and there, and smote on the right hand and on the left hand, and all the folk might well espy where that he rode. And by fortune he met with his brother Sir Gawaine, and there he put Sir Gawaine to the worse, for he put off his helm, and so he served five or six knights of the Round Table, that all men said he put him in the most pain, and best he did his devoir. For when Sir Tristram beheld him how he first jousted and after fought so well with a sword, then he rode unto Sir Ironside and to Sir Persant of Inde, and asked them, by their faith, What manner a knight is yonder knight that seemeth in so many divers colours? Truly, meseemeth, said Tristram, that he putteth himself in great pain, for he never ceaseth. Wot ye not what he is? said Sir Ironside. No, said Sir Tristram. Then shall ye know that this is he that loveth the lady of the castle, and she him again; and this is he that won me when I besieged the lady of this castle, and this is he that won Sir Persant of Inde, and his three brethren. What is his name, said Sir Tristram, and of what blood is he come? He was called in the court of King

Arthur, Beaumains, but his right name is Sir Gareth of Orkney, brother to Sir Gawaine. By my head, said Sir Tristram, he is a good knight, and a big man of arms, and if he be young he shall prove a full noble knight. He is but a child, they all said, and of Sir Launcelot he was made knight. Therefore he is mickle the better, said Tristram. And then Sir Tristram, Sir Ironside, Sir Persant, and his brother, rode together for to help Sir Gareth ; and then there were given many strong strokes. And then Sir Gareth rode out on the one side to amend his helm ; and then said his dwarf: Take me your ring, that ye lose it not while that ye drink. And so when he had drunk he gat on his helm, and eagerly took his horse and rode into the field, and left his ring with his dwarf ; and the dwarf was glad the ring was from him, for then he wist well he should be known. And then when Sir Gareth was in the field all folks saw him well and plainly that he was in yellow colours ; and there he rased off helms and pulled down knights, that King Arthur had marvel what knight he was, for the king saw by his hair that it was the same knight.

CHAPTER XXX

HOW SIR GARETH WAS ESPIED BY THE HERALDS, AND HOW HE ESCAPED OUT OF THE FIELD

BUT before he was in so many colours, and now he is but in one colour ; that is yellow. Now go, said King Arthur unto divers heralds, and ride about him, and espy what manner knight he is, for I have speryd of many knights this day that be upon his party, and all say they know him not. And so an herald rode nigh Gareth as he could ; and there he saw written about his helm in gold, This helm is Sir Gareth of Orkney. Then the herald cried as he were wood, and many heralds with him :—This is Sir Gareth of Orkney in the yellow arms ; that by all kings and knights of Arthur's beheld him and awaited ; and then they pressed all to behold him, and ever the heralds cried: This is Sir Gareth of Orkney, King Lot's son. And when Sir Gareth espied that he was discovered, then he doubled his strokes, and smote down Sir Sagramore, and his brother Sir Gawaine. O brother, said Sir Gawaine, I weened ye would not have stricken me. So when he heard him say so he thrang here and there, and so with great pain he gat out of the press, and there he met with his dwarf. O boy, said Sir Gareth, thou hast beguiled me foul this day that thou kept my ring; give it me anon again, that I may hide my body withal; and so he took it him. And then they all wist not where he was become; and Sir Gawaine had in manner espied where Sir Gareth rode, and then he rode after with all his might. That espied Sir Gareth, and rode lightly into the forest, that Sir Gawaine wist not where he was become. And when Sir Gareth wist that Sir Gawaine was passed, he asked the dwarf of best counsel. Sir, said the dwarf, meseemeth it were best, now that ye are escaped from spying, that ye send my lady Dame Liones her ring. It is well advised, said Sir Gareth; now have it here and bear it to her, and say that I recommend me unto her good grace, and say her I will come when I may, and I pray her to be true and faithful to me as I will be to her. Sir, said the dwarf, it shall be done as ye command: and so he rode his way, and did his errand unto the lady. Then she said, Where is my knight, Sir Gareth? Madam, said the dwarf, he bad me say that he would not be long from you. And so lightly the dwarf came again unto Sir Gareth, that would full fain have had a lodging, for he had need to be reposed. And then fell there a thunder and a rain, as heaven and earth should go together. And Sir Gareth was not a little weary, for of all that day he had but little rest, neither his horse nor he. So this Sir Gareth rode so long in that forest until the night came. And ever it lightened and thundered, as it had been wood. At the last by fortune he came to a castle, and there he heard the waits upon the walls.

CHAPTER XXXI

HOW SIR GARETH CAME TO A CASTLE WHERE HE WAS WELL LODGED, AND HE JOUSTED WITH A KNIGHT AND SLEW HIM

THEN Sir Gareth rode unto the barbican of the castle, and prayed the porter fair to let him into the castle. The porter answered ungoodly again, and said, Thou gettest no lodging here. Fair sir, say not so, for I am a knight of King Arthur's, and pray the lord or the lady of this castle

to give me harbour for the love of King Arthur.   Then the
porter went unto the duchess, and told her how there was a
knight of King Arthur's would have harbour.   Let him in,
said the duchess, for I will see that knight, and for King
Arthur's sake he shall not be harbourless.   Then she yode
up into a tower over the gate, with great torch-light.   When
Sir Gareth saw that torch-light he cried on high : Whether
thou be lord or lady, giant or champion, I take no force so
that I may have harbour this night ; and if it so be that
I must needs fight, spare me not to-morn when I have
rested me, for both I and mine horse be weary.   Sir knight,
said the lady, thou speakest knightly and boldly ; but wit
thou well the lord of this castle loveth not King Arthur, nor
none of his court, for my lord hath ever been against him ;
and therefore thou were better not to come within this
castle ; for an thou come in this night, thou must come in
under such form, that wheresomever thou meet my lord, by
stigh or by street, thou must yield thee to him as prisoner.
Madam, said Sir Gareth, what is your lord, and what is his
name ?   Sir, my lord's name is the Duke de la Rowse.
Well madam, said Sir Gareth, I shall promise you in what
place I meet your lord I shall yield me unto him and to his
good grace ; with that I understand he will do me no harm :
and if I understand that he will, I will release myself an I
can with my spear and my sword.   Ye say well, said the
duchess ; and then she let the drawbridge down, and so he
rode into the hall, and there he alit, and his horse was led
into a stable ; and in the hall he unarmed him and said,
Madam, I will not out of this hall this night ; and when
it is daylight, let see who will have ado with me, he shall
find me ready.   Then was he set unto supper, and had
many good dishes.   Then Sir Gareth list well to eat, and
knightly he ate his meat, and eagerly ; there was many
a fair lady by him, and some said they never saw a goodlier
man nor so well of eating.   Then they made him passing
good cheer, and shortly when he had supped his bed was
made there ; so he rested him all night.   And on the morn
he heard mass, and brake his fast and took his leave at the
duchess, and at them all ; and thanked her goodly of her
lodging, and of his good cheer ; and then she asked him his
name.   Madam, he said, truly my name is Gareth of Orkney,
and some men call me Beaumains.   Then knew she well it
was the same knight that fought for Dame Liones.   So Sir

Gareth departed and rode up into a mountain, and there met him a knight, his name was Sir Bendelaine, and said to Sir Gareth : Thou shalt not pass this way, for either thou shalt joust with me, or else be my prisoner. Then will I joust, said Sir Gareth. And so they let their horses run, and there Sir Gareth smote him throughout the body ; and Sir Bendelaine rode forth to his castle there beside, and there died. So Sir Gareth would have rested him, and he came riding to Bendelaine's castle. Then his knights and servants espied that it was he that had slain their lord. Then they armed twenty good men, and came out and assailed Sir Gareth ; and so he had no spear, but his sword, and put his shield afore him ; and there they brake their spears upon him, and they assailed him passingly sore. But ever Sir Gareth defended him as a knight.

CHAPTER XXXII

HOW SIR GARETH FOUGHT WITH A KNIGHT THAT HELD WITHIN HIS CASTLE THIRTY LADIES, AND HOW HE SLEW HIM

So when they saw that they might not overcome him, they rode from him, and took their counsel to slay his horse ; and so they came in upon Sir Gareth, and with spears they slew his horse, and then they assailed him hard. But when he was on foot, there was none that he fought but he gave him such a buffet that he did never recover. So he slew them by one and one till they were but four, and there they fled ; and Sir Gareth took a good horse that was one of theirs, and rode his way. Then he rode a great pace till that he came to a castle, and there he heard much mourning of ladies and gentlewomen. So there came by him a page. What noise is this, said Sir Gareth, that I hear within this castle ? Sir knight, said the page, here be within this castle thirty ladies, and all they be widows ; for here is a knight that waiteth daily upon this castle, and his name is the brown knight without pity, and he is the periloust knight that now liveth ; and therefore sir, said the page, I rede you flee. Nay, said Sir Gareth, I will not flee though thou be afeard of him. And then the page saw where came the brown knight : Lo, said the page, yonder he cometh. Let me deal with him, said Sir Gareth. And when either of other had a sight they let their horses run, and the brown knight brake his spear, and Sir Gareth smote him throughout the body, that he overthrew him to the ground stark dead. So Sir Gareth rode into the castle, and prayed the ladies that he might repose him. Alas, said the ladies, ye may not be lodged here. Make him good cheer, said the page, for this knight hath slain your enemy. Then they all made him good cheer as lay in their power. But wit ye well they made him good cheer, for they might none otherwise do, for they were but poor. And so on the morn he went to mass, and there he saw the thirty ladies kneel, and lay grovelling upon divers tombs, making great dole and sorrow. Then Sir Gareth wist well that in the tombs lay their lords. Fair ladies, said Sir Gareth, ye must at the next feast of Pentecost be at the court of King Arthur, and say that I, Sir Gareth, sent you thither. We shall do this, said the ladies. So he departed, and by fortune he came to a mountain, and there he found a goodly knight that bad him, Abide sir knight, and joust with me. What are ye? said Sir Gareth. My name is, said he, the Duke de la Rowse. Ah sir, ye are the same knight that I lodged once in your castle; and there I made promise unto your lady that I should yield me unto you. Ah, said the duke, art thou that proud knight that profferest to fight with my knights; therefore make thee ready, for I will have ado with you. So they let their horses run, and there Sir Gareth smote the duke down from his horse. But the duke lightly avoided his horse, and dressed his shield and drew his sword, and bad Sir Gareth alight and fight with him. So he did alight, and they did great battle together more than an hour, and either hurt other full sore. At the last Sir Gareth gat the duke to the earth, and would have slain him, and then he yield him to him. Then must ye go, said Sir Gareth, unto Sir Arthur my lord at the next feast, and say that I, Sir Gareth of Orkney, sent you unto him. It shall be done, said the duke, and I will do to you homage and fealty with an hundred knights with me; and all the days of my life to do you service where ye will command me.

CHAPTER XXXIII

HOW SIR GARETH AND SIR GAWAINE FOUGHT EACH AGAINST OTHER,
AND HOW THEY KNEW EACH OTHER BY THE DAMOSEL LINET

So the duke departed, and Sir Gareth stood there alone ; and there he saw an armed knight coming toward him. Then Sir Gareth took the duke's shield, and mounted upon horseback, and so without bidding they ran together as it had been the thunder. And there that knight hurt Sir Gareth under the side with his spear. And then they alit and drew their swords, and gave great strokes that the blood trailed to the ground. And so they fought two hours. At the last there came the damosel Linet, that some men called the damosel Savage, and she came riding upon an ambling mule ; and there she cried all on high, Sir Gawaine, Sir Gawaine, leave thy fighting with thy brother Sir Gareth. And when he heard her say so he threw away his shield and his sword, and ran to Sir Gareth, and took him in his arms, and sythen kneeled down and asked him mercy. What are ye, said Sir Gareth, that right now were so strong and so mighty, and now so suddenly yield you to me ? O Gareth, I am your brother Sir Gawaine, that for your sake have had great sorrow and labour. Then Sir Gareth unlaced his helm, and kneeled down to him, and asked him mercy. Then they rose both, and embraced either other in their arms, and wept a great while or they might speak, and either of them gave other the prize of the battle. And there were many kind words between them. Alas, my fair brother, said Sir Gawaine, perdy I owe of right to worship you an ye were not my brother, for ye have worshipped King Arthur and all his court, for ye have sent me more worshipful knights this twelvemonth than six the best of the Round Table have done, except Sir Lancelot. Then came the damosel Savage that was the Lady Linet, that rode with Sir Gareth so long and there she did staunch Sir Gareth's wounds and Sir Gawaine's. Now what will ye do ? said the damosel Savage ; meseemeth that it were well done that Arthur had witting of you both, for your horses are so bruised that they may not bear. Now, fair damosel, said Sir Gawaine, I pray you ride unto my lord mine uncle, King Arthur, and tell him what adventure is to me betid here, and I suppose he will not tarry long. Then she took her mule, and lightly she came to King Arthur that was but two mile thence. And when she had told him tidings the king bad get him a palfrey. And when he was upon his back he bad the lords and ladies come after, who that would; and there was saddling and bridling of queens' horses and princes' horses, and well was him that soonest might be ready. So when the king came thereas they were, he saw Sir Gawaine and Sir Gareth sit upon a little hill-side, and then the king avoided his horse. And when he came nigh Sir Gareth he would have spoken but he might not; and therewith he sank down in a swoon for gladness. And so they stert unto their uncle, and required him of his good grace to be of good comfort. Wit ye well the king made great joy, and many a piteous complaint he made to Sir Gareth, and ever he wept as he had been a child. With that came his mother, the queen of Orkney, Dame Morgawse, and when she saw Sir Gareth readily in the visage she might not weep, but suddenly fell down in a swoon, and lay there a great while like as she had been dead. And then Sir Gareth recomforted his mother in such wise that she recovered and made good cheer. Then the king commanded that all manner of knights that were under his obeissance should make their lodging right there for the love of his nephews. And so it was done, and all manner of purveyance purveyed, that there lacked nothing that might be gotten of tame nor wild for gold or silver. And then by the means of the damosel Savage Sir Gawaine and Sir Gareth were healed of their wounds; and there they sojourned eight days. Then said King Arthur unto the damosel Savage: I marvel that your sister, Dame Liones, cometh not here to me, and in especial that she cometh not to visit her knight, my nephew Sir Gareth, that hath had so much travail for her love. My lord, said the damosel Linet, ye must of your good grace hold her excused, for she knoweth not that my lord, Sir Gareth, is here. Go then for her, said King Arthur, that we may be appointed what is best to be done, according to the pleasure of my nephew. Sir, said the damosel, that shall be done, and so she rode unto her sister. And as lightly as she might she made her ready; and she came on the morn with her brother Sir Gringamore, and with her forty knights. And so when she was come she had all the cheer that might be done, both of the King, and of many other kings and queens.

CHAPTER XXXIV

HOW SIR GARETH ACKNOWLEDGED THAT THEY LOVED EACH OTHER TO KING ARTHUR, AND OF THE APPOINTMENT OF THEIR WEDDING

AND among all these ladies she was named the fairest, and peerless. Then when Sir Gawaine saw her there was many a goodly look and goodly words, that all men of worship had joy to behold them. Then came King Arthur and many other kings, and Dame Guenever, and the queen of Orkney. And there the king asked his nephew, Sir Gareth, whether he would have that lady as paramour, or to have her to his wife. My lord, wit you well that I love her above all ladies living. Now, fair lady, said King Arthur, what say ye? Most noble King, said Dame Liones, wit you well that my lord, Sir Gareth, is to me more lever to have and welde as my husband, than any king or prince that is christened ; and if I may not have him I promise you I will never have none. For, my lord Arthur, said Dame Liones, wit ye well he is my first love, and he shall be the last ; and if ye will suffer him to have his will and free choice I dare say he will have me. That is truth, said Sir Gareth ; an I have not you and welde not you as my wife, there shall never lady nor gentlewoman rejoice me. What, nephew, said the king, is the wind in that door? for wit ye well I would not for the stint of my crown to be causer to withdraw your hearts ; and wit ye well ye cannot love so well but I shall rather increase it than distress it. And also ye shall have my love and my lordship in the uttermost wise that may lie in my power. And in the same wise said Sir Gareth's mother. Then there was made a provision for the day of marriage ; and by the king's advice it was provided that it should be at Michaelmas following, at Kink Kenadon by the seaside, for there is a plentiful country. And so it was cried in all the places through the realm. And then Sir Gareth sent his summons to all these knights and ladies that he had won in battle tofore, that they should be at his day of marriage at Kink Kenadon by the sands. And then Dame Liones, and the damosel Linet with Sir Gringamore, rode to their castle ; and a goodly and a rich ring she gave to Sir Gareth, and he gave her another. And King Arthur gave her a rich bee of gold ; and so she departed ; and King Arthur and his fellowship rode toward Kink Kenadon, and Sir Gareth brought his lady on the way, and so came to the king again and rode with him. Lord ! the great cheer that Sir Launcelot made of Sir Gareth and he of him, for there was never no knight that Sir Gareth loved so well as he did Sir Launcelot ; and ever for the most part he would be in Sir Launcelot's company ; for after Sir Gareth had espied Sir Gawaine's conditions, he withdrew himself from his brother, Sir Gawaine's, fellowship, for he was vengeable, and where he hated he would be avenged with murder, and that hated Sir Gareth.

CHAPTER XXXV

OF THE GREAT ROYALTY, AND WHAT OFFICERS WERE MADE AT THE FEAST OF THE WEDDING, AND OF THE JOUSTS AT THE FEAST

So it drew fast to Michaelmas ; and thither came Dame Liones, the lady of the Castle Perilous, and her sister, Dame Linet, with Sir Gringamore, her brother, with them, for he had the conduct of these ladies. And there they were lodged at the device of King Arthur. And upon Michaelmas Day the Bishop of Canterbury made the wedding betwixt Sir Gareth and the Lady Liones with great solemnity. And King Arthur made Gaheris to wed the damosel Savage, that was Dame Linet ; and King Arthur made Sir Agravaine to wed Dame Liones' niece, a fair lady, her name was Dame Laurel. And so when this solemnization was done, then came in the green knight, Sir Pertolepe, with thirty knights, and there he did homage and fealty to Sir Gareth, and these knights to hold of him for evermore. Also Sir Pertolepe said : I pray you that at this feast I may be your chamberlain. With a good will, said Sir Gareth, syth it liketh you to take so simple an office. Then came in the red knight, with three score knights with him, and did to Sir Gareth homage and fealty, and all those knights to hold of him for evermore. And then this Sir Perimones prayed Sir Gareth to grant him to be his chief butler at that high feast. I will well, said Sir Gareth, that ye have this office, and it were better. Then came in Sir Persant of Inde, with an hundred knights with him, and there he did homage and fealty, and all his knights should do him service, and hold their lands of him for ever; and there he prayed Sir Gareth to make him his sewer-chief at the feast. I will well, said Sir Gareth, that ye have it, and it were better. Then came the Duke de la Rowse, with an hundred knights with him, and there he did homage and fealty to Sir Gareth, and so to hold their lands of him for ever. And he required Sir Gareth that he might serve him of the wine that day of that feast. I will well, said Sir Gareth, and it were better. Then came in the red knight of the red laundes, that was Sir Ironside, and he brought with him three hundred knights, and there he did homage and fealty, and all these knights to hold their lands of him for ever. And then he asked Sir Gareth to be his carver. I will well, said Sir Gareth, an it please you. Then came into the court thirty ladies, and all they seemed widows, and those thirty ladies brought with them many fair gentle-women. And all they kneeled down at once unto King Arthur and unto Sir Gareth, and there all those ladies told the king how Sir Gareth delivered them from the dolorous tower, and slew the brown knight without pity: And there-fore we, and our heirs for evermore, will do homage unto Sir Gareth of Orkney. So then the kings and queens, princes and earls, barons and many bold knights, went unto meat; and well may ye wit there were all manner of meat plenteously, all manner revels and games, with all manner of minstrelsy that was used in those days. Also there was great jousts three days. But the king would not suffer Sir Gareth to joust, by cause of his new bride; for, as the French book sayeth, that Dame Liones desired of the king that none that were wedded should joust at that feast. So the first day there jousted Sir Lamorak de Galis, for he over-threw thirty knights, and did passing marvellously deeds of arms; and then King Arthur made Sir Persant and his two brethren knights of the Round Table to their lives' end, and gave them great lands. Also the second day there jousted Tristram best, and he overthrew forty knights, and did there marvellous deeds of arms. And there King Arthur made Ironside, that was the red knight of the red laundes, a knight of the Table Round to his life's end, and gave him great lands. The third day there jousted Sir Launcelot du Lake, and he overthrew fifty knights, and did many marvellous deeds of arms, that all men wondered on him. And there King Arthur made the Duke de la Rowse a knight of the Round Table to his life's end, and gave him great lands to spend. But when these jousts were done, Sir Lamorak and Sir Tristram departed suddenly, and would not be known, for the which King Arthur and all the court were sore displeased. And so they held the court forty days with great solemnity. And this Sir Gareth was a noble knight, and a well-ruled, and fair-languaged.

Thus endeth this tale of Sir Gareth of Orkney that wedded Dame Liones of the Castle Perilous. And also Sir Gaheris wedded her sister, Dame Linet, that was called the damosel Savage. And Sir Agravaine wedded Dame Laurel, a fair lady and great, and mighty lands with great riches gave with them King Arthur, that royally they might live till their lives' end.

Here followeth the viii. book, the which is the first book of Sir Tristram de Liones, and who was his father and his mother, and how he was born and fostered, and how he was made knight.

BOOK VIII

CHAPTER I

HOW SIR TRISTRAM DE LIONES WAS BORN, AND HOW HIS MOTHER DIED AT HIS BIRTH, WHEREFORE SHE NAMED HIM TRISTRAM

IT was a king that hight Meliodas, and he was lord and king of the country of Liones, and this Meliodas was a likely knight as any was that time living. And by fortune he wedded King Mark's sister of Cornwall, and she was called Elizabeth, that was called both good and fair. And at that time King Arthur reigned, and he was whole king of England, Wales, and Scotland, and of many other realms : howbeit there were many kings that were lords of many countries, but all they held their lands of King Arthur ; for in Wales were two kings, and in the north were many kings ; and in Cornwall and in the west were two kings; also in Ireland were two or three kings, and all were under the obeissance of King Arthur. So was the King of France, and the King of Brittany, and all the lordships unto Rome. So when this King Meliodas had been with his wife, within a while she waxed great with child, and she was a full meek lady, and well she loved her lord, and he her again, so there was great joy betwixt them. Then there was a lady in that country that had loved King Meliodas long, and by no mean she never could get his love; therefore she let ordain upon a day, as King Meliodas rode on hunting, for he was a great chaser, and there by an enchantment she made him chase an hart by himself alone till that he came to an old castle, and there anon he was taken prisoner by the lady that him loved. When Elizabeth, King Meliodas' wife, missed her lord, and she was nigh out of her wit, and also as great with child as she was, she took a gentlewoman with her, and ran into the forest to seek her lord. And when she was far in the forest she might no farther, for she began to travail fast of her child. And she had many grimly throes; her gentlewoman helped her all that she might, and so by miracle of Our Lady of Heaven she was delivered with great pains. But she had taken such cold for the default of help that deep draughts of death took her, that needs she must die and depart out of this world, there was none other bote. And when this Queen Elizabeth saw that there was none other bote, then she made great dole, and said unto her gentlewoman: When ye see my lord, King Meliodas, recommend me unto him, and tell him what pains I endure here for his love, and how I must die here for his sake for default of good help; and let him wit that I am full sorry to depart out of this world from him, therefore pray him to be friend to my soul. Now let me see my little child, for whom I have had all this sorrow. And when she saw him she said thus: Ah, my little son, thou hast murdered thy mother, and therefore I suppose, thou that art a murderer so young, thou art full likely to be a manly man in thine age. And by cause I shall die of the birth of thee, I charge thee, gentlewoman, that thou pray my lord, King Meliodas, that when he is christened let call him Tristram, that is as much to say as a sorrowful birth. And therewith this queen gave up the ghost and died. Then the gentlewoman laid her under an umbre of a great tree, and then she lapped the child as well as she might for cold. Right so there came the barons, following after the queen, and when they saw that she was dead, and understood none other but the king was destroyed.

CHAPTER II

HOW THE STEPMOTHER OF SIR TRISTRAM HAD ORDAINED POISON FOR TO HAVE POISONED SIR TRISTRAM

THEN certain of them would have slain the child, by cause they would have been lords of the country of Liones. But then through the fair speech of the gentlewoman, and by the means that she made, the most part of the barons would not assent thereto. And then they let carry home the dead queen, and much dole was made for her. Then this meanwhile Merlin delivered King Meliodas out of prison on the morn after his queen was dead. And so when the king was come home the most part of the barons made great joy. But the sorrow that the king made for his queen that might no tongue tell. So then the king let inter her richly, and after he let christen his child as his wife had commanded afore her death. And then he let call him Tristram, the sorrowful born child. Then the King Meliodas endured seven years without a wife, and all this time Tristram was nourished well. Then it befell that King Meliodas wedded King Howell's daughter of Brittany, and anon she had children of King Meliodas: then was she heavy and wroth that her children should not rejoice the country of Liones, wherefore this queen ordained for to poison young Tristram. So she let poison be put in a piece of silver in the chamber whereas Tristram and her children were together, unto that intent that when Tristram were thirsty he should drink that drink. And so it fell upon a day, the queen's son, as he was in that chamber, espied the piece with poison, and he weened it had been good drink, and by cause the child was thirsty he took the piece with poison and drank freely; and therewithal suddenly the child brast and was dead. When the queen of Meliodas wist of the death of her son, wit ye well that she was heavy. But yet the king understood nothing of her treason. Notwithstanding the queen would not leave this, but efte she let ordain more poison, and put it in a piece. And by fortune King Meliodas, her husband, found the piece with wine where was the poison, and he that was much thirsty took the piece for to drink thereout. And as he would have drunken thereof the queen espied him, and then she ran unto him, and pulled the piece from him suddenly. The king marvelled why she did so, and remembered him how her son was suddenly slain with poison. And then he took her by the hand, and said: Thou false traitress, thou shalt tell me what manner of drink this is, or else I shall slay thee. And therewith he pulled out his sword, and sware a great oath that he should slay her but if she told him truth. Ah! mercy, my lord, said she, and I shall tell you all. And then she told him why she would have slain Tristram, by cause her children should rejoice his land. Well, said King Meliodas, and therefore shall ye have the law. And so she was condemned by the assent of the barons to be burnt; and then was there made a great fire, and right as she was at the fire to take her execution, young Tristram kneeled afore King Meliodas, and besought him to give him a boon. I will well, said the king again. Then said young Tristram, Give me the life of thy queen, my stepmother. That is unrightfully asked, said King Meliodas, for thou ought of right to hate her, for she would have slain thee with that poison an she might have had her will; and for thy sake most is my cause that she should die. Sir, said Tristram, as for that, I beseech you of your mercy that you will forgive it her, and as for my part, God forgive it her, and I do; and so much it liked your highness to grant me my boon, for God's love I require you hold your promise. Sythen it is so, said the king, I will that ye have her life. Then, said the king, I give her to you, and go ye to the fire and take her, and do with her what ye will. So Sir Tristram went to the fire, and by the commandment of the king delivered her from the death. But after that King Meliodas would never have ado with her as at bed and board. But by the good means of young Tristram he made the king and her accorded. But then the king would not suffer young Tristram to abide no longer in his court.

CHAPTER III

HOW SIR TRISTRAM WAS SENT INTO FRANCE, AND HAD ONE TO GOVERN HIM NAMED GOUVERNAIL, AND HOW HE LEARNED TO HARP, HAWK, AND HUNT

AND then he let ordain a gentleman that was well learned and taught, his name was Gouvernail; and then he sent young Tristram with Gouvernail into France to learn the language, and nurture, and deeds of arms. And there was Tristram more than seven years. And then when he well could speak the language, and had learned all that he might learn in that country, then he came home to his father, King Meliodas, again. And so Tristram learned to be an harper passing all other, that there was none such called in no country, and so on harping and on instruments of music he applied him in his youth for to learn. And after, as he growed in might and strength, he laboured ever in hunting and in hawking, so that never gentleman more, that ever we heard read of. And as the book saith, he began good measures of blowyng of beasts of venery, and beasts of chase, and all manner of vermin, and all these terms we have yet of hawking and hunting. And therefore the book of venery, of hawking, and hunting, is called the book of Sir Tristram. Wherefore, as meseemeth, all gentlemen that bear old arms ought of right to honour Sir Tristram for the goodly terms that gentlemen have and use, and shall to the day of doom, that thereby in a manner all men of worship may dissever a gentleman from a yeoman, and from a yeoman a villain. For he that gentle is will draw him unto gentle tatches, and to follow the customs of noble gentlemen. Thus Sir Tristram endured in Cornwall until he was big and strong, of the age of nineteen years. And then the King Meliodas had great joy of Sir Tristram, and so had the queen, his wife. For ever after in her life, by cause Sir Tristram saved her from the fire, she did never hate him more after, but loved him ever after, and gave Tristram many great gifts; for every estate loved him, where that he went.

CHAPTER IV

HOW SIR MARHAUS CAME OUT OF IRELAND FOR TO ASK TRUAGE OF CORNWALL, OR ELSE HE WOULD FIGHT THEREFOR

THEN it befell that King Anguish of Ireland sent unto King Mark of Cornwall for his truage, that Cornwall had paid many winters. And all that time King Mark was behind of the truage for seven years. And King Mark and his barons gave unto the messenger of Ireland these words and answer, that they would none pay; and bad the messenger go unto his King Anguish, And tell him we will pay him no truage, but tell your lord, an he will always have truage of us of Cornwall, bid him send a trusty knight of his land, that will fight for his right, and we shall find another for to defend our right. With this answer the messengers departed into Ireland. And when King Anguish understood the answer of the messengers he was wonderly wroth. And then he called unto him Sir Marhaus, the good knight, that was nobly proved, and a Knight of the Table Round. And this Marhaus was brother unto the queen of Ireland. Then the king said thus : Fair brother, Sir Marhaus, I pray you go into Cornwall for my sake, and do battle for our truage that of right we ought to have ; and whatsomever ye spend ye shall have sufficiently more than ye shall need. Sir, said Marhaus, wit ye well that I shall not be loth to do battle in the right of you and your land with the best knight of the Table Round ; for I know them, for the most part, what be their deeds ; and for to advance my deeds and to increase my worship I will right gladly go unto this journey for our right. So in all haste there was made purveyance for Sir Marhaus, and he had all things that to him needed ; and so he departed out of Ireland, and arrived up in Cornwall even fast by the Castle of Tintagil. And when King Mark understood that he was there arrived to fight for Ireland, then made King Mark great sorrow when he understood that the good and noble knight Sir Marhaus was come. For they knew no knight that durst have ado with him. For at that time Sir Marhaus was called one of the famousest and renowned knights of the world. And thus Sir Marhaus abode in the sea, and every day he sent unto King Mark for to pay the truage that was behind of seven year, other-else to find a knight to fight with him for the truage. This manner of message Sir Marhaus sent daily unto King Mark. Then they of Cornwall let make cries in every place, that what knight would fight for to save the truage of Cornwall, he should be rewarded so that he should fare the better the term of his life. Then some of the barons said to King Mark, and counselled him to send to the Court of King Arthur for to seek Sir Launcelot du Luke, that was that time named for the marvelloust knight of all the world. Then there were some other barons that counselled the king not to do so, and said that it was labour in vain, by cause Sir Marhaus was a knight of the Round Table, therefore any of them will be loth to have ado with other, but if it were any knight at his own request would fight disguised and unknown. So the king and all his barons assented that it was no bote to seek any knight of the Round Table. This meanwhile came the language and the noise unto King Meliodas, how that Sir Marhaus abode battle fast by Tintagil, and how King Mark could find no manner knight to fight for him. When young Tristram heard of this he was wroth, and sore ashamed that there durst no knight in Cornwall have ado with Sir Marhaus of Ireland.

CHAPTER V

HOW TRISTRAM ENTERPRIZED THE BATTLE TO FIGHT FOR THE TRUAGE OF CORNWALL, AND HOW HE WAS MADE KNIGHT

THERE withal Tristram went unto his father, King Meliodas, and asked him counsel what was best to do for to recover Cornwall from truage. For, as meseemeth, said Sir Tristram, it were shame that Sir Marhaus, the queen's brother of Ireland, should go away unless that he were foughten withal. As for that, said King Meliodas, wit you well, son Tristram, that Sir Marhaus is called one of the best knights of the world, and knight of the Table Round; and therefore I know no knight in this country that is able to match with him. Alas, said Sir Tristram, that I am not made knight; and if Sir Marhaus should thus depart into Ireland, God let me never have worship: an I were made knight I should match him. And sir, said Tristram, I pray you give me leave to ride to King Mark; and so ye be not displeased of King Mark will I be made knight. I will well, said King Meliodas, that ye be ruled as your courage will rule you. Then Sir Tristram thanked his father much. And then he made him ready to ride into Cornwall. In the meanwhile there came a messenger with letters of love from King Faramon of France's daughter unto Sir Tristram, that were full piteous letters, and in them were written many complaints of love; but Sir Tristram had no joy of her letters nor regard unto her. Also she sent him a little brachet that was passing fair. But when the king's daughter understood that Sir Tristram would not love her, as the book saith, she died for sorrow. And then the same squire that brought the letter and the brachet came again unto Sir Tristram, as after ye shall hear in the tale. So this young Sir Tristram rode unto his eme King Mark of Cornwall. And when he came there he heard say that there would no knight fight with Sir Marhaus. Then yede Sir Tristram unto his eme and said: Sir, if ye will give me the order of knighthood, I will do battle with Sir Marhaus. What are ye, said the king, and from whence be ye come? Sir, said Tristram, I come from King Meliodas that wedded your sister, and a gentleman wit ye well I am. King Mark beheld Sir Tristram and saw that he was but a young man of age, but he was passingly well made and big. Fair sir, said the king, what is your name, and where were ye born? Sir, said he again, my name is Tristram, and in the country of Liones was I born. Ye say well, said the king; and if ye will do this battle I shall make you knight. Therefore I come to you, said Sir Tristram, and for none other cause. But then King Mark made him knight. And therewithal, anon as he had made him knight, he sent a messenger unto Sir Marhaus with letters that said that he had found a young knight ready for to take the battle to the uttermost. It may well be, said Sir Marhaus; but tell King Mark I will not fight with no knight but he be of blood royal, that is to say, outher king's son, outher queen's son, born of a prince or princess. When King Mark understood that, he sent for Sir Tristram de Liones and told him what was the answer of Sir Marhaus. Then said Sir Tristram: Sythen that he sayeth so, let him wit that I am come of father side and mother side of as noble blood as he is: for, sir, now shall ye know that I am King Meliodas' son, born of your own sister, Dame Elizabeth, that died in the forest in the birth of me. O Jesu, said King Mark, ye are welcome fair nephew to me. Then in all the haste the king let horse Sir Tristram, and armed him in the best manner that might be had or gotten for gold or silver. And then King Mark sent unto Sir Marhaus, and did him to wit that a better born man than he was himself should fight with him, and his name is Sir Tristram de Liones, gotten of King Meliodas, and born of King Mark's sister. Then was Sir Marhaus glad and blithe that he should fight with such a gentleman. And so by the assent of King Mark and of Sir Marhaus that let ordain that they should fight within an island nigh Sir Marhaus' ships; and so was Sir Tristram put into a vessel both his horse and he, and all that to him longed both for his body and for his horse. Sir Tristram lacked nothing. And when King Mark and his barons of Cornwall beheld how young Sir Tristram departed with such a carriage to fight for the right of Cornwall, there was neither man nor woman of worship but they wept to see and understand so young a knight to jeopardy himself for their right.

CHAPTER VI

HOW SIR TRISTRAM ARRIVED INTO THE ISLAND FOR TO FURNISH THE BATTLE WITH SIR MARHAUS

So to shorten this tale, when Sir Tristram was arrived within the island he looked to the farther side, and there he saw at an anchor six ships nigh to the land ; and under the shadow of the ships upon the land, there hoved the noble knight, Sir Marhaus of Ireland. Then Sir Tristram commanded his servant Gouvernail to bring his horse to the land, and dress his harness at all manner of rights. And then when he had so done he mounted upon his horse ; and when he was in his saddle well apparelled, and his shield dressed upon his shoulder, Tristram asked Gouvernail, Where is this knight that I shall have ado withal ? Sir, said Gouvernail, see ye him not ? I weened ye had seen him ; yonder he hoveth under the umbre of his ships on horseback, with his spear in his hand and his shield upon his shoulder. That is truth, said the noble knight, Sir Tristram, now I see him well enough. Then he commanded his servant Gouvernail to go to his vessel again : And commend me unto mine eme King Mark, and pray him if that I be slain in this battle for to inter my body as him seemed best ; and as for me, let him wit that I will never yield me for cowardice ; and if I be slain and flee not, then they have lost no truage for me ; and if so be that I flee or yield me as recreant, bid mine eme never bury me in Christian burials. And upon thy life, said Sir Tristram to Gouvernail, come thou not nigh this island till that thou see me overcome or slain, or else that I win yonder knight. So either departed from other sore weeping.

CHAPTER VII

HOW SIR TRISTRAM FOUGHT AGAINST SIR MARHAUS AND ACHIEVED HIS BATTLE, AND HOW SIR MARHAUS FLED TO HIS SHIP

AND then Sir Marhaus avised Sir Tristram, and said thus : Young knight, Sir Tristram, what dost thou here ? me sore repenteth of thy courage, for wit thou well I have been assayed, and the best knights of this land have been assayed of my hand ; and also I have matched with the best knights of the world, and therefore by my counsel return again unto thy vessel. And fair knight, and well-proved knight, said Sir Tristram, thou shalt well wit I may not forsake thee in this quarrel, for I am for thy sake made knight. And thou shalt well wit that I am a king's son born, and gotten upon a queen ; and such promise I have made at my uncle's request and mine own seeking, that I shall fight with thee unto the uttermost, and deliver Cornwall from the old truage. And also wit thou well, Sir Marhaus, that this is the greatest cause that thou couragest me to have ado with thee, for thou art called one of the most renowned knights of the world, and by cause of that noise and fame that thou hast thou givest me courage to have ado with thee, for never yet was I proved with good knight ; and sythen I took the order of knighthood this day, I am well pleased that I may have ado with so good a knight as thou art. And now wit thou well, Sir Marhaus, that I cast me to get worship on thy body ; and if that I be not proved, I trust to God that I shall be worshipfully proved upon thy body, and to deliver the country of Cornwall for ever from all manner of truage from Ireland for ever. When Sir Marhaus had heard him say what he would, he said then thus again : Fair knight, sythen it is so that thou castest to win worship of me, I let thee wit worship may thou none lose by me if thou mayest stand me three strokes ; for I let thee wit for my noble deeds, proved and seen, King Arthur made me knight of the Table Round. Then they began to feutre their spears, and they met so fiercely together that they smote either other down, both horse and all. But Sir Marhaus smote Sir Tristram a great wound in the side with his spear, and then they avoided their horses, and pulled out their swords, and threw their shields afore them. And then they lashed together as men that were wild and courageous. And when they had stricken so together long, then they left their strokes, and foyned at their breaths and visors ; and when they saw that that might not prevail them, then they hurtled together like rams to bear either other down. Thus they fought still more than half a day, and either were wounded passing sore, that the blood ran down freshly from them upon the ground. By then Sir Tristram waxed more fresher than Sir Marhaus, and better winded and bigger; and with a mighty stroke he smote Sir Marhaus upon the helm such a buffet that it went through his helm, and through the coif of steel, and through the brain-pan, and the sword stuck so fast in the helm and in his brain-pan that Sir Tristram pulled thrice at his sword or ever he might pull it out from his head; and there Marhaus fell down on his knees, the edge of Tristram's sword left in his brain-pan. And suddenly Sir Marhaus rose grovelling, and threw his sword and his shield from him, and so ran to his ships and fled his way, and Sir Tristram had ever his shield and his sword. And when Sir Tristram saw Sir Marhaus withdraw him, he said: Ah! sir knight of the Round Table, why withdrawest thou thee? thou dost thyself and thy kin great shame, for I am but a young knight, or now I was never proved, and rather than I should withdraw me from thee, I had rather be hewn in an hundred pieces. Sir Marhaus answered no word but yede his way sore groaning. Well, sir knight, said Sir Tristram, I promise thee thy sword and thy shield shall be mine; and thy shield shall I wear in all places where I ride on mine adventures, and in the sight of King Arthur and all the Round Table.

CHAPTER VIII

HOW SIR MARHAUS AFTER THAT HE WAS ARRIVED IN IRELAND DIED OF THE STROKE THAT SIR TRISTRAM HAD GIVEN HIM, AND HOW TRISTRAM WAS HURT

ANON Sir Marhaus and his fellowship departed into Ireland. And as soon as he came to the king, his brother, he let search his wounds. And when his head was searched a piece of Sir Tristram's sword was found therein, and might never be had out of his head for no surgeons, and so he died of Sir Tristram's sword; and that piece of the sword the queen, his sister, kept it for ever with her, for she thought to be revenged an she might. Now turn we again unto Sir Tristram, that was sore wounded, and full sore bled that he might not within a little while, when he had taken cold, unnethe stir him of his limbs. And then he set him down softly upon a little hill, and bled fast. Then anon came Gouvernail, his man, with his vessel; and the king and his barons came with procession against him. And when he was come unto the land, King Mark took him in his arms, and the king and Sir Dinas, the seneschal, led Sir Tristram into the castle of Tintagil. And then was he searched in the best manner, and laid in his bed. And when King Mark saw his wounds he wept heartily, and so did all his lords. So God me help, said King Mark, I would not for all my lands that my nephew died. So Sir Tristram lay there a month and more, and ever he was like to die of that stroke that Sir Marhaus smote him first with the spear. For, as the French book saith, the spear's head was envenomed, that Sir Tristram might not be whole. Then was King Mark and all his barons passing heavy, for they deemed none other but that Sir Tristram should not recover. Then the king let send after all manner of leeches and surgeons, both unto men and women, and there was none that would behote him the life. Then came there a lady that was a right wise lady, and she said plainly unto King Mark, and to Sir Tristram, and to all his barons, that he should never be whole but if Sir Tristram went in the same country that the venom came from, and in that country should he be holpen or else never. Thus said the lady unto the king. When King Mark understood that, he let purvey for Sir Tristram a fair vessel, well victualled, and therein was put Sir Tristram, and Gouvernail with him, and Sir Tristram took his harp with him, and so he was put into the sea to sail into Ireland; and so by good fortune he arrived up in Ireland, even fast by a castle where the king and the queen was; and at his arrival he sat and harped in his bed a merry lay, such one heard they never none in Ireland before that time. And when it was told the king and the queen of such a knight that was such an harper, anon the king sent for him, and let search his wounds, and then asked him his name. Then he answered, I am of the country of Liones, and my name is Tramtrist, that thus was wounded in a battle as I fought for a lady's right. So God me help, said King Anguish, ye shall have all the help in this land that ye may have here; but I let you wit, in Cornwall I had a great loss as ever had king, for there I lost the best knight of the world; his name was Marhaus, a full noble knight, and Knight of the Table Round; and there he told Sir Tristram wherefore Sir Marhaus was slain. Sir Tristram made semblant as he had been sorry, and better knew he how it was than the king.

CHAPTER IX

THEN the king for great favour made Tramtrist to be put in his daughter's ward and keeping, because she was a noble surgeon. And when she had searched him she found in the bottom of his wound that therein was poison, and so she healed him within a while; and therefore Tramtrist cast great love to La Beale Isoud, for she was at that time the fairest maid and lady of the world. And there Tramtrist learned her to harp, and she began to have a great fantasy unto him. And at that time Sir Palamides, the Saracen, was in that country, and well cherished with the king and the queen. And every day Sir Palamides drew unto La Beale Isoud and proffered her many gifts, for he loved her passingly well. All that espied Tramtrist, and full well knew he Sir Palamides for a noble knight and a mighty man. And wit you well Sir Tramtrist had great despite at Sir Palamides, for La Beale Isoud told Tramtrist that Palamides was in will to be christened for her sake. Thus was there great envy betwixt Tramtrist and Sir Palamides. Then it befell that King Anguish let cry a great jousts and a great tournament for a lady that was called the lady of the laundes, and she was nigh cousin unto the king. And what man won her, three days after he should wed her and have all her lands. This cry was made in England, Wales, Scotland, and also in France and in Brittany. It befell upon a day La Beale Isoud came unto Sir Tramtrist, and told him of this tournament. He answered and said : Fair lady, I am but a feeble knight, and but late I had been dead had not your good ladyship been. Now, fair lady, what would ye I should do in this matter? Well ye wot, my lady, that I may not joust. Ah, Tramtrist, said La Beale Isoud, why will ye not have ado at that tournament? well I wot Sir Palamides shall be there, and to do what he may ; and therefore Tramtrist, I pray you for to be there, for else Sir Palamides is like to win the degree. Madam, said Tramtrist, as for that, it may be so, for he is a proved knight, and I am but a young knight and late made ; and the first battle that I did it mishapped me to be sore wounded as ye see. But an I wist ye would be my better lady, at that tournament I will be, so that ye will keep my counsel and let no creature have knowledge that I shall joust but yourself, and such as ye will to keep your counsel; my poor person shall I jeopard there for your sake, that, peradventure, Sir Palamides shall know when that I come. Thereto, said La Beale Isoud, do your best, and as I can, said La Beale Isoud, I shall purvey horse and armour for you at my device. As ye will so be it, said Sir Tramtrist, I will be at your commandment. So at the day of jousts there came Sir Palamides with a black shield, and he overthrew many knights, that all the people had marvel of him. For he put to the worse Sir Gawaine, Gaheris, Agravaine, Bagdemagus, Kay, Dodias le Savage, Sagramore le Desirous, Gumret le Petit, and Griflet le Fise de Dieu. All these the first day Sir Palamides struck down to the earth. And then all manner of knights were adread of Sir Palamides, and many called him the knight with the black shield. So that day Sir Palamides had great worship. Then came King Anguish unto Tramtrist, and asked him why he would not joust. Sir, he said, I was but late hurt, and as yet I dare not adventure me. Then came there the same squire that was sent from the king's daughter of France unto Sir Tristram. And when he had espied Sir Tristram he fell flat to his feet. All that espied La Beale Isoud, what courtesy the squire made unto Sir Tristram. And therewithal suddenly Sir Tristram ran unto his squire, whose name was Hebes le Renoumes, and prayed him heartily in no wise to tell his name. Sir, said Hebes, I will not discover your name but if ye command me.

CHAPTER X

HOW SIR TRISTRAM WON THE DEGREE AT A TOURNAMENT IN IRELAND, AND THERE MADE PALAMIDES TO BEAR NO MORE HARNESS IN A YEAR

THEN Sir Tristram asked him what he did in those countries. Sir, he said, I came hither with Sir Gawaine for to be made knight, and if it please you, of your hands that I may be made knight. Await upon me as tomorn secretly, and in the field I shall make you a knight. Then had La Beale Isoud great suspicion unto Tramtrist, that he was some man of worship proved, and therewith she comforted herself, and cast more love unto him than she had done to-fore. And so on the morn Sir Palamides made him ready to come into the field as he did the first day. And there he smote down the king with the hundred knights, and the King of Scots. Then had La Beale Isoud ordained and well arrayed Sir Tristram in white horse and harness. And right so she let put him out at a privy postern, and so he came into the field as it had been a bright angel. And anon Sir Palamides espied him, and therewith he feutred a spear unto Sir Tramtrist, and he again unto him. And there Sir Tristram smote down Sir Palamides unto the earth. And then there was a great noise of people: some said Sir Palamides had a fall, some said the knight with the black shield had a fall. And wit you well La Beale Isoud was passing glad. And then Sir Gawaine and his fellows nine had marvel what knight it might be that had smitten down Sir Palamides. Then would there none joust with Tramtrist, but all that there were forsook him, most and least. Then Sir Tristram made Hebes a knight, and caused him to put himself forth, and did right well that day. So after Sir Hebes held him with Sir Tristram. And when Sir Palamides had received this fall, wit ye well that he was sore ashamed, and as privily as he might he withdrew him out of the field. All that espied Sir Tristram, and lightly he rode after Sir Palamides and overtook him, and bad him turn, for better he would essay him or ever he departed. Then Sir Palamides turned him, and either lashed at other with their swords. But at the first stroke Sir Tristram smote down Palamides, and gave him such a stroke upon the head that he fell to the earth. So then Tristram bad yield him, and do his commandment, or else he would slay him. When Sir Palamides beheld his countenance, he dread his buffets so, that he granted all his askings. Well said, said Sir Tristram, this shall be your charge. First, upon pain of your life that ye forsake my lady La Beale Isoud, and in no manner wise that ye draw not to her. Also this twelvemonth and a day that ye bear none armour nor none harness of war. Now promise me this, or here shalt thou die. Alas, said Palamides, for ever am I ashamed. Then he sware as Sir Tristram had commanded him. Then for despite and anger Sir Palamides cut off his harness, and threw them away. And so Sir Tristram turned again to the castle where was La Beale Isoud ; and by the way he met with a damosel that asked after Sir Launcelot, that won the Dolorous Guard worshipfully; and this damosel asked Sir Tristram what he was. For it was told her that it was he that smote down Sir Palamides, by whom the ten knights of King Arthur's were smitten down. Then the damosel prayed Sir Tristram to tell her what he was, and whether that he were Sir Launcelot du Lake, for she deemed that there was no knight in the world might do such deeds of arms but if it were Launcelot. Fair damosel, said Sir Tristram, wit ye well that I am not Sir Launcelot, for I was never of such prowess, but in God is all that he may make me as good a knight as the good knight Sir Launcelot. Now, gentle knight, said she, put up thy visor; and when she beheld his visage she thought she saw never a better man's visage, nor a better faring knight. And then when the damosel knew certainly that he was not Sir Launcelot, then she took her leave, and departed from him. And then Sir Tristram rode privily unto the postern, where kept him La Beale Isoud, and there she made him good cheer, and thanked God of his good speed. So anon, within a while the king and the queen understood that it was Tramtrist that smote down Sir Palamides; then was he much made of, more than he was before.

CHAPTER XI

HOW THE QUEEN ESPIED THAT SIR TRISTRAM HAD SLAIN HER BROTHER SIR MARHAUS BY HIS SWORD, AND IN WHAT JEOPARDY HE WAS

THUS was Sir Tramtrist long there well cherished with the king and the queen, and namely with La Beale Isoud. So upon a day the queen and La Beale Isoud made a bayne for Sir Tramtrist. And when he was in his bayne the queen and Isoud, her daughter, roamed up and down in the chamber; and therewhiles Gouvernail and Hebes attended upon Tramtrist, and the queen beheld his sword there as it lay upon his bed. And then by unhap the queen drew out his sword and beheld it a long while, and both they thought it a passing fair sword; but within a foot and an half of the point there was a great piece thereof out broken of the edge. And when the queen espied that gap in the sword, she remembered her of a piece of a sword that was found in the brain-pan of Sir Marhaus, the good knight that was her brother. Alas then, said she unto her daughter, La Beale Isoud, this is the same traitor knight that slew my brother, thine eme. When Isoud heard her say so she was passing sore abashed, for passing well she loved Tramtrist, and full well she knew the cruelness of her mother the queen. Anon therewithal the queen went unto her own chamber, and sought her coffer, and there she took out the piece of the sword that was pulled out of Sir Marhaus' head after that he was dead. And then she ran with that piece of iron to the sword that lay upon the bed. And when she put that piece of steel and iron unto the sword, it was as meet as it might be when it was new broken. And then the queen gripped that sword in her hand fiercely, and with all her might she ran straight upon Tramtrist where he sat in his bayne, and there she had rived him through had not Sir Hebes gotten her in his arms, and pulled the sword from her, and else she had thrust him through. Then when she was let of her evil will she ran to the King Anguish, her husband, and said on her knees: O my lord, here have ye in your house that traitor knight that slew my brother and your servant, that noble knight, Sir Marhaus. Who is that, said King Anguish, and where is he? Sir, she said, it is Sir Tramtrist, the same knight that my daughter healed. Alas, said the king, therefore am I right heavy, for he is a full noble knight as ever I saw in field. But I charge you, said the king to the queen, that ye have not ado with that knight, but let me deal with him. Then the king went into the chamber unto Sir Tramtrist, and then was he gone unto his chamber, and the king found him all ready armed to mount upon his horse. When the king saw him all ready armed to go unto horseback, the king said: Nay, Tramtrist, it will not avail to compare thee against me; but thus much I shall do for my worship and for thy love; in so much as thou art within my court it were no worship for me to slay thee: therefore upon this condition I will give thee leave for to depart from this court in safety, so thou wilt tell me who was thy father, and what is thy name, and if thou slew Sir Marhaus, my brother.

CHAPTER XII

HOW SIR TRISTRAM DEPARTED FROM THE KING AND LA BEALE
ISOUD OUT OF IRELAND FOR TO COME INTO CORNWALL

SIR, said Tristram, now I shall tell you all the truth: my father's name is Sir Meliodas, King of Liones, and my mother hight Elizabeth, that was sister unto King Mark of Cornwall; and my mother died of me in the forest, and by cause thereof she commanded or she died that when I were christened they should christen me Tristram; and by cause I would not be known in this country I turned my name and let me call Tramtrist; and for the truage of Cornwall I fought for my eme's sake, and for the right of Cornwall that ye had possessed many years. And wit ye well, said Tristram unto the king, I did the battle for the love of mine uncle, King Mark, and for the love of the country of Cornwall, and for to increase mine honour; for that same day that I fought with Sir Marhaus I was made knight, and never or then did I battle with no knight, and from me he went alive, and left his shield and his sword behind. So God me help, said the king, I may not say but ye did as a knight should, and it was your part to do for your quarrel, and to increase your worship as a knight should; howbeit I may not maintain you in this country with my worship, unless that I should displease my barons, and my wife and her kin. Sir, said Tristram, I thank you of your good lordship that I have had with you here, and the great goodness my lady, your daughter, hath shewed me, and therefore, said Sir Tristram, it may so happen that ye shall win more by my life than by my death, for in the parts of England it may happen I may do you service at some season, that ye shall be glad that ever ye shewed me your good lordship. With more I promise you as I am true knight, that in all places I shall be my lady, your daughter's, servant and knight in right and in wrong, and I shall never fail her to do as much as a knight may do. Also I beseech your good grace that I may take my leave at my lady, your daughter, and at all the barons and knights. I will well, said the king. Then Sir Tristram went unto La Beale Isoud and took his leave of her. And then he told her all, what he was, and how he had changed his name by cause he would not be known, and how a lady told him that he should never be whole till he came into this country where the poison was made, wherethrough I was near my death had not your ladyship been. O gentle knight, said La Beale Isoud, full woe am I of thy departing, for I saw never man that I owed so good will to. And therewithal she wept heartily. Madam, said Sir Tristram, ye shall understand that my name is Sir Tristram de Liones, gotten of King Meliodas, and born of his queen. And I promise you faithfully that I shall be all the days of my life your knight. Gramercy, said La Beale Isoud, and I promise you thereagainst that I shall not be married this seven years but by your assent; and to whom that ye will I shall be married to him will I have, and he will have me if ye will consent. And then Sir Tristram gave her a ring, and she gave him another; and therewith he departed from her, leaving her making great dole and lamentation; and he straight went unto the court among all the barons, and there he took his leave at most and least, and openly he said among them all: Fair lords, now it is so that I must depart: if there be any man here that I have offended unto, or that any man be with me grieved, let complain him here afore me or that ever I depart, and I shall amend it unto my power. And if there be any that will proffer me wrong, or say of me wrong or shame behind my back, say it now or never, and here is my body to make it good, body against body. And all they stood still, there was not one that would say one word; yet were there some knights that were of the queen's blood, and of Sir Marhaus' blood, but they would not meddle with him.

CHAPTER XIII

HOW SIR TRISTRAM AND KING MARK HURTED EACH OTHER FOR THE LOVE OF A KNIGHT'S WIFE

So Sir Tristram departed, and took the sea, and with good wind he arrived up at Tintagil in Cornwall; and when King Mark was whole in his prosperity there came tidings that Sir Tristram was arrived, and whole of his wounds: thereof was King Mark passing glad, and so were all the barons; and when he saw his time he rode unto his father, King Meliodas, and there he had all the cheer that the king and the queen could make him. And then largely King Meliodas and his queen departed of their lands and goods to Sir Tristram. Then by the license of King Meliodas, his father, he returned again unto the court of King Mark, and there he lived in great joy long time, until at the last there befell a jealousy and an unkindness betwixt King Mark and Sir Tristram, for they loved both one lady. And she was an earl's wife that hight Sir Segwarides. And this lady loved Sir Tristram passingly well. And he loved her again, for she was a passing fair lady, and that espied Sir Tristram well. Then King Mark understood that and was jealous, for King Mark loved her passingly well. So it fell upon a day this lady sent a dwarf unto Sir Tristram, and bad him, as he loved her, that he would be with her the night next following. Also she charged you that ye come not to her but if ye be well armed, for her lover was called a good knight. Sir Tristram answered to the dwarf: Recommend me unto my lady, and tell her I will not fail but I will be with her the term that she hath set me. And with this answer the dwarf departed. And King Mark espied that the dwarf was with Sir Tristram upon message from Segwarides' wife; then King Mark sent for the dwarf, and when he was come he made the dwarf by force to tell him all, why and wherefore that he came on message from Sir Tristram. Now, said King Mark, go where thou wilt, and upon pain of death that thou say no word that thou spakest with me; so the dwarf departed from the king. And that same night that the steven was set betwixt Segwarides' wife and Sir Tristram, King Mark armed him, and made him ready, and took two knights of his council with him; and so he rode afore for to abide by the way, for to wait upon Sir Tristram. And as Sir Tristram came riding upon his way with his spear in his hand, King Mark came hurtling upon him with his two knights suddenly. And all three smote him with their spears, and King Mark hurt Sir Tristram on the breast right sore. And then Sir Tristram feutred his spear, and smote his uncle, King Mark, so sore, that he rashed him to the earth, and bruised him that he lay still in a swoon, and long it was or ever he might welde himself. And then he ran to the one knight, and efte to the other, and smote them to the cold earth, that they lay still. And therewithal Sir Tristram rode forth sore wounded to the lady, and found her abiding him at a postern.

CHAPTER XIV

HOW SIR TRISTRAM LAY WITH THE LADY, AND HOW HER HUSBAND
FOUGHT WITH SIR TRISTRAM

AND there she welcomed him fair, and either halsed other in arms, and so she let put up his horse in the best wise, and then she unarmed him. And so they supped lightly, and went to bed with great joy and pleasaunce; and so in his raging he took no keep of his green wound that King Mark had given him. And so Sir Tristram bled both the over sheet and the nether, and pillows, and head sheet. And within a while there came one afore, that warned her that her lord was near hand within a bow draught. So she made Sir Tristram to arise, and so he armed him, and took his horse, and so departed. By then was come Segwarides, her lord, and when he found her bed troubled and broken, and went near and beheld it by candle light, then he saw that there had lain a wounded knight. Ah, false traitress, then he said, why hast thou betrayed me? And therewithal he swang out a sword, and said: But if thou tell me who hath been here, here thou shalt die. Ah, my lord, mercy, said the lady, and held up her hands, saying: Slay me not, and I shall tell you all who hath been here. Tell anon, said Segwarides, to me all the truth. Anon for dread she said: Here was Sir Tristram with me, and by the way as he came to me ward, he was sore wounded. Ah, false traitress, said Segwarides, where is he become? Sir, she said, he is armed, and departed on horseback, not yet hence half a mile. Ye say well, said Segwarides. Then he armed him lightly, and gat his horse, and rode after Sir Tristram that rode straightway unto Tintagil. And within a while he overtook Sir Tristram, and then he bad him, Turn, false traitor-knight. And Sir Tristram anon turned him against him. And therewithal Segwarides smote Sir Tristram with a spear that it all to brast; and then he swang out his sword and smote fast at Sir Tristram. Sir knight, said Sir Tristram, I counsel you that ye smite no more, howbeit for the wrongs that I have done you I will forbear you as long as I may. Nay, said Segwarides, that shall not be, for either thou shalt die or I. Then Sir Tristram drew out his sword, and hurtled his horse unto him fiercely, and through the waist of the body he smote Sir Segwarides that he fell to the earth in a swoon. And so Sir Tristram departed and left him there. And so he rode unto Tintagil and took his lodging secretly, for he would not be known that he was hurt. Also Sir Segwarides' men rode after their master, whom they found lying in the field sore wounded, and brought him home on his shield, and there he lay long or that he were whole, but at the last he recovered. Also King Mark would not be aknown of that Sir Tristram and he had met that night. And as for Sir Tristram, he knew not that King Mark had met with him. And so the king askance came to Sir Tristram, to comfort him as he lay sick in his bed. But as long as King Mark lived he loved never Sir Tristram after that; though there was fair speech, love was there none. And thus it passed many weeks and days, and all was forgiven and forgotten; for Sir Segwarides durst not have ado with Sir Tristram, because of his noble prowess, and also because he was nephew unto King Mark; therefore he let it overslip: for he that hath a privy hurt is loth to have a shame outward.

CHAPTER XV

HOW SIR BLEOBERIS DEMANDED THE FAIREST LADY IN KING MARK'S COURT, WHOM HE TOOK AWAY, AND HOW HE WAS FOUGHT WITH

THEN it befell upon a day that the good knight Bleoberis de Ganis, brother to Blamore de Ganis, and nigh cousin unto the good knight Sir Launcelot du Lake, this Bleoberis came unto the court of King Mark, and there he asked of King Mark a boon, to give him what gift that he would ask in his court. When the king heard him ask so, he marvelled of his asking, but because he was a knight of the Round Table, and of a great renown, King Mark granted him his whole asking. Then, said Sir Bleoberis, I will have the fairest lady in your court that me list to choose. I may not say nay, said King Mark; now choose at your adventure. And so Sir Bleoberis did choose Sir Segwarides' wife, and took her by the hand, and so went his way with her; and so he took his horse and gart set her behind his squire, and rode upon his way. When Sir Segwarides heard tell that his lady was gone with a knight of King Arthur's court, then he

armed him and rode after that knight for to rescue his lady.
So when Bleoberis was gone with this lady, King Mark and
all the court was wroth that she was away. Then were
there certain ladies that knew that there were great love
between Sir Tristram and her, and also that lady loved Sir
Tristram above all other knights. Then there was one lady
that rebuked Sir Tristram in the horriblest wise, and called
him coward knight, that he would for shame of his knighthood see a lady so shamefully be taken away from his uncle's
court. But she meant that either of them had loved other
with entire heart. But Sir Tristram answered her thus : Fair
lady, it is not my part to have ado in such matters while her
lord and husband is present here ; and if it had been that
her lord had not been here in this court, then for the
worship of this court peradventure I would have been her
champion, and if so be Sir Segwarides speed not well, it may
happen that I will speak with that good knight or ever he
pass from this country. Then within a while came one of
Sir Segwarides' squires, and told in the court that Sir
Segwarides was beaten sore and wounded to the point of
death ; as he would have rescued his lady Sir Bleoberis overthrew him and sore hath wounded him. Then was King
Mark heavy thereof, and all the court. When Sir Tristram
heard of this he was ashamed and sore grieved ; and then
was he soon armed and on horseback, and Gouvernail, his
servant, bare his shield and spear. And so as Sir Tristram
rode fast he met with Sir Andret his cousin, that by the
commandment of King Mark was sent to bring forth, an ever
it lay in his power, two knights of Arthur's court, that rode
by the country to seek their adventures. When Sir Tristram
saw Sir Andret he asked him what tidings. So God me help,
said Sir Andret, there was never worse with me, for here by
the commandment of King Mark I was sent to fetch two
knights of King Arthur's court, and that one beat me and
wounded me, and set nought by my message. Fair cousin,
said Sir Tristram, ride on your way, and if I may meet them
it may happen I shall revenge you. So Sir Andret rode into
Cornwall, and Sir Tristram rode after the two knights, the
which one hight Sagramore Le Desirous, and the other
hight Dodinas Le Savage.

CHAPTER XVI

THEN within a while Sir Tristram saw them afore him, two likely knights. Sir, said Gouvernail unto his master, Sir, I would counsel you not to have ado with them, for they be two proved knights of Arthur's court. As for that, said Sir Tristram, have ye no doubt but I will have ado with them to increase my worship, for it is many day sythen I did any deeds of arms. Do as ye list, said Gouvernail. And therewithal anon Sir Tristram asked them from whence they came, and whither they would, and what they did in those marches. Sir Sagramore looked upon Sir Tristram, and had scorn of his words, and asked him again, Fair knight, be ye a knight of Cornwall? Whereby ask ye it? said Sir Tristram. For it is seldom seen, said Sir Sagramore, that ye Cornish knights be valiant men of arms; for within these two hours there met us one of your Cornish knights, and great words he spake, and anon with little might he was laid to the earth. And, as I trow, said Sir Sagramore, ye shall have the same handsel that he had. Fair lords, said Sir Tristram, it may so happen that I may better withstand than he did, and whether ye will or no I will have ado with you, because he was my cousin that ye beat. And therefore here do your best, and wit ye well but if ye quit you the better here upon this ground, one knight of Cornwall shall beat you both. When Sir Dodinas le Savage heard him say so he gat a spear in his hand, and said, Sir knight, keep well thyself. And then they departed and came together as it had been thunder. And Sir Dodinas' spear brast in sunder, but Sir Tristram smote him with a more might, that he smote him clean over the horse croup, that nigh he had broken his neck. When Sir Sagramore saw his fellow have such a fall he marvelled what knight he might be. And he dressed his spear with all his might, and Sir Tristram against him, and they came together as the thunder, and there Sir Tristram smote Sir Sagramore a strong buffet, that he bare his horse and him to the earth, and in the falling he brake his thigh. When this was done Sir Tristram asked them: Fair knights, will ye any more? Be there no bigger knights in the court of King Arthur? it is to you shame to say of us knights of

Cornwall dishonour, for it may happen a Cornish knight may match you. That is truth, said Sir Sagramore, that have we well proved ; but I require thee, said Sir Sagramore, tell us your right name, by the faith and troth that ye owe to the high order of knighthood. Ye charge me with a great thing, said Sir Tristram, and sythen ye list to wit it, ye shall know and understand that my name is Sir Tristram de Liones, King Meliodas' son, and nephew unto King Mark. Then were they two knights fain that they had met with Tristram, and so they prayed him to abide in their fellowship. Nay, said Sir Tristram, for I must have ado with one of your fellows, his name is Sir Bleoberis de Ganis. God speed you well, said Sir Sagramore and Dodinas. Sir Tristram departed and rode onward on his way. And then was he ware before him in a valley where rode Sir Bleoberis with Sir Segwarides' lady that rode behind his squire upon a palfrey.

CHAPTER XVII

HOW SIR TRISTRAM FOUGHT WITH SIR BLEOBERIS FOR A LADY, AND HOW THE LADY WAS PUT TO CHOICE TO WHOM SHE WOULD GO

THEN Sir Tristram rode more than a pace until that he had overtaken him. Then spake Sir Tristram : Abide, he said, Knight of Arthur's court, bring again that lady, or deliver her to me. I will do neither, said Bleoberis, for I dread no Cornish knight so sore that me list to deliver her. Why, said Sir Tristram, may not a Cornish knight do as well as another knight? this same day two knights of your court within this three mile met with me, and or ever we departed they found a Cornish knight good enough for them both. What were their names? said Bleoberis. They told me, said Sir Tristram, that the one of them hight Sir Sagramore le Desirous, and the other hight Dodinas le Savage. Ah, said Sir Bleoberis, have ye met with them? so God me help, they were two good knights and men of great worship, and if ye have beat them both ye must needs be a good knight ; but if it so be ye have beat them both, yet shall ye not fear me, but ye shall beat me or ever ye have this lady. Then defend you, said Sir Tristram. So they departed and came together like thunder, and either bare other down, horse and all, to the earth. Then they avoided their horses, and lashed together eagerly with swords, and mightily, now tracing and traversing on the right hand and on the left hand more than two hours. And sometime they rushed together with such a might that they lay both grovelling on the ground. Then Sir Bleoberis de Ganis start aback, and said thus: Now, gentle good knight, a while hold your hands, and let us speak together. Say what ye will, said Tristram, and I will answer you. Sir, said Bleoberis, I would wit of whence ye be, and of whom ye be come, and what is your name? So God me help, said Sir Tristram, I fear not to tell you my name. Wit ye well I am King Meliodas' son, and my mother is King Mark's sister, and my name is Sir Tristram de Liones, and King Mark is mine uncle. Truly, said Bleoberis, I am right glad of you, for ye are he that slew Marhaus the knight, hand for hand in an island, for the truage of Cornwall; also ye overcame Sir Palamides the good knight, at a tournament in an island, where ye beat Sir Gawaine and his nine fellows. So God me help, said Sir Tristram, wit ye well that I am the same knight; now I have told you my name, tell me yours with good will. Wit ye well that my name is Sir Bleoberis de Ganis, and my brother hight Sir Blamore de Ganis, that is called a good knight, and we be sister's children unto my lord Sir Launcelot du Lake, that we call one of the best knights of the world. That is truth, said Sir Tristram, Sir Launcelot is called peerless of courtesy and of knighthood; and for his sake, said Sir Tristram, I will not with my good will fight no more with you, for the great love I have to Sir Launcelot du Lake. In good faith, said Bleoberis, as for me I will be loth to fight with you; but sythen ye follow me here to have this lady, I shall proffer you kindness, courtesy, and gentleness right here upon this ground. This lady shall be betwixt us both, and to whom that she will go, let him have her in peace. I will well, said Tristram, for, as I deem, she will leave you and come to me. Ye shall prove it anon, said Bleoberis.

CHAPTER XVIII

HOW THE LADY FORSOOK SIR TRISTRAM AND ABODE WITH SIR BLEOBERIS, AND HOW SHE DESIRED TO GO TO HER HUSBAND

So when she was set betwixt them both she said these words unto Sir Tristram: Wit ye well, Sir Tristram de

Liones, that but late thou wast the man in the world that I most loved and trusted, and I weened thou hadst loved me again above all ladies; but when thou sawest this knight lead me away thou madest no cheer to rescue me, but suffered my lord Segwarides ride after me; but until that time I weened thou haddest loved me, and therefore now I will leave thee, and never love thee more. And therewithal she went unto Sir Bleoberis. When Sir Tristram saw her do so he was wonderly wroth with that lady, and ashamed to come to the court. Sir Tristram, said Sir Bleoberis, ye are in the default, for I hear by this lady's words she before this day trusted you above all earthly knights, and, as she sayeth, ye have deceived her, therefore wit ye well, there may no man hold that will away; and rather than ye should be heartily displeased with me I would ye had her, an she would abide with you. Nay, said the lady, so God me help I will never go with him; for he that I loved most I weened he had loved me. And therefore, Sir Tristram, she said, ride as thou came, for though thou haddest overcome this knight, as ye was likely, with thee never would I have gone. And I shall pray this knight so fair of his knighthood, that or ever he pass this country that he will lead me to the abbey where my lord Sir Segwarides lieth. So God me help, said Bleoberis, I let you wit, good knight Sir Tristram, because King Mark gave me the choice of a gift in this court, and so this lady liked me best, notwithstanding she is wedded and hath a lord; and I have fulfilled my quest: she shall be sent unto her husband again, and in especial most for your sake, Sir Tristram; and if she would go with you I would ye had her. I thank you, said Sir Tristram, but for her love I shall beware what manner a lady I shall love or trust; for had her lord, Sir Segwarides, been away from the court, I should have been the first that should have followed you; but sythen that ye have refused me, as I am true knight I shall her know passingly well that I shall love or trust. And so they took their leave one from the other and departed. And so Sir Tristram rode unto Tintagil, and Sir Bleoberis rode unto the abbey where Sir Segwarides lay sore wounded, and there he delivered his lady, and departed as a noble knight; and when Sir Segwarides saw his lady, he was greatly comforted; and then she told him that Sir Tristram had done great battle with Sir Bleoberis, and caused him to bring her again. These words pleased Sir Segwarides right well, that Sir Tristram would do so much; and so that lady told all the battle unto King Mark betwixt Sir Tristram and Sir Bleoberis.

CHAPTER XIX

HOW KING MARK SENT SIR TRISTRAM FOR LA BEALE ISOUD TOWARD IRELAND, AND HOW BY FORTUNE HE ARRIVED INTO ENGLAND

THEN when this was done King Mark cast always in his heart how he might destroy Sir Tristram. And then he imagined in himself to send Sir Tristram into Ireland for La Beale Isoud. For Sir Tristram had so praised her beauty and her goodness that King Mark said that he would wed her, whereupon he prayed Sir Tristram to take his way into Ireland for him on message. And all this was done to the intent to slay Sir Tristram. Notwithstanding, Sir Tristram would not refuse the message for no danger nor peril that might fall, for the pleasure of his uncle, but to go he made him ready in the most goodliest wise that might be devised. For Sir Tristram took with him the most goodliest knights that he might find in the court; and they were arrayed, after the guise that was then used, in the goodliest manner. So Sir Tristram departed and took the sea with all his fellowship. And anon, as he was in the broad sea a tempest took him and his fellowship, and drove them back into the coast of England; and there they arrived fast by Camelot, and full fain they were to take the land. And when they were landed Sir Tristram set up his pavilion upon the land of Camelot, and there he let hang his shield upon the pavilion. And that same day came two knights of King Arthur's, that one was Sir Ector de Maris, and Sir Morganor. And they touched the shield, and bade him come out of the pavilion for to joust an he would joust. Ye shall be answered, said Sir Tristram, an ye will tarry a little while. So he made him ready, and first he smote down Sir Ector de Maris, and after he smote down Sir Morganor, all with one spear, and sore bruised them. And when they lay upon the earth they asked Sir Tristram what he was, and of what country he was knight. Fair lords, said Sir Tristram, wit ye well that I am of Cornwall. Alas, said Sir Ector, now am I ashamed that ever any

Cornish knight should overcome me. And then for despite Sir Ector put off his armour from him, and went on foot, and would not ride.

CHAPTER XX

HOW KING ANGUISH OF IRELAND WAS SUMMONED TO COME TO KING ARTHUR'S COURT FOR TREASON

THEN it fell that Sir Bleoberis and Sir Blamore de Ganis, that were brethren, they had summoned the King Anguish of Ireland for to come to Arthur's court upon pain of forfeiture of King Arthur's good grace. And if the King of Ireland came not in at the day assigned and set the king should lose his hands. So by it happened that at the day assigned, King Arthur neither Sir Launcelot might not be there for to give the judgment, for King Arthur was with Sir Launcelot at the Castle Joyous Gard. And so King Arthur assigned King Carados and the King of Scots to be there that day as judges. So when the kings were at Camelot King Anguish of Ireland was come to know his accusers. Then was there Sir Blamore de Ganis, and appeled the King of Ireland of treason, that he had slain a cousin of his in his court in Ireland by treason. The king was sore abashed of his accusation, for why? he was come at the summons of King Arthur, and or he came at Camelot he wist not wherefore he was sent after. And when the king heard Sir Blamore say his will, he understood well there was none other remedy but for to answer him knightly; for the custom was such in those days, that an any man were appeled of any treason or murder he should fight body for body, or else to find another knight for him. And all manner of murderers in those days were called treason. So when King Anguish understood his accusing he was passing heavy, for he knew Sir Blamore de Ganis that he was a noble knight, and of noble knights come. Then the King of Ireland was simply purveyed of his answer; therefore the judges gave him respite by the third day to give his answer. So the king departed unto his lodging. The meanwhile there came a lady by Sir Tristram's pavilion making great dole. What aileth you, said Sir Tristram, that ye make such dole? Ah, fair knight, said the lady, I am ashamed unless that some good knight help me; for a great lady of worship sent by me a fair child and a rich, unto Sir Launcelot du Lake, and hereby there met with me a knight, and threw me down from my palfrey, and took away the child from me. Well, my lady, said Sir Tristram, and for my lord Sir Launcelot's sake I shall get you that child again, or else I shall be beaten for it. And so Sir Tristram took his horse, and asked the lady which way the knight rode; and then she told him. And he rode after him, and within a while he overtook that knight. And then Sir Tristram bad him turn and give again the child.

CHAPTER XXI

HOW SIR TRISTRAM RESCUED A CHILD FROM A KNIGHT, AND HOW GOUVERNAIL TOLD HIM OF KING ANGUISH

THE knight turned his horse and made him ready to fight. And then Sir Tristram smote him with a sword such a buffet that he tumbled to the earth. And then he yielded him unto Sir Tristram. Then come thy way, said Sir Tristram, and bring the child to the lady again. So he took his horse meekly and rode with Sir Tristram; and then by the way Sir Tristram asked him his name. Then he said, My name is Breuse Saunce Pité. So when he had delivered that child to the lady, he said: Sir, as in this the child is well remedied. Then Sir Tristram let him go again that sore repented him after, for he was a great foe unto many good knights of King Arthur's court. Then when Sir Tristram was in his pavilion Gouvernail, his man, came and told him how that King Anguish of Ireland was come thither, and he was put in great distress; and there Gouvernail told Sir Tristram how King Anguish was summoned and appeled of murder. So God me help, said Sir Tristram, these be the best tidings that ever came to me these seven years, for now shall the king of Ireland have need of my help; for I daresay there is no knight in this country that is not of Arthur's court dare do battle with Sir Blamore de Ganis; and for to win the love of the King of Ireland I will take the battle upon me; and therefore Gouvernail bring me, I charge thee, to the king. Then Gouvernail went unto King Anguish of Ireland, and saluted him fair. The king welcomed him and asked him what he would. Sir, said Gouvernail, here is a knight near hand that desireth to speak with you: he bad me say he would do you service. What knight is he? said the king. Sir, said he, it is Sir Tristram de Liones, that for your good grace that ye showed him in your lands will reward you in this country. Come on, fellow, said the king, with me anon and show me unto Sir Tristram. So the king took a little hackney and but few fellowship with him, until he came unto Sir Tristram's pavilion. And when Sir Tristram saw the king he ran unto him and would have holden his stirrup. But the king leapt from his horse lightly, and either halsed other in their arms. My gracious lord, said Sir Tristram, gramercy of your great goodnesses showed unto me in your marches and lands: and at that time I promised you to do you service an ever it lay in my power. And, gentle knight, said the king unto Sir Tristram, now have I great need of you, never had I so great need of no knight's help. How so, my good lord? said Sir Tristram. I shall tell you, said the king: I am summoned and appeled from my country for the death of a knight that was kin unto the good knight Sir Launcelot; wherefore Sir Blamore de Ganis, brother to Sir Bleoberis hath appeled me to fight with him, outher to find a knight in my stead. And well I wot, said the king, these that are come of King Ban's blood, as Sir Launcelot and these other, are passing good knights, and hard men for to win in battle as any that I know now living. Sir, said Sir Tristram, for the good lordship ye showed me in Ireland, and for my lady your daughter's sake, La Beale Isoud, I will take the battle for you upon this condition that ye shall grant me two things: that one is that ye shall swear to me that ye are in the right, that ye were never consenting to the knight's death; Sir, then said Sir Tristram, when that I have done this battle, if God give me grace that I speed, that ye shall give me a reward, what thing reasonable that I will ask of you. So God me help, said the king, ye shall have whatsomever ye will ask. It is well said, said Sir Tristram.

CHAPTER XXII

HOW SIR TRISTRAM FOUGHT FOR SIR ANGUISH AND OVERCAME HIS
ADVERSARY, AND HOW HIS ADVERSARY WOULD NEVER YIELD HIM

Now make your answer that your champion is ready, for I shall die in your quarrel rather than to be recreant. I have no doubt of you, said the king, that, an ye should have ado with Sir Launcelot du Lake. Sir, said Sir Tristram, as for Sir Launcelot, he is called the noblest knight of the world, and wit ye well that the knights of his blood are noble men, and dread shame ; and as for Bleoberis, brother unto Sir Blamore, I have done battle with him, therefore upon my head it is no shame to call him a good knight. It is noised, said the king, that Blamore is the hardier knight. Sir, as for that let him be, he shall never be refused, an as he were the best knight that now beareth shield or spear. So King Anguish departed unto King Carados and the kings that were that time as judges, and told them that he had found his champion ready. Then by the command-ment of the kings Sir Blamore de Ganis and Sir Tristram were sent for to hear the charge. And when they were come before the judges there were many kings and knights beheld Sir Tristram, and much speech they had of him because that he slew Sir Marhaus, the good knight, and because he forjousted Sir Palamides the good knight. So when they had taken their charge they withdrew them to make them ready to do battle. Then said Sir Bleoberis unto his brother, Sir Blamore : Fair dear brother, remember of what kin we be come of, and what a man is Sir Launcelot du Lake, neither farther nor nearer but brother's children, and there was never none of our kin that ever was shamed in battle ; and rather suffer death, brother, than to be shamed. Brother, said Blamore, have ye no doubt of me, for I shall never shame none of my blood ; howbeit I am sure that yonder knight is called a passing good knight as of his time one of the world, yet shall I never yield me, nor say the loth word : well may he happen to smite me down with his great might of chivalry, but rather shall he slay me than I shall yield me as recreant. God speed you well, said Sir Bleoberis, for ye shall find him the mightiest knight that ever ye had ado withal, for I know him, for I have had ado with him. God me speed, said Sir Blamore de Ganis ; and

therewith he took his horse at the one end of the lists, and
Sir Tristram at the other end of the lists, and so they feutred
their spears and came together as it had been thunder; and
there Sir Tristram through great might smote down Sir
Blamore and his horse to the earth. Then anon Sir Blamore
avoided his horse and pulled out his sword and threw his
shield afore him, and bad Sir Tristram alight: For though
an horse hath failed me, I trust to God the earth will not
fail me. And then Sir Tristram alit, and dressed him unto
battle; and there they lashed together strongly as racing
and tracing, foyning and dashing, many sad strokes, that
the kings and knights had great wonder that they might
stand; for ever they fought like wood men, so that there
was never knights seen fight more fiercely than they did;
for Sir Blamore was so hasty that he would have no rest,
that all men wondered that they had breath to stand on
their feet; and all the place was bloody that they fought in.
And at the last, Sir Tristram smote Sir Blamore such a
buffet upon the helm that he there fell down upon his side,
and Sir Tristram stood and beheld him.

CHAPTER XXIII

HOW SIR BLAMORE DESIRED TRISTRAM TO SLAY HIM, AND HOW SIR TRISTRAM SPARED HIM, AND HOW THEY TOOK APPOINTMENT

THEN when Sir Blamore might speak, he said thus: Sir
Tristram de Liones, I require thee, as thou art a noble
knight, and the best knight that ever I found, that thou wilt
slay me out, for I would not live to be made lord of all the
earth, for I have lever die with worship than live with shame;
and needs, Sir Tristram, thou must slay me, or else thou
shalt never win the field, for I will never say the loth word.
And therefore if thou dare slay me, slay me, I require thee.
When Sir Tristram heard him say so knightly, he wist not
what to do with him; he remembering him of both parties,
of what blood he was come, and for Sir Launcelot's sake he
would be loth to slay him; and in the other party in no
wise he might not choose, but that he must make him to
say the loth word, or else to slay him. Then Sir Tristram
start aback, and went to the kings that were judges, and
there he kneeled down tofore them, and besought them for
their worships, and for King Arthur's and Sir Launcelot's

sake, that they would take this matter in their hands. For, my fair lords, said Sir Tristram, it were shame and pity that this noble knight that yonder lieth should be slain; for ye hear well, shamed will he not be, and I pray to God that he never be slain nor shamed for me. And as for the king for whom I fight for, I shall require him, as I am his true champion and true knight in this field, that he will have mercy upon this good knight. So God me help, said King Anguish, I will for your sake, Sir Tristram, be ruled as ye will have me, for I know you for my true knight; and therefore I will heartily pray the kings that be here as judges to take it in their hands. And the kings that were judges called Sir Bleoberis to them, and asked him his advice. My lords, said Bleoberis, though my brother be beaten, and hath the worse through might of arms, I dare say, though Sir Tristram hath beaten his body he hath not beaten his heart, and I thank God he is not shamed this day; and rather than he should be shamed I require you, said Bleoberis, let Sir Tristram slay him out. It shall not be so, said the kings, for his part adversary, both the king and the champion, have pity of Sir Blamore's knighthood. My lords, said Bleoberis, I will right well as ye will. Then the kings called the king of Ireland, and found him goodly and treatable. And then, by all their advices, Sir Tristram and Sir Bleoberis took up Sir Blamore, and the two brethren were accorded with King Anguish, and kissed and made friends for ever. And then Sir Blamore and Sir Tristram kissed together, and there they made their oaths that they would never none of them two brethren fight with Sir Tristram, and Sir Tristram made the same oath. And for that gentle battle all the blood of Sir Launcelot loved Sir Tristram for ever. Then King Anguish and Sir Tristram took their leave, and sailed into Ireland with great noblesse and joy. So when they were in Ireland the king let make it known throughout all the land how and in what manner Sir Tristram had done for him. Then the queen and all that there were made the most of him that they might. But the joy that La Beale Isoud made of Sir Tristram there might no tongue tell, for of all men earthly she loved him most.

CHAPTER XXIV

HOW SIR TRISTRAM DEMANDED LA BEALE ISOUD FOR KING MARK,
AND HOW SIR TRISTRAM AND ISOUD DRANK THE LOVE DRINK

THEN upon a day King Anguish asked Sir Tristram why he asked not his boon, for whatsomever he had promised him he should have it without fail. Sir, said Sir Tristram, now is it time; this is all that I will desire, that ye will give me La Beale Isoud, your daughter, not for myself, but for mine uncle, King Mark, that shall have her to wife, for so have I promised him. Alas, said the king, I had liefer than all the land that I have ye would wed her yourself. Sir, an I did then I were shamed for ever in this world, and false of my promise. Therefore, said Sir Tristram, I pray you hold your promise that ye promised me; for this is my desire, that ye will give me La Beale Isoud to go with me into Cornwall for to be wedded to King Mark, mine uncle. As for that, said King Anguish, ye shall have her with you to do with her what it please you; that is for to say if that ye list to wed her yourself, that is me liefest, and if ye will give her unto King Mark, your uncle, that is in your choice. So to make short conclusion, La Beale Isoud was made ready to go with Sir Tristram, and Dame Bragwaine went with her for her chief gentlewoman, with many other. Then the queen, Isoud's mother, gave to her and Dame Bragwaine, her daughter's gentlewoman, and unto Gouvernail, a drink, and charged them that what day King Mark should wed, that same day they should give him that drink, so that King Mark should drink to La Beal Isoud, and then, said the queen, I undertake either shall love other the days of their life. So this drink was given unto Dame Bragwaine, and unto Gouvernail. And then anon Sir Tristram took the sea, and La Beale Isoud; and when they were in their cabin, it happed so that they were thirsty, and they saw a little flacket of gold stand by them, and it seemed by the colour and the taste that it was noble wine. Then Sir Tristram took the flacket in his hand, and said, Madam Isoud, here is the best drink that ever ye drank, that Dame Bragwaine, your maiden, and Gouvernail, my servant, have kept for themself. Then they laughed and made good cheer, and either drank to other freely, and they thought never drink that ever they drank to other was so sweet nor so good. But by that their drink was in their bodies, they loved either other so well that never their love departed for weal neither for woe. And thus it happed the love first betwixt Sir Tristram and La Beale Isoud, the which love never departed the days of their life. So then they sailed till by fortune they came nigh a castle that hight Pluere, and thereby arrived for to repose them, weening to them to have had good harbourage. But anon as Sir Tristram was within the castle they were taken prisoners; for the custom of the castle was such, who that rode by that castle and brought any lady, he must needs fight with the lord, that hight Breunor. And if it were so that Breunor won the field, then should the knight stranger and his lady be put to death, what that ever they were; and if it were so that the strange knight won the field of Sir Breunor, then should he die and his lady both. This custom was used many winters, for it was called the Castle Pluere, that is to say the Weeping Castle.

CHAPTER XXV

HOW SIR TRISTRAM AND ISOUD WERE IN PRISON, AND HOW HE FOUGHT FOR HER BEAUTY, AND SMOTE OFF ANOTHER LADY'S HEAD

THUS as Sir Tristram and La Beale Isoud were in prison, it happed a knight and a lady came unto them where they were, to cheer them. I have marvel, said Tristram unto the knight and the lady, what is the cause the lord of this castle holdeth us in prison: it was never the custom of no place of worship that ever I came in, when a knight and a lady asked harbour, and they to receive them, and after to destroy them that be his guests. Sir, said the knight, this is the old custom of this castle, that when a knight cometh here he must needs fight with our lord, and he that is the weaker must lose his head. And when that is done, if his lady that he bringeth be fouler than our lord's wife, she must lose her head: and if she be fairer proved than is our lady, then shall the lady of this castle lose her head. So God me help, said Sir Tristram, this is a foul custom and a shameful. But one advantage have I, said Sir Tristram, I have a lady is fair enough, fairer saw I never in all my life days, and I doubt not for lack of beauty she shall not lose her head; and rather than I should lose my head I will fight for it on a fair field. Wherefore, sir knight, I pray you tell your lord that I will be ready as tomorn with my lady, and myself to do battle, if it be so I may have my horse and mine armour. Sir, said that knight, I undertake that your desire shall be sped right well. And then he said: Take your rest, and look that ye be up by times and make you ready and your lady, for ye shall want no thing that you behoveth. And therewith he departed, and on the morn betimes that same knight came to Sir Tristram, and fetched him out and his lady, and brought him horse and armour that was his own, and bade him make him ready to the field, for all the estates and commons of that lordship were there ready to behold that battle and judgment. Then came Sir Breunor, the lord of that castle, with his lady in his hand, muffled, and asked Sir Tristram where was his lady: For an thy lady be fairer than mine, with thy sword smite off my lady's head; and if my lady be fairer than thine, with my sword I must strike off her head. And if I may win thee, yet shall thy lady be mine, and thou shalt lose thy head. Sir, said Tristram, this is a foul custom and horrible; and rather than my lady should lose her head, yet had I lever lose my head. Nay, nay, said Sir Breunor, the ladies shall be first showed together, and the one shall have her judgment. Nay, I will not so, said Sir Tristram, for here is none that will give righteous judgment. But I doubt not, said Sir Tristram, my lady is fairer than thine, and that will I prove and make good with my hand. And whosomever he be that will say the contrary I will prove it on his head. And therewith Sir Tristram showed La Beale Isoud, and turned her thrice about with his naked sword in his hand. And when Sir Breunor saw that, he did the same wise turn his lady. But when Sir Breunor beheld La Beale Isoud, him thought he saw never a fairer lady, and then he dread his lady's head should be off. And so all the people that were there present gave judgment that La Beale Isoud was the fairer lady and the better made. How now, said Sir Tristram, meseemeth it were pity that my lady should lose her head, but because thou and she of long time have used this wicked custom, and by you both have many good knights and ladies been destroyed, for that cause it were no loss to destroy you both. So God me help, said Sir Breunor, for to say the

sooth, thy lady is fairer than mine, and that me sore
repenteth. And so I hear the people privily say, for of
all women I saw none so fair; and therefore, an thou wilt
slay my lady, I doubt not but I shall slay thee and have
thy lady. Thou shalt win her, said Sir Tristram, as dear
as ever knight won lady. And by cause of thine own
judgment, as thou wouldst have done to my lady if that
she had been fouler, and because of the evil custom, give
me thy lady, said Sir Tristram. And therewithal Sir
Tristram strode unto him and took his lady from him,
and with an awk stroke he smote off her head clene. Well,
knight, said Sir Breunor, now hast thou done me a despite.

CHAPTER XXVI

HOW SIR TRISTRAM FOUGHT WITH SIR BREUNOR, AND AT THE LAST SMOTE OFF HIS HEAD

Now take thine horse: sythen I am ladyless I will win
thy lady an I may. Then they took their horses and came
together as it had been the thunder; and Sir Tristram smote
Sir Breunor clean from his horse, and lightly he rose up;
and as Sir Tristram came again by him he thrust his horse
throughout both the shoulders, that his horse hurled here
and there and fell dead to the ground. And ever Sir
Breunor ran after to have slain Sir Tristram, but Sir Tristram was light and nimble, and voided his horse lightly.
And or ever Sir Tristram might dress his shield and his
sword the other gave him three or four sad strokes. Then
they rushed together like two boars, tracing and traversing
mightily and wisely as two noble knights. For this Sir
Breunor was a proved knight, and had been or then the
death of many good knights, that it was pity that he had so
long endured. Thus they fought, hurling here and there
nigh two hours, and either were wounded sore. Then at
the last Sir Breunor rushed upon Sir Tristram and took him
in his arms, for he trusted much in his strength. Then was
Sir Tristram called the strongest and the highest knight of
the world; for he was called bigger than Sir Launcelot, but
Sir Launcelot was better breathed. So anon Sir Tristram
thrust Sir Breunor down grovelling, and then he unlaced
his helm and struck off his head. And then all they that
longed to the catle came to him, and did him homage and

fealty, praying him that he would abide there still a little while to fordo that foul custom. Sir Tristram granted thereto. The meanwhile one of the knights of the castle rode unto Sir Galahad, the haut prince, the which was Sir Breunor's son, which was a noble knight, and told him what misadventure his father had and his mother.

CHAPTER XXVII

HOW SIR GALAHAD FOUGHT WITH SIR TRISTRAM, AND HOW SIR TRISTRAM YIELDED HIM AND PROMISED TO FELLOWSHIP WITH LAUNCELOT

THEN came Sir Galahad, and the king with the hundred knights with him ; and this Sir Galahad proffered to fight with Sir Tristram hand for hand. And so they made them ready to go unto battle on horseback with great courage. Then Sir Galahad and Sir Tristram met together so hard that either bare other down, horse and all, to the earth. And then they avoided their horses as noble knights, and dressed their shields, and drew their swords with ire and rancour, and they lashed together many sad strokes, and one while striking, another while foyning, tracing and traversing as noble knights; thus they fought long, near half a day, and either were sore wounded. At the last Sir Tristram waxed light and big, and doubled his strokes, and drove Sir Galahad aback on the one side and on the other, so that he was like to have been slain. With that came the king with the hundred knights, and all that fellowship went fiercely upon Sir Tristram. When Sir Tristram saw them coming upon him, then he wist well he might not endure. Then as a wise knight of war, he said to Sir Galahad, the haut prince : Sir, ye show to me no knighthood, for to suffer all your men to have ado with me all at once ; and as meseemeth ye be a noble knight of your hands it is great shame to you. So God me help, said Sir Galahad, there is none other way but thou must yield thee to me, other else to die, said Sir Galahad to Sir Tristram. I will rather yield me to you than die, for that is more for the might of your men than of your hands. And therewithal Sir Tristram took his own sword by the point, and put the pommel in the hand of Sir Galahad. Therewithal came the king with the hundred knights, and hard began to assail Sir Tristram.

Let be, said Sir Galahad, be ye not so hardy to touch him, for I have given this knight his life. That is your shame, said the king with the hundred knights; hath he not slain your father and your mother? As for that, said Sir Galahad, I may not wyte him greatly, for my father had him in prison, and inforced him to do battle with him; and my father had such a custom that was a shameful custom, that what knight came there to ask harbour his lady must needs die but if she were fairer than my mother; and if my father overcame that knight he must needs die. This was a shameful custom and usage, a knight for his harbour asking to have such harbourage. And for this custom I would never draw about him. So God me help, said the king, this was a shameful custom. Truly, said Sir Galahad, so seemed me; and meseemed it had been great pity that this knight should have been slain, for I dare say he is the noblest man that beareth life, but if it were Sir Lancelot du Lake. Now, fair knight, said Sir Galahad, I require thee tell me thy name, and of whence thou art, and whither thou wilt. Sir, he said, my name is Sir Tristram de Liones, and from King Mark of Cornwall I was sent on message unto King Anguish of Ireland, for to fetch his daughter to be his wife, and here she is ready to go with me into Cornwall, and her name is La Beale Isoud. And, Sir Tristram, said Sir Galahad, the haut prince, well be ye found in these marches, and so ye will promise me to go unto Sir Launcelot du Lake, and accompany with him, ye shall go where ye will, and your fair lady with you; and I shall promise you never in all my days shall such customs be used in this castle as have been used. Sir, said Sir Tristram, now I let you wit, so God me help, I weened ye had been Sir Launcelot du Lake when I saw you first, and therefore I dread you the more; and sir, I promise you, said Sir Tristram, as soon as I may I will see Sir Launcelot and infellowship me with him; for of all the knights of the world I most desire his fellowship.

CHAPTER XXVIII

HOW SIR LAUNCELOT MET WITH SIR CARADOS BEARING AWAY SIR GAWAINE, AND OF THE RESCUE OF SIR GAWAINE

AND then Sir Tristram took his leave when he saw his time, and took the sea. And in the meanwhile word came unto Sir Launcelot and to Sir Tristram that Sir Carados, the mighty king, that was made like a giant, fought with Sir Gawaine, and gave him such strokes that he swooned in his saddle, and after that he took him by the collar and pulled him out of his saddle, and fast bound him to the saddle-bow, and so rode his way with him toward his castle. And as he rode, by fortune Sir Launcelot met with Sir Carados, and anon he knew Sir Gawaine that lay bound after him. Ah, said Sir Launcelot unto Sir Gawaine, how stands it with you? Never so hard, said Sir Gawaine, unless that ye help me, for so God me help, without ye rescue me I know no knight that may, but outher you or Sir Tristram. Wherefore Sir Launcelot was heavy of Sir Gawaine's words. And then Sir Launcelot bad Sir Carados : Lay down that knight and fight with me. Thou art but a fool, said Sir Carados, for I will serve you in the same wise. As for that, said Sir Launcelot, spare me not, for I warn thee I will not spare thee. And then he bound Sir Gawaine hand and foot, and so threw him to the ground. And then he gat his spear of his squire, and departed from Sir Launcelot to fetch his course. And so either met with other, and brake their spears to their hands ; and then they pulled out swords, and hurtled together on horseback more than an hour. And at the last Sir Launcelot smote Sir Carados such a buffet upon the helm that it pierced his brain pan. So then Sir Launcelot took Sir Carados by the collar and pulled him under his horse's feet, and then he alit and pulled off his helm and struck off his head. And then Sir Launcelot unbound Sir Gawaine. So this same tale was told to Sir Galahad and to Sir Tristram :—here may ye hear the nobleness that followeth Sir Launcelot. Alas, said Sir Tristram, an I had not this message in hand with this fair lady, truly I would never stint or I had found Sir Launcelot. Then Sir Tristram and La Beale Isoud went to the sea and came into Cornwall, and there all the barons met them.

CHAPTER XXIX

OF THE WEDDING OF KING MARK TO LA BEALE ISOUD, AND OF BRAGWAINE HER MAID, AND OF PALAMIDES

AND anon they were richly wedded with great noblesse. But ever, as the French book saith, Sir Tristram and La Beale Isoud loved ever together. Then was there great jousts and great tourneying, and many lords and ladies were at that feast, and Sir Tristram was most praised of all other. Thus dured the feast long, and after the feast was done, within a little while after, by the assent of two ladies that were with Queen Isoud, they ordained for hate and envy for to destroy Dame Bragwaine, that was maiden and lady unto La Beale Isoud ; and she was sent into the forest for to fetch herbs, and there she was met, and bound feet and hand to a tree, and so she was bounden three days. And by fortune, Sir Palamides found Dame Bragwaine, and there he delivered her from the death, and brought her to a nunnery there beside, for to be recovered. When Isoud the queen missed her maiden, wit ye well she was right heavy as ever was any queen, for of all earthly women she loved her best : the cause was for she came with her out of her country. And so upon a day Queen Isoud walked into the forest to put away her thoughts, and there she went herself unto a well and made great moan. And suddenly there came Palamides to her, and had heard all her complaint, and said : Madam Isoud, an ye will grant me my boon, I shall bring to you Dame Bragwaine safe and sound. And the queen was so glad of his proffer that suddenly unadvised she granted all his asking. Well, madam, said Palamides, I trust to your promise, and if ye will abide here half an hour I shall bring her to you. I shall abide you, said La Beale Isoud. And Sir Palamides rode forth his way to that nunnery, and lightly he came again with Dame Bragwaine ; but by her good will she would not have come again, by cause for love of the queen she stood in adventure of her life. Notwithstanding, half against her will, she went with Sir Palamides unto the queen. And when the queen saw her she was passing glad. Now, madam, said Palamides, remember upon your promise, for I have fulfilled my promise. Sir Palamides, said the queen, I wot not what is your desire, but I will that ye wit, howbeit I promised you largely, I thought none evil, nor I warn you none evil will I do. Madam, said Sir Palamides, as at this time, ye shall not know my desire, but before my lord your husband there shall ye know that I will have my desire that ye have promised me. And therewith the queen departed, and rode home to the king, and Sir Palamides rode after her. And when Sir Palamides came before the king, he said : Sir King, I require you as ye be a righteous king, that ye will judge me the right. Tell me your cause, said the king, and ye shall have right.

CHAPTER XXX

HOW PALAMIDES DEMANDED QUEEN ISOUD, AND HOW LAMBEGUS
RODE AFTER TO RESCUE HER, AND OF THE ESCAPE OF ISOUD

SIR, said Palamides, I promised your Queen Isoud to bring again Dame Bragwaine that she had lost, upon this covenant, that she should grant me a boon that I would ask, and without grudging, outher advisement, she granted me. What say ye, my lady? said the king. It is as he saith, so God me help, said the queen; to say thee sooth I promised him his asking for love and joy that I had to see her. Well, madam, said the king, and if ye were hasty to grant him what boon he would ask, I will well that ye perform your promise. Then, said Palamides, I will that ye wit that I will have your queen to lead her and govern her whereas me list. Therewith the king stood still, and bethought him of Sir Tristram, and deemed that he would rescue her. And then hastily the king answered: Take her with the adventures that shall fall of it, for as I suppose thou wilt not enjoy her no while. As for that, said Palamides, I dare right well abide the adventure. And so, to make short tale, Sir Palamides took her by the hand and said: Madam, grudge not to go with me, for I desire nothing but your own promise. As for that, said the queen, I fear not greatly to go with thee, howbeit thou hast me at advantage upon my promise, for I doubt not I shall be worshipfully rescued from thee. As for that, said Sir Palamides, be it as it be may. So Queen Isoud was set behind Palamides, and rode his way. Anon the king sent after Sir Tristram, but in no wise he could be found, for he was in the forest an hunting; for that was always his custom, but if he used arms, to chase and to hunt in the forests. Alas, said the king, now I am shamed for ever, that by mine own assent my lady and my queen shall be devoured. Then came forth a knight, his name was Lambegus, and he was a knight of Sir Tristram. My lord, said this knight, sith ye have trust in my lord, Sir Tristram, wit ye well for his sake I will ride after your queen and rescue her, or else I shall be beaten. Gramercy, said the king, as I live, Sir Lambegus, I shall deserve it. And then Sir Lambegus armed him, and rode after as fast as he might. And then within a while he overtook Sir Palamides. And then Sir Palamides left the queen. What art thou, said

Palamides, art thou Tristram? Nay, he said, I am his servant, and my name is Sir Lambegus. That me repenteth, said Palamides. I had liefer thou haddest been Sir Tristram. I believe you well, said Lambegus, but when thou meetest with Sir Tristram thou shalt have thy hands full. And then they hurtled together and all to brast their spears, and then they pulled out their swords, and hewed on helms and hauberks. At the last Sir Palamides gave Sir Lambegus such a wound that he fell down like a dead knight to the earth. Then he looked after La Beale Isoud, and then she was gone he nyst where. Wit ye well Sir Palamides was never so heavy. So the queen ran into the forest, and there she found a well, and therein she had thought to have drowned herself. And as good fortune would, there came a knight to her that had a castle thereby, his name was Sir Adtherp. And when he found the queen in that mischief he rescued her, and brought her to his castle. And when he wist what she was he armed him, and took his horse, and said he would be avenged upon Palamides; and so he rode on till he met with him, and there Sir Palamides wounded him sore, and by force he made him to tell him the cause why he did battle with him, and how he had led the queen unto his castle. Now bring me there, said Palamides, or thou shalt die of my hands. Sir, said Sir Adtherp, I am so wounded I may not follow, but ride you this way and it shall bring you into my castle, and there within is the queen. Then Sir Palamides rode still till he came to the castle. And at a window La Beale Isoud saw Sir Palamides; then she made the gates to be shut strongly. And when he saw he might not come within the castle, he put off his bridle and his saddle, and put his horse to pasture, and set himself down at the gate like a man that was out of his wit that recked not of himself.

CHAPTER XXXI

HOW SIR TRISTRAM RODE AFTER PALAMIDES, AND HOW HE FOUND HIM AND FOUGHT WITH HIM, AND BY THE MEANS OF ISOUD THE BATTLE CEASED

Now turn we unto Sir Tristram, that when he was come home and wist La Beale Isoud was gone with Sir Palamides, wit ye will he was wroth out of measure. Alas, said Sir

Tristram, I am this day shamed. Then he cried to Gouvernail his man: Haste thee that I were armed and on horseback, for well I wot Lambegus hath no might nor strength to withstand Sir Palamides: alas that I have not been in his stead! So anon as he was armed and horsed Sir Tristram and Gouvernail rode after into the forest, and within a while he found his knight Lambegus almost wounded to the death; and Sir Tristram bare him to a forester, and charged him to keep him well. And then he rode forth, and there he found Sir Adtherp sore wounded, and he told him how the queen would have drowned herself had he not been, and how for her sake and love he had taken upon him to do battle with Sir Palamides. Where is my lady? said Sir Tristram. Sir, said the knight, she is sure enough within my castle, an she can hold her within it. Gramercy, said Sir Tristram, of thy great goodness. And so he rode till he came nigh to that castle; and then Sir Tristram saw where Sir Palamides sat at the gate sleeping, and his horse pastured fast afore him. Now go thou, Gouvernail, said Sir Tristram, and bid him awake, and make him ready. So Gouvernail rode unto him and said: Sir Palamides, arise, and take to thine harness. But he was in such a study he heard not what Gouvernail said. So Gouvernail came again and told Sir Tristram he slept, or else he was mad. Go thou again, said Sir Tristram, and bid him arise, and tell him that I am here, his mortal foe. So Gouvernail rode again and put upon him the butt of his spear, and said: Sir Palamides, make thee ready, for wit ye well Sir Tristram hoveth yonder, and sendeth thee word he is thy mortal foe. And therewithal Sir Palamides arose stilly, without words, and gat his horse, and saddled him and bridled him, and lightly he leapt upon, and gat his spear in his hand, and either feutred their spears and hurtled fast together; and there Tristram smote down Sir Palamides over his horse's tail. Then lightly Sir Palamides put his shield afore him and drew his sword. And there began strong battle on both parts, for both they fought for the love of one lady, and ever she lay on the walls and beheld them how they fought out of measure, and either were wounded passing sore, but Palamides was much sorer wounded. Thus they fought tracing and traversing more than two hours, that

well-nigh for dole and sorrow La Beale Isoud swooned.
Alas, she said, that one I loved and yet do, and the
other I love not, yet it were great pity that I should see
Sir Palamides slain; for well I know by that time the
end be done Sir Palamides is but a dead knight: because
he is not christened I would be loath that he should die
a Saracen. And therewithal she came down and besought
Sir Tristram to fight no more. Ah, madam, said he, what
mean you, will ye have me shamed? Well ye know I
will be ruled by you. I will not your dishonour, said
La Beale Isoud, but I would that ye would for my sake
spare this unhappy Saracen Palamides. Madam, said Sir
Tristram, I will leave fighting at this time for your sake.
Then she said to Sir Palamides: This shall be your
charge, that thou shalt go out of this country while I
am therein. I will obey your commandment, said Sir
Palamides, the which is sore against my will. Then take
thy way, said La Beale Isoud, unto the court of King
Arthur, and there recommend me unto Queen Guenever,
and tell her that I send her word that there be within
this land but four lovers, that is, Sir Launcelot du Lake
and Queen Guenever, and Sir Tristram de Liones and
Queen Isoud.

CHAPTER XXXII

HOW SIR TRISTRAM BROUGHT QUEEN ISOUD HOME, AND OF THE
DEBATE OF KING MARK AND SIR TRISTRAM

AND so Sir Palamides departed with great heaviness.
And Sir Tristram took the queen and brought her again
to King Mark, and then was there made great joy of
her home-coming. Who was cherished but Sir Tristram!
Then Sir Tristram let fetch Sir Lambegus, his knight,
from the forester's house, and it was long or he was whole,
but at the last he was well recovered. Thus they lived
with joy and play a long while. But ever Sir Andred,
that was nigh cousin to Sir Tristram, lay in a watch to
wait betwixt Sir Tristram and La Beale Isoud, for to take
them and slander them. So upon a day Sir Tristram
talked with La Beale Isoud in a window, and that espied
Sir Andred, and told it to the king. Then King Mark

took a sword in his hand and came to Sir Tristram, and
called him false traitor, and would have stricken him.
But Sir Tristram was nigh him, and ran under his sword,
and took it out of his hand. And then the king cried :
Where are my knights and my men ? I charge you slay
this traitor. But at that time there was not one would
move for his words. When Sir Tristram saw that there
was not one would be against him, he shook the sword
to the king, and made countenance as though he would
have stricken him. And then King Mark fled, and Sir
Tristram followed him, and smote upon him five or six
strokes flatling on the neck, that he made him to fall
upon the nose. And then Sir Tristram yede his way
and armed him, and took his horse and his man, and so
he rode into that forest. And there upon a day Sir
Tristram met with two brethren that were knights with
King Mark, and there he struck off the head of the one,
and wounded the other to the death ; and he made him
to bear his brother's head in his helm unto the king, and
thirty more there he wounded. And when that knight
came before the king to say his message, he there died
afore the king and the queen. Then King Mark called
his council unto him, and asked advice of his barons
what was best to do with Sir Tristram. Sir, said the
barons, in especial Sir Dinas, the Seneschal, Sir, we will
give you counsel for to send for Sir Tristram, for we will
that ye wit many men will hold with Sir Tristram an he
were hard bestad. And sir, said Sir Dinas, ye shall
understand that Sir Tristram is called peerless and
makeless of any Christian knight, and of his might and
hardiness we knew none so good a knight, but if it be Sir
Launcelot du Lake. And if he depart from your court and
go to King Arthur's court, wit ye well he will get him such
friends there that he will not set by your malice. And
therefore, sir, I counsel you to take him to your grace. I
will well, said the king, that he be sent for, that we may
be friends. Then the barons sent for Sir Tristram under
a safe conduct. And so when Sir Tristram came to the
king he was welcome, and no rehearsal was made, and
there was game and play. And then the king and the
queen went a-hunting, and Sir Tristram.

CHAPTER XXXIII

HOW SIR LAMORAK JOUSTED WITH THIRTY KNIGHTS, AND SIR
TRISTRAM AT THE REQUEST OF KING MARK SMOTE HIS HORSE
DOWN

THE king and the queen made their pavilions and their
tents in that forest beside a river, and there was daily hunting
and jousting, for there were ever thirty knights ready to
joust unto all them that came in at that time. And there
by fortune came Sir Lamorak de Galis and Sir Driant ; and
there Sir Driant jousted right well, but at the last he had a
fall. Then Sir Lamorak proffered to joust. And when he
began he fared so with the thirty knights that there was not
one of them but that he gave him a fall, and some of them
were sore hurt. I marvel, said King Mark, what knight he
is that doth such deeds of arms. Sir, said Sir Tristram, I
know him well for a noble knight as few now be living, and
his name is Sir Lamorak de Galis. It were great shame,
said the king, that he should go thus away, unless that some
of you meet with him better. Sir, said Sir Tristram, meseemeth it were no worship for a noble man to have ado
with him : and for by cause at this time he hath done over
much for any mean knight living, therefore, as meseemeth,
it were great shame and villainy to tempt him any more at
this time, insomuch as he and his horse are weary both ; for
the deeds of arms that he hath done this day, an they be
well considered, it were enough for Sir Launcelot du Lake.
As for that, said King Mark, I require you, as ye love me
and my lady the queen, La Beale Isoud, take your arms and
joust with Sir Lamorak de Galis. Sir, said Sir Tristram, ye
bid me do a thing that is against knighthood, and well I can
deem that I shall give him a fall, for it is no mastery, for
my horse and I be fresh both, and so is not his horse and
he ; and wit ye well that he will take it for great unkindness,
for ever one good knight is loath to take another at dis-
advantage ; but by cause I will not displease you, as ye
require me so will I do, and obey your commandment. And
so Sir Tristram armed him and took his horse, and put him
forth, and there Sir Lamorak met him mightily, and what
with the might of his own spear, and of Sir Tristram's spear,
Sir Lamorak's horse fell to the earth, and he sitting in the
saddle. Then anon as lightly as he might he avoided the

saddle and his horse, and put his shield afore him and drew his sword. And then he bad Sir Tristram : Alight, thou knight, an thou durst. Nay, said Sir Tristram, I will no more have ado with thee, for I have done to thee over much unto my dishonour and to thy worship. As for that, said Sir Lamorak, I can thee no thank ; syn thou hast for-jousted me on horseback I require thee and I beseech thee, an thou be Sir Tristram, fight with me on foot. I will not so, said Sir Tristram ; and wit ye well my name is Sir Tristram de Liones, and well I know ye be Sir Lamorak de Galis, and this that I have done to you was against my will, but I was required thereto ; but to say that I will do at your request as at this time, I will have no more ado with you, for me shameth of that I have done. As for the shame, said Sir Lamorak, on thy part or on mine, bear thou it an thou wilt, for though a mare's son hath failed me, now a queen's son shall not fail thee ; and therefore, an thou be such a knight as men call thee, I require thee, alight, and fight with me. Sir Lamorak, said Sir Tristram, I understand your heart is great, and cause why ye have, to say thee sooth ; for it would grieve me an any knight should keep him fresh and then to strike down a weary knight, for that knight nor horse was never formed that alway might stand or endure. And therefore, said Sir Tristram, I will not have ado with you, for me forthinketh of that I have done. As for that, said Sir Lamorak, I shall quit you and ever I see my time.

CHAPTER XXXIV

HOW SIR LAMORAK SENT AN HORN TO KING MARK IN DESPITE OF SIR TRISTRAM, AND HOW SIR TRISTRAM WAS DRIVEN INTO A CHAPEL

So he departed from him with Sir Driant, and by the way they met with a knight that was sent from Morgan le Fay unto King Arthur ; and this knight had a fair horn harnessed with gold, and the horn had such a virtue that there might no lady nor gentlewoman drink of that horn but if she were true to her husband, and if she were false she should spill all the drink, and if she were true to her lord she might drink peaceable. And by cause of the Queen Guenever, and in the despite of Sir Launcelot, this horn was sent unto

King Arthur; and by force Sir Lamorak made that knight
to tell all the cause why he bare that horn. Now shalt thou
bear this horn, said Lamorak, unto King Mark, or else
choose thou to die for it; for I tell thee plainly, in despite
and reproof of Sir Tristram thou shalt bear that horn unto
King Mark, his uncle, and say thou to him that I sent it him
for to assay his lady, and if she be true to him he shall prove
her. So the knight went his way unto King Mark, and
brought him that rich horn, and said that Sir Lamorak sent
it him, and thereto he told him the virtue of that horn.
Then the king made Queen Isoud to drink thereof, and an
hundred ladies, and there were but four ladies of all those
that drank clene. Alas, said King Mark, this is a great
despite, and sware a great oath that she should be burnt and
the other ladies. Then the barons gathered them together,
and said plainly they would not have those ladies burnt for
an horn made by sorcery, that came from as false a sorceress
and witch as then was living. For that horn did never
good, but caused strife and debate, and always in her days
she had been an enemy to all true lovers. So there were
many knights made their avow an ever they met with Morgan
le Fay that they would show her short courtesy. Also Sir
Tristram was passing wroth that Sir Lamorak sent that horn
unto King Mark, for well he knew that it was done in the
despite of him. And therefore he thought to requite Sir
Lamorak. Then Sir Tristram used daily and nightly to go
to Queen Isoud when he might, and ever Sir Andred his
cousin watched him night and day for to take him with La
Beale Isoud. And so upon a night Sir Andred espied the
hour and the time when Sir Tristram went to his lady. Then
Sir Andred gat unto him twelve knights, and at midnight he
set upon Sir Tristram secretly and suddenly, and there Sir
Tristram was taken naked abed with La Beale Isoud, and
then was he bound hand and foot, and so was he kept until
day. And then by the assent of King Mark, and of Sir
Andred, and of some of the barons, Sir Tristram was led
unto a chapel that stood upon the sea rocks, there for to
take his judgment: and so he was led bounden with forty
knights. And when Sir Tristram saw that there was none
other boot but needs that he must die, then said he: Fair
lords, remember what I have done for the country of Cornwall, and in what jeopardy I have been in for the weal of you
all; for when I fought for the truage of Cornwall with Sir

Marhaus, the good knight, I was promised for to be better rewarded, when ye all refused to take the battle; therefore, as ye be good gentle knights, see me not thus shamefully to die, for it is shame to all knighthood thus to see me die; for I daresay, said Sir Tristram, that I never met with no knight but I was as good as he, or better. Fie upon thee, said Sir Andred, false traitor that thou art, with thine avaunting; for all thy boast thou shalt die this day. O Andred, Andred, said Sir Tristram, thou shouldst be my kinsman, and now thou art to me full unfriendly, but an there were no more but thou and I, thou wouldst not put me to death. No, said Sir Andred, and therewith he drew his sword, and would have slain him. When Sir Tristram saw him make such countenance he looked upon both his hands that were fast bounden unto two knights, and suddenly he pulled them both to him, and unwrast his hands, and then he leapt unto his cousin, Sir Andred, and wrested his sword out of his hands; then he smote Sir Andred that he fell to the earth, and so Sir Tristram fought till that he had killed ten knights. So then Sir Tristram gat the chapel and kept it mightily. Then the cry was great, and the people drew fast unto Sir Andred, more than an hundred. When Sir Tristram saw the people draw unto him, he remembered he was naked, and sperd fast the chapel door, and brake the bars of a window, and so he leapt out and fell upon the crags in the sea. And so at that time Sir Andred nor none of his fellows might get to him at that time.

CHAPTER XXXV

HOW SIR TRISTRAM WAS HOLPEN BY HIS MEN, AND OF QUEEN ISOUD WHICH WAS PUT IN A LAZAR-COTE, AND HOW TRISTRAM WAS HURT

So when they were departed, Gouvernail, and Sir Lambegus, and Sir Sentraille de Lushon, that were Sir Tristram's men, sought their master. When they heard he was escaped then they were passing glad; and on the rocks they found him, and with towels they pulled him up. And then Sir Tristram asked them where was La Beale Isoud, for he weened she had been had away of Andred's people. Sir, said Gouvernail, she is put in a lazar-cote. Alas, said Sir

Tristram, this is a full ungoodly place for such a fair lady, and if I may she shall not be long there. And so he took his men and went there as was La Beale Isoud, and fetched her away, and brought her into a forest to a fair manor, and Sir Tristram there abode with her. So the good knight bad his men go from him: For at this time I may not help you. So they departed all save Gouvernail. And so upon a day Sir Tristram yede into the forest for to disport him, and then it happened that there he fell on sleep; and there came a man that Sir Tristram aforehand had slain his brother, and when this man had found him he shot him through the shoulder with an arrow, and Sir Tristram leapt up and killed that man. And in the meantime it was told King Mark how Sir Tristram and La Beale Isoud were in that same manor, and as soon as ever he might thither he came with many knights to slay Sir Tristram. And when he came there he found him gone; and there he took La Beale Isoud home with him, and kept her straight that by no means never she might wit nor send unto Tristram, nor he unto her. And then when Sir Tristram came toward the old manor he found the track of many horses, and thereby he wist his lady was gone. And then Sir Tristram took great sorrow, and endured with great pain long time, for the arrow that he was hurt withal was envenomed. Then by the mean of La Beale Isoud she told a lady that was cousin unto Dame Bragwaine, and she came to Sir Tristram, and told him that he might not be whole by no means. For thy lady, La Beale Isoud, may not help thee, therefore she biddeth you haste into Brittany to King Howel, and there ye shall find his daughter, Isoud La Blanche Mains, and she shall help thee. Then Sir Tristram and Gouvernail gat them shipping, and so sailed into Brittany. And when King Howel wist that it was Sir Tristram he was full glad of him. Sir, he said, I am come into this country to have help of your daughter, for it is told me that there is none other may heal me but she; and so within a while she healed him.

CHAPTER XXXVI

HOW SIR TRISTRAM SERVED IN WAR KING HOWEL OF BRITTANY,
AND SLEW HIS ADVERSARY IN THE FIELD

THERE was an earl that hight Grip, and this earl made great war upon the king, and put the king to the worse, and besieged him. And on a time Sir Kehydius, that was son to King Howel, as he issued out he was sore wounded nigh to the death. Then Gouvernail went to the king and said: Sir, I counsel you to desire my lord, Sir Tristram, as in your need to help you. I will do by your counsel, said the king. And so he yede unto Sir Tristram, and prayed him in his wars to help him: For my son, Sir Kehydius, may not go into the field. Sir, said Sir Tristram, I will go to the field and do what I may. Then Sir Tristram issued out of the town with such fellowship as he might make, and did such deeds that all Brittany spake of him. And then, at the last, by great might and force, he slew the Earl Grip with his own hands, and more than an hundred knights he slew that day. And then Sir Tristram was received worshipfully with procession. Then King Howel embraced him in his arms, and said: Sir Tristram, all my kingdom I will resign to thee. God defend, said Sir Tristram, for I am beholden unto you for your daughter's sake to do for you. Then by the great means of King Howel and Kehydius his son, by great proffers, there grew great love betwixt Isoud and Sir Tristram, for that lady was both good and fair, and a woman of noble blood and fame. And for by cause Sir Tristram had such cheer and riches, and all other pleasaunce that he had, almost he had forsaken La Beale Isoud. And so upon a time Sir Tristram agreed to wed Isoud La Blanche Mains. And at the last they were wedded, and solemnly held their marriage. And so when they were abed both Sir Tristram remembered him of his old lady La Beale Isoud. And then he took such a thought suddenly that he was all dismayed, and other cheer made he none but with clipping and kissing; as for other fleshly lusts Sir Tristram never thought nor had ado with her: such mention maketh the French book; also it maketh mention that the lady weened there had been no pleasure but kissing and clipping. And in the meantime there was a knight in Brittany, his name was Suppinabiles, and he came over the sea into England, and then he came

into the court of King Arthur, and there he met with Sir
Launcelot du Lake, and told him of the marriage of Sir
Tristram. Then said Sir Launcelot: Fie upon him, untrue
knight to his lady that so noble a knight as Sir Tristram is
should be found to his first lady false, La Beale Isoud,
Queen of Cornwall; but say ye him this, said Sir Launcelot,
that of all knights in the world I loved him most, and had
most joy of him, and all was for his noble deeds; and let
him wit the love between him and me is done for ever, and
that I give him warning from this day forth as his mortal
enemy

CHAPTER XXXVII

HOW SIR SUPPINABILES TOLD SIR TRISTRAM HOW HE WAS DEFAMED IN THE COURT OF KING ARTHUR, AND OF SIR LAMORAK

THEN departed Sir Suppinabiles unto Brittany again, and
there he found Sir Tristram, and told him that he had been
in King Arthur's court. Then said Sir Tristram: Heard ye
anything of me? So God me help, said Sir Suppinabiles,
there I heard Sir Launcelot speak of you great shame, and
that ye be a false knight to your lady, and he bad me do
you to wit that he will be your mortal enemy in every place
where he may meet you. That me repenteth, said Tristram,
for of all knights I loved to be in his fellowship. So Sir
Tristram made great moan and was ashamed that noble
knights should defame him for the sake of his lady. And
in this meanwhile La Beale Isoud made a letter unto Queen
Guenever, complaining her of the untruth of Sir Tristram,
and how he had wedded the king's daughter of Brittany.
Queen Guenever sent her another letter, and bad her be
of good cheer, for she should have joy after sorrow, for Sir
Tristram was so noble a knight called, that by crafts of
sorcery, ladies would make such noble men to wed them.
But in the end, Queen Guenever said, it shall be thus, that
he shall hate her, and love you better than ever he did
tofore. So leave we Sir Tristram in Brittany, and speak we
of Sir Lamorak de Galis, that as he sailed his ship fell on a
rock and perished all, save Sir Lamorak and his squire;
and there he swam mightily, and fishers of the Isle of
Servage took him up, and his squire was drowned, and the

shipmen had great labour to save Sir Lamorak's life for all the comfort that they could do. And the lord of that isle, hight Sir Nabon le Noire, a great mighty giant. And this Sir Nabon hated all the knights of King Arthur's, and in no wise he would do them favour. And these fishers told Sir Lamorak all the guise of Sir Nabon; how there came never knight of King Arthur's but he destroyed him. And at the last battle that he did was slain Sir Nanowne le Petite, the which he put to a shameful death in despite of King Arthur, for he was drawn lymme meale. That forthinketh me, said Sir Lamorak, for that knight's death, for he was my cousin; and if I were at mine ease as well as ever I was, I would revenge his death. Peace, said the fishers, and make here no words, for or ever ye depart from hence Sir Nabon must know that ye have been here, or else we should die for your sake. So that I be whole, said Lamorak, of my disease that I have taken in the sea, I will that ye tell him that I am a knight of King Arthur's, for I was never afeared to deny my lord.

CHAPTER XXXVIII

HOW SIR TRISTRAM AND HIS WIFE ARRIVED IN WALES, AND HOW HE MET THERE WITH SIR LAMORAK

Now turn we unto Sir Tristram, that upon a day he took a little barge, and his wife Isoud La Blanche Mains, with Sir Kehydius her brother, to play them in the coasts. And when they were from the land, there was a wind drove them in to the coast of Wales upon this Isle of Servage, where as was Sir Lamorak, and there the barge all to rove; and there Dame Isoud was hurt; and as well as they might they gat into the forest, and there by a well he saw Sagwarides and a damosel. And then either saluted other. Sir, said Sagwarides, I know you for Sir Tristram de Liones, the man in the world that I have most cause to hate, because ye departed the love between me and my wife; but as for that, said Sir Sagwarides, I will never hate a noble knight for a light lady; and therefore, I pray you, be my friend, and I will be yours unto my power; for wit ye well ye are hard bestead in this valley, and we shall have enough to do either of us to succour other. And then Sir Sagwarides

brought Sir Tristram to a lady there by that was born in
Cornwall, and she told him all the perils of that valley, and
how there came never knight there but he were taken prisoner
or slain. Wit you well, fair lady, said Sir Tristram, that I
slew Sir Marhaus and delivered Cornwall from the truage of
Ireland, and I am he that delivered the king of Ireland
from Sir Blamore de Ganis, and I am he that beat Sir
Palamides; and wit ye well I am Sir Tristram de Liones,
that by the grace of God shall deliver this woful Isle of
Servage. So Sir Tristram was well eased. Then one told
him there was a knight of King Arthur's that was wrecked
on the rocks. What is his name? said Sir Tristram. We
wot not, said the fishers, but he keepeth it no counsel but
that he is a knight of King Arthur's, and by the mighty lord
of this isle he setteth nought by. I pray you, said Sir
Tristram, an ye may, bring him hither that I may see him,
and if he be any of the knights of Arthur's I shall know him.
Then the lady prayed the fishers to bring him to her place.
So on the morrow they brought him thither in a fisher's
raiment; and as soon as Sir Tristram saw him he smiled
upon him and knew him well, but he knew not Sir
Tristram. Fair sir, said Sir Tristram, meseemeth by your
cheer ye have been diseased but late, and also methinketh
I should know you heretofore. I will well, said Sir
Lamorak, that ye have seen me and met with me. Fair
sir, said Sir Tristram, tell me your name. Upon a covenant
I will tell you, said Sir Lamorak, that is, that ye will tell
me whether ye be lord of this island or no, that is called
Nabon le Noire. Forsooth, said Sir Tristram, I am not he,
nor I hold not of him; I am his foe as well as ye be, and
so shall I be found or I depart out of this isle. Well, said
Sir Lamorak, syn ye have said so largely unto me, my name
is Sir Lamorak de Galis, son unto King Pellinore. Forsooth, I trow well, said Sir Tristram, for an ye said other I
know the contrary. What are ye, said Sir Lamorak, that
knoweth me? I am Sir Tristram de Liones. Ah, sir,
remember ye not of the fall ye did give me once, and after
ye refused me to fight on foot. That was not for fear I had
of you, said Sir Tristram, but me shamed at that time to
have more ado with you, for meseemed ye had enough; but,
Sir Lamorak, for my kindness many ladies ye put to a
reproof when ye sent the horn from Morgan le Fay to King
Mark, where as ye did this in despite of me. Well, said he,

an it were to do again, so would I do, for I had liefer strife
and debate fell in King Mark's court rather than Arthur's
court, for the honour of both courts be not alike. As to
that, said Sir Tristram, I know well ; but that that was done
it was for despite of me, but all your malice, I thank God,
hurt not greatly. Therefore, said Sir Tristram, ye shall
leave all your malice, and so will I, and let us assay how we
may win worship between you and me upon this giant, Sir
Nabon le Noire that is lord of this island, to destroy him.
Sir, said Sir Lamorak, now I understand your knighthood,
it may not be false that all men say, for of your bounty,
noblesse, and worship, of all knights ye are peerless, and for
your courtesy and gentleness I showed you ungentleness,
and that now me repenteth.

CHAPTER XXXIX

HOW SIR TRISTRAM FOUGHT WITH SIR NABON, AND OVERCAME HIM, AND MADE SIR SAGWARIDES LORD OF THE ISLE

In the meantime there came word that Sir Nabon had
made a cry that all the people of that isle should be at his
castle the fifth day after. And the same day the son of
Nabon should be made knight, and all the knights of that
valley and thereabout should be there to joust, and all those
of the realm of Logris should be there to joust with them of
North Wales : and thither came five hundred knights, and
they of the country brought thither Sir Lamorak, and Sir
Tristram, and Sir Kehydius, and Sir Sagwarides, for they
durst none otherwise do ; and then Sir Nabon lent Sir
Lamorak horse and armour at Sir Lamorak's desire, and Sir
Lamorak jousted and did such deeds of arms that Nabon
and all the people said there was never knight that ever they
saw do such deeds of arms ; for, as the French book saith,
he forjousted all that were there for the most part of five
hundred knights, that none abode him in his saddle. Then
Sir Nabon proffered to play with him his play : For I saw
never no knight do so much upon a day. I will well, said
Sir Lamorak, play as I may, but I am weary and sore
bruised. And there either gat a spear, but Nabon would
not encounter with Sir Lamorak, but smote his horse in the
forehead, and so slew him ; and then Sir Lamorak yede on

foot, and turned his shield and drew his sword, and there began strong battle on foot. But Sir Lamorak was so sore bruised and short breathed, that he traced and traversed somewhat aback. Fair fellow, said Sir Nabon, hold thy hand and I shall show thee more courtesy than ever I showed knight, by cause I have seen this day thy noble knighthood, and therefore stand thou by, and I will wit whether any of thy fellows will have ado with me. Then when Sir Tristram heard that, he stepped forth and said: Nabon, lend me horse and sure armour, and I will have ado with thee. Well, fellow, said Sir Nabon, go thou to yonder pavilion, and arm thee of the best thou findest there, and I shall play a marvellous play with thee. Then said Sir Tristram: Look ye play well, or else peradventure I shall learn you a new play. That is well said, fellow, said Sir Nabon. So when Sir Tristram was armed as him liked best, and well shielded and sworded, he dressed to him on foot; for well he knew that Sir Nabon would not abide a stroke with a spear, therefore he would slay all knights' horses. Now, fair fellow, Sir Nabon, let us play. So then they fought long on foot, tracing and traversing, smiting and foyning long without any rest. At the last Sir Nabon prayed him to tell him his name. Sir Nabon, I tell thee my name is Sir Tristram de Liones, a knight of Cornwall under King Mark. Thou art welcome, said Sir Nabon, for of all knights I have most desired to fight with thee or with Sir Launcelot. So then they went eagerly together, and Sir Tristram slew Sir Nabon, and so forthwith he leapt to his son, and struck off his head; and then all the country said they would hold of Sir Tristram. Nay, said Sir Tristram, I will not so; here is a worshipful knight, Sir Lamorak de Galis, that for me he shall be lord of this country, for he hath done here great deeds of arms. Nay, said Sir Lamorak, I will not be lord of this country, for I have not deserved it as well as ye, therefore give ye it where ye will, for I will none have. Well, said Sir Tristram, syn ye nor I will not have it, let us give it to him that hath not so well deserved it. Do as ye list, said Sagwarides, for the gift is yours, for I will none have an I had deserved it. So was it given to Sagwarides, whereof he thanked them; and so was he lord, and worshipfully he did govern it. And then Sir Sagwarides delivered all prisoners, and set good governance in that valley; and so he returned into Cornwall, and told

King Mark and La Beale Isoud how Sir Tristram had advanced him to the Isle of Servage, and there he proclaimed in all Cornwall of all the adventures of these two knights, so was it openly known. But full woe was La Beale Isoud when she heard tell that Sir Tristram was wedded to Isoud La Blanche Mains.

CHAPTER XL

HOW SIR LAMORAK DEPARTED FROM SIR TRISTRAM, AND HOW HE MET WITH SIR FROL, AND AFTER WITH SIR LAUNCELOT

So turn we unto Sir Lamorak, that rode toward Arthur's court, and Sir Tristram's wife and Kehydius took a vessel and sailed into Brittany, unto King Howel, where he was welcome. And when he heard of these adventures they marvelled of his noble deeds. Now turn we unto Sir Lamorak, that when he was departed from Sir Tristram he rode out of the forest, till he came to an hermitage. When the hermit saw him, he asked him from whence he came. Sir, said Sir Lamorak, I come from this valley. Sir, said the hermit: Thereof I marvel. For this twenty winter I saw never no knight pass this country but he was either slain or villainously wounded, or pass as a poor prisoner. Those ill customs, said Sir Lamorak, are fordone, for Sir Tristram slew your lord, Sir Nabon, and his son. Then was the hermit glad, and all his brethren, for he said there was never such a tyrant among christian men. And therefore, said the hermit, this valley and franchise we will hold of Sir Tristram. So on the morrow Sir Lamorak departed ; and as he rode he saw four knights fight against one, and that one knight defended him well, but at the last the four knights had him down. And then Sir Lamorak went betwixt them, and asked them why they would slay that one knight, and said it was shame, four against one. Thou shalt well wit, said the four knights, that he is false. That is your tale, said Sir Lamorak, and when I hear him also speak, I will say as ye say. Then said Lamorak : Ah, knight, can ye not excuse you, but that ye are a false knight. Sir, said he, yet can I excuse me both with my word and with my hands, that I will make good upon one of the best of them, my body to his body.

Then spake they all at once : We will not jeopardy our bodies as for thee. But wit thou well, they said, an King Arthur were here himself, it should not lie in his power to save his life. That is too much said, said Sir Lamorak, but many speak behind a man more than they will say to his face ; and by cause of your words ye shall understand that I am one of the simplest of King Arthur's court ; in the worship of my lord now do your best, and in despite of you I shall rescue him. And then they lashed all at once to Sir Lamorak, but anon at two strokes Sir Lamorak had slain two of them, and then the other two fled. So then Sir Lamorak turned again to that knight, and asked him his name. Sir, he said, my name is Sir Frol of the Out Isles. Then he rode with Sir Lamorak and bare him company. And as they rode by the way they saw a seemly knight riding against them, and all in white. Ah, said Frol, yonder knight jousted late with me and smote me down, therefore I will joust with him. Ye shall not do so, said Sir Lamorak, by my counsel, an ye will tell me your quarrel, whether ye jousted at his request, or he at yours. Nay, said Sir Frol, I jousted with him at my request. Sir, said Lamorak, then will I counsel you deal no more with him, for meseemeth by his countenance he should be a noble knight, and no japer ; for methinketh he should be of the Table Round. Therefore I will not spare, said Sir Frol. And then he cried and said : Sir knight, make thee ready to joust. That needeth not, said the White Knight, for I have no lust to joust with thee ; but yet they feutred their spears, and the White Knight overthrew Sir Frol, and then he rode his way a soft pace. Then Sir Lamorak rode after him, and prayed him to tell him his name : For meseemeth ye should be of the fellowship of the Round Table. Upon a covenant, said he, I will tell you my name, so that ye will not discover my name, and also that ye will tell me yours. Then, said he, my name is Sir Lamorak de Galis. And my name is Sir Launcelot du Lake. Then they put up their swords, and kissed heartily together, and either made great joy of other. Sir, said Sir Lamorak, an it please you I will do you service. God defend, said Launcelot, that any of so noble a blood as ye be should do me service. Then he said : More, I am in a quest that I must do myself alone. Now God speed you, said Sir Lamorak, and so they departed. Then Sir Lamorak came to Sir Frol and horsed him again. What knight is that ? said

Sir Frol. Sir, he said, it is not for you to know, nor it is no point of my charge. Ye are the more uncourteous, said Sir Frol, and therefore I will depart from you. Ye may do as ye list, said Sir Lamorak, and yet by my company ye have saved the fairest flower of your garland; so they departed.

CHAPTER XLI

HOW SIR LAMORAK SLEW SIR FROL, AND OF THE COURTEOUS FIGHTING WITH SIR BELLIANCE HIS BROTHER

THEN within two or three days Sir Lamorak found a knight at a well sleeping, and his lady sat with him and waked. Right so came Sir Gawaine and took the knight's lady, and set her up behind his squire. So Sir Lamorak rode after Sir Gawaine, and said: Sir Gawaine, turn again. And then said Sir Gawaine: What will ye do with me? for I am nephew unto King Arthur. Sir, said he, for that cause I will spare you, else that lady should abide with me, or else ye should joust with me. Then Sir Gawaine turned him and ran to him that ought the lady, with his spear, but the knight with pure might smote down Sir Gawaine, and took his lady with him. All this Sir Lamorak saw, and said to himself: But I revenge my fellow he will say of me dishonour in King Arthur's court. Then Sir Lamorak returned and proffered that knight to joust. Sir, said he, I am ready. And there they came together with all their might, and there Sir Lamorak smote the knight through both sides that he fell to the earth dead. Then that lady rode to that knight's brother that hight Belliance le Orgulus, that dwelt fast thereby, and then she told him how his brother was slain. Alas, said he, I will be revenged. And so he horsed him, and armed him, and within a while he overtook Sir Lamorak, and bad him: Turn and leave that lady, for thou and I must play a new play; for thou hast slain my brother Sir Frol, that was a better knight than ever wert thou. It might well be, said Sir Lamorak, but this day in the field I was found the better. So they rode together, and unhorsed other, and turned their shields, and drew their swords, and fought mightily as noble knights proved, by the space of two hours. So then Sir Belliance prayed him to tell him his name. Sir, said he, my name is Sir Lamorak de Galis. Ah, said Sir Belliance, thou art the man in the world that I most hate, for I slew my sons for thy sake, where I saved thy life, and now thou hast slain my brother Sir Frol. Alas, how should I be accorded with thee ; therefore defend thee, for thou shalt die, there is none other remedy. Alas, said Sir Lamorak, full well me ought to know you, for ye are the man that most have done for me. And therewithal Sir Lamorak kneeled down, and besought him of grace. Arise, said Sir Belliance, or else thereas thou kneelest I shall slay thee. That shall not need, said Sir Lamorak, for I will yield me unto you, not for fear of you, nor for your strength, but your goodness maketh me full loath to have ado with you ; wherefore I require you for God's sake, and for the honour of knighthood, forgive me all that I have offended unto you. Alas, said Belliance, leave thy kneeling, or else I shall slay thee without mercy. Then they yede again unto battle, and either wounded other, that all the ground was bloody there as they fought. And at the last Belliance withdrew him aback and set him down softly upon a little hill, for he was so faint for bleeding that he might not stand. Then Sir Lamorak threw his shield upon his back, and asked him what cheer. Well, said Sir Belliance. Ah, sir, yet shall I show you favour in your mal-ease. Ah, knight Sir Belliance, said Sir Lamorak, thou art a fool, for an I had had thee at such advantage as thou hast done me, I should slay thee ; but thy gentleness is so good and so large, that I must needs forgive thee mine evil will. And then Sir Lamorak kneeled down, and unlaced first his umberere, and then his own, and then either kissed other with weeping tears. Then Sir Lamorak led Sir Belliance to an abbey fast by, and there Sir Lamorak would not depart from Belliance till he was whole. And then they sware together that none of them should never fight against other. So Sir Lamorak departed and went to the court of King Arthur.

Here leave we of Sir Lamorak
and of Sir Tristram. And
here beginneth the history
of La Cote Male Taile.

BOOK IX

CHAPTER I

HOW A YOUNG MAN CAME INTO THE COURT OF KING ARTHUR, AND
HOW SIR KAY CALLED HIM IN SCORN LA COTE MALE TAILE

AT the court of King Arthur there came a young man
bigly made, and he was richly bisene : and he desired to be
made knight of the king, but his over-garment sat over-
thwartly, howbeit it was rich cloth of gold. What is your
name? said King Arthur. Sir, said he, my name is Breunor
le Noire, and within short space ye shall know that I am of
good kin. It may well be, said Sir Kay, the Seneschal, but
in mockage ye shall be called La Cote Male Taile, that is
as much to say, the evil-shapen coat. It is a great thing
that thou askest, said the king ; and for what cause wearest
thou that rich coat? tell me, for I can well think for some
cause it is. Sir, he answered, I had a father, a noble knight,
and as he rode a-hunting, upon a day it happed him to
lay him down to sleep ; and there came a knight that had
been long his enemy, and when he saw he was fast on sleep
he all to hewed him ; and this same coat had my father on
the same time ; and that maketh this coat to sit so evil upon
me, for the strokes be on it as I found it, and never shall
be amended for me. Thus to have my father's death in
remembrance I wear this coat till I be revenged ; and by
cause ye are called the most noblest king of the world I
come to you that ye should make me knight. Sir, said Sir
Lamorak and Sir Gaheris, it were well done to make him
knight ; for him beseemeth well of person and of countenance, that he shall prove a good man, and a good knight,
and a mighty ; for, sir, an ye be remembered, even such
one was Sir Launcelot du Lake when he came first into this
court, and full few of us knew from whence he came ; and
now is he proved the man of most worship in the world ;
and all your court and all your Round Table is by Sir
Launcelot worshipped and amended more than by any
knight now living. That is truth, said the king, and to-
morrow at your request I shall make him knight. So on

the morrow there was an hart found, and thither rode King Arthur with a company of his knights to slay the hart. And this young man that Sir Kay named La Cote Male Taile was there left behind with Queen Guenever; and by sudden adventure there was an horrible lion kept in a strong tower of stone, and it happened that he at that time brake loose, and came hurling afore the queen and her knights. And when the queen saw the lion she cried and fled, and prayed her knights to rescue her. And there was none of them all but twelve that abode, and all the other fled. Then said La Cote Male Taile: Now I see well that all coward knights be not dead; and therewithal he drew his sword and dressed him afore the lion. And that lion gaped wide and came upon him ramping to have slain him. And he then smote him in the middes of the head such a mighty stroke that it clave his head in sunder, and dashed to the earth. Then was it told the queen how the young man that Sir Kay named by scorn La Cote Male Taile had slain the lion. With that the king came home. And when the queen told him of that adventure, he was well pleased, and said: Upon pain of mine head he shall prove a noble man and a faithful knight, and true of his promise: then the king forthwithal made him knight. Now sir, said this young knight, I require you and all the knights of your court, that ye call me by none other name but La Cote Male Taile: in so much as Sir Kay hath so named me so will I be called. I assent me well thereto, said the king.

CHAPTER II

HOW A DAMOSEL CAME INTO THE COURT AND DESIRED A KNIGHT TO TAKE ON HIM AN ENQUEST, WHICH LA COTE MALE TAILE EMPRISED

THEN that same day there came a damosel into the court, and she brought with her a great black shield, with a white hand in the middes holding a sword. Other picture was there none in that shield. When King Arthur saw her he asked her from whence she came and what she would. Sir, she said, I have ridden long and many a day with this shield many ways, and for this cause I am come to your court: there was a good knight that ought this shield, and this knight had undertaken a great deed of arms to achieve it; and so it misfortuned him another strong knight met with him by sudden adventure, and there they fought long, and either wounded other passing sore; and they were so wary that they left that battle even hand. So this knight that ought this shield saw none other way but he must die; and then he commanded me to bear this shield to the court of King Arthur, he requiring and praying some good knight to take this shield, and that he would fulfil the quest that he was in. Now what say ye to this quest? said King Arthur; is there any of you here that will take upon him to welde this shield? Then was there not one that would speak one word. Then Sir Kay took the shield in his hands. Sir knight, said the damosel, what is your name? Wit ye well, said he, my name is Sir Kay, the Seneschal, that wide-where is known. Sir, said that damosel, lay down that shield, for wit ye well it falleth not for you, for he must be a better knight than ye that shall welde this shield. Damosel, said Sir Kay, wit ye well I took this shield in my hands by your leave for to behold it, not to that intent; but go wheresomever thou wilt, for I will not go with you. Then the damosel stood still a great while and beheld many of those knights. Then spake the knight, La Cote Male Taile: Fair damosel, I will take the shield and that adventure upon me, so I wist I should know whitherward my journey might be; for by cause I was this day made knight I would take this adventure upon me. What is your name, fair young man? said the damosel. My name is, said he, La Cote Male Taile. Well mayest thou be called so, said the damosel, the knight with the evil-shapen coat; but an thou be so hardy to take upon thee to bear that shield and to follow me, wit thou well thy skin shall be as well hewn as thy coat. As for that, said La Cote Male Taile, when I am so hewn I will ask you no salve to heal me withal. And forthwithal there came into the court two squires and brought him great horses, and his armour, and his spears, and anon he was armed and took his leave. I would not by my will, said the king, that ye took upon you that hard adventure. Sir, said he, this adventure is mine, and the first that ever I took upon me, and that will I follow whatsomever come of me. Then that damosel departed, and La Cote Male Taile fast followed after. And within a while he overtook the damosel, and anon she missaid him in the foulest manner.

CHAPTER III

HOW LA COTE MALE TAILE OVERTHREW SIR DAGONET THE KING'S
FOOL, AND OF THE REBUKE THAT HE HAD OF THE DAMOSEL

THEN Sir Kay ordained Sir Dagonet, King Arthur's fool, to follow after La Cote Male Taile; and there Sir Kay ordained that Sir Dagonet was horsed and armed, and bad him follow La Cote Male Taile and proffer him to joust, and so he did; and when he saw La Cote Male Taile, he cried and bad him make him ready to joust. So Sir La Cote Male Taile smote Sir Dagonet over his horse's croup. Then the damosel mocked La Cote Male Taile, and said: Fie for shame! now art thou shamed in Arthur's court, when they send a fool to have ado with thee, and specially at thy first jousts; thus she rode long, and chid. And within a while there came Sir Bleoberis, the good knight, and there he jousted with La Cote Male Taile, and there Sir Bleoberis smote him so sore, that horse and all fell to the earth. Then La Cote Male Taile arose up lightly, and dressed his shield, and drew his sword, and would have done battle to the utterance, for he was wood wroth. Not so, said Sir Bleoberis de Ganis, as at this time I will not fight upon foot. Then the damosel Maledisant rebuked him in the foulest manner, and bad him: Turn again, coward. Ah, damosel, he said, I pray you of mercy to missay me no more, my grief is enough though ye give me no more; I call myself never the worse knight when a mare's son faileth me, and also I count me never the worse knight for a fall of Sir Bleoberis. So thus he rode with her two days; and by fortune there came Sir Palomides and encountered with him, and he in the same wise served him as did Bleoberis tofore hand. What dost thou here in my fellowship? said the damosel Maledisant, thou canst not sit no knight, nor withstand him one buffet, but if it were Sir Dagonet. Ah, fair damosel, I am not the worse to take a fall of Sir Palomides, and yet great disworship have I none, for neither Bleoberis nor yet Palomides would not fight with me on foot. As for that, said the damosel, wit thou well they have disdain and scorn to light off their horses to fight with such a lewd knight as thou art. So in the meanwhile there came Sir Mordred, Sir Gawaine's brother, and so he fell in the fellowship with the damosel Maledisant. And then they came afore the Castle Orgulous, and there was such a custom that there might no knight come by that castle but either he must joust or be prisoner, or at the least to lose his horse and his harness. And there came out two knights against them, and Sir Mordred jousted with the foremost, and that knight of the castle smote Sir Mordred down off his horse. And then La Cote Male Taile jousted with that other, and either of them smote other down, horse and all, to the earth. And when they avoided their horses, then either of them took other's horses. And then La Cote Male Taile rode unto that knight that smote down Sir Mordred, and jousted with him. And there Sir La Cote Male Taile hurt and wounded him passing sore, and put him from his horse as he had been dead. So he turned unto him that met him afore, and he took the flight towards the castle, and Sir La Cote Male Taile rode after him into the Castle Orgulous, and there La Cote Male Taile slew him.

CHAPTER IV

HOW LA COTE MALE TAILE FOUGHT AGAINST AN HUNDRED KNIGHTS, AND HOW HE ESCAPED BY THE MEAN OF A LADY

AND anon there came an hundred knights about him and assailed him ; and when he saw his horse should be slain he alit and voided his horse, and put the bridle under his feet, and so put him out of the gate. And when he had so done he hurled in among them, and dressed his back unto a lady's chamber-wall, thinking himself that he had liefer die there with worship than to abide the rebukes of the damosel Maledisant. And in the meantime as he stood and fought, that lady whose was the chamber went out slily at her postern, and without the gates she found La Cote Male Taile's horse, and lightly she gat him by the bridle, and tied him to the postern. And then she went unto her chamber slily again for to behold how that one knight fought against an hundred knights. And when she had beheld him long she went to a window behind his back, and said : Thou knight, thou fightest wonderly well, but for all that at the last thou must needs die, but an thou canst through thy mighty prowess win unto yonder postern, for there have I fastened thy horse to abide thee : but wit thou well thou must think on thy worship, and think not to die, for thou mayst not win unto that postern without thou do nobly and mightily. When La Cote Male Taile heard her say so he gripped his sword in his hands, and put his shield fair afore him, and through the thickest press he thrulled through them. And when he came to the postern he found there ready four knights, and at two the first strokes he slew two of the knights, and the other fled; and so he won his horse and rode from them. And all as it was it was rehearsed in King Arthur's court, how he slew twelve knights within the Castle Orgulous; and so he rode on his way. And in the meanwhile the damosel said to Sir Mordred: I ween my foolish knight be either slain or taken prisoner: then were they ware where he came riding. And when he was come unto them he told all how he had sped and escaped in despite of them all: And some of the best of them will tell no tales. Thou liest falsely, said the damosel, that dare I make good, but as a fool and a dastard to all knighthood they have let thee pass. That may ye prove, said La Cote Male Taile. With that she sent a courier of hers that rode alway with her for to know the truth of this deed; and so he rode thither lightly, and asked how and in what manner that La Cote Male Taile was escaped out of the castle. Then all the knights cursed him, and said that he was a fiend and no man: for he hath slain here twelve of our best knights, and we weened unto this day that it had been too much for Sir Launcelot du Lake or for Sir Tristram de Liones. And in despite of us all he is departed from us and maugre our heads. With this answer the courier departed and came to Maledisant his lady, and told her all how Sir La Cote Male Taile had sped at the Castle Orgulous. Then she smote down her head, and said little. By my head, said Sir Mordred to the damosel, ye are greatly to blame so to rebuke him, for I warn you plainly he is a good knight, and I doubt not but he shall prove a noble knight; but as yet he may not yet sit sure on horseback, for he that shall be a good horseman it must come of usage and exercise. But when he cometh to the strokes of his sword he is then noble and mighty, and that saw Sir Bleoberis and Sir Palomides, for wit ye well they are wily men of arms, and anon they know when they see a young knight by his riding, how they are sure to give him a fall from his horse or a great buffet. But for the most part they will not light on foot with young knights, for they are wight and strongly armed. For in likewise Sir Launcelot du Lake, when he was first made knight, he was often put to the worse upon horseback, but ever upon foot he recovered his renown, and slew and defoiled many knights of the Round Table. And therefore the rebukes that Sir Launcelot did unto many knights causeth them that be men of prowess to beware; for often I have seen the old proved knights rebuked and slain by them that were but young beginners. Thus they rode sure talking by the way together. Here leave we off a while of this tale, and speak we of Sir Launcelot du Lake;

CHAPTER V

HOW SIR LAUNCELOT CAME TO THE COURT AND HEARD OF LA COTE MALE TAILE, AND HOW HE FOLLOWED AFTER HIM, AND HOW LA COTE MALE TAILE WAS PRISONER

THAT when he was come to the court of King Arthur, then heard he tell of the young knight La Cote Male Taile, how he slew the lion, and how he took upon him the adventure of the black shield, the which was named at that time the hardiest adventure of the world. So God me save, said Sir Launcelot unto many of his fellows, it was shame to all the noble knights to suffer such a young knight to take such adventure upon him for his destruction; for I will that ye wit, said Sir Launcelot, that that damosel Maledisant hath borne that shield many a day for to seek the most proved knights, and that was she that Breuse Saunce Pité took that shield from her, and after Tristram de Liones rescued that shield from him and gave it to the damosel again, a little afore that time that Sir Tristram fought with my nephew Sir Blamore de Ganis, for a quarrel that was betwixt the King of Ireland and him. Then many knights were sorry that Sir La Cote Male Taile was gone forth to that adventure. Truly, said Sir Launcelot, I cast me to ride after him. And within seven days Sir Launcelot overtook La Cote Male Taile, and then he saluted him and the damosel Maledisant. And when Sir Mordred saw Sir Launcelot, then he left their fellowship; and so Sir Launcelot rode with them all a day, and ever that damosel rebuked La Cote Male Taile, and then Sir Launcelot answered for him; then she left off, and rebuked Sir Launcelot. So this meantime Sir Tristram sent by a damosel a letter unto Sir Launcelot, excusing him of the wedding of Isoud la Blanche Mains; and said in the letter, as he was a true knight he had never ado fleshly with Isoud la Blanche Mains; and passing courteously and gently Sir Tristram wrote unto Sir Launcelot, ever beseeching him to be his good friend and unto La Beale Isoud of Cornwall, and that Sir Launcelot would excuse him if that ever he saw her. And within short time by the grace of God, said Sir Tristram, that he would speak with La Beale Isoud, and with him right hastily. Then Sir Launcelot departed from the damosel and from Sir La Cote Male Taile, for to oversee that letter, and to write another letter unto Sir Tristram de Liones. And in the meanwhile La Cote Male Taile rode with the damosel until they came to a castle that hight Pendragon; and there were six knights stood afore him, and one of them proffered to joust with La Cote Male Taile. And there La Cote Male Taile smote him over his horse's croup. And then the five knights set upon him all at once with their spears, and there they smote La Cote Male Taile down, horse and man. And then they alit suddenly, and set their hands upon him all at once, and took him prisoner, and so led him unto the castle and kept him as prisoner. And on the morn Sir Launcelot arose, and delivered the damosel with letters unto Sir Tristram, and then he took his way after La Cote Male Taile; and by the way upon a bridge there was a knight proffered Sir Launcelot to joust, and Sir Launcelot smote him down, and then they fought upon foot a noble battle together, and a mighty; and at the last Sir Launcelot smote him down grovelling upon his hands and his knees. And then that knight yielded him, and Sir Launcelot received him fair. Sir, said the knight, I require thee tell me your name, for much my heart giveth unto you. Nay, said Sir Launcelot, as at this time I will not tell you my name, unless then that ye tell me your name. Certainly, said the knight, my name is Sir Nerovens, that was made knight of my lord Sir Launcelot du Lake. Ah, Nerovens de Lile, said Sir Launcelot, I am right glad that ye are proved a good knight, for now wit ye well my name is Sir Launcelot du Lake. Alas, said Sir Nerovens de Lile, what have I done! And therewithal flatling he fell to his feet, and would have kissed them, but Sir Launcelot would

not let him ; and then either made great joy of other. And
then Sir Nerovens told Sir Launcelot that he should not go
by the Castle of Pendragon : For there is a lord, a mighty
knight, and many knights with him, and this night I heard
say that they took a knight prisoner yesterday that rode
with a damosel, and they say he is a Knight of the Round
Table.

CHAPTER VI

HOW SIR LAUNCELOT FOUGHT WITH SIX KNIGHTS, AND AFTER
WITH SIR BRIAN, AND HOW HE DELIVERED THE PRISONERS

AH, said Sir Launcelot, that knight is my fellow, and him
shall I rescue or else I shall lose my life therefor. And
therewithal he rode fast till he came before the Castle of
Pendragon ; and anon therewithal there came six knights,
and all made them ready to set upon Sir Launcelot at
once ; then Sir Launcelot feutred his spear, and smote the
foremost that he brake his back insunder, and three of
them hit and three failed. And then Sir Launcelot passed
through them, and lightly he turned in again, and smote
another knight through the breast and throughout the back
more than an ell, and therewithal his spear brake. So then
all the remnant of the four knights drew their swords and
lashed at Sir Launcelot. And at every stroke Sir Launcelot
bestowed so his strokes that at four strokes sundry they
avoided their saddles, passing sore wounded ; and forthwithal he rode hurling into that castle. And anon the lord
of the castle, that was that time cleped Sir Brian de les Isles,
the which was a noble man and a great enemy unto King
Arthur, within a while he was armed and upon horseback.
And then they feutred their spears and hurled together so
strongly that both their horses rashed to the earth. And
then they avoided their saddles, and dressed their shields,
and drew their swords, and flang together as woodmen, and
there were many strokes given in a while. At the last Sir
Launcelot gave to Sir Brian such a buffet that he kneeled
upon his knees, and then Sir Launcelot rushed upon him,
and with great force he pulled off his helm ; and when Sir
Brian saw that he should be slain he yielded him, and put
him in his mercy and in his grace. Then Sir Launcelot

made him to deliver all his prisoners that he had within his castle, and therein Sir Launcelot found of Arthur's knights thirty, and forty ladies, and so he delivered them ; and then he rode his way. And anon as La Cote Male Taile was delivered he gat his horse, and his harness, and his Damosel Maledisant. The meanwhile Sir Nerovens, that Sir Launcelot had foughten withal afore at the bridge, he sent a damosel after Sir Launcelot to wit how he sped at the Castle of Pendragon. And then they within the castle marvelled what knight he was, when Sir Brian and his knights delivered all those prisoners. Have ye no marvel, said the damosel, for the best knight in this world was here, and did this journey, and wit ye well, she said, it was Sir Launcelot. Then was Sir Brian full glad, and so was his lady, and all his knights, that such a man should win them. And when the damosel and La Cote Male Taile understood that it was Sir Launcelot du Lake that had ridden with them in fellowship, and that she remembered her how she had rebuked him and called him coward, then was she passing heavy.

CHAPTER VII

So then they took their horses and rode forth a pace after Sir Launcelot. And within two mile they overtook him, and saluted him, and thanked him, and the damosel cried Sir Launcelot mercy of her evil deed and saying : For now I know the flower of all knighthood is departed even between Sir Tristram and you. For God knoweth, said the damosel, that I have sought you my lord, Sir Launcelot, and Sir Tristram long, and now I thank God I have met with you ; and once at Camelot I met with Sir Tristram, and there he rescued this black shield with the white hand holding a naked sword that Sir Breuse Saunce Pité had taken from me. Now, fair damosel, said Sir Launcelot, who told you my name ? Sir, said she, there came a damosel from a knight that ye fought withal at the bridge, and she told me your name was Sir Launcelot du Lake. Blame have she then, said Sir Launcelot, but her lord, Sir Nerovens, hath told her. But, damosel, said Sir Launcelot, upon this

covenant I will ride with you, so that ye will not rebuke this
knight Sir La Cote Male Taile no more; for he is a good
knight, and I doubt not he shall prove a noble knight, and
for his sake and pity that he should not be destroyed I
followed him to succour him in this great need. Ah, Jesu
thank you, said the damosel, for now I will say unto you
and to him both, I rebuked him never for no hate that I
hated him, but for great love that I had to him. For ever
I supposed that he had been too young and too tender to
take upon him these adventures. And therefore by my
will I would have driven him away for jealousy that I had
of his life, for it may be no young knight's deed that shall
achieve this adventure to the end. Pardie, said Sir Launcelot, it is well said, and where ye are called the Damosel
Maledisant I will call you the Damosel Bienpensant. And
so they rode forth a great while unto they came to the border
of the country of Surluse, and there they found a fair village
with a strong bridge like a fortress. And when Sir Launcelot and they were at the bridge there start forth afore them
of gentlemen and yeomen many, that said: Fair lords, ye
may not pass this bridge and this fortress by cause of that
black shield that I see one of you bear, and therefore there
shall not pass but one of you at once; therefore choose you
which of you shall enter within this bridge first. Then Sir
Launcelot proffered himself first to enter within this bridge.
Sir, said La Cote Male Taile, I beseech you let me enter
within this fortress, and if I may speed well I will send for
you, and if it happened that I be slain, there it goeth. And
if so be that I am a prisoner taken, then may ye rescue me.
I am loth, said Sir Launcelot, to let you pass this passage.
Sir, said La Cote Male Taile, I pray you let me put my body
in this adventure. Now go your way, said Sir Launcelot,
and Jesu be your speed. So he entered, and anon there
met with him two brethren, the one hight Sir Plaine de Force,
and the other hight Sir Plaine de Amours. And anon they
met with Sir La Cote Male Taile; and first La Cote Male
Taile smote down Plaine de Force, and after he smote down
Plaine de Amours; and then they dressed them to their
shields and swords, and bad La Cote Male Taile alight,
and so he did; and there was dashing and foining with
swords, and so they began to assail full hard La Cote Male
Taile, and many great wounds they gave him upon his head,
and upon his breast, and upon his shoulders. And as he

might ever among he gave sad strokes again. And then the two brethren traced and traversed for to be of both hands of Sir La Cote Male Taile, but he by fine force and knightly prowess gat them afore him. And then when he felt himself so wounded, then he doubled his strokes, and gave them so many wounds that he felled them to the earth, and would have slain them had they not yielded them. And right so Sir La Cote Male Taile took the best horse that there was of them three, and so rode forth his way to the other fortress and bridge; and there he met with the third brother whose name was Sir Plenorius, a full noble knight, and there they jousted together, and either smote other down, horse and man, to the earth. And then they avoided their horses, and dressed their shields, and drew their swords, and gave many sad strokes, and one while the one knight was afore on the bridge, and another while the other. And thus they fought two hours and more, and never rested. And ever Sir Launcelot and the damosel beheld them. Alas, said the damosel, my knight fighteth passing sore and over long. Now may ye see, said Sir Launcelot, that he is a noble knight, for to consider his first battle, and his grievous wounds; and even forthwithal so wounded as he is, it is marvel that he may endure this long battle with that good knight.

CHAPTER VIII

HOW LA COTE MALE TAILE WAS TAKEN PRISONER, AND AFTER RESCUED BY SIR LAUNCELOT, AND HOW SIR LAUNCELOT OVERCAME FOUR BRETHREN

THIS meanwhile Sir La Cote Male Taile sank right down upon the earth, what forwounded and what forbled he might not stand. Then the other knight had pity of him, and said : Fair young knight, dismay you not, for had ye been fresh when ye met with me, as I was, I wot well that I should not have endured so long as ye have done ; and therefore for your noble deeds of arms I shall show to you kindness and gentleness in all that I may. And forthwithal this noble knight, Sir Plenorius, took him up in his arms, and led him into his tower. And then he commanded him the wine, and made to search him and to stop his bleeding wounds. Sir, said La Cote Male Taile, withdraw you from me, and hie you to yonder bridge again, for there will meet with you another manner knight than ever was I. Why, said Plenorius, is there another manner knight behind of your fellowship? Yea, said La Cote Male Taile, there is a much better knight than I am. What is his name? said Plenorius. Ye shall not know for me, said La Cote Male Taile. Well, said the knight, he shall be encountered withal whatsomever he be. Then Sir Plenorius heard a knight call that said: Sir Plenorius, where art thou? either thou must deliver me the prisoner that thou hast led unto thy tower, or else come and do battle with me. Then Plenorius gat his horse, and came with a spear in his hand walloping toward Sir Launcelot; and then they began to feuter their spears, and came together as thunder, and smote either other so mightily that their horses fell down under them. And then they avoided their horses, and pulled out their swords, and like two bulls they lashed together with great strokes and foynes; but ever Sir Launcelot recovered ground upon him, and Sir Plenorius traced to have gone about him. But Sir Launcelot would not suffer that, but bare him backer and backer, till he came nigh his tower gate. And then said Sir Launcelot: I know thee well for a good knight, but wit thou well thy life and death is in my hand, and therefore yield thee to me, and thy prisoner. The other answered no word, but struck mightily upon Sir Launcelot's helm, that the fire sprang out of his eyes. Then Sir Launcelot doubled his strokes so thick, and smote at him so mightily, that he made him kneel upon his knees. And therewith Sir Launcelot leapt upon him, and pulled him grovelling down. Then Sir Plenorius yielded him, and his tower, and all his prisoners at his will. Then Sir Launcelot received him and took his troth; and then he rode to the other bridge, and there Sir Launcelot jousted with other three of his brethren, the one hight Pillounes, and the other hight Pellogris, and the third Sir Pellandris. And first upon horseback Sir Launcelot smote them down, and afterward he beat them on foot, and made them to yield them unto him; and then he returned unto Sir Plenorius, and there he found in his prison King Carados of Scotland, and many other knights, and all they were delivered. And then Sir La Cote Male Taile came to Sir Launcelot, and then Sir Launcelot would have given him all these fortresses and these bridges. Nay, said La Cote Male Taile, I will not have Sir Plenorius' livelihood; with that he will grant you, my lord Sir Launcelot, to come unto King Arthur's court, and to be his knight, and all his brethren, I will pray you, my lord, to let him have his livelihood. I will well, said Sir Launcelot, with this that he will come to the court of King Arthur and become his man, and his brethren five. And as for you, Sir Plenorius, I will undertake, said Sir Launcelot, at the next feast, so there be a place voided, that ye shall be Knight of the Round Table. Sir, said Plenorius, at the next feast of Pentecost I will be at Arthur's court, and at that time I will be guided and ruled as King Arthur and ye will have me. Then Sir Launcelot and Sir La Cote Male Taile reposed them there, unto the time that Sir La Cote Male Taile was whole of his wounds, and there they had merry cheer, and good rest, and many good games, and there were many fair ladies.

CHAPTER IX

HOW SIR LAUNCELOT MADE LA COTE MALE TAILE LORD OF THE CASTLE OF PENDRAGON, AND AFTER WAS MADE KNIGHT OF THE ROUND TABLE

AND in the meanwhile came Sir Kay, the Seneschal, and Sir Brandiles, and anon they fellowshipped with them. And then within ten days, then departed those knights of Arthur's court from these fortresses. And as Sir Launcelot came by the Castle of Pendragon there he put Sir Brian de les Isles from his lands, for cause he would never be withhold with King Arthur; and all that Castle of Pendragon and all the lands thereof he gave to Sir La Cote Male Taile. And then Sir Launcelot sent for Nerovens that he made once knight, and he made him to have all the rule of that castle and of that country, under La Cote Male Taile; and so they rode to Arthur's court all wholly together. And at Pentecost next following there was Sir Plenorius and Sir La Cote Male Taile, called otherwise by right Sir Breunor le Noire, both made Knights of the Table Round; and great lands King Arthur gave them, and there Breunor le Noire wedded that damosel Maledisant. And after she was called Beauvivante, but ever after for the more part he was called La Cote Male Taile; and he proved a passing noble knight, and mighty; and many worshipful deeds he did after in his life; and Sir Plenorius proved a noble knight and full of prowess, and all the days of their life for the most part they awaited upon Sir Launcelot; and Sir Plenorius' brethren were ever knights of King Arthur. And also, as the French book maketh mention, Sir La Cote Male Taile avenged his father's death.

CHAPTER X

HOW LA BEALE ISOUD SENT LETTERS TO SIR TRISTRAM BY HER MAID BRAGWAINE, AND OF DIVERS ADVENTURES OF SIR TRISTRAM

Now leave we here Sir La Cote Male Taile, and turn we unto Sir Tristram de Liones that was in Brittany. When La Beale Isoud understood that he was wedded she sent to him by her maiden Bragwaine as piteous letters as could be thought and made, and her conclusion was that, an it pleased Sir Tristram, that he would come to her court, and bring with him Isoud La Blanche Mains, and they should be kept as well as she herself. Then Sir Tristram called unto him Sir Kehydius, and asked him whether he would go with him into Cornwall secretly. He answered him that he was ready at all times. And then he let ordain privily a little vessel, and therein they went, Sir Tristram, Kehydius, Dame Bragwaine, and Gouvernail, Sir Tristram's squire. So when they were in the sea a contrarious wind blew them on the coasts of North Wales, nigh the Castle Perilous. Then said Sir Tristram: Here shall ye abide me these ten days, and Gouvernail, my squire, with you. And if so be I come not again by that day take the next way into Cornwall; for in this forest are many strange adventures, as I have heard say, and some of them I cast me to prove or I depart. And when I may I shall hie me after you. Then Sir Tristram and Kehydius took their horses and departed from their fellowship. And so they rode within that forest a mile and more; and at the last Sir Tristram saw afore him a likely knight armed sitting by a well, and a strong mighty horse passing nigh him tied to an oak, and a man hoving and riding by him leading an horse laden with spears. And this knight that sat at the well seemed by his countenance to be passing heavy. Then Sir Tristram rode near him and said: Fair knight, why sit ye so drooping? ye seem to be a knight-errant by your arms and harness, and therefore dress you to joust with one of us, or with both. Therewithal that knight made no words, but took his shield and buckled it about his neck, and lightly he took his horse and leapt upon him. And then he took a great spear of his squire, and departed his way a furlong. Sir Kehydius asked leave of Sir Tristram to joust first. Do your best, said Sir Tristram. So they met together, and there Sir Kehydius had a fall, and was sore wounded on high above the paps. Then Sir Tristram said: Knight, that is well jousted, now make you ready unto me. I am ready, said the knight. And then that knight took a greater spear in his hand, and encountered with Sir Tristram, and there by great force that knight smote down Sir Tristram from his horse and had a great fall. Then Sir Tristram was sore ashamed, and lightly he avoided his horse, and put his shield afore his shoulder, and drew his sword. And then Sir Tristram required that knight of his knighthood to alight upon foot and fight with him. I will well, said the knight; and so he alit upon foot, and avoided his horse, and cast his shield upon his shoulder, and drew his sword, and there they fought a long battle together full nigh two hours. Then Sir Tristram said: Fair knight, hold thine hand, and tell me of whence thou art, and what is thy name. As for that, said the knight, I will be avised; but an thou wilt tell me thy name peradventure I will tell thee mine.

CHAPTER XI

HOW SIR TRISTRAM MET WITH SIR LAMORAK DE GALIS, AND HOW THEY FOUGHT, AND AFTER ACCORDED NEVER TO FIGHT TOGETHER

Now fair knight, he said, my name is Sir Tristram de Liones. Sir, said the other knight, and my name is Sir Lamorak de Galis. Ah, Sir Lamorak, said Sir Tristram, well be we met, and bethink thee now of the despite thou didst me of the sending of the horn unto King Mark's court, to the intent to have slain or dishonoured my lady the Queen, La Beale Isoud; and therefore wit thou well, said Sir Tristram, the one of us shall die or we depart. Sir, said Sir Lamorak, remember that we were together in the Isle of Servage, and at that time ye promised me great friendship. Then Sir Tristram would make no longer delays, but lashed at Sir Lamorak; and thus they fought long till either were weary of other. Then Sir Tristram said to Sir Lamorak: In all my life met I never with such a knight that was so big and well breathed as ye be, therefore, said Sir Tristram, it were pity that any of us both should here be mischieved. Sir, said Sir Lamorak, for your renown and name I will that ye have the worship of this battle, and therefore I will yield me unto you. And therewith he took the point of his sword to yield him. Nay, said Sir Tristram, ye shall not do so, for well I know your proffers, and more of your gentleness than for any fear or dread ye have of me. And therewithal Sir Tristram proffered him his sword and said: Sir Lamorak, as an overcome knight I yield me unto you as to a man of the most noble prowess that ever I met withal. Nay, said Sir Lamorak, I will do you gentleness; I require you let us be sworn together that never none of us shall after this day have ado with other. And therewithal Sir Tristram and Sir Lamorak sware that never none of them should fight against other, nor for weal nor for woe.

CHAPTER XII

HOW SIR PALOMIDES FOLLOWED THE QUESTING BEAST, AND SMOTE DOWN SIR TRISTRAM AND SIR LAMORAK WITH ONE SPEAR

AND this meanwhile there came Sir Palomides, the good knight, following the questing beast that had in shape a head like a serpent's head, and a body like a leopard, buttocks like a lion, and footed like an hart; and in his body there was such a noise as it had been the noise of thirty couple of hounds questing, and such a noise that beast made wheresomever he went; and this beast evermore Sir Palomides followed, for it was called his quest. And right so as he followed this beast it came by Sir Tristram, and soon after came Palomides. And to brief this matter he smote down Sir Tristram and Sir Lamorak both with one spear; and so he departed after the beast Galtisant, that was called the questing beast; wherefore these two knights were passing wroth that Sir Palomides would not fight on foot with them. Here men may understand that be of worship, that he was never formed that all times might stand, but sometime he was put to the worse by mal-fortune; and at sometime the worse knight put the better knight to a rebuke. Then Sir Tristram and Sir Lamorak gat Sir Kehydius upon a shield betwixt them both, and led him to a forester's lodge, and there they gave him in charge to keep him well, and with him they abode three days. Then the two knights took their horses and at the cross they departed. And then said Sir Tristram to Sir Lamorak: I require you if ye hap to meet with Sir Palomides, say him that he shall find me at the same well where I met him, and there I, Sir Tristram, shall prove whether he be better knight than I. And so either departed from other a sundry way, and Sir Tristram rode nigh there as was Sir Kehydius; and Sir Lamorak rode until he came to a chapel, and there he put his horse unto pasture. And anon there came Sir Meliagaunce, that was King Bagdemagus' son, and he there put his horse to pasture, and was not ware of Sir Lamorak; and then this knight Sir Meliagaunce made his moan of the love that he had to Queen Guenever, and there he made a woful complaint. All this heard Sir Lamorak, and on the morn Sir Lamorak took his horse and rode unto the forest, and there he met with two knights hoving under the wood shaw. Fair knights, said Sir Lamorak, what do ye hoving here and watching? and if ye be knights-errant that will joust, lo I am ready. Nay, sir knight, they said, not so, we abide not here to joust with you, but we lie here in await of a knight that slew our brother. What knight was that, said Sir Lamorak, that you would fain meet withal? Sir, they said, it is Sir Launcelot that slew our brother, and if ever we may meet with him he shall not escape, but we shall slay him. Ye take upon you a great charge, said Sir Lamorak, for Sir Launcelot is a noble proved knight. As for that we doubt not, for there nys none of us but we are good enough for him. I will not believe that, said Sir Lamorak, for I heard never yet of no knight the days of my life but Sir Launcelot was too big for him.

CHAPTER XIII

RIGHT so as they stood talking thus Sir Lamorak was ware how Sir Launcelot came riding straight toward them ; then Sir Lamorak saluted him, and he him again. And then Sir Lamorak asked Sir Launcelot if there were anything that he might do for him in these marches. Nay, said Sir Launcelot, not at this time I thank you. Then either departed from other, and Sir Lamorak rode again there as he left the two knights, and then he found them hid in the leaved wood. Fie on you, said Sir Lamorak, false cowards, pity and shame it is that any of you should take the high order of knighthood. So Sir Lamorak departed from them, and within a while he met with Sir Meliagaunce. And then Sir Lamorak asked him why he loved Queen Guenever as he did : For I was not far from you when ye made your complaint by the chapel. Did ye so? said Sir Meliagaunce, then will I abide by it : I love Queen Guenever, what will ye with it? I will prove and make good that she is the fairest lady and most of beauty in the world. As to that, said Sir Lamorak, I say nay thereto, for Queen Morgawse of Orkney, mother to Sir Gawaine, and his mother is the fairest queen and lady that beareth the life. That is not so, said Sir Meliagaunce, and that will I prove with my hands upon thy body. Will ye so? said Sir Lamorak, and in a better quarrel keep I not to fight. Then they departed either from other in great wrath. And then they came riding together as it had been thunder, and either smote other so sore that their horses fell backward to the earth. And then they avoided their horses, and dressed their shields, and drew their swords. And then they hurtled together as wild boars, and thus they fought a great while. For Meliagaunce was a good man and of great might, but Sir Lamorak was hard big for him, and put him always aback, but either had wounded other sore. And as they stood thus fighting, by fortune came Sir Launcelot and Sir Bleoberis riding. And then Sir Launcelot rode betwixt them, and asked them for what cause they fought so together : And ye are both knights of King Arthur ! Sir, said Meliagaunce, I shall tell you for what cause we do this battle.

I praised my lady, Queen Guenever, and said she was the fairest lady of the world, and Sir Lamorak said nay thereto, for he said Queen Morgawse of Orkney was fairer than she and more of beauty. Ah, Sir Lamorak, why sayest thou so? it is not thy part to dispraise thy princess that thou art under their obeisance, and we all. And therewith he alit on foot, and said: For this quarrel, make thee ready, for I will prove upon thee that Queen Guenever is the fairest lady and most of bounte in the world. Sir, said Sir Lamorak, I am loath to have ado with you in this quarrel, for every man thinketh his own lady fairest; and though I praise the lady that I love most ye should not be wroth; for though my lady, Queen Guenever, be fairest in your eye, wit ye well Queen Morgawse of Orkney is fairest in mine eye, and so every knight thinketh his own lady fairest; and wit ye well, sir, ye are the man in the world except Sir Tristram that I am most loathest to have ado withal, but, an ye will needs fight with me I shall endure you as long as I may. Then spake Sir Bleoberis and said: My lord Sir Launcelot, I wist you never so misadvised as ye are now, for Sir Lamorak sayeth you but reason and knightly; for I warn you I have a lady, and methinketh that she is the fairest lady of the world. Were this a great reason that ye should be wroth with me for such language? And well ye wot, that Sir Lamorak is as noble a knight as I know, and he hath ought you and us ever good will, and therefore I pray you be good friends. Then Sir Launcelot said unto Sir Lamorak: I pray you forgive me mine evil will, and if I was misadvised I will amend it. Sir, said Sir Lamorak, the amends is soon made betwixt you and me. And so Sir Launcelot and Sir Bleoberis departed, and Sir Meliagaunce and Sir Lamorak took their horses, and either departed from other. And within a while came King Arthur, and met with Sir Lamorak, and jousted with him; and there he smote down Sir Lamorak, and wounded him sore with a spear, and so he rode from him; wherefore Sir Lamorak was wroth that he would not fight with him on foot, howbeit that Sir Lamorak knew not King Arthur.

CHAPTER XIV

HOW SIR KAY MET WITH SIR TRISTRAM, AND AFTER OF THE
SHAME SPOKEN OF THE KNIGHTS OF CORNWALL, AND HOW
THEY JOUSTED

Now leave we of this tale, and speak we of Sir Tristram, that as he rode he met with Sir Kay, the Seneschal; and there Sir Kay asked Sir Tristram of what country he was. He answered that he was of the country of Cornwall. It may well be, said Sir Kay, for yet heard I never that ever good knight came out of Cornwall. That is evil spoken, said Sir Tristram, but an it please you to tell me your name I require you. Sir, wit ye well, said Sir Kay, that my name is Sir Kay, the Seneschal. Is that your name? said Sir Tristram, now wit ye well that ye are named the shamefullest knight of your tongue that now is living; howbeit ye are called a good knight, but ye are called unfortunate, and passing overthwart of your tongue. And thus they rode together till they came to a bridge. And there was a knight would not let them pass till one of them jousted with him; and so that knight jousted with Sir Kay, and there that knight gave Sir Kay a fall: his name was Sir Tor, Sir Lamorak's half-brother. And then they two rode to their lodging, and there they found Sir Brandiles, and Sir Tor came thither anon after. And as they sat at supper these four knights, three of them spake all shame by Cornish knights. Sir Tristram heard all that they said and he said but little, but he thought the more, but at that time he discovered not his name. Upon the morn Sir Tristram took his horse and abode them upon their way. And there Sir Brandiles proffered to joust with Sir Tristram, and Sir Tristram smote him down, horse and all, to the earth. Then Sir Tor le Fise de Vayshoure encountered with Sir Tristram, and there Sir Tristram smote him down, and then he rode his way, and Sir Kay followed him, but he would not of his fellowship. Then Sir Brandiles came to Sir Kay and said: I would wit fain what is that knight's name. Come on with me, said Sir Kay, and we shall pray him to tell us his name. So they rode together till they came nigh him, and then they were ware where he sat by a well, and had put off his helm to drink at the well. And when he saw them come he laced on his helm lightly, and took his horse, and proffered them to joust. Nay, said Sir Brandiles, we jousted late enough with you, we come not in that intent. But for this we come to require you of knighthood to tell us your name. My fair knights, sythen that is your desire, and to please you, ye shall wit that my name is Sir Tristram de Liones, nephew unto King Mark of Cornwall. In good time, said Sir Brandiles, and well be ye found, and wit ye well that we be right glad that we have found you, and we be of a fellowship that would be right glad of your company. For ye are the knight in the world that the noble fellowship of the Round Table most desireth to have the company of. God thank them, said Sir Tristram, of their great goodness, but as yet I feel well that I am unable to be of their fellowship, for I was never yet of such deeds of worthiness to be in the company of such a fellowship. Ah, said Sir Kay, an ye be Sir Tristram de Liones, ye are the man called now most of prowess except Sir Launcelot du Lake; for he beareth not the life, Christian nor heathen, that can find such another knight, to speak of his prowess, and of his hands, and his truth withal. For yet could there never creature say of him dishonour and make it good. Thus they talked a great while, and then they departed either from other such ways as them seemed best.

CHAPTER XV

HOW KING ARTHUR WAS BROUGHT INTO THE FOREST PERILOUS, AND HOW SIR TRISTRAM SAVED HIS LIFE

Now shall ye hear what was the cause that King Arthur came into the Forest Perilous, that was in North Wales, by the means of a lady. Her name was Annowre, and this lady came to King Arthur at Cardiff; and she by fair promise and fair behests made King Arthur to ride with her into that Forest Perilous; and she was a great sorceress; and many days she had loved King Arthur, and by cause she would have him to lie by her she came into that country. So when the king was gone with her many of his knights followed after King Arthur when they missed him, as Sir Launcelot, Brandiles, and many other; and when she had brought him to her tower she desired him to lie by her; and then the king remembered him of his lady, and would not lie by

her for no craft that she could do. Then every day she
would make him ride into that forest with his own knights,
to the intent to have had King Arthur slain. For when
this Lady Annowre saw that she might not have him at her
will, then she laboured by false means to have destroyed
King Arthur, and slain. Then the lady of the lake that was
alway friendly to King Arthur, she understood by her
subtle crafts that King Arthur was like to be destroyed.
And therefore this lady of the lake that hight Nimue, came
into that forest to seek after Sir Launcelot du Lake or Sir
Tristram for to help King Arthur ; foras that same day this
lady of the lake knew well that King Arthur should be slain,
unless that he had help of one of these two knights. And
thus she rode up and down till she met with Sir Tristram,
and anon as she saw him she knew him. O my lord Sir
Tristram, she said, well be ye met, and blessed be the time
that I have met with you ; for this same day, and within
these two hours, shall be done the foulest deed that ever
was done in this land. O fair damosel, said Sir Tristram,
may I amend it. Come on with me, she said, and that in all
the haste ye may, for ye shall see the most worshipfullest
knight of the world hard bested. Then said Sir Tristram :
I am ready to help such a noble man. He is neither better
nor worse, said the lady of the lake, but the noble King
Arthur himself. God defend, said Sir Tristram, that ever he
should be in such distress. Then they rode together a great
pace, until they came to a little turret or castle ; and underneath that castle they saw a knight standing upon foot
fighting with two knights ; and so Sir Tristram beheld them,
and at the last the two knights smote down the one knight,
and that one of them unlaced his helm to have slain him.
And the Lady Annowre gat King Arthur's sword in her hand
to have stricken off his head. And therewithal came Sir
Tristram with all his might, crying : Traitress, traitress,
leave that. And anon there Sir Tristram smote the one of
the knights through the body that he fell dead ; and then
he rushed to the other and smote his back in sunder ; and
in the meanwhile the lady of the lake cried to King Arthur :
Let not that false lady escape. Then King Arthur overtook her, and with the same sword he smote off her head,
and the lady of the lake took up her head and hung it up
by the hair of her saddle-bow. And then Sir Tristram
horsed King Arthur and rode forth with him, but he

charged the lady of the lake not to discover his name as at that time. When the king was horsed he thanked heartily Sir Tristram, and desired to wit his name; but he would not tell him, but that he was a poor knight adventurous; and so he bare King Arthur fellowship till he met with some of his knights. And within a while he met with Sir Ector de Maris, and he knew not King Arthur nor Sir Tristram, and he desired to joust with one of them. Then Sir Tristram rode unto Sir Ector, and smote him from his horse. And when he had done so he came again to the king and said: My lord, yonder is one of your knights, he may bare you fellowship, and another day that deed that I have done for you I trust to God ye shall understand that I would do you service. Alas, said King Arthur, let me wit what ye are? Not at this time, said Sir Tristram. So he departed and left King Arthur and Sir Ector together.

CHAPTER XVI

HOW SIR TRISTRAM CAME TO LA BEALE ISOUD, AND HOW KE-
HYDIUS BEGAN TO LOVE BEALE ISOUD, AND OF A LETTER
THAT TRISTRAM FOUND

AND then at a day set Sir Tristram and Sir Lamorak met at the well; and then they took Kehydius at the forester's house, and so they rode with him to the ship where they left Dame Bragwaine and Gouvernail, and so they sailed into Cornwall all wholly together. And by assent and information of Dame Bragwaine when they were landed they rode unto Sir Dinas, the Seneschal, a trusty friend of Sir Tristram's. And so Dame Bragwaine and Sir Dinas rode to the court of King Mark, and told the queen, La Beale Isoud, that Sir Tristram was nigh her in that country. Then for very pure joy La Beale Isoud swooned; and when she might speak she said: Gentle knight Seneschal, help that I might speak with him, outher my heart will brast. Then Sir Dinas and Dame Bragwaine brought Sir Tristram and Kehydius privily unto the court, unto a chamber where as La Beale Isoud had assigned it; and to tell the joys that were betwixt La Beale Isoud and Sir Tristram, there is no tongue can tell it, nor heart think it, nor pen write it. And as the French book maketh mention, at the first time that ever Sir Kehydius saw La Beale Isoud he was so enamoured upon her that for very pure love he might never withdraw it. And at the last, as ye shall hear or the book be ended, Sir Kehydius died for the love of La Beale Isoud. And then privily he wrote unto her letters and ballads of the most goodliest that were used in those days. And when La Beale Isoud understood his letters she had pity of his complaint, and unavised she wrote another letter to comfort him withal. And Sir Tristram was all this while in a turret at the commandment of La Beale Isoud, and when she might she came unto Sir Tristram. So on a day King Mark played at the chess under a chamber window; and at that time Sir Tristram and Sir Kehydius were within the chamber over King Mark, and as it mishapped Sir Tristram found the letter that Kehydius sent unto La Beale Isoud, also he had found the letter that she wrote unto Kehydius, and at that same time La Beale Isoud was in the same chamber. Then Sir Tristram came unto La Beale Isoud and said: Madam, here is a letter that was sent unto you, and here is the letter that ye sent unto him that sent you that letter. Alas, Madam, the good love that I have loved you; and many lands and riches have I forsaken for your love, and now ye are a traitress to me, the which doth me great pain. But as for thee, Sir Kehydius, I brought thee out of Brittany into this country, and thy father, King Howel, I won his lands, howbeit I wedded thy sister Isoud La Blanche Mains for the goodness she did unto me. And yet, as I am true knight, she is a clene maiden for me; but wit thou well, Sir Kehydius, for this falsehood and treason thou hast done me, I will revenge it upon thee. And therewithal Sir Tristram drew out his sword and said: Sir Kehydius, keep thee, and then La Beale Isoud swooned to the earth. And when Sir Kehydius saw Sir Tristram come upon him he saw none other boot, but leapt out at a bay-window even over the head where sat King Mark playing at the chess. And when the king saw one come hurling over his head he said: Fellow, what art thou, and what is the cause thou leapest out at that window? My lord the king, said Kehydius, it fortuned me that I was asleep in the window above your head, and as I slept I slumbered, and so I fell down. And thus Sir Kehydius excused him.

CHAPTER XVII

THEN Sir Tristram dread sore lest he were discovered unto the king that he was there ; wherefore he drew him to the strength of the Tower, and armed him in such armour as he had for to fight with them that would withstand him. And so when Sir Tristram saw there was no resistance against him he sent Gouvernail for his horse and his spear, and knightly he rode forth out of the castle openly, that was called the Castle of Tintagil. And even at gate he met with Gingalin, Sir Gawaine's son. And anon Sir Gingalin put his spear in his rest, and ran upon Sir Tristram and brake his spear ; and Sir Tristram at that time had but a sword, and gave him such a buffet upon the helm that he fell down from his saddle, and his sword slid adown, and carved asunder his horse's neck. And so Sir Tristram rode his way into the forest, and all this doing saw King Mark. And then he sent a squire unto the hurt knight, and commanded him to come to him, and so he did. And when King Mark wist that it was Sir Gingalin he welcomed him and gave him an horse, and asked him what knight it was that had encountered with him. Sir, said Gingalin, I wot not what knight he was, but well I wot that he sigheth and maketh great dole. Then Sir Tristram within a while met with a knight of his own, that hight Sir Fergus. And when he had met with him he made great sorrow, insomuch that he fell down off his horse in a swoon, and in such sorrow he was in three days and three nights. Then at the last Sir Tristram sent unto the court by Sir Fergus, for to spere what tidings. And so as he rode by the way he met with a damosel that came from Sir Palomides, to know and seek how Sir Tristram did. Then Sir Fergus told her how he was almost out of his mind. Alas, said the damosel, where shall I find him ? In such a place, said Sir Fergus. Then Sir Fergus found Queen Isoud sick in her bed, making the greatest dole that ever any earthly woman made. And when the damosel found Sir Tristram she made great dole by cause she might not amend him, for the more she made of him the more was his pain. And at the last Sir Tristram took his horse and rode away from her. And then was it three days or that she could find him, and then she brought him meat and drink, but he would none; and then another time Sir Tristram escaped away from the damosel, and it happed him to ride by the same castle where Sir Palomides and Sir Tristram did battle when La Beale Isoud departed them. And there by fortune the damosel met with Sir Tristram again, making the greatest dole that ever earthly creature made; and she yede to the lady of that castle and told her of the misadventure of Sir Tristram. Alas, said the lady of that castle, where is my lord, Sir Tristram? Right here by your castle, said the damosel. In good time, said the lady, is he so nigh me; he shall have meat and drink of the best; and an harp I have of his whereupon he taught me, for of goodly harping he beareth the prize in the world. So this lady and damosel brought him meat and drink, but he ate little thereof. Then upon a night he put his horse from him, and then he unlaced his armour, and then Sir Tristram would go into the wilderness, and brast down the trees and boughs; and otherwhile when he found the harp that the lady sent him, then would he harp, and play thereupon and weep together. And sometime when Sir Tristram was in the wood that the lady wist not where he was, then would she sit her down and play upon that harp: then would Sir Tristram come to that harp, and hearken thereto, and sometime he would harp himself. Thus he there endured a quarter of a year. Then at the last he ran his way, and she wist not where he was become. And then was he naked and waxed lean and poor of flesh; and so he fell in the fellowship of herdmen and shepherds, and daily they would give him some of their meat and drink. And when he did any shrewd deed they would beat him with rods, and so they clipped him with shears and made him like a fool.

CHAPTER XVIII

HOW SIR TRISTRAM SOUSED DAGONET IN A WELL, AND HOW PALOMIDES SENT A DAMOSEL TO SEEK TRISTRAM, AND HOW PALOMIDES MET WITH KING MARK

AND upon a day Dagonet, King Arthur's fool, came into Cornwall with two squires with him; and as they rode through that forest they came by a fair well where Sir

Tristram was wont to be; and the weather was hot, and they alit to drink of that well, and in the meanwhile their horses brake loose. Right so Sir Tristram came unto them, and first he soused Sir Dagonet in that well, and after his squires, and thereat laughed the shepherds; and forthwithal he ran after their horses and brought them again one by one, and right so, wet as they were, he made them leap up and ride their ways. Thus Sir Tristram endured there an half year naked, and would never come in town nor village. The meanwhile the damosel that Sir Palomides sent to seek Sir Tristram, she yede unto Sir Palomides and told him all the mischief that Sir Tristram endured. Alas, said Sir Palomides, it is great pity that ever so noble a knight should be so mischieved for the love of a lady; but nevertheless, I will go and seek him, and comfort him an I may. Then a little before that time La Beale Isoud had commanded Sir Kehydius out of the country of Cornwall. So Sir Kehydius departed with a dolorous heart, and by adventure he met with Sir Palomides, and they enfellowshipped together; and either complained to other of their hot love that they loved La Beale Isoud. Now let us, said Sir Palomides, seek Sir Tristram, that loved her as well as we, and let us prove whether we may recover him. So they rode into that forest, and three days and three nights they would never take their lodging, but ever sought Sir Tristram. And upon a time, by adventure, they met with King Mark that was ridden from his men all alone. When they saw him Sir Palomides knew him, but Sir Kehydius knew him not. Ah, false king, said Sir Palomides, it is pity thou hast thy life, for thou art a destroyer of all worshipful knights, and by thy mischief and thy vengeance thou hast destroyed that most noble knight, Sir Tristram de Liones. And therefore defend thee, said Sir Palomides, for thou shalt die this day. That were shame, said King Mark, for ye two are armed and I am unarmed. As for that, said Sir Palomides, I shall find a remedy therefor; here is a knight with me, and thou shalt have his harness. Nay, said King Mark, I will not have ado with you, for cause have ye none to me; for all the misease that Sir Tristram hath was for a letter that he found; for as to me I did to him no displeasure, and God knoweth I am full sorry for his disease and malady. So when the king had thus excused him they were friends, and King Mark would have had them unto Tintagil; but Sir Palomides would not, but turned unto the realm of Logris, and Sir Kehydius said that he would go into Brittany. Now turn we unto Sir Dagonet again, that when he and his squires were upon horseback he deemed that the shepherds had sent that fool to array them so, by cause that they laughed at them, and so they rode unto the keepers of beasts and all to beat them. Sir Tristram saw them beat that were wont to give him meat and drink, then he ran thither and gat Sir Dagonet by the head, and gave him such a fall to the earth that he bruised him sore so that he lay still. And then he wrast his sword out of his hand, and therewith he ran to one of his squires and smote off his head, and the other fled. And so Sir Tristram took his way with that sword in his hand, running as he had been wild wood. Then Sir Dagonet rode to King Mark and told him how he had sped in that forest. And therefore, said Sir Dagonet, beware, King Mark, that thou come not about that well in the forest, for there is a fool naked, and that fool and I fool met together, and he had almost slain me. Ah, said King Mark, that is Sir Matto le Breune, that fell out of his wit by cause he lost his lady; for when Sir Gaheris smote down Sir Matto and won his lady of him, never since was he in his mind, and that was pity, for he was a good knight.

CHAPTER XIX

HOW IT WAS NOISED HOW SIR TRISTRAM WAS DEAD, AND HOW
LA BEALE ISOUD WOULD HAVE SLAIN HERSELF

THEN Sir Andred, that was cousin unto Sir Tristram, made a lady that was his paramour to say and to noise it that she was with Sir Tristram or ever he died. And this tale she brought unto King Mark's court, that she buried him by a well, and that or he died he besought King Mark to make his cousin, Sir Andred, king of the country of Liones, of the which Sir Tristram was lord of. All this did Sir Andred by cause he would have had Sir Tristram's lands. And when King Mark heard tell that Sir Tristram was dead he wept and made great dole. But when Queen Isoud heard of these tidings she made such sorrow that she was nigh out of her mind; and so upon a day she thought to slay herself and never to live after Sir Tristram's death.

And so upon a day La Beale Isoud gat a sword privily and bare it to her garden, and there she pitched the sword through a plum tree up to the hilt, so that it stuck fast, and it stood breast high. And as she would have run upon the sword and to have slain herself all this espied King Mark, how she kneeled down and said: Sweet Lord Jesu, have mercy upon me, for I may not live after the death of Sir Tristram de Liones, for he was my first love and he shall be the last. And with these words came King Mark and took her in his arms, and then he took up the sword, and bare her away with him into a tower; and there he made her to be kept, and watched her surely, and after that she lay long sick, nigh at the point of death. This meanwhile ran Sir Tristram naked in the forest with the sword in his hand, and so he came to an hermitage, and there he laid him down and slept; and in the meanwhile the hermit stole away his sword, and laid meat down by him. Thus was he kept there ten days; and at the last he departed and came to the herdmen again. And there was a giant in that country that hight Tawleas, and for fear of Sir Tristram more than seven year he durst never much go at large, but for the most part he kept him in a sure castle of his own; and so this Tawleas heard tell that Sir Tristram was dead, by the noise of the court of King Mark. Then this Tawleas went daily at large. And so he happed upon a day he came to the herdmen wandering and lingering, and there he set him down to rest among them. The meanwhile there came a knight of Cornwall that led a lady with him, and his name was Sir Dinaunt; and when the giant saw him he went from the herdmen and hid him under a tree, and so the knight came to that well, and there he alit to repose him. And as soon as he was from his horse this giant Tawleas came betwixt this knight and his horse, and took the horse and leapt upon him. So forthwith he rode unto Sir Dinaunt and took him by the collar, and pulled him afore him upon his horse, and there would have stricken off his head. Then the herdmen said unto Sir Tristram: Help yonder knight. Help ye him, said Sir Tristram. We dare not, said the herdmen. Then Sir Tristram was ware of the sword of the knight thereas it lay; and so thither he ran and took up the sword and struck off Sir Tawleas' head, and so he yede his way to the herdmen.

CHAPTER XX

THEN the knight took up the giant's head and bare it with him unto King Mark, and told him what adventure betid him in the forest, and how a naked man rescued him from the grimly giant, Tawleas. Where had ye this adventure? said King Mark. Forsooth, said Sir Dinaunt, at the fair fountain in your forest where many adventurous knights meet, and there is the mad man. Well, said King Mark, I will see that wild man. So within a day or two King Mark commanded his knights and his hunters that they should be ready on the morn for to hunt, and so upon the morn he went unto that forest. And when the king came to that well he found there lying by that well a fair naked man, and a sword by him. Then King Mark blew and straked, and therewith his knights came to him; and then the king commanded his knights to: Take that naked man with fairness, and bring him to my castle. So they did softly and fair, and cast mantles upon Sir Tristram, and so led him unto Tintagil; and there they bathed him, and washed him, and gave hot suppings till they had brought him well to his remembrance; but all this while there was no creature that knew Sir Tristram, nor what man he was. So it fell upon a day that the Queen, La Beale Isoud, heard of such a man, that ran naked in the forest, and how the king had brought him home to the court. Then La Beale Isoud called unto her Dame Bragwaine and said: Come on with me, for we will go see this man that my lord brought from the forest the last day. So they passed forth, and spered where was the sick man. And then a squire told the queen that he was in the garden taking his rest, and reposing him against the sun. So when the queen looked upon Sir Tristram she was not remembered of him. But ever she said unto Dame Bragwaine: Meseemeth I should have seen him heretofore in many places. But as soon as Sir Tristram saw her he knew her well enough. And then he turned away his visage and wept. Then the queen had always a little brachet with her that Sir Tristram gave her the first time that ever she came into Cornwall, and never would that brachet depart from her but if Sir Tristram was nigh there as was La Beale Isoud; and this brachet was sent from the king's daughter of France unto Sir Tristram for great love. And anon as this little brachet felt a savour of Sir Tristram, she leapt upon him and licked his learys and his ears, and then she whined and quested, and she smelled at his feet and at his hands, and on all parts of his body that she might come to. Ah, my lady, said Dame Bragwaine unto La Beale Isoud, alas, alas, said she, I see it is mine own lord, Sir Tristram. And thereupon Isoud fell down in a swoon, and so lay a great while. And when she might speak she said: My lord Sir Tristram, blessed be God ye have your life, and now I am sure ye shall be discovered by this little brachet, for she will never leave you. And also I am sure as soon as my lord, King Mark, do know you he will banish you out of the country of Cornwall, or else he will destroy you; for God's sake, mine own lord, grant King Mark his will, and then draw you unto the court of King Arthur, for there are ye beloved, and ever when I may I shall send unto you; and when ye list ye may come to me, and at all times early and late I will be at your commandment, to live as poor a life as ever did queen or lady. O madam, said Sir Tristram, go from me, for mickle anger and danger have I escaped for your love.

CHAPTER XXI

HOW KING MARK, BY THE ADVICE OF HIS COUNCIL, BANISHED SIR TRISTRAM OUT OF CORNWALL THE TERM OF TEN YEARS

THEN the queen departed, but the brachet would not from him; and therewithal came King Mark, and the brachet set upon him, and bayed at them all. Therewithal Sir Andred spake and said: Sir, this is Sir Tristram, I see by the brachet. Nay, said the king, I cannot suppose that. Then the king asked him upon his faith what he was, and what was his name. So God me help, said he, my name is Sir Tristram de Liones; now do by me what ye list. Ah, said King Mark, me repenteth of your recovery. And then he let call his barons to judge Sir Tristram to the death. Then many of his barons would not assent thereto, and in especial Sir Dinas, the Seneschal, and Sir Fergus. And so by the advice of them all Sir Tristram was banished out of the country for ten year, and thereupon he took his oath upon a book before the king and his barons. And so he was made to depart out of the country of Cornwall; and there were many barons brought him unto his ship, of the which some were his friends and some his foes. And in the meanwhile there came a knight of King Arthur's, his name was Dinadan, and his coming was for to seek after Sir Tristram; then they showed him where he was armed at all points going to the ship. Now fair knight, said Sir Dinadan, or ye pass this court that ye will joust with me I require thee. With a good will, said Sir Tristram, an these lords will give me leave. Then the barons granted thereto, and so they ran together, and there Sir Tristram gave Sir Dinadan a fall. And then he prayed Sir Tristram to give him leave to go in his fellowship. Ye shall be right welcome, said then Sir Tristram. And so they took their horses and rode to their ships together, and when Sir Tristram was in the sea he said: Greet well King Mark and all mine enemies, and say them I will come again when I may; and well am I rewarded for the fighting with Sir Marhaus, and delivered all this country from servage; and well am I rewarded for the fetching and costs of Queen Isoud out of Ireland, and the danger that I was in first and last, and by the way coming home what danger I had to bring again Queen Isoud from the Castle Pluere; and well am I rewarded when I fought with Sir Bleoberis for Sir Sagwarides' wife; and well am I rewarded when I fought with Sir Blamore de Ganis for King Anguish, father unto La Beale Isoud; and well am I rewarded when I smote down the good knight, Sir Lamorak de Galis, at King Mark's request; and well am I rewarded when I fought with the King with the hundred knights, and the King of Northgalis, and both these would have put his land in servage, and by me they were put to a rebuke; and well am I rewarded for the slaying of Tawleas, the mighty giant, and many other deeds have I done for him, and now have I my warison. And tell King Mark that many noble knights of the Table Round have spared the barons of this country for my sake. Also am I not well rewarded when I fought with the good knight Sir Palomides and rescued Queen Isoud from him; and at that time King Mark said afore all his barons I should have been better rewarded. And forthwithal he took the sea.

CHAPTER XXII

HOW A DAMOSEL SOUGHT HELP TO HELP SIR LAUNCELOT AGAINST
THIRTY KNIGHTS, AND HOW SIR TRISTRAM FOUGHT WITH
THEM

AND at the next landing, fast by the sea, there met with
Sir Tristram and with Sir Dinadan, Sir Ector de Maris
and Sir Bors de Ganis; and there Sir Ector jousted
with Sir Dinadan, and he smote him and his horse
down. And then Sir Tristram would have jousted with
Sir Bors, and Sir Bors said that he would not joust
with no Cornish knights, for they are not called men of
worship; and all this was done upon a bridge. And with
this came Sir Bleoberis and Sir Driant, and Sir Bleoberis
proffered to joust with Sir Tristram, and there Sir Tristram
smote down Sir Bleoberis. Then said Sir Bors de Ganis : I
wist never Cornish knight of so great valour nor so valiant
as that knight that beareth the trappours embroidered with
crowns. And then Sir Tristram and Sir Dinadan departed
from them into a forest, and there met them a damosel that
came for the love of Sir Launcelot to seek after some noble
knights of King Arthur's court for to rescue Sir Launcelot.
And so Sir Launcelot was ordained, for by the treason of
Queen Morgan le Fay to have slain Sir Launcelot, and for
that cause she ordained thirty knights to lie in await for
Sir Launcelot, and this damsel knew this treason. And for
this cause the damosel came for to seek noble knights to
help Sir Launcelot. For that night, or the day after, Sir
Launcelot should come where these thirty knights were.
And so this damosel met with Sir Bors and Sir Ector and
with Sir Driant, and there she told them all four of the
treason of Morgan le Fay ; and then they promised her that
they would be nigh where Sir Launcelot should meet
with the thirty knights. And if so be they set upon him we
will do rescues as we can. So the damosel departed, and by
adventure the damosel met with Sir Tristram and with Sir
Dinadan, and there the damosel told them all the treason
that was ordained for Sir Launcelot. Fair damosel, said
Sir Tristram, bring me to that same place where they should
meet with Sir Launcelot. Then said Sir Dinadan : What
will ye do? it is not for us to fight with thirty knights, and
wit you well I will not thereof ; as to match one knight two

or three is enough an they be men, but for to match fifteen knights that will I never undertake. Fie for shame, said Sir Tristram, do but your part. Nay, said Sir Dinadan, I will not thereof but if ye will lend me your shield, for ye bear a shield of Cornwall; and for the cowardice that is named to the knights of Cornwall, by your shields ye be ever forborne. Nay, said Sir Tristram, I will not depart from my shield for her sake that gave it me. But one thing, said Sir Tristram, I promise thee, Sir Dinadan, but if thou wilt promise me to abide with me, here I shall slay thee, for I desire no more of thee but answer one knight. And if thy heart will not serve thee, stand by and look upon me and them. Sir, said Sir Dinadan, I promise you to look upon and to do what I may to save myself, but I would I had not met with you. So then anon these thirty knights came fast by these four knights, and they were ware of them, and either of other. And so these thirty knights let them pass, for this cause, that they would not wrath them, if cause be that they had ado with Sir Launcelot; and the four knights let them pass to this intent, that they would see and behold what they would do with Sir Launcelot. And so the thirty knights passed on and came by Sir Tristram and by Sir Dinadan, and then Sir Tristram cried on high: Lo, here is a knight against you for the love of Sir Launcelot. And there he slew two with one spear and ten with his sword. And then came in Sir Dinadan and he did passing well, and so of the thirty knights there went but ten away, and they fled. All this battle saw Sir Bors de Ganis and his three fellows, and then they saw well it was the same knight that jousted with them at the bridge; then they took their horses and rode unto Sir Tristram, and praised him and thanked him of his good deeds, and they all desired Sir Tristram to go with them to their lodging; and he said: Nay, he would not go to no lodging. Then they all four knights prayed him to tell them his name. Fair lords, said Sir Tristram, as at this time I will not tell you my name.

CHAPTER XXIII

THEN Sir Tristram and Sir Dinadan rode forth their way till they came to the shepherds and to the herdmen, and there they asked them if they knew any lodging or harbour there nigh hand. Forsooth, Sirs, said the herdmen, hereby is good lodging in a castle; but there is such a custom that there shall no knight be harboured but if he joust with two knights, and if he be but one knight he must joust with two. And as ye be therein soon shall ye be matched. There is shrewd harbour, said Sir Dinadan; lodge where ye will, for I will not lodge there. Fie for shame, said Sir Tristram, are ye not a knight of the Table Round? wherefore ye may not with your worship refuse your lodging. Not so, said the herdmen, for an ye be beaten and have the worse ye shall not be lodged there, and if ye beat them ye shall be well harboured. Ah, said Sir Dinadan, they are two sure knights. Then Sir Dinadan would not lodge there in no manner but as Sir Tristram required him of his knighthood; and so they rode thither. And to make short tale, Sir Tristram and Sir Dinadan smote them down both, and so they entered into the castle and had good cheer as they could think or devise. And when they were unarmed, and thought to be merry and in good rest, there came in at the gates Sir Palomides and Sir Gaheris, requiring to have the custom of the castle. What array is this? said Sir Dinadan, I would have my rest. That may not be, said Sir Tristram; now must we needs defend the custom of this castle, insomuch as we have the better of the lords of this castle, and therefore, said Sir Tristram, needs must ye make you ready. In the devil's name, said Sir Dinadan, came I into your company. And so they made them ready; and Sir Gaheris encountered with Sir Tristram, and Sir Gaheris had a fall; and Sir Palomides encountered with Sir Dinadan, and Sir Dinadan had a fall: then was it fall for fall. So then must they fight on foot. That would not Sir Dinadan, for he was so sore bruised of the fall that Sir Palomides gave him. Then Sir Tristram unlaced Sir Dinadan's helm, and prayed him to help him. I will not, said Sir Dinadan, for I am sore wounded of the thirty knights that we had but late ago to do withal. But ye fare, said Sir Dinadan unto Sir Tristram, as a madman and as a man that is out of his mind that would cast himself away, and I may curse the time that ever I saw you, for in all the world are not two such knights that be so wood as is Sir Launcelot and ye Sir Tristram; for once I fell in the fellowship of Sir Launcelot as I have done now with you, and he set me a work that a quarter of a year I kept my bed. Jesu defend me, said Sir Dinadan, from such two knights, and specially from your fellowship. Then, said Sir Tristram, I will fight with them both. Then Sir Tristram bade them come forth both, for I will fight with you. Then Sir Palomides and Sir Gaheris dressed them, and smote at them both. Then Dinadan smote at Sir Gaheris a stroke or two, and turned from him. Nay, said Sir Palomides, it is too much shame for us two knights to fight with one. And then he did bid Sir Gaheris stand aside with that knight that hath no list to fight. Then they rode together and fought long, and at the last Sir Tristram doubled his strokes, and drove Sir Palomides aback more than three strides. And then by one assent Sir Gaheris and Sir Dinadan went betwixt them, and departed them in sunder. And then by assent of Sir Tristram they would have lodged together. But Sir Dinadan would not lodge in that castle. And then he cursed the time that ever he came in their fellowship, and so he took his horse, and his harness, and departed. Then Sir Tristram prayed the lords of that castle to lend him a man to bring him to a lodging, and so they did, and overtook Sir Dinadan, and rode to their lodging two mile thence with a good man in a priory, and there they were well at ease. And that same night Sir Bors and Sir Bleoberis, and Sir Ector and Sir Driant, abode still in the same place thereas Sir Tristram fought with the thirty knights; and there they met with Sir Launcelot the same night, and had made promise to lodge with Sir Colgrevance the same night.

CHAPTER XXIV

HOW SIR TRISTRAM JOUSTED WITH SIR KAY AND SIR SAGRAMORE
LE DESIROUS, AND HOW SIR GAWAINE TURNED SIR TRISTRAM
FROM MORGAN LE FAY

But anon as the noble knight, Sir Launcelot, heard of the shield of Cornwall, then wist he well that it was Sir Tristram that fought with his enemies. And then Sir Launcelot praised Sir Tristram, and called him the man of most worship in the world. So there was a knight in that priory that hight Pellinore, and he desired to wit the name of Sir Tristram, but in no wise he could not; and so Sir Tristram departed and left Sir Dinadan in the priory, for he was so weary and so sore bruised that he might not ride. Then this knight, Sir Pellinore, said to Sir Dinadan: Sithen that ye will not tell me that knight's name I will ride after him and make him to tell me his name, or he shall die therefor. Beware, sir knight, said Sir Dinadan, for an ye follow him ye shall repent it. So that knight, Sir Pellinore, rode after Sir Tristram and required him of jousts. Then Sir Tristram smote him down and wounded him through the shoulder, and so he passed on his way. And on the next day following Sir Tristram met with pursuivants, and they told him that there was made a great cry of tournament between King Carados of Scotland and the King of North Wales, and either should joust against other at the Castle of Maidens; and these pursuivants sought all the country after the good knights, and in especial King Carados let make seeking for Sir Launcelot du Lake, and the King of North-galis let seek after Sir Tristram de Liones. And at that time Sir Tristram thought to be at that jousts; and so by adventure they met with Sir Kay, the Seneschal, and Sir Sagramore le Desirous; and Sir Kay required Sir Tristram to joust, and Sir Tristram in a manner refused him, by cause he would not be hurt nor bruised against the great jousts that should be before the Castle of Maidens, and therefore thought to repose him and to rest him. And alway Sir Kay cried: Sir knight of Cornwall, joust with me, or else yield thee to me as recreant. When Sir Tristram heard him say so he turned to him, and then Sir Kay refused him and turned his back. Then Sir Tristram said: As I find thee I shall take thee. Then Sir Kay turned with evil will, and

Sir Tristram smote Sir Kay down, and so he rode forth.
Then Sir Sagramore le Desirous rode after Sir Tristram, and
made him to joust with him, and there Sir Tristram smote
down Sir Sagramore le Desirous from his horse, and rode
his way; and the same day he met with a damosel that told
him that he should win great worship of a knight adventurous
that did much harm in all that country. When Sir Tristram
heard her say so, he was glad to go with her to win worship.
So Sir Tristram rode with that damosel a six mile, and then
met him Sir Gawaine, and therewithal Sir Gawaine knew the
damosel, that she was a damosel of Queen Morgan le Fay.
Then Sir Gawaine understood that she led that knight to
some mischief.   Fair knight, said Sir Gawaine, whither ride
you now with that damosel?   Sir, said Sir Tristram, I wot
not whither I shall ride but as the damosel will lead me.
Sir, said Sir Gawaine, ye shall not ride with her, for she and
her lady did never good, but ill.   And then Sir Gawaine,
pulled out his sword and said: Damosel, but if thou tell me
anon for what cause thou leadest this knight with thee thou
shalt die for it right anon: I know all your lady's treason,
and yours. Mercy, Sir Gawaine, she said, and if ye will save
my life I will tell you.   Say on, said Sir Gawaine, and thou
shalt have thy life.   Sir, she said, Queen Morgan le Fay,
my lady, hath ordained a thirty ladies to seek and espy after
Sir Launcelot or Sir Tristram, and by the trains of these
ladies, who that may first meet any of these two knights, they
should turn them unto Morgan le Fay's castle, saying that
they should do deeds of worship; and if any of the two
knights came there, there be thirty knights lying and watching in a tower to wait upon Sir Launcelot or upon Sir
Tristram.   Fie for shame, said Sir Gawaine, that ever such
false treason should be wrought or used in a queen, and a
king's sister, and a king and queen's daughter.

CHAPTER XXV

HOW SIR TRISTRAM AND SIR GAWAINE RODE TO HAVE FOUGHTEN
    WITH THE THIRTY KNIGHTS, BUT THEY DURST NOT COME
    OUT

SIR, said Sir Gawaine, will ye stand with me, and we will
see the malice of these thirty knights. Sir, said Sir Tristram,
go ye to them, an it please you, and ye shall see I will not

tail you, for it is not long ago syn I and a fellow met with thirty knights of that queen's fellowship ; and God speed us so that we may win worship. So then Sir Gawaine and Sir Tristram rode toward the castle where Morgan le Fay was, and ever Sir Gawaine deemed well that he was Sir Tristram de Liones, by cause he heard that two knights had slain and beaten thirty knights. And when they came afore the castle Sir Gawaine spake on high and said : Queen Morgan le Fay, send out your knights that ye have laid in a watch for Sir Launcelot and for Sir Tristram. Now, said Sir Gawaine, I know your false treason, and through all places where that I ride men shall know of your false treason ; and now let see Sir Gawaine whether ye dare come out of your castle, ye thirty knights. Then the queen spake and all the thirty knights at once, and said : Sir Gawaine, full well wotest thou what thou dost and sayest ; for by God we know thee passing well, but all that thou speakest and dost, thou sayest it upon pride of that good knight that is there with thee. For there be some of us that know full well the hands of that knight over all well. And wit thou well, Sir Gawaine, it is more for his sake than for thine that we will not come out of this castle. For wit ye well, Sir Gawaine, the knight that beareth the arms of Cornwall, we know him and what he is. Then Sir Gawaine and Sir Tristram departed and rode on their ways a day or two together ; and there by adventure, they met with Sir Kay and Sir Sagramore le Desirous. And then they were glad of Sir Gawaine, and he of them, but they wist not what he was with the shield of Cornwall, but by deeming. And thus they rode together a day or two. And then they were ware of Sir Breuse Saunce Pité chasing a lady for to have slain her, for he had slain her paramour afore. Hold you all still, said Sir Gawaine, and show none of you forth, and ye shall see me reward yonder false knight ; for an he espy you he is so well horsed that he will escape away. And then Sir Gawaine rode betwixt Sir Breuse and the lady, and said : False knight, leave her, and have ado with me. When Sir Breuse saw no more but Sir Gawaine he feutred his spear, and Sir Gawaine against him ; and there Sir Breuse overthrew Sir Gawaine, and then he rode over him, and overthwart him twenty times to have destroyed him ; and when Sir Tristram saw him do so villainous a deed, he hurled out against him. And when Sir Breuse saw him with the shield of Cornwall he knew him well that it was Sir Tristram, and then he fled, and Sir Tristram followed after him ; and Sir Breuse Saunce Pité was so horsed that he went his way quite, and Sir Tristram followed him long, for he would fain have been avenged upon him. And so when he had long chased him, he saw a fair well, and thither he rode to repose him, and tied his horse till a tree.

CHAPTER XXVI

HOW DAMOSEL BRAGWAINE FOUND TRISTRAM SLEEPING BY A WELL, AND HOW SHE DELIVERED LETTERS TO HIM FROM LA BEALE ISOUD

AND then he pulled off his helm and washed his visage and his hands, and so he fell on sleep. In the meanwhile came a damosel that had sought Sir Tristram many ways and days within this land. And when she came to the well she looked upon him, and had forgotten him as in remembrance of Sir Tristram, but by his horse she knew him, that hight Passe-Brewel that had been Sir Tristram's horse many years. For when he was mad in the forest Sir Fergus kept him. So this lady, Dame Bragwaine, abode still till he was awake. So when she saw him wake she saluted him, and he her again, for either knew other of old acquaintance ; then she told him how she had sought him long and broad, and there she told him how she had letters from Queen La Beale Isoud. Then anon Sir Tristram read them, and wit ye well he was glad, for therein was many a piteous complaint. Then Sir Tristram said : Lady Bragwaine, ye shall ride with me till that tournament be done at the Castle of Maidens, and then shall bear letters and tidings with you. And then Sir Tristram took his horse and sought lodging, and there he met with a good ancient knight and prayed him to lodge with him. Right so came Gouvernail unto Sir Tristram, that was glad of that lady. So this old knight's name was Sir Pellounes, and he told of the great tournament that should be at the Castle of Maidens. And there Sir Launcelot and thirty-two knights of his blood had ordained shields of Cornwall. And right so there came one unto Sir Pellounes, and told him that Sir Persides de Bloise was come home ; then that knight held up his hands and thanked God of his coming home. And there Sir Pellounes told Sir Tristram that in two years he had not seen his son, Sir Persides. Sir, said Sir Tristram, I know your son well enough for a good knight. So on a time Sir Tristram and Sir Persides came to their lodging both at once, and so they unarmed them, and put upon them their clothing. And then these two knights each welcomed other. And when Sir Persides understood that Sir Tristram was of Cornwall, he said he was once in Cornwall: And there I jousted afore King Mark; and so it happed me at that time to overthrow ten knights, and then came to me Sir Tristram de Liones and overthrew me, and took my lady away from me, and that shall I never forget, but I shall remember me an ever I see my time. Ah, said Sir Tristram, now I understand that ye hate Sir Tristram. What deem ye, ween ye that Sir Tristram is not able to withstand your malice? Yes, said Sir Persides, I know well that Sir Tristram is a noble knight, and a much better knight than I, yet shall I not owe him my good will. Right as they stood thus talking at a bay-window of that castle, they saw many knights riding to and fro toward the tournament. And then was Sir Tristram ware of a likely knight riding upon a great black horse, and a black-covered shield. What knight is that, said Sir Tristram, with the black horse and the black shield? he seemeth a good knight. I know him well, said Sir Persides, he is one of the best knights of the world. Then is it Sir Launcelot, said Tristram. Nay, said Sir Persides, it is Sir Palomides, that is yet unchristened.

CHAPTER XXVII

HOW SIR TRISTRAM HAD A FALL WITH SIR PALOMIDES, AND HOW LAUNCELOT OVERTHREW TWO KNIGHTS

THEN they saw much people of the country salute Sir Palomides. And within a while after there came a squire of the castle, that told Sir Pellounes that was lord of that castle, that a knight with a black shield had smitten down thirteen knights. Fair brother, said Sir Tristram unto Sir Persides, let us cast upon us cloaks, and let us go see the play. Not so, said Sir Persides, we will not go like knaves thither, but we will ride like men and good knights to withstand our enemies. So they armed them, and took their horses and great spears, and thither they went there as many knights assayed themself before the tournament. And anon Sir Palomides saw Sir Persides, and then he sent a squire unto him and said: Go thou to the yonder knight with the green shield and therein a lion of gold, and say him I require him to joust with me, and tell him that my name is Sir Palomides. When Sir Persides understood that request of Sir Palomides, he made him ready, and there anon they met together, but Sir Persides had a fall. Then Sir Tristram dressed him to be revenged upon Sir Palomides, and that saw Sir Palomides that was ready and so was not Sir Tristram, and took him at an advantage and smote him over his horse's tail when he had no spear in his rest. Then start up Sir Tristram and took his horse lightly, and was wroth out of measure, and sore ashamed of that fall. Then Sir Tristram sent unto Sir Palomides by Gouvernail, and prayed him to joust with him at his request. Nay, said Sir Palomides, as at this time I will not joust with that knight, for I know him better than he weeneth. And if he be wroth he may right it tomorn at the Castle of Maidens, where he may see me and many other knights. With that came Sir Dinadan, and when he saw Sir Tristram wroth he list not to jape. Lo, said Sir Dinadan, here may a man prove, be a man never so good yet may he have a fall, and he was never so wise but he might be overseen, and he rideth well that never fell. So Sir Tristram was passing wroth, and said to Sir Persides and to Sir Dinadan : I will revenge me. Right so as they stood talking there, there came by Sir Tristram a likely knight riding passing soberly and heavily with a black shield. What knight is that? said Sir Tristram unto Sir Persides. I know him well, said Sir Persides, for his name is Sir Briant of North Wales; so he passed on among other knights of North Wales. And there came in Sir Launcelot du Lake with a shield of the arms of Cornwall, and he sent a squire unto Sir Briant, and required him to joust with him. Well, said Sir Briant, sithen I am required to joust I will do what I may; and there Sir Launcelot smote down Sir Briant from his horse a great fall. And then Sir Tristram marvelled what knight he was that bare the shield of Cornwall. Whatsoever he be, said Sir Dinadan, I warrant you he is of King Ban's blood, the which be knights of the most noble prowess in the world, for to account so many for so many. Then there came two knights of Northgalis, that one hight Hew de la Montaine, and the other Sir Maddok de la Montaine, and they challenged Sir Launcelot foot hot. Sir Launcelot not refusing them but made him ready, with one spear he smote them down both over their horse's croups ; and so Sir Launcelot rode his way. By the good lord, said Sir Tristram, he is a good knight that beareth the shield of Cornwall, and meseemeth he rideth in the best manner that ever I saw knight ride. Then the King of Northgalis rode unto Sir Palomides, and prayed him heartily for his sake to joust with that knight that hath done us of Northgalis despite. Sir, said Sir Palomides, I am full loath to have ado with that knight, and cause why is, for as tomorn the great tournament shall be ; and therefore I will keep myself fresh by my will. Nay, said the King of Northgalis, I pray you require him of jousts. Sir, said Sir Palomides, I will joust at your request, and require that knight to joust with me, and often I have seen a man have a fall at his own request.

CHAPTER XXVIII

HOW SIR LAUNCELOT JOUSTED WITH PALOMIDES AND OVERTHREW HIM, AND AFTER HE WAS ASSAILED WITH TWELVE KNIGHTS

THEN Sir Palomides sent unto Sir Launcelot a squire, and required him of jousts. Fair fellow, said Sir Launcelot, tell me thy lord's name. Sir, said the squire, my lord's name is Sir Palomides, the good knight. In good hour, said Sir Launcelot, for there is no knight that I saw this seven years that I had liefer ado withal than with him. And so either knights made them ready with two great spears. Nay, said Sir Dinadan, ye shall see that Sir Palomides will quit him right well. It may be so, said Sir Tristram, but I undertake that knight with the shield of Cornwall shall give him a fall. I believe it not, said Sir Dinadan. Right so they spurred their horses and feutred their spears, and either hit other, and Sir Palomides brake a spear upon Sir Launcelot, and he sat and moved not ; but Sir Launcelot smote him so lightly that he made his horse to avoid the saddle, and the stroke brake his shield and the hauberk, and had he not fallen he had been slain. How now, said Sir Tristram, I wist well by the manner of their riding both that Sir

Palomides should have a fall. Right so Sir Launcelot rode his way, and rode to a well to drink and to repose him, and they of Northgalis espied him whither he rode ; and then there followed him twelve knights for to have mischieved him, for this cause that upon the morn at the tournament of the Castle of Maidens that he should not win the victory. So they came upon Sir Launcelot suddenly, and unnethe he might put upon him his helm and take his horse, but they were in hands with him ; and then Sir Launcelot gat his spear, and rode through them, and there he slew a knight and brake a spear in his body. Then he drew his sword and smote upon the right hand and upon the left hand, so that within a few strokes he had slain other three knights, and the remnant that abode he wounded them sore all that did abide. Thus Sir Launcelot escaped from his enemies of North Wales, and then Sir Launcelot rode his way till a friend, and lodged him till on the morn ; for he would not the first day have ado in the tournament by cause of his great labour. And on the first day he was with King Arthur there as he was set on high upon a scaffold to discern who was best worthy of his deeds. So Sir Launcelot was with King Arthur, and jousted not the first day.

CHAPTER XXIX

HOW SIR TRISTRAM BEHAVED HIM THE FIRST DAY OF THE TOURNAMENT, AND THERE HE HAD THE PRIZE

Now turn we unto Sir Tristram de Liones, that commanded Gouvernail, his servant, to ordain him a black shield with none other remembrance therein. And so Sir Persides and Sir Tristram departed from their host Sir Pellounes, and they rode early toward the tournament, and then they drew them to King Carados' side, of Scotland ; and anon knights began the field what of King Northgalis' part, and what of King Carados' part, and there began great party. Then there was hurling and rushing. Right so came in Sir Persides and Sir Tristram, and so they did fare that they put the king of Northgalis aback. Then came in Sir Bleoberis de Ganis and Sir Gaheris with them of Northgalis, and then was Sir Persides smitten down and almost slain, for more than forty horsemen went over him.

For Sir Bleoberis did great deeds of arms, and Sir Gaheris failed him not. When Sir Tristram beheld them, and saw them do such deeds of arms, he marvelled what they were. Also Sir Tristram thought shame that Sir Persides was so done to; and then he gat a great spear in his hand, and then he rode to Sir Gaheris and smote him down from his horse. And then was Sir Bleoberis wroth, and gat a spear and rode against Sir Tristram in great ire; and there Sir Tristram met with him, and smote Sir Bleoberis from his horse. So then the king with the hundred knights was wroth, and he horsed Sir Bleoberis and Sir Gaheris again, and there began a great medley; and ever Sir Tristram held them passing short, and ever Sir Bleoberis was passing busy upon Sir Tristram; and there came Sir Dinadan against Sir Tristram, and Sir Tristram gave him such a buffet that he swooned in his saddle. Then anon Sir Dinadan came to Sir Tristram and said: Sir, I know thee better than thou weenest; but here I promise thee my troth I will never come against thee more, for I promise thee that sword of thine shall never come on mine helm. With that came Sir Bleoberis, and Sir Tristram gave him such a buffet that down he laid his head; and then he caught him so sore by the helm that he pulled him under his horse's feet. And then King Arthur blew to lodging. Then Sir Tristram departed to his pavilion, and Sir Dinadan rode with him; and Sir Persides and King Arthur then, and the kings upon both parties, marvelled what knight that was with the black shield. Many said their advice, and some knew him for Sir Tristram, and held their peace and would nought say. So that first day King Arthur, and all the kings and lords that were judges, gave Sir Tristram the prize; howbeit they knew him not, but named him the knight with the black shield.

CHAPTER XXX

HOW SIR TRISTRAM RETURNED AGAINST KING ARTHUR'S PARTY BY CAUSE HE SAW SIR PALOMIDES ON THAT PARTY

THEN upon the morn Sir Palomides returned from the king of Northgalis, and rode to King Arthur's side, where was King Carados, and the king of Ireland, and Sir Launcelot's kin and Sir Gawaine's kin. So Sir Palomides sent the damosel unto Sir Tristram that he sent to seek him when he was out of his mind in the forest, and this damosel asked Sir Tristram what he was and what was his name? As for that, said Sir Tristram, tell Sir Palomides ye shall not wit as at this time unto the time I have broken two spears upon him. But let him wit thus much, said Sir Tristram, that I am the same knight that he smote down in over evening at the tournament; and tell him plainly on what party that Sir Palomides be I will be of the contrary party. Sir, said the damosel, ye shall understand that Sir Palomides will be on King Arthur's side, where the most noble knights of the world be. In the name of God, said Sir Tristram, then will I be with the king of Northgalis, because Sir Palomides will be on King Arthur's side, and else I would not but for his sake. So when King Arthur was come they blew unto the field; and then there began a great party, and so King Carados jousted with the king of the hundred knights, and there King Carados had a fall: then was there hurling and rushing, and right so came in knights of King Arthur's, and they bare aback the king of Northgalis' knights. Then Sir Tristram came in, and began so roughly and so bigly that there was none might withstand him, and thus Sir Tristram dured long. And at the last Sir Tristram fell among the fellowship of King Ban, and there fell upon him Sir Bors de Ganis, and Sir Ector de Maris, and Sir Blamore de Ganis, and many other knights. And then Sir Tristram smote on the right hand and on the left hand, that all lords and ladies spake of his noble deeds. But at the last Sir Tristram should have had the worse had not the king with the hundred knights been. And then he came with his fellowship and rescued Sir Tristram, and brought him away from those knights that bare the shields of Cornwall. And then Sir Tristram saw another fellowship by themself, and there were a forty knights together, and Sir Kay, the Seneschal, was their governor. Then Sir Tristram rode in amongst them, and there he smote down Sir Kay from his horse; and there he fared among those knights like a greyhound among conies. Then Sir Launcelot found a knight that was sore wounded upon the head. Sir, said Sir Launcelot, who wounded you so sore? Sir, he said, a knight that beareth a black shield, and I may curse the time that ever I met with him, for he is a devil and no man. So Sir Launcelot departed from him and thought to meet with Sir Tristram, and so he rode with his sword drawn in his hand to seek Sir Tristram; and then he espied him how he hurled here and there, and at every stroke Sir Tristram well-nigh smote down a knight. O mercy Jesu! said the king, sith the times I bare arms saw I never no knight do so marvellous deeds of arms. And if I should set upon this knight, said Sir Launcelot to himself, I did shame to myself, and therewithal Sir Launcelot put up his sword. And then the king with the hundred knights and an hundred more of North Wales set upon the twenty of Sir Launcelot's kin: and they twenty knights held them ever together as wild swine, and none would fail other. And so when Sir Tristram beheld the noblesse of these twenty knights he marvelled of their good deeds, for he saw by their fare and by their rule that they had liefer die than avoid the field. Now Jesu, said Sir Tristram, well may he be valiant and full of prowess that hath such a sort of noble knights unto his kin, and full like is he to be a noble man that is their leader and governor. He meant it by Sir Launcelot du Lake. So when Sir Tristram had beholden them long he thought shame to see two hundred knights battering upon twenty knights. Then Sir Tristram rode unto the king with the hundred knights and said: Sir, leave your fighting with those twenty knights, for ye win no worship of them, ye be so many and they so few; and wit ye well they will not out of the field I see by their cheer and countenance; and worship get ye none an ye slay them. Therefore leave your fighting with them, for I to increase my worship I will ride to the twenty knights and help them with all my might and power. Nay, said the king with the hundred knights, ye shall not do so; now I see your courage and courtesy I will withdraw my knights for your pleasure, for evermore a good knight will favour another, and like will draw to like.

CHAPTER XXXI

HOW SIR TRISTRAM FOUND PALOMIDES BY A WELL, AND BROUGHT HIM WITH HIM TO HIS LODGING

THEN the king with the hundred knights withdrew his knights. And all this while, and long tofore, Sir Launcelot had watched upon Sir Tristram with a very purpose to have fellowshipped with him. And then suddenly Sir Tristram, Sir Dinadan, and Gouvernail, his man, rode their way into the forest, that no man perceived where they went. So then King Arthur blew unto lodging, and gave the king of Northgalis the prize by cause Sir Tristram was upon his side. Then Sir Launcelot rode here and there, so wood as lion that fauted his fill, by cause he had lost Sir Tristram, and so he returned unto King Arthur. And then in all the field was a noise that with the wind it might be heard two mile thence, how the lords and ladies cried : The knight with the black shield hath won the field. Alas, said King Arthur, where is that knight become? It is shame to all those in the field so to let him escape away from you ; but with gentleness and courtesy ye might have brought him unto me to the Castle of Maidens. Then the noble King Arthur went unto his knights and comforted them in the best wise that he could, and said : My fair fellows, be not dismayed, howbeit ye have lost the field this day. And many were hurt and sore wounded, and many were whole. My fellows, said King Arthur, look that ye be of good cheer, for to-morn I will be in the field with you and revenge you of your enemies. So that night King Arthur and his knights reposed themself. The damosel that came from La Beale Isoud unto Sir Tristram, all the while the tournament was adoing she was with Queen Guenever, and ever the queen asked her for what cause she came into that country. Madam, she answered, I come for none other cause but from my lady La Beale Isoud to wit of your welfare. For in no wise she would not tell the queen that she came for Sir Tristram's sake. So this lady, Dame Bragwaine, took her leave of Queen Guenever, and she rode after Sir Tristram. And as she rode through the forest she heard a great cry ; then she commanded her squire to go into the forest to wit what was that noise. And so he came to a well, and there he found a knight bounden till a tree crying as he had been wood, and his horse and his harness standing by him. And when he espied that squire, therewith he abraide and brake himself loose, and took his sword in his hand, and ran to have slain the squire. Then he took his horse and fled all that ever he might unto Dame Bragwaine, and told her of his adventure. Then she rode unto Sir Tristram's pavilion, and told Sir Tristram what adventure she had found in

the forest. Alas, said Sir Tristram, upon my head there
is some good knight at mischief. Then Sir Tristram took
his horse and his sword and rode thither, and there he
heard how the knight complained unto himself and said:
I, woful knight Sir Palomides, what misadventure befalleth
me, that thus am defoiled with falsehood and treason,
through Sir Bors and Sir Ector. Alas, he said, why live I so
long! And then he gat his sword in his hands, and made
many strange signs and tokens; and so through his raging
he threw his sword into that fountain. Then Sir Palomides
wailed and wrang his hands. And at the last for pure sorrow
he ran into that fountain, over his belly, and sought after
his sword. Then Sir Tristram saw that, and ran upon Sir
Palomides, and held him in his arms fast. What art thou,
said Palomides, that holdeth me so? I am a man of this
forest that would thee none harm. Alas, said Sir Palomides,
I may never win worship where Sir Tristram is; for ever
where he is an I be there, then get I no worship; and if he
be away for the most part I have the gree, unless that Sir
Launcelot be there or Sir Lamorak. Then Sir Palomides
said: Once in Ireland Sir Tristram put me to the worse,
and another time in Cornwall, and in other places in this
land. What would ye do, said Sir Tristram, an ye had Sir
Tristram? I would fight with him, said Sir Palomides, and
ease my heart upon him; and yet, to say thee sooth, Sir
Tristram is the gentlest knight in this world living. What
will ye do, said Sir Tristram, will ye go with me to your
lodging? Nay, said he, I will go to the king with the hundred knights, for he rescued me from Sir Bors de Ganis and
Sir Ector, and else had I been slain traitourly. Sir Tristram
said him such kind words that Sir Palomides went with him
to his lodging. Then Gouvernail went tofore, and charged
Dame Bragwaine to go out of the way to her lodging. And
bid ye Sir Persides that he make him no quarrels. And so
they rode together till they came to Sir Tristram's pavilion,
and there Sir Palomides had all the cheer that might be
had all that night. But in no wise Sir Palomides might not
know what was Sir Tristram; and so after supper they yede
to rest, and Sir Tristram for great travail slept till it was day.
And Sir Palomides might not sleep for anguish; and in the
dawning of the day he took his horse privily, and rode his
way unto Sir Gaheris and unto Sir Sagramore le Desirous,
where they were in their pavilions; for they three were

fellows at the beginning of the tournament. And then upon the morn the king blew unto the tournament upon the third day.

CHAPTER XXXII

So the king of Northgalis and the king with the hundred knights, they two encountered with King Carados and with the king of Ireland; and there the king with the hundred knights smote down King Carados, and the king of Northgalis smote down the king of Ireland. With that came in Sir Palomides, and when he came he made great work, for by his indented shield he was well known. So came in King Arthur, and did great deeds of arms together, and put the king of Northgalis and the king with the hundred knights to the worse. With this came in Sir Tristram with his black shield, and anon he jousted with Sir Palomides, and there by fine force Sir Tristram smote Sir Palomides over his horse's croup. Then King Arthur cried: Knight with the black shield, make thee ready to me, and in the same wise Sir Tristram smote King Arthur. And then by force of King Arthur's knights the king and Sir Palomides were horsed again. Then King Arthur with a great eager heart he gat a spear in his hand, and there upon the one side he smote Sir Tristram over his horse. Then foot-hot Sir Palomides came upon Sir Tristram, as he was upon foot, to have overridden him. Then Sir Tristram was ware of him, and there he stooped aside, and with great ire he gat him by the arm, and pulled him down from his horse. Then Sir Palomides lightly arose, and then they dashed together mightily with their swords; and many kings, queens, and lords, stood and beheld them. And at the last Sir Tristram smote Sir Palomides upon the helm three mighty strokes, and at every stroke that he gave him he said: Have this for Sir Tristram's sake. With that Sir Palomides fell to the earth grovelling. Then came the king with the hundred knights, and brought Sir Tristram an horse, and so was he horsed again. By then was Sir Palomides horsed, and with great ire he jousted upon Sir

Tristram with his spear as it was in the rest, and gave him
a great dash with his sword. Then Sir Tristram avoided
his spear, and gat him by the neck with his both hands,
and pulled him clean out of his saddle, and so he bare him
afore him the length of ten spears, and then in the presence
of them all he let him fall at his adventure. Then Sir
Tristram was ware of King Arthur with a naked sword in
his hand, and with his spear Sir Tristram ran upon
King Arthur; and then King Arthur boldly abode him
and with his sword he smote a-two his spear, and therewithal Sir Tristram stonied; and so King Arthur gave him
three or four strokes or he might get out his sword, and at
the last Sir Tristram drew his sword and assailed the other
passing hard. With that the great press departed. Then
Sir Tristram rode here and there and did his great pain,
that eleven of the good knights of the blood of King Ban,
that was of Sir Launcelot's kin, that day Sir Tristram smote
down; that all the estates marvelled of his great deeds and
all cried upon the knight with the black shield.

CHAPTER XXXIII

HOW SIR LAUNCELOT HURT SIR TRISTRAM, AND HOW AFTER SIR
TRISTRAM SMOTE DOWN SIR PALOMIDES

THEN this cry was so large that Sir Launcelot heard it.
And then he gat a great spear in his hand and came towards
the cry. Then Sir Launcelot cried: The knight with the
black shield, make thee ready to joust with me. When Sir
Tristram heard him say so he gat his spear in his hand, and
either abashed down their heads, and came together as
thunder; and Sir Tristram's spear brake in pieces, and Sir
Launcelot by malfortune struck Sir Tristram on the side a
deep wound nigh to the death; but yet Sir Tristram avoided
not his saddle, and so the spear brake. Therewithal Sir
Tristram that was wounded gat out his sword, and he rushed
to Sir Launcelot, and gave him three great strokes upon the
helm that the fire sprang thereout, and Sir Launcelot abashed
his head lowly toward his saddle-bow. And therewithal Sir
Tristram departed from the field, for he felt him so wounded
that he weened he should have died; and Sir Dinadan
espied him and followed him into the forest. Then Sir

Launcelot abode and did many marvellous deeds. So when Sir Tristram was departed by the forest's side he alit, and unlaced his harness and freshed his wound; then weened Sir Dinadan that he should have died. Nay, nay, said Sir Tristram, Dinadan never dread thee, for I am heart whole, and of this wound I shall soon be whole, by the mercy of God. By that Sir Dinadan was ware where came Palomides riding straight upon them. And then Sir Tristram was ware that Sir Palomides came to have destroyed him. And so Sir Dinadan gave him warning, and said: Sir Tristram, my lord, ye are so sore wounded that ye may not have ado with him, therefore I will ride against him and do to him what I may, and if I be slain ye may pray for my soul; and in the meanwhile ye may withdraw you and go into the castle, or in the forest, that he shall not meet with you. Sir Tristram smiled and said: I thank you, Sir Dinadan, of your good will, but ye shall wit that I am able to handle him. And then anon hastily he armed him, and took his horse, and a great spear in his hand, and said to Sir Dinadan: Adieu; and rode toward Sir Palomides a soft pace. Then when Sir Palomides saw that, he made countenance to amend his horse, but he did it for this cause, for he abode Sir Gaheris that came after him. And when he was come he rode toward Sir Tristram. Then Sir Tristram sent unto Sir Palomides, and required him to joust with him; and if he smote down Sir Palomides he would do no more to him; and if it so happened that Sir Palomides smote down Sir Tristram, he bade him do his utterance. So they were accorded. Then they met together, and Sir Tristram smote down Sir Palomides that he had a grievous fall, so that he lay still as he had been dead. And then Sir Tristram ran upon Sir Gaheris, and he would not have jousted; but whether he would or not Sir Tristram smote him over his horse's croup, that he lay still as though he had been dead. And then Sir Tristram rode his way and left Sir Persides' squire within the pavilions, and Sir Tristram and Sir Dinadan rode to an old knight's place to lodge them. And that old knight had five sons at the tournament, for whom he prayed God heartily for their coming home. And so, as the French book saith, they came home all five well beaten. And when Sir Tristram departed into the forest Sir Launcelot held alway the stoure like hard, as a man araged that took no heed to himself, and wit ye well there was many a noble knight against him. And when King Arthur saw Sir Launcelot do so marvellous deeds of arms he then armed him, and took his horse and his armour, and rode into the field to help Sir Launcelot; and so many knights came in with King Arthur. And to make short tale in conclusion, the king of Northgalis and the king of the hundred knights were put to the worse; and by cause Sir Launcelot abode and was the last in the field the prize was given him. But Sir Launcelot would neither for king, queen, nor knight, have the prize, but where the cry was cried through the field: Sir Launcelot, Sir Launcelot hath won the field this day, Sir Launcelot let make another cry contrary: Sir Tristram hath won the field, for he began first, and last he hath endured, and so hath he done the first day, the second, and the third day.

CHAPTER XXXIV

HOW THE PRIZE OF THE THIRD DAY WAS GIVEN TO SIR LAUNCELOT, AND SIR LAUNCELOT GAVE IT TO SIR TRISTRAM

THEN all the estates and degrees high and low said of Sir Launcelot great worship, for the honour that he did unto Sir Tristram; and for that honour doing to Sir Tristram he was at that time more praised and renowned than an he had overthrown five hundred knights; and all the people wholly for this gentleness, first the estates both high and low, and after the commonalty cried at once: Sir Launcelot hath won the field whosoever say nay. Then was Sir Launcelot wroth and ashamed, and so therewithal he rode to King Arthur. Alas, said the king, we are all dismayed that Sir Tristram is thus departed from us. By God, said King Arthur, he is one of the noblest knights that ever I saw hold spear or sword in hand, and the most courteoust knight in his fighting; for full hard I saw him, said King Arthur, when he smote Sir Palomides upon the helm thrice, that he abashed his helm with his strokes, and also he said: Here is a stroke for Sir Tristram, and thus thrice he said. Then King Arthur, Sir Launcelot, and Sir Dodinas le Savage took their horses to seek Sir Tristram, and by the means of Sir Persides he had told King Arthur where Sir Tristram was in his pavilion. But when they came there, Sir Tristram and Sir Dinadan were gone. Then King Arthur and Sir Launcelot were heavy, and returned again to the Castle of Maidens making great dole for the hurt of Sir Tristram, and his sudden departing. So God me help, said King Arthur, I am more heavy that I cannot meet with him than for all the hurts that all my knights have had at the tournament. Right so came Sir Gaheris and told King Arthur how Sir Tristram had smitten down Sir Palomides, and it was at Sir Palomides' own request. Alas, said King Arthur, that was great dishonour to Sir Palomides, in as much as Sir Tristram was sore wounded, and now may we all, kings and knights, and men of worship, say that Sir Tristram may be called a noble knight, and one of the best knights that ever I saw the days of my life. For I will that ye all, kings and knights, know, said King Arthur, that I never saw knight do so marvellously as he hath done these three days; for he was the first that began and that longest held on, save this last day. And though he was hurt, it was a manly adventure of two noble knights, and when two noble men encounter needs must the one have the worse, like as God will suffer at that time. As for me, said Sir Launcelot, for all the lands that ever my father left me I would not have hurt Sir Tristram an I had known him at that time; that I hurt him was for I saw not his shield. For an I had seen his black shield, I would not have meddled with him for many causes; for late he did as much for me as ever did knight, and that is well known that he had ado with thirty knights, and no help save Sir Dinadan. And one thing shall I promise, said Sir Launcelot, Sir Palomides shall repent it as in his unkindly dealing for to follow that noble knight that I by mishap hurted thus. Sir Launcelot said all the worship that might be said by Sir Tristram. Then King Arthur made a great feast to all that would come. And thus we let pass King Arthur, and a little we will turn unto Sir Palomides, that after he had a fall of Sir Tristram, he was nigh hand araged out of his wit for despite of Sir Tristram. And so he followed him by adventure. And as he came by a river, in his woodness he would have made his horse to have leapt over; and the horse failed footing and fell in the river, wherefore Sir Palomides was adread lest he should have been drowned; and then he avoided his horse, and swam to the land, and let his horse go down by adventure.

CHAPTER XXXV

HOW PALOMIDES CAME TO THE CASTLE WHERE SIR TRISTRAM WAS, AND OF THE QUEST THAT SIR LAUNCELOT AND TEN KNIGHTS MADE FOR SIR TRISTRAM

AND when he came to the land he took off his harness, and sat roaring and crying as a man out of his mind. Right so came a damosel even by Sir Palomides, that was sent from Sir Gawaine and his brother unto Sir Mordred, that lay sick in the same place with that old knight where Sir Tristram was. For, as the French book saith, Sir Persides hurt so Sir Mordred a ten days afore; and had it not been for the love of Sir Gawaine and his brother, Sir Persides had slain Sir Mordred. And so this damosel came by Sir Palomides, and she and he had language together, the which pleased neither of them; and so the damosel rode her ways till she came to the old knight's place, and there she told that old knight how she met with the woodest knight by adventure that ever she met withal. What bare he in his shield? said Sir Tristram. It was indented with white and black, said the damosel. Ah, said Sir Tristram, that was Sir Palomides, the good knight. For well I know him, said Sir Tristram, for one of the best knights living in this realm. Then that old knight took a little hackney, and rode for Sir Palomides, and brought him unto his own manor; and full well knew Sir Tristram Sir Palomides, but he said but little, for at that time Sir Tristram was walking upon his feet, and well amended of his hurts; and always when Sir Palomides saw Sir Tristram he would behold him full marvellously, and ever him seemed that he had seen him. Then would he say unto Sir Dinadan: An ever I may meet with Sir Tristram he shall not escape mine hands. I marvel, said Sir Dinadan, that ye boast behind Sir Tristram, for it is but late that he was in your hands, and ye in his hands; why would ye not hold him when ye had him? for I saw myself twice or thrice that ye gat but little worship of Sir Tristram. Then was Sir Palomides ashamed. So leave we them a little while in the old castle with the old knight Sir Darras. Now shall we speak of King Arthur, that said to Sir Launcelot: Had not ye been we had not lost Sir Tristram, for he was here daily unto the time ye met with him, and in an evil time, said Arthur, ye encountered with him. My lord Arthur, said

Launcelot, ye put upon me that I should be cause of his departtion; God knoweth it was against my will. But when men be hot in deeds of arms oft they hurt their friends as well as their foes. And my lord, said Sir Launcelot, ye shall understand that Sir Tristram is a man that I am loath to offend, for he hath done for me more than ever I did for him as yet. But then Sir Launcelot made bring forth a book: and then Sir Launcelot said: Here we are ten knights that will swear upon a book never to rest one night where we rest another this twelvemonth until that we find Sir Tristram. And as for me, said Sir Launcelot, I promise you upon this book that an I may meet with him, either with fairness or foulness I shall bring him to this court, or else I shall die therefor. And the names of these ten knights that had undertaken this quest were these following: First was Sir Launcelot, Sir Ector de Maris, Sir Bors de Ganis, and Bleoberis, and Sir Blamore de Ganis, and Lucan the Butler, Sir Uwaine, Sir Galihud, Lionel, and Galiodin. So these ten noble knights departed from the court of King Arthur, and so they rode upon their quest together until they came to a cross where departed four ways, and there departed the fellowship in four to seek Sir Tristram. And as Sir Launcelot rode by adventure he met with Dame Bragwaine that was sent into that country to seek Sir Tristram, and she fled as fast as her palfrey might go. So Sir Launcelot met with her and asked her why she fled. Ah, fair knight, said Dame Bragwaine, I flee for dread of my life, for here followeth me Sir Breuse Saunce Pité to slay me. Hold you nigh me, said Sir Launcelot. Then when Sir Launcelot saw Sir Breuse Saunce Pité, Sir Launcelot cried unto him, and said: False knight, destroyer of ladies and damosels, now thy last days be come. When Sir Breuse Saunce Pité saw Sir Launcelot's shield he knew it well, for at that time he bare not the arms of Cornwall, but he bare his own shield. And then Sir Breuse fled, and Sir Launcelot followed after him. But Sir Breuse was so well horsed that when him list to flee he might well flee, and also abide when him list. And then Sir Launcelot returned unto Dame Bragwaine, and she thanked him of his great labour.

CHAPTER XXXVI

HOW SIR TRISTRAM, SIR PALOMIDES, AND SIR DINADAN WERE TAKEN AND PUT IN PRISON

Now will we speak of Sir Lucan the butler, that by fortune he came riding to the same place there as was Sir Tristram, and in he came in none other intent but to ask harbour. Then the porter asked what was his name. Tell your lord that my name is Sir Lucan, the butler, a knight of the Round Table. So the porter went unto Sir Darras, lord of the place, and told him who was there to ask harbour. Nay, nay, said Sir Daname, that was nephew to Sir Darras, say him that he shall not be lodged here, but let him wit that I, Sir Daname, will meet with him anon, and bid him make him ready. So Sir Daname came forth on horseback, and there they met together with spears, and Sir Lucan smote down Sir Daname over his horse's croup, and then he fled into that place, and Sir Lucan rode after him, and asked after him many times. Then Sir Dinadan said to Sir Tristram: It is shame to see the lord's cousin of this place defoiled. Abide, said Sir Tristram, and I shall redress it. And in the meanwhile Sir Dinadan was on horseback, and he jousted with Lucan the butler, and there Sir Lucan smote Dinadan through the thick of the thigh, and so he rode his way; and Sir Tristram was wroth that Sir Dinadan was hurt, and followed after, and thought to avenge him; and within a while he overtook Sir Lucan, and bade him turn; and so they met together so that Sir Tristram hurt Sir Lucan passing sore and gave him a fall. With that came Sir Uwaine, a gentle knight, and when he saw Sir Lucan so hurt he called Sir Tristram to joust with him. Fair knight, said Sir Tristram, tell me your name I require you. Sir knight, wit ye well my name is Sir Uwaine le Fise de Roy Ureine. Ah, said Sir Tristram, by my will I would not have ado with you at no time. Ye shall not so, said Sir Uwaine, but ye shall have ado with me. And then Sir Tristram saw none other boot, but rode against him, and overthrew Sir Uwaine and hurt him in the side, and so he departed unto his lodging again. And when Sir Dinadan understood that Sir Tristram had hurt Sir Lucan he would have ridden after Sir Lucan for to have slain him, but Sir Tristram would not suffer him. Then Sir Uwaine let ordain an horse litter, and brought Sir Lucan to the abbey of Ganis, and the castle thereby hight the Castle of Ganis, of the which Sir Bleoberis was lord. And at that castle Sir Launcelot promised all his fellows to meet in the quest of Sir Tristram. So when Sir Tristram was come to his lodging there came a damosel that told Sir Darras that three of his sons were slain at that tournament, and two grievously wounded that they were never like to help themself. And all this was done by a noble knight that bare the black shield, and that was he that bare the prize. Then came there one and told Sir Darras that the same knight was within, him that bare the black shield. Then Sir Darras yede unto Sir Tristram's chamber, and there he found his shield and showed it to the damosel. Ah sir, said the damosel, that same is he that slew your three sons. Then without any tarrying Sir Darras put Sir Tristram, and Sir Palomides, and Sir Dinadan, within a strong prison, and there Sir Tristram was like to have died of great sickness ; and every day Sir Palomides would reprove Sir Tristram of old hate betwixt them. And ever Sir Tristram spake fair and said little. But when Sir Palomides saw the falling of sickness of Sir Tristram, then was he heavy for him, and comforted him in all the best wise he could. And as the French book saith, there came forty knights to Sir Darras that were of his own kin, and they would have slain Sir Tristram and his two fellows, but Sir Darras would not suffer that, but kept them in prison, and meat and drink they had. So Sir Tristram endured there great pain, for sickness had undertaken him, and that is the greatest pain a prisoner may have. For all the while a prisoner may have his health of body he may endure under the mercy of God and in hope of good deliverance ; but when sickness toucheth a prisoner's body, then may a prisoner say all wealth is him bereft, and then he hath cause to wail and to weep. Right so did Sir Tristram when sickness had undertaken him, for then he took such sorrow that he had almost slain himself.

CHAPTER XXXVII

HOW KING MARK WAS SORRY FOR THE GOOD RENOWN OF SIR
TRISTRAM. SOME OF KING ARTHUR'S KNIGHTS JOUSTED WITH
KNIGHTS OF CORNWALL

Now will we speak, and leave Sir Tristram, Sir Palomides, and Sir Dinadan in prison, and speak we of other knights that sought after Sir Tristram many divers parts of this land. And some yede into Cornwall; and by adventure Sir Gaheris, nephew unto King Arthur, came unto King Mark, and there he was well received and sat at King Mark's own table and ate of his own mess. Then King Mark asked Sir Gaheris what tidings there were in the realm of Logris. Sir, said Sir Gaheris, the king reigneth as a noble knight; and now but late there was a great jousts and tournament as ever I saw any in the realm of Logris, and the most noble knights were at that jousts. But there was one knight that did marvellously three days, and he bare a black shield, and of all knights that ever I saw he proved the best knight. Then, said King Mark, that was Sir Launcelot, or Sir Palomides the paynim. Not so, said Sir Gaheris, for both Sir Launcelot and Sir Palomides were on the contrary party against the knight with the black shield. Then was it Sir Tristram, said the king. Yea, said Sir Gaheris. And therewithal the king smote down his head, and in his heart he feared sore that Sir Tristram should get him such worship in the realm of Logris wherethrough that he himself should not be able to withstand him. Thus Sir Gaheris had great cheer with King Mark, and with Queen La Beale Isoud, the which was glad of Sir Gaheris' words; for well she wist by his deeds and manners that it was Sir Tristram. And then the king made a feast royal, and to that feast came Sir Uwaine le Fise de Roy Ureine, and some called him Uwaine le Blanche Mains. And this Sir Uwaine challenged all the knights of Cornwall. Then was the king wood wroth that he had no knights to answer him. Then Sir Andred, nephew unto King Mark, leapt up and said: I will encounter with Sir Uwaine. Then he yede and armed him and horsed him in the best manner. And there Sir Uwaine met with Sir Andred, and smote him down that he swooned on the earth. Then was King Mark sorry and wroth out of measure that he had no knight to revenge his nephew, Sir Andred. So the king called unto him Sir Dinas, the Seneschal, and prayed him for his sake to take upon him to joust with Sir Uwaine. Sir, said Sir Dinas, I am full loath to have ado with any knight of the Round Table. Yet, said the King, for my love take upon thee to joust. So Sir Dinas made him ready, and anon they encountered together with great spears, but Sir Dinas was overthrown, horse and man, a great fall. Who was wroth but King Mark! Alas, he said, have I no knight that will encounter with yonder knight? Sir, said Sir Gaheris, for your sake I will joust. So Sir Gaheris made him ready, and when he was armed he rode into the field. And when Sir Uwaine saw Sir Gaheris's shield he rode to him and said: Sir, ye do not your part. For, sir, the first time ye were made knight of the Round Table ye sware that ye should not have ado with your fellowship wittingly. And pardie, Sir Gaheris, ye knew me well enough by my shield, and so do I know you by your shield, and though ye would break your oath I would not break mine; for there is not one here nor ye that shall think I am afeared of you, but I durst right well have ado with you, and yet we be sisters' sons. Then was Sir Gaheris ashamed, and so therewithal every knight went their way, and Sir Uwaine rode into the country. Then King Mark armed him, and took his horse and his spear, with a squire with him. And then he rode afore Sir Uwaine, and suddenly at a gap he ran upon him as he that was not ware of him, and there he smote him almost through the body, and there left him. So within a while there came Sir Kay and found Sir Uwaine, and asked him how he was hurt. I wot not, said Sir Uwaine, why nor wherefore, but by treason I am sure I gat this hurt; for there came a knight suddenly upon me or that I was ware, and suddenly hurt me. Then there was come Sir Andred to seek King Mark. Thou traitor knight, said Sir Kay, an I wist it were thou that thus traitorly hast hurt this noble knight thou shouldst never pass my hands. Sir, said Sir Andred, I did never hurt him, and that I will report me to himself. Fie on you false knight, said Sir Kay, for ye of Cornwall are nought worth. So Sir Kay made carry Sir Uwaine to the Abbey of the Black Cross, and there he was healed. And then Sir Gaheris took his leave of King Mark, but or he departed he said: Sir king, ye did a foul shame unto you and your court, when ye banished Sir Tristram out of this country, for ye needed not to have doubted no knight an he had been here. And so he departed.

CHAPTER XXXVIII

OF THE TREASON OF KING MARK, AND HOW SIR GAHERIS SMOTE HIM DOWN AND ANDRED HIS COUSIN

THEN there came Sir Kay, the Seneschal, unto King Mark, and there he had good cheer showing outward. Now fair lords, said he, will ye prove any adventure in the forest of Morris, in the which I know well is as hard an adventure as I know any. Sir, said Sir Kay, I will prove it. And Sir Gaheris said he would be avised, for King Mark was ever full of treason: and therewithal Sir Gaheris departed and rode his way. And by the same way that Sir Kay should ride he laid him down to rest, charging his squire to wait upon Sir Kay; And warn me when he cometh. So within a while Sir Kay came riding that way, and then Sir Gaheris took his horse and met him, and said: Sir Kay, ye are not wise to ride at the request of King Mark, for he dealeth all with treason. Then said Sir Kay: I require you let us prove this adventure. I shall not fail you, said Sir Gaheris. And so they rode that time til a lake that was that time called the Perilous Lake, and there they abode under the shaw of the wood. The meanwhile King Mark within the castle of Tintagil avoided all his barons, and all other save such as were privy with him were avoided out of his chamber. And then he let call his nephew Sir Andred, and bad arm him and horse him lightly; and by that time it was midnight. And so King Mark was armed in black, horse and all; and so at a privy postern they two issued out with their varlets with them, and rode till they came to that lake. Then Sir Kay espied them first, and gat his spear, and proffered to joust. And King Mark rode against him, and smote each other full hard, for the moon shone as the bright day. And there at that jousts Sir Kay's horse fell down, for his horse was not so big as the king's horse, and Sir Kay's horse bruised him full sore. Then Sir Gaheris was wroth that Sir Kay had a fall. Then he cried: Knight, sit thou fast in thy saddle, for I will revenge my fellow. Then King Mark was afeard of Sir Gaheris, and so with evil will King Mark rode against him, and Sir Gaheris gave him such a stroke that he fell down. So then forthwithal Sir Gaheris ran unto Sir Andred and smote him from his horse quite, that his helm smote in the earth, and nigh had broken his neck. And therewithal Sir Gaheris alit, and gat up Sir Kay. And then they yode both on foot to them, and bad them yield them, and tell their names outher they should die. Then with great pain Sir Andred spake first, and said: It is King Mark of Cornwall, therefore be ye ware what ye do, and I am Sir Andred, his cousin. Fie on you both, said Sir Gaheris, for a false traitor, and false treason hast thou wrought and he both, under the feigned cheer that ye made us! it were pity, said Sir Gaheris, that thou shouldst live any longer. Save my life, said King Mark, and I will make amends; and consider that I am a king anointed. It were the more shame, said Sir Gaheris, to save thy life; thou art a king anointed with chrism, and therefore thou shouldest hold with all men of worship; and therefore thou art worthy to die. With that he lashed at King Mark without saying any more, and covered him with his shield and defended him as he might. And then Sir Kay lashed at Sir Andred, and therewithal King Mark yielded him unto Sir Gaheris. And then he kneeled adown, and made his oath upon the cross of the sword, that never while he lived he would be against errant-knights. And also he sware to be good friend unto Sir Tristram if ever he came into Cornwall. By then Sir Andred was on the earth, and Sir Kay would have slain him. Let be, said Sir Gaheris, slay him not I pray you. It were pity, said Sir Kay, that he should live any longer, for this is nigh cousin unto Sir Tristram, and ever he hath been a traitor unto him, and by him he was exiled out of Cornwall, and therefore I will slay him, said Sir Kay. Ye shall not, said Sir Gaheris; sythen I have given the king his life, I pray you give him his life. And therewithal Sir Kay let him go. And so Sir Kay and Sir Gaheris rode their way unto Dinas, the Seneschal, for by cause they heard say that he loved well Sir Tristram. So they reposed them there, and soon after they rode unto the realm of Logris. And so within a little while they met with Sir Launcelot that always had Dame Bragwaine with him, to that intent he weened to have met the sooner with Sir Tristram; and

Sir Launcelot asked what tidings in Cornwall, and whether they heard of Sir Tristram or not. Sir Kay and Sir Gaheris answered and said, that they heard not of him. Then they told Sir Launcelot word by word of their adventure. Then Sir Launcelot smiled and said: Hard it is to take out of the flesh that is bred in the bone; and so made them merry together.

CHAPTER XXXIX

HOW AFTER THAT SIR TRISTRAM, SIR PALOMIDES, AND SIR DINADAN HAD BEEN LONG IN PRISON THEY WERE DELIVERED

Now leave we off this tale, and speak we of Sir Dinas that had within the castle a paramour, and she loved another knight better than him. And so when Sir Dinas went out on hunting she slipped down by a towel, and took with her two brachets, and so she yede to the knight that she loved, and he her again. And when Sir Dinas come home and missed his paramour and his brachets, then was he the more wrother for his brachets than for the lady. So then he rode after the knight that had his paramour, and bad him turn and joust. So Sir Dinas smote him down, that with the fall he brake his leg and his arm. And then his lady and paramour cried Sir Dinas' mercy, and said she would love him better than ever she did. Nay, said Sir Dinas, I shall never trust them that once betrayed me, and therefore as ye have begun so end, for I will never meddle with you. And so Sir Dinas departed, and took his brachets with him, and so rode to his castle. Now will we turn unto Sir Launcelot, that was right heavy that he could never hear no tidings of Sir Tristram, for all this while he was in prison with Sir Darras, Palomides, and Dinadan. Then Dame Bragwaine took her leave to go into Cornwall, and Sir Launcelot, Sir Kay, and Sir Gaheris rode to seek Sir Tristram in the country of Surleuse. Now speaketh this tale of Sir Tristram and of his two fellows, for every day Sir Palomides brawled and said language against Sir Tristram. I marvel, said Sir Dinadan, of thee, Sir Palomides, an thou hadest Sir Tristram here thou wouldst do him no harm; for an a wolf and a sheep were together in a prison the wolf would suffer the sheep to be in peace. And wit thou well, said Sir Dinadan, this same is Sir Tristram at a word, and now must thou do thy best with him, and let see now if ye can skift it with your hands. Then was Sir Palomides abashed and said little. Sir Palomides, then said Sir Tristram, I have heard much of your maugre against me, but I will not meddle with you as at this time by my will, by cause I dread the lord of this place that hath us in governance; for an I dread him not more than I do thee, soon it should be skift: so they peaced themself. Right so came in a damosel and said: Knights, be of good cheer, for ye are sure of your lives, and that I heard say my lord, Sir Darras. Then were they glad all three, for daily they weened they should have died. Then soon after this Sir Tristram fell sick that he weened to have died; then Sir Dinadan wept, and so did Sir Palomides under them both making great sorrow. So a damosel came in to them and found them mourning. Then she went unto Sir Darras, and told him how that mighty knight that bare the black shield was likely to die. That shall not be, said Sir Darras, for God defend when knights come to me for succour that I should suffer them to die within my prison. Therefore, said Sir Darras to the damosel, fetch that knight and his fellows afore me. And then anon Sir Darras saw Sir Tristram brought afore him. He said: Sir knight, me repenteth of thy sickness, for thou art called a full noble knight, and so it seemeth by thee; and wit ye well it shall never be said that Sir Darras shall destroy such a noble knight as thou art in prison, howbeit that thou hast slain three of my sons, whereby I was greatly aggrieved. But now shalt thou go and thy fellows, and your harness and horses have been fair and clean kept, and ye shall go where it liketh you, upon this covenant, that thou, knight, wilt promise me to be good friend to my sons two that be now on live and also that thou tell me thy name. Sir, said he, as for me my name is Sir Tristram de Liones, and in Cornwall was I born, and nephew I am unto King Mark. And as for the death of your sons I might not do withal, for an they had been the next kin that I have I might have done none otherwise. And if I had slain them by treason or treachery I had been worthy to have died. All this I consider, said Sir Darras, that all that ye did was by force of knighthood, and that was the cause I would not put you to death. But syth ye be Sir Tristram, the good knight, I pray you heartily to be my good friend and to my sons. Sir, said Sir Tristram,

I promise you by the faith of my body, ever while I live I will do you service, for ye have done to us but as a natural knight ought to do. Then Sir Tristram reposed him there till that he was amended of his sickness; and when he was big and strong they took their leave, and every knight took their horses, and so departed and rode together till they came to a cross way. Now fellows, said Sir Tristram, here will we depart in sundry ways. And by cause Sir Dinadan had the first adventure of him I will begin.

CHAPTER XL

HOW SIR DINADAN RESCUED A LADY FROM SIR BREUSE SAUNCE PITÉ, AND HOW SIR TRISTRAM RECEIVED A SHIELD OF MORGAN LE FAY

So as Sir Dinadan rode by a well he found a lady making great dole. What aileth you? said Sir Dinadan. Sir knight, said the lady, I am the wofullest lady of the world, for within these five days here came a knight called Sir Breuse Saunce Pité, and he slew mine own brother, and ever since he hath kept me at his own will, and of all men in the world I hate him most; and therefore I require you of knighthood to avenge me, for he will not tarry, but be here anon. Let him come, said Sir Dinadan, and by cause of honour of all women I will do my part. With this came Sir Breuse, and when he saw a knight with his lady he was wood wroth. And then he said: Sir knight, keep thee from me. So they hurtled together as thunder, and either smote other passing sore, but Sir Dinadan put him through the shoulder a grievous wound, and or ever Sir Dinadan might turn him Sir Breuse was gone and fled. Then the lady prayed him to bring her to a castle there beside but four mile thence; and so Sir Dinadan brought her there, and she was welcome, for the lord of that castle was her uncle; and so Sir Dinadan rode his way upon his adventure. Now turn we this tale unto Sir Tristram, that by adventure he came to a castle to ask lodging, wherein was Queen Morgan le Fay; and so when Sir Tristram was let into that castle he had good cheer all that night. And upon the morn when he would have departed the queen said: Wit ye well ye shall not depart lightly, for ye are here as a prisoner. Jesu defend! said Sir Tristram, for I was but late a prisoner. Fair knight, said the queen, ye shall abide with me till that I wit what ye are and from whence ye come. And ever the queen would set Sir Tristram on her own side, and her paramour on the other side. And ever Queen Morgan would behold Sir Tristram, and there at the knight was jealous, and was in will suddenly to have run upon Sir Tristram with a sword, but he left it for shame. Then the queen said to Sir Tristram: Tell me thy name, and I shall suffer you to depart when ye will. Upon that covenant I tell you my name is Sir Tristram de Liones. Ah, said Morgan le Fay, an I had wist that, thou shouldst not have departed so soon as thou shalt. But sythen I have made a promise I will hold it, with that thou wilt promise me to bear upon thee a shield that I shall deliver thee, unto the castle of the Hard Rock, where King Arthur had cried a great tournament, and there I pray you that ye will be, and to do for me as much deeds of arms as ye may do. For at the Castle of Maidens, Sir Tristram, ye did marvellous deeds of arms as ever I heard knight do. Madam, said Sir Tristram, let me see the shield that I shall bear. Then the shield was brought forth, and the field was goldish with a king and a queen therein painted, and a knight standing above them upon the king's head, and the other upon the queen's. Madam, said Sir Tristram, this is a fair shield and a mighty; but what signifieth this king and this queen, and the knight standing upon both their heads? I shall tell you, said Morgan le Fay, it signifieth King Arthur and Queen Guenever, and a knight who holdeth them both in bondage and in servage. Who is that knight? said Sir Tristram. That shall ye not wit as at this time, said the Queen. But as the French book saith, Queen Morgan loved Sir Launcelot best, and ever she desired him, and he would never love her nor do nothing at her request, and therefore she held many knights together for to have taken him by strength. And by cause she deemed that Sir Launcelot loved Queen Guenever paramour, and she him again, therefore Queen Morgan le Fay ordained that shield to put Sir Launcelot to a rebuke, to that intent that King Arthur might understand the love between them. Then Sir Tristram took that shield and promised her to bear it at the tournament at the Castle of the Hard Rock. But Sir Tristram knew not that that shield was ordained against Sir Launcelot, but afterward he knew it.

CHAPTER XLI

HOW SIR TRISTRAM TOOK WITH HIM THE SHIELD, AND ALSO HOW HE
SLEW THE PARAMOUR OF MORGAN LE FAY

So then Sir Tristram took his leave of the queen, and
took the shield with him. Then came the knight that held
Queen Morgan le Fay, his name was Sir Hemison, and he
made him ready to follow Sir Tristram. Fair friend, said
Morgan, ride not after that knight, for ye shall not win no
worship of him. Fie on him, coward, said Sir Hemison,
for I wist never good knight come out of Cornwall but if it
were Sir Tristram de Liones. What an that be he? said
she. Nay, nay, said he, he is with La Beale Isoud, and this
is but a daffish knight. Alas, my fair friend, ye shall find
him the best knight that ever ye met withal, for I know him
better than ye do. For your sake, said Sir Hemison, I
shall slay him. Ah, fair friend, said the Queen, me
repenteth that ye will follow that knight, for I fear me sore
of your again coming. With this this knight rode his way
wood wroth, and he rode after Sir Tristram as fast as he
had been chased with knights. When Sir Tristram heard
a knight come after him so fast he returned about, and saw
a knight coming against him. And when he came nigh to
Sir Tristram he cried on high : Sir knight, keep thee from
me. Then they rushed together as it had been thunder,
and Sir Hemison bruised his spear upon Sir Tristram, but
his harness was so good that he might not hurt him. And
Sir Tristram smote him harder, and bare him through the
body, and he fell over his horse's croup. Then Sir Tristram
turned to have done more with his sword, but he saw so
much blood go from him that him seemed he was likely to
die, and so he departed from him and came to a fair manor
to an old knight, and there Sir Tristram lodged.

CHAPTER XLII

HOW MORGAN LE FAY BURIED HER PARAMOUR, AND HOW SIR TRIST-
RAM PRAISED SIR LAUNCELOT AND HIS KIN

Now leave to speak of Sir Tristram, and speak we of the
knight that was wounded to the death. Then his varlet
alit, and took off his helm, and then he asked his lord
whether there were any life in him. There is in me life,
said the knight, but it is but little ; and therefore leap thou

up behind me when thou hast holpen me up, and hold me fast that I fall not, and bring me to Queen Morgan le Fay; for deep draughts of death draw to my heart that I may not live, for I would fain speak with her or I died: for else my soul will be in great peril an I die. For with great pain his varlet brought him to the castle, and there Sir Hemison fell down dead. When Morgan le Fay saw him dead she made great sorrow out of reason; and then she let despoil him unto his shirt, and so she let him put into a tomb. And about the tomb she let write: Here lieth Sir Hemison, slain by the hands of Sir Tristram de Liones. Now turn we unto Sir Tristram, that asked the knight his host if he saw late any knight's adventurous. Sir, he said, the last night here lodged with me Ector de Maris and a damosel with him, and that damosel told me that he was one of the best knights of the world. That is not so, said Sir Tristram, for I know four better knights of his own blood, and the first is Sir Launcelot du Lake, call him the best knight, and Sir Bors de Ganis, Sir Bleoberis, Sir Blamore de Ganis, and Sir Gaheris. Nay, said his host, Sir Gawaine is a better knight than he. That is not so, said Sir Tristram, for I have met with them both, and I felt Sir Gaheris for the better knight, and Sir Lamorak I call him as good as any of them except Sir Launcelot. Why name ye not Sir Tristram? said his host, for I account him as good as any of them. I know not Sir Tristram, said Tristram. Thus they talked and bourded as long as them list, and then went to rest. And on the morn Sir Tristram departed, and took his leave of his host, and rode toward the Roche Dure, and none adventure had Sir Tristram but that; and so he rested not till he came to the castle where he saw five hundred tents.

CHAPTER XLIII

HOW SIR TRISTRAM AT A TOURNAMENT BARE THE SHIELD THAT MORGAN LE FAY DELIVERED TO HIM

THEN the King of Scots and the King of Ireland held against King Arthur's knights, and there began a great medley. So came in Sir Tristram and did marvellous deeds of arms, for there he smote down many knights. And ever he was afore King Arthur with that shield. And when King Arthur saw that shield he marvelled greatly in what intent it was made ; but Queen Guenever deemed as it was, wherefore she was heavy. Then was there a damosel of Queen Morgan in a chamber by King Arthur, and when she heard King Arthur speak of that shield, then she spake openly unto King Arthur. Sir King, wit ye well this shield was ordained for you, to warn you of your shame and dishonour, and that longeth to you and your queen. And then anon that damosel pyked her away privily, that no man wist where she was become. Then was King Arthur sad and wroth, and asked from whence came that damosel. There was not one that knew her nor wist where she was become. Then Queen Guenever called to her Sir Ector de Maris, and there she made her complaint to him, and said : I wot well this shield was made by Morgan le Fay in despite of me and of Sir Launcelot, wherefore I dread me sore lest I should be destroyed. And ever the King beheld Sir Tristram, that did so marvellous deeds of arms that he wondered sore what knight he might be, and well he wist it was not Sir Launcelot. And it was told him that Sir Tristram was in Petit Britain with Isoud La Blanche Mains, for he deemed an he had been in the realm of Logris Sir Launcelot or some of his fellows that were in the quest of Sir Tristram that they should have found him or that time. So King Arthur had marvel what knight he might be. And ever Sir Arthur's eye was on that shield. All that espied the queen, and that made her sore afeard. Then ever Sir Tristram smote down knights wonderly to behold, what upon the right hand and upon the left hand, that unnethe no knight might withstand him. And the king of Scots and the king of Ireland began to withdraw them. When Arthur espied that, he thought that that knight with the strange shield should not escape him. Then he called unto him Sir Uwaine Le Blanche Mains, and bad him arm him and make him ready. So anon King Arthur and Sir Uwaine dressed them before Sir Tristram, and required him to tell them where he had that shield. Sir, he said, I had it of Queen Morgan le Fay, sister unto King Arthur.

So here endeth this history of
this book, for it is the first
book of Sir Tristram de
Liones and the second
book of Sir Tristram
followeth.

BOOK X

CHAPTER I

HOW SIR TRISTRAM JOUSTED, AND SMOTE DOWN KING ARTHUR, BECAUSE HE TOLD HIM NOT THE CAUSE WHY HE BARE THAT SHIELD

AND if so be ye can descrive what ye bear, ye are worthy to bear the arms. As for that, said Sir Tristram, I will answer you; this shield was given me, not desired, of Queen Morgan le Fay; and as for me, I can not descrive these arms, for it is no point of my charge, and yet I trust to God to bear them with worship. Truly, said King Arthur, ye ought not to bear none arms but if ye wist what ye bear: but I pray you tell me your name. To what intent? said Sir Tristram. For I would wit, said Arthur. Sir, ye shall not wit as at this time. Then shall ye and I do battle together, said King Arthur. Why, said Sir Tristram, will ye do battle with me but if I tell you my name? and that little needeth you an ye were a man of worship, for ye have seen me this day have had great travail, and therefore ye are a villainous knight to ask battle of me, considering my great travail; howbeit I will not fail you, and have ye no doubt that I fear not you, though you think you have me at a great advantage yet shall I right well endure you. And therewithal King Arthur dressed his shield and his spear, and Sir Tristram against him, and they came so eagerly together. And there King Arthur brake his spear all to pieces upon Sir Tristram's shield. But Sir Tristram hit Arthur again, that horse and man fell to the earth. And there was King Arthur wounded on the left side, a great wound and a perilous. Then when Sir Uwaine saw his lord Arthur lie on the ground sore wounded, he was passing heavy. And then he dressed his shield and his spear, and cried aloud unto Sir Tristram and said: Knight, defend thee. So they came together as thunder, and Sir Uwaine brysed his spear all to pieces upon Sir Tristram's shield, and Sir Tristram smote him harder and sorer, with such a might that he bare him clean out of his saddle to the earth. With that Sir Tristram turned about and said: Fair knights, I had no need to joust with you, for I have had enough to do this day. Then arose Arthur and went to Sir Uwaine, and said to Sir Tristram: We have as we have deserved, for through our orgulyte we demanded battle of you, and yet we knew not your name. Nevertheless, by Saint Cross, said Sir Uwaine, he is a strong knight at mine advice as any is now living. Then Sir Tristram departed, and in every place he asked and demanded after Sir Launcelot, but in no place he could not hear of him whether he were dead or on live; wherefore Sir Tristram made great dole and sorrow. So Sir Tristram rode by a forest, and then was he ware of a fair tower by a marsh on that one side, and on that other side a fair meadow. And there he saw ten knights fighting together. And ever the nearer he came he saw how there was but one knight did battle against nine knights, and that one did so marvellously that Sir Tristram had great wonder that ever one knight might do so great deeds of arms. And then within a little while he had slain half their horses and unhorsed them, and their horses ran in the fields and forest. Then Sir Tristram had so great pity of that one knight that endured so great pain, and ever he thought it should be Sir Palomides, by his shield. And so he rode unto the knights and cried unto them, and bade them cease of their battle, for they did themselves great shame so many knights to fight with one. Then answered the master of those knights, his name was called Breuse Saunce Pité, that was at that time the most mischievoust knight living, and said thus: Sir knight, what have ye ado with us to meddle? and therefore, an ye be wise, depart on your way as ye came, for this knight shall not escape us. That were pity, said Sir Tristram, that so good a knight as he is should be slain so cowardly; and therefore I warn you I will succour him with all my puissance.

CHAPTER II

HOW SIR TRISTRAM SAVED SIR PALOMIDES' LIFE, AND HOW THEY PROMISED TO FIGHT TOGETHER WITHIN A FORTNIGHT

So Sir Tristram alit off his horse by cause they were on foot, that they should not slay his horse, and then dressed his shield, with his sword in his hand, and he smote on the right hand and on the left hand passing sore, that well-nigh at every stroke he struck down a knight. And when they espied his strokes they fled all with Breuse Saunce Pité unto the tower, and Sir Tristram followed fast after with his sword in his hand, but they escaped into the tower, and shut Sir Tristram without the gate. And when Sir Tristram saw this he returned aback unto Sir Palomides, and found him sitting under a tree sore wounded. Ah, fair knight, said Sir Tristram, well be ye found. Gramercy, said Sir Palomides, of your great goodness, for ye have rescued me of my life, and saved me from my death. What is your name? said Sir Tristram. He said: My name is Sir Palomides. O Jesu, said Sir Tristram, thou hast a fair grace of me this day that I should rescue thee, and thou art the man in the world that I most hate; but now make thee ready, for I will do battle with thee. What is your name? said Sir Palomides. My name is Sir Tristram, your mortal enemy. It may be so, said Sir Palomides; but ye have done over much for me this day that I should fight with you; for inasmuch as ye have saved my life it will be no worship for you to have ado with me, for ye are fresh and I am wounded sore, and therefore, an ye will needs have ado with me, assign me a day and then I shall meet with you without fail. Ye say well, said Sir Tristram, now I assign you to meet me in the meadow by the river of Camelot, where Merlin set the peron. So they were agreed. Then Sir Tristram asked Sir Palomides why the ten knights did battle with him. For this cause, said Sir Palomides; as I rode upon mine adventures in a forest here beside I espied where lay a dead knight, and a lady weeping beside him. And when I saw her making such dole, I asked her who slew her lord. Sir, she said, the falsest knight of the world now living, and he is the most villain that ever man heard speak of, and his name is Sir Breuse Saunce Pité. Then for pity I made the damosel to leap on her palfrey, and I promised her to be her warrant, and to help her to inter her lord. And so, suddenly, as I came riding by this tower, there came out Sir Breuse Saunce Pité, and suddenly he struck me from my horse. And then or I might recover my horse this Sir Breuse slew the damosel. And so I took my horse again, and I was sore ashamed, and so began the medley betwixt us; and this is the cause wherefore we did this battle. Well, said Sir Tristram, now I understand the manner of your battle, but in any wise have remembrance of your promise that ye have made with me to do battle with me this day fortnight. I shall not fail you, said Sir Palomides. Well, said Sir Tristram, as at this time I will not fail you till that ye be out of the danger of your enemies. So they mounted upon their horses, and rode together unto that forest, and there they found a fair well, with clear water bubbling. Fair sir, said Sir Tristram, to drink of that water have I courage; and then they alit off their horses. And then were they ware by them where stood a great horse tied to a tree, and ever he neighed. And then were they ware of a fair knight armed, under a tree, lacking no piece of harness, save his helm lay under his head. By the good lord, said Sir Tristram, yonder lieth a well-faring knight; what is best to do? Awake him, said Sir Palomides. So Sir Tristram awaked him with the butt of his spear. And so the knight rose up hastily and put his helm upon his head, and gat a great spear in his hand; and without any more words he hurled unto Sir Tristram, and smote him clean from his saddle to the earth, and hurt him on the left side, that Sir Tristram lay in great peril. Then he wallopped farther, and fetched his course, and came hurling upon Sir Palomides, and there he struck him a part through the body, that he fell from his horse to the earth. And then this strange knight left them there, and took his way through the forest. With this Sir Palomides and Sir Tristram were on foot, and gat their horses again, and either asked counsel of other, what was best to do. By my head, said Sir Tristram, I will follow this strong knight that thus hath shamed us. Well, said Sir Palomides, and I will repose me hereby with a friend of mine. Beware, said Sir Tristram unto Palomides, that ye fail not that day that ye have set with me to do battle, for, as I deem, ye will not hold your day, for I am much bigger than ye. As for that, said Sir Palomides, be it as it be may, for I fear you not, for an I be not sick nor prisoner, I will not fail you; but I have cause to have more doubt of you that ye will not meet with me, for ye ride after yonder strong knight. And if ye meet with him it is an hard adventure an ever ye escape his hands. Right so Sir Tristram and Sir Palomides departed, and either took their ways diverse.

CHAPTER III

HOW SIR TRISTRAM SOUGHT A STRONG KNIGHT THAT HAD SMITTEN
HIM DOWN, AND MANY OTHER KNIGHTS OF THE ROUND
TABLE

AND so Sir Tristram rode long after this strong knight. And at the last he saw where lay a lady overthwart a dead knight. Fair lady, said Sir Tristram, who hath slain your lord? Sir, she said, here came a knight riding, as my lord and I rested us here, and asked him of whence he was, and my lord said of Arthur's court. Therefore, said the strong knight, I will joust with thee, for I hate all these that be of Arthur's court. And my lord that lieth here dead amounted upon his horse, and the strong knight and my lord encountered together, and there he smote my lord throughout with his spear, and thus he hath brought me in great woe and damage. That me repenteth, said Sir Tristram, of your great anger; an it please you tell me your husband's name. Sir, said she, his name was Galardoun, that would have proved a good knight. So departed Sir Tristram from that dolorous lady, and had much evil lodging. Then on the third day Sir Tristram met with Sir Gawaine and with Sir Bleoberis in a forest at a lodge, and either were sore wounded. Then Sir Tristram asked Sir Gawaine and Sir Bleoberis if they met with such a knight, with such a cognisance, with a covered shield. Fair sir, said these knights, such a knight met with us to our great damage. And first he smote down my fellow, Sir Bleoberis, and sore wounded him because he bade me I should not have ado with him, for why he was overstrong for me. That strong knight took his words at scorn, and said he said it for mockery. And then they rode together, and so he hurt my fellow. And when he had done so I might not for shame but I must joust with him. And at the first course he smote me down and my horse to the earth. And there he had almost slain me, and from us he took his horse and departed, and in an evil time we met with him. Fair knights, said Sir Tristram, so he met with me, and with another knight that hight Palomides, and he smote us both down with one spear, and hurt us right sore. By my faith, said Sir Gawaine, by my counsel ye shall let him pass and seek him no further; for at the next feast of the Round

Table, upon pain of my head ye shall find him there. By my faith, said Sir Tristram, I shall never rest till that I find him. And then Sir Gawaine asked him his name. Then he said : My name is Sir Tristram. And so either told other their names, and then departed Sir Tristram and rode his way. And by fortune in a meadow Sir Tristram met with Sir Kay, the Seneschal, and Sir Dinadan. What tidings with you, said Sir Tristram, with you knights ? Not good, said these knights. Why so ? said Sir Tristram ; I pray you tell me, for I ride to seek a knight. What cognisance beareth he ? said Sir Kay. He beareth, said Sir Tristram, a covered shield close with cloth. By my head, said Sir Kay, that is the same knight that met with us, for this night we were lodged within a widow's house, and there was that knight lodged ; and when he wist we were of Arthur's court he spoke great villainy by the king, and specially by the Queen Guenever, and then on the morn was waged battle with him for that cause. And at the first recounter, said Sir Kay, he smote me down from my horse and hurt me passing sore ; and when my fellow, Sir Dinadan, saw me smitten down and hurt he would not revenge me, but fled from me ; and thus he departed. And then Sir Tristram asked them their names, and so either told other their names. And so Sir Tristram departed from Sir Kay, and from Sir Dinadan, and so he passed through a great forest into a plain, till he was ware of a priory, and there he reposed him with a good man six days.

CHAPTER IV

HOW SIR TRISTRAM SMOTE DOWN SIR SAGRAMORE LE DESIROUS AND SIR DODINAS LE SAVAGE

AND then he sent his man that hight Gouvernail, and commanded him to go to a city thereby to fetch him new harness ; for it was long time afore that that Sir Tristram had been refreshed, his harness was bruised and broken. And when Gouvernail, his servant, was come with his apparel, he took his leave at the widow, and mounted upon his horse, and rode his way early on the morn. And by sudden adventure Sir Tristram met with Sir Sagramore le Desirous, and with Sir Dodinas le Savage. And these two knights met with Sir Tristram and questioned with him, and asked him if he would joust with them. Fair knights, said Sir Tristram, with a good will I would joust with you, but I have promised at a day set, near hand, to do battle with a strong knight; and therefore I am loth to have ado with you, for an it misfortuned me here to be hurt I should not be able to do my battle which I promised. As for that, said Sagramore, maugre your head, ye shall joust with us or ye pass from us. Well, said Sir Tristram, if ye enforce me thereto I must do what I may. And then they dressed their shields, and came running together with great ire. But through Sir Tristram's great force he struck Sir Sagramore from his horse. Then he hurled his horse farther, and said to Sir Dodinas: Knight, make thee ready; and so through fine force Sir Tristram struck Dodinas from his horse. And when he saw them lie on the earth he took his bridle, and rode forth on his way, and his man Gouvernail with him. Anon as Sir Tristram was passed, Sir Sagramore and Sir Dodinas gat again their horses, and mounted up lightly and followed after Sir Tristram. And when Sir Tristram saw them come so fast after him he returned with his horse to them, and asked them what they would. It is not long ago sythen I smote you to the earth at your own request and desire: I would have ridden by you, but ye would not suffer me, and now meseemeth ye would do more battle with me. That is truth, said Sir Sagramore and Sir Dodinas, for we will be revenged of the despite ye have done to us. Fair knights, said Sir Tristram, that shall little need you, for all that I did to you ye caused it; wherefore I require you of your knighthood leave me as at this time, for I am sure an I do battle with you I shall not escape without great hurts, and as I suppose ye shall not escape all lotless. And this is the cause why I am so loth to have ado with you; for I must fight within these three days with a good knight, and as valiant as any is now living, and if I be hurt I shall not be able to do battle with him. What knight is that, said Sir Sagramore, that ye shall fight withal? Sirs, said he, it is a good knight called Sir Palomides. By my head, said Sir Sagramore and Sir Dodinas, ye have cause to dread him, for ye shall find him a passing good knight, and a valiant. And by cause ye shall have ado with him we will forbear you as at this time, and else ye should not escape us lightly. But, fair knight, said Sir Sagramore, tell us your name. Sir, said he, my name is Sir Tristram de Liones. Ah, said Sagramore and Sir Dodinas, well be ye found, for much worship have we heard of you. And then either took leave of other, and departed on their way.

CHAPTER V

HOW SIR TRISTRAM MET AT THE PERON WITH SIR LAUNCELOT, AND HOW THEY FOUGHT TOGETHER UNKNOWN

THEN departed Sir Tristram and rode straight unto Camelot, to the peron that Merlin had made tofore, where Sir Lanceor, that was the king's son of Ireland, was slain by the hands of Balin. And in that same place was the fair lady Colombe slain, that was love unto Sir Lanceor; for after he was dead she took his sword and thrust it through her body. And by the craft of Merlin he made to inter this knight, Lanceor, and his lady, Colombe, under one stone. And at that time Merlin prophesied that in that same place should fight two the best knights that ever were in Arthur's days, and the best lovers. So when Sir Tristram came to the tomb where Lanceor and his lady were buried he looked about him after Sir Palomides. Then was he ware of a seemly knight came riding against him all in white, with a covered shield. When he came nigh Sir Tristram he said on high : Ye be welcome, sir knight, and well and truly have ye holden your promise. And then they dressed their shields and spears, and came together with all their might of their horses ; and they met so fiercely that both their horses and knights fell to the earth, and as fast as they might avoided their horses, and put their shields afore them ; and they struck together with bright swords, as men that were of might, and either wounded other wonderly sore, that the blood ran out upon the grass. And thus they fought the space of four hours, that never one would speak to other one word, and of their harness they had hewn off many pieces. O Lord Jesu, said Gouvernail, I marvel greatly of the strokes my master hath given to your master. By my head, said Sir Launcelot's servant, your master hath not given so many but your master has received as many or more. O Jesu, said Gouvernail, it is too much for Sir

Palomides to suffer or Sir Launcelot, and yet pity it were
that either of these good knights should destroy other's
blood. So they stood and wept both, and made great dole
when they saw the bright swords over-covered with blood of
their bodies. Then at the last spake Sir Launcelot and
said: Knight, thou fightest wonderly well as ever I saw
knight, therefore, an it please you, tell me your name. Sir,
said Sir Tristram, that is me loth to tell any man my name.
Truly, said Sir Launcelot, an I were required I was never
loth to tell my name. It is well said, said Sir Tristram,
then I require you to tell me your name? Fair knight, he
said, my name is Sir Launcelot du Lake. Alas, said Sir
Tristram, what have I done! for ye are the man in the world
that I love best. Fair knight, said Sir Launcelot, tell me
your name? Truly, said he, my name is Sir Tristram de
Liones. O Jesu, said Sir Launcelot, what adventure is
befallen me! And therewith Sir Launcelot kneeled down
and yielded him up his sword. And therewithal Sir Tristram
kneeled adown, and yielded him up his sword. And so either
gave other the degree. And then they both forthwithal went
to the stone, and set them down upon it, and took off their
helms to cool them, and either kissed other an hundred times.
And then anon after they took off their helms and rode to
Camelot. And there they met with Sir Gawaine and with
Sir Gaheris that had made promise to Arthur never to come
again to the court till they had brought Sir Tristram with
them.

CHAPTER VI

HOW SIR LAUNCELOT BROUGHT SIR TRISTRAM TO THE COURT, AND
OF THE GREAT JOY THAT THE KING AND OTHER MADE FOR
THE COMING OF SIR TRISTRAM

RETURN again, said Sir Launcelot, for your quest is done,
for I have met with Sir Tristram: lo, here is his own person!
Then was Sir Gawaine glad, and said to Sir Tristram: Ye
are welcome, for now have ye eased me greatly of my labour.
For what cause, said Sir Gawaine, came ye into this court?
Fair sir, said Sir Tristram, I came into this country because
of Sir Palomides; for he and I had assigned at this day to
have done battle together at the peron, and I marvel I
hear not of him. And thus by adventure my lord, Sir

Launcelot, and I met together. With this came King Arthur, and when he wist that there was Sir Tristram, then he ran unto him and took him by the hand and said : Sir Tristram, ye are as welcome as any knight that ever came to this court. And when the king had heard how Sir Launcelot and he had foughten, and either had wounded other wonderly sore, then the king made great dole. Then Sir Tristram told the king how he came thither for to have had ado with Sir Palomides. And then he told the king how he had rescued him from the nine knights and Breuse Saunce Pité ; and how he found a knight lying by a well, and that knight smote down Sir Palomides and me, but his shield was covered with a cloth. So Sir Palomides left me, and I followed after that knight ; and in many places I found where he had slain knights, and forjousted many. By my head, said Sir Gawaine, that same knight smote me down and Sir Bleoberis, and hurt us sore both, he with the covered shield. Ah, said Sir Kay, that knight smote me adown and hurt me passing sore, and fain would I have known him, but I might not. Jesu, mercy, said Arthur, what knight was that with the covered shield ? I know not, said Sir Tristram ; and so said they all. Now, said King Arthur, then wot I, for it is Sir Launcelot. Then they all looked upon Sir Launcelot and said : Ye have beguiled us with your covered shield. It is not the first time, said Arthur, he hath done so. My lord, said Sir Launcelot, truly wit ye well I was the same knight that bare the covered shield ; and by cause I would not be known that I was of your court I said no worship of your house. That is truth, said Sir Gawaine, Sir Kay, and Sir Bleoberis. Then King Arthur took Sir Tristram by the hand and went to the Table Round. Then came Queen Guenever and many ladies with her, and all the ladies said at one voice : Welcome, Sir Tristram ! Welcome, said the damosels. Welcome, said knights. Welcome, said Arthur, for one of the best knights, and the gentlest of the world, and the man of most worship ; for of all manner of hunting thou bearest the prize, and of all measures of blowing thou art the beginning, and of all the terms of hunting and hawking ye are the beginner, of all instruments of music ye are the best ; therefore, gentle knight, said Arthur, ye are welcome to this court. And also, I pray you, said Arthur, grant me a boon. It shall be at your commandment, said Tristram. Well, said Arthur,

I will desire of you that ye will abide in my court. Sir, said Sir Tristram, thereto is me loth, for I have ado in many countries. Not so, said Arthur, ye have promised it me, ye may not say nay. Sir, said Sir Tristram, I will as ye will. Then went Arthur unto the sieges about the Round Table, and looked in every siege the which were void that lacked knights. And then the king saw in the siege of Marhaus letters that said: This is the siege of the noble knight, Sir Tristram. And then Arthur made Sir Tristram Knight of the Table Round, with great nobley and great feast as might be thought. For Sir Marhaus was slain afore by the hands of Sir Tristram in an island; and that was well known at that time in the court of Arthur, for this Marhaus was a worthy knight. And for evil deeds that he did unto the country of Cornwall Sir Tristram and he fought. And they fought so long, tracing and traversing, till they fell bleeding to the earth; for they were so sore wounded that they might not stand for bleeding. And Sir Tristram by fortune recovered, and Sir Marhaus died through the stroke on the head. So leave we of Sir Tristram and speak we of King Mark.

CHAPTER VII

HOW FOR THE DESPITE OF SIR TRISTRAM KING MARK CAME WITH TWO KNIGHTS INTO ENGLAND, AND HOW HE SLEW ONE OF THE KNIGHTS

THEN King Mark had great despite of the renown of Sir Tristram, and then he chased him out of Cornwall: yet was he nephew unto King Mark, but he had great suspicion unto Sir Tristram by cause of his queen, La Beale Isoud; for him seemed that there was too much love between them both. So when Sir Tristram departed out of Cornwall into England King Mark heard of the great prowess that Sir Tristram did there, the which grieved him sore. So he sent on his part men to espy what deeds he did. And the queen sent privily on her part spies to know what deeds he had done, for great love was between them twain. So when the messengers were come home they told the truth as they had heard, that he passed all other knights but if it were Sir Launcelot. Then King Mark was right heavy of these tidings, and as glad was La Beale Isoud. Then in great despite he took with him two good knights and two squires, and disguised himself, and took his way into England, to the intent for to slay Sir Tristram. And one of these two knights hight Bersules, and the other knight was called Amant. So as they rode King Mark asked a knight that he met, where he should find King Arthur. He said: At Camelot. Also he asked that knight after Sir Tristram, whether he heard of him in the court of King Arthur. Wit you well, said that knight, ye shall find Sir Tristram there for a man of as great worship as is now living; for through his prowess he won the tournament of the Castle of Maidens that standeth by the Hard Rock. And sithen he hath won with his own hands thirty knights that were men of great honour. And the last battle that ever he did he fought with Sir Launcelot; and that was a marvellous battle. And not by force Sir Launcelot brought Sir Tristram to the court, and of him King Arthur made passing great joy, and so made him knight of the Table Round; and his seat was where the good knight's, Sir Marhaus, seat was. Then was King Mark passing sorry when he heard of the honour of Sir Tristram; and so they departed. Then said King Mark unto his two knights: Now will I tell you my counsel: ye are the men that I trust most to on live, and I will that ye wit my coming hither is to this intent, for to destroy Sir Tristram by wiles or by treason; and it shall be hard if ever he escape our hands. Alas, said Sir Bersules, what mean you? for ye be set in such a way ye are disposed shamefully; for Sir Tristram is the knight of most worship that we know living, and therefore I warn you plainly I will never consent to do him to the death; and therefore I will yield my service, and forsake you. When King Mark heard him say so, suddenly he drew his sword and said: Ah, traitor; and smote Sir Bersules on the head, that the sword went to his teeth. When Amant, the knight, saw him do that villainous deed, and his squires, they said it was foul done, and mischievously: Wherefore we will do thee no more service, and wit ye well, we will appeach thee of treason afore Arthur. Then was King Mark wonderly wroth and would have slain Amant; but he and the two squires held them together, and set nought by his malice. When King Mark saw he might not be revenged on them, he said thus unto the knight, Amant: Wit thou well, an thou appeach me of treason I shall thereof defend me afore

King Arthur; but I require thee that thou tell not my name, that I am King Mark, whatsomever come of me. As for that, said Sir Amant, I will not discover your name; and so they departed, and Amant and his fellows took the body of Bersules and buried it.

CHAPTER VIII

HOW KING MARK CAME TO A FOUNTAIN WHERE HE FOUND SIR LAMORAK COMPLAINING FOR THE LOVE OF KING LOT'S WIFE

THEN King Mark rode till he came to a fountain, and there he rested him, and stood in a doubt whether he would ride to Arthur's court or none, or return again to his country. And as he thus rested him by that fountain there came by him a knight well armed on horseback; and he alit, and tied his horse until a tree, and set him down by the brink of the fountain; and there he made great languor and dole, and made the dolefullest complaint of love that ever man heard; and all this while was he not ware of King Mark. And this was a great part of his complaint: he cried and wept, saying: O fair Queen of Orkney, King Lot's wife, and mother of Sir Gawaine, and to Sir Gaheris, and mother to many other, for thy love I am in great pains. Then King Mark arose and went near him and said: Fair knight, ye have made a piteous complaint. Truly, said the knight, it is an hundred part more ruefuller than my heart can utter. I require you, said King Mark, tell me your name. Sir, said he, as for my name I will not hide it from no knight that beareth a shield, and my name is Sir Lamorak de Galis. But when Sir Lamorak heard King Mark speak, then wist he well by his speech that he was a Cornish knight. Sir, said Sir Lamorak, I understand by your tongue ye be of Cornwall, wherein there dwelleth the shamefullest king that is now living, for he is a great enemy to all good knights; and that proveth well, for he hath chased out of that country Sir Tristram, that is the worshipfullest knight that now is living, and all knights speak of him worship; and for jealousness of his queen he hath chased him out of his country. It is pity, said Sir Lamorak, that ever any such false knightcoward as King Mark is, should be matched with such a fair lady and good as La Beale Isoud is, for all

the world of him speaketh shame, and of her worship that
any queen may have. I have not ado in this matter, said
King Mark, neither nought will I speak thereof. Well said,
said Sir Lamorak. Sir, can ye tell me any tidings? I can
tell you, said Sir Lamorak, that there shall be a great tournament in haste beside Camelot, at the Castle of Jagent; and
the King with the hundred knights and the King of Ireland,
as I suppose, make that tournament. Then there came a
knight that was called Sir Dinadan, and saluted them both.
And when he wist that King Mark was a knight of Cornwall
he reproved him for the love of King Mark a thousand fold
more than did Sir Lamorak. Then he proffered to joust with
King Mark. And he was full loth thereto, but Sir Dinadan
edged him so, that he jousted with Sir Lamorak. And Sir
Lamorak smote King Mark so sore that he bare him on his
spear end over his horse's tail. And then King Mark arose
again, and followed after Sir Lamorak. But Sir Dinadan
would not joust with Sir Lamorak, but he told King Mark
that Sir Lamorak was Sir Kay, the Seneschal. That is not
so, said King Mark, for he is much bigger than Sir Kay;
and so he followed and overtook him, and bad him abide.
What will you do? said Sir Lamorak. Sir, he said, I will
fight with a sword, for ye have shamed me with a spear;
and therewith they dashed together with swords, and Sir
Lamorak suffered him and forbare him. And King Mark
was passing hasty, and smote thick strokes. Sir Lamorak
saw he would not stint, and waxed somewhat wroth, and
doubled his strokes, for he was one of the noblest knights
of the world; and he beat him so on the helm that his
head hung nigh on the saddle bow. When Sir Lamorak
saw him fare so, he said: Sir knight, what cheer? meseemeth
you have nigh your fill of fighting, it were pity to do you
any more harm, for ye are but a mean knight, therefore I
give you leave to go where ye list. Gramercy, said King
Mark, for ye and I be not matches. Then Sir Dinadan
mocked King Mark and said: Ye are not able to match a
good knight. As for that, said King Mark, at the first time
I jousted with this knight ye refused him. Think ye that it
is a shame to me? said Sir Dinadan: nay, sir, it is ever
worship to a knight to refuse that thing that he may not
attain, therefore your worship had been much more to have
refused him as I did; for I warn you plainly he is able to
beat such five as ye and I be; for ye knights of Cornwall

are no men of worship as other knights are. And by cause
ye are no men of worship ye hate all men of worship, for
never was bred in your country such a knight as is Sir
Tristram.

CHAPTER IX

HOW KING MARK, SIR LAMORAK, AND SIR DINADAN CAME TO A
CASTLE, AND HOW KING MARK WAS KNOWN THERE

THEN they rode forth all together, King Mark, Sir Lamorak,
and Sir Dinadan, till that they came to a bridge, and at the
end thereof stood a fair tower. Then saw they a knight
on horseback well armed, brandishing a spear, crying and
proffering himself to joust. Now, said Sir Dinadan unto
King Mark, yonder are two brethren, that one hight Alein,
and the other hight Trian, that will joust with any that
passeth this passage. Now proffer yourself, said Dinadan to
King Mark, for ever ye be laid to the earth. Then King
Mark was ashamed, and therewith he feutred his spear,
and hurtled to Sir Trian, and either brake their spears all
to pieces, and passed through anon. Then Sir Trian sent
King Mark another spear to joust more; but in no wise
he would not joust no more. Then they came to the
castle all three knights, and prayed the lord of the castle
of harbour. Ye are right welcome, said the knights of the
castle, for the love of the lord of this castle, the which
hight Sir Tor le Fise Aries. And then they came into a
fair court well repaired, and they had passing good cheer,
till the lieutenant of this castle, that hight Berluse, espied
King Mark of Cornwall. Then said Berluse: Sir knight,
I know you better than you ween, for ye are King Mark
that slew my father afore mine own eyen; and me had ye
slain had I not escaped into a wood; but wit ye well, for
the love of my lord of this castle I will neither hurt you
nor harm you, nor none of your fellowship. But wit ye
well, when ye are past this lodging I shall hurt you an I
may, for ye slew my father traitorly. But first for the love
of my lord, Sir Tor, and for the love of Sir Lamorak, the
honourable knight that here is lodged, ye shall have none ill
lodging; for it is pity that ever ye should be in the company
of good knights; for ye are the most villainous knight or
king that is now known on live, for ye are a destroyer of
good knights, and all that ye do is but treason.

CHAPTER X

HOW SIR BERLUSE MET WITH KING MARK, AND HOW SIR DINADAN TOOK HIS PART

THEN was King Mark sore ashamed, and said but little again. But when Sir Lamorak and Sir Dinadan wist that he was King Mark they were sorry of his fellowship. So after supper they went to lodging. So on the morn they arose early, and King Mark and Sir Dinadan rode together; and three mile from their lodging there met with them three knights, and Sir Berluse was one, and that other his two cousins. Sir Berluse saw King Mark, and then he cried on high: Traitor, keep thee from me, for wit thou well that I am Berluse. Sir knight, said Sir Dinadan, I counsel you to leave off at this time, for he is riding to King Arthur; and by cause I have promised to conduct him to my lord King Arthur needs must I take a part with him; howbeit I love not his condition, and fain I would be from him. Well, Dinadan, said Sir Berluse, me repenteth that ye will take part with him, but now do your best. And then he hurtled to King Mark, and smote him sore upon the shield, that he bare him clean out of his saddle to the earth. That saw Sir Dinadan, and he feutred his spear, and ran to one of Berluse's fellows, and smote him down off his saddle. Then Dinadan turned his horse, and smote the third knight in the same wise to the earth, for Sir Dinadan was a good knight on horseback; and there began a great battle, for Berluse and his fellows held them together strongly on foot. And so through the great force of Sir Dinadan King Mark had Berluse to the earth, and his two fellows fled; and had not been Sir Dinadan King Mark would have slain him. And so Sir Dinadan rescued him of his life, for King Mark was but a murderer. And then they took their horses and departed, and left Sir Berluse there sore wounded. Then King Mark and Sir Dinadan rode forth a four leagues English, till that they came to a bridge where hoved a knight on horseback, armed and ready to joust. Lo, said Sir Dinadan unto King Mark, yonder hoveth a knight that will joust, for there shall none pass this bridge but he must joust with that knight. It is well, said King Mark, for this jousts falleth with thee. Sir Dinadan knew the knight well that he was a noble knight, and fain he would have jousted, but he had had lever King Mark had jousted with him, but by no mean King Mark would not joust. Then Sir Dinadan might not refuse him in no manner. And then either dressed their spears and their shields, and smote together, so that through fine force Sir Dinadan was smitten to the earth; and lightly he rose up and gat his horse, and required that knight to do battle with swords. And he answered and said: Fair knight, as at this time I may not have ado with you no more, for the custom of this passage is such. Then was Sir Dinadan passing wroth that he might not be revenged of that knight; and so he departed, and in no wise would that knight tell his name. But ever Sir Dinadan thought he should know him by his shield that it should be Sir Tor.

CHAPTER XI

HOW KING MARK MOCKED SIR DINADAN, AND HOW THEY MET WITH SIX KNIGHTS OF THE ROUND TABLE

So as they rode by the way King Mark then began to mock Sir Dinadan, and said: I weened you knights of the Table Round might not in no wise find their matches. Ye say well, said Sir Dinadan; as for you, on my life I call you none of the best knights; but sith ye have such a despite at me I require you to joust with me to prove my strength. Not so, said King Mark, for I will not have ado with you in no manner; but I require you of one thing, that when ye come to Arthur's court discover not my name, for I am there so hated. It is shame to you, said Sir Dinadan, that ye govern you so shamefully; for I see by you ye are full of cowardice, and ye are a murderer, and that is the greatest shame that a knight may have; for never a knight being a murderer hath worship, nor never shall have; for I saw but late through my force ye would have slain Sir Berluse, a better knight than ye, or ever ye shall be, and more of prowess. Thus they rode forth talking till they came to a fair place, where stood a knight, and prayed them to take their lodging with him. So at the request of that knight they reposed them there, and made them well at ease, and had great cheer. For all errant-knights were welcome to him, and specially all those of Arthur's court.

Then Sir Dinadan demanded his host what was the knight's name that kept the bridge. For what cause ask you it? said the host. For it is not long ago, said Sir Dinadan, sythen he gave me a fall. Ah, fair knight, said his host, thereof have ye no marvel, for he is a passing good knight, and his name is Sir Tor, the son of Aries le Vaysher. Ah, said Sir Dinadan, was that Sir Tor? for truly so ever me thought. Right as they stood thus talking together they saw come riding to them over a plain six knights of the court of King Arthur, well armed at all points. And there by their shields Sir Dinadan knew them well. The first was the good knight Sir Uwaine, the son of King Uriens, the second was the noble knight Sir Brandiles, the third was Ozana le Cure Hardy, the fourth was Uwaine les Adventurous, the fifth was Sir Agravaine, the sixth Sir Mordred, brother to Sir Gawaine. When Sir Dinadan had seen these six knights he thought in himself he would bring King Mark by some wile to joust with one of them. And anon they took their horses and ran after these knights well a three mile English. Then was King Mark ware where they sat all six about a well, and ate and drank such meats as they had, and their horses walking and some tied, and their shields hung in divers places about them. Lo, said Sir Dinadan, yonder are knights errant that will joust with us. God forbid, said King Mark, for they be six and we but two. As for that, said Sir Dinadan, let us not spare, for I will assay the foremost; and therewith he made him ready. When King Mark saw him do so, as fast as Sir Dinadan rode toward them, King Mark rode froward them with all his menial meyne. So when Sir Dinadan saw King Mark was gone, he set the spear out of the rest, and threw his shield upon his back, and came riding to the fellowship of the Table Round. And anon Sir Uwaine knew Sir Dinadan, and welcomed him, and so did all his fellowship.

CHAPTER XII

AND then they asked him of his adventures, and whether he had seen Sir Tristram or Sir Launcelot. So God me help, said Sir Dinadan, I saw none of them sythen I departed from Camelot. What knight is that, said Sir Brandiles, that so suddenly departed from you, and rode over yonder field? Sir, said he, it was a knight of Cornwall, and the most horrible coward that ever bestrode horse. What is his name? said all these knights. I wot not, said Sir Dinadan. So when they had reposed them, and spoken together, they took their horses and rode to a castle where dwelt an old knight that made all knights errant good cheer. Then in the meanwhile that they were talking came into the castle Sir Griflet le Fise de Dieu, and there was he welcome; and they all asked him whether he had seen Sir Launcelot or Sir Tristram. Sirs, he answered, I saw him not sythen he departed from Camelot. So as Sir Dinadan walked and beheld the castle, thereby in a chamber he espied King Mark, and then he rebuked him, and asked him why he departed so. Sir, said he, for I durst not abide by cause they were so many. But how escaped ye? said King Mark. Sir, said Sir Dinadan, they were better friends than I weened they had been. Who is captain of that fellowship? said the king. Then for to fear him Sir Dinadan said that it was Sir Launcelot. O Jesu, said the king, might I know Sir Launcelot by his shield? Yea, said Dinadan, for he beareth a shield of silver and black bends. All this he said to fear the king, for Sir Launcelot was not in his fellowship. Now I pray you, said King Mark, that ye will ride in my fellowship. That is me loth to do, said Sir Dinadan, by cause ye forsook my fellowship. Right so Sir Dinadan went from King Mark, and went to his own fellowship; and so they mounted upon their horses, and rode on their ways, and talked of the Cornish knight, for Dinadan told them that he was in the castle where they were lodged. It is well said, said Sir Griflet, for here have I brought Sir Dagonet, King Arthur's fool, that is the best fellow and the merriest in the world. Will ye do well? said Sir Dinadan: I have told the Cornish knight that here is Sir Launcelot, and the

Cornish knight asked me what shield he bare. Truly, I told him that he bare the same shield that Sir Mordred beareth. Will ye do well? said Sir Mordred; I am hurt and may not well bear my shield nor harness, and therefore put my shield and my harness upon Sir Dagonet, and let him set upon the Cornish knight. That shall be done, said Sir Dagonet, by my faith. Then anon was Dagonet armed him in Mordred's harness and his shield, and he was set on a great horse, and a spear in his hand. Now, said Dagonet, shew me the knight, and I trow I shall bear him down. So all these knights rode to a woodside, and abode till King Mark came by the way. Then they put forth Sir Dagonet, and he came on all the while his horse might run, straight upon King Mark. And when he came nigh King Mark, he cried as he were wood, and said: Keep thee, knight of Cornwall, for I will slay thee. Anon, as King Mark beheld his shield, he said to himself: Yonder is Sir Launcelot; alas, now am I destroyed; and therewithal he made his horse to run as fast as it might through wind and thin. And ever Sir Dagonet followed after King Mark, crying and rating him as a wood man, through a great forest. When Sir Uwaine and Sir Brandiles saw Dagonet so chase King Mark, they laughed all as they were wood. And then they took their horses, and rode after to see how Sir Dagonet sped, for they would not for no good that Sir Dagonet were shent, for King Arthur loved him passing well, and made him knight with his own hands. And at every tournament he began to make King Arthur to laugh. Then the knights rode here and there, crying and chasing after King Mark, that all the forest rang of the noise.

CHAPTER XIII

HOW SIR PALOMIDES BY ADVENTURE MET KING MARK FLYING, AND HOW HE OVERTHREW DAGONET AND OTHER KNIGHTS

So King Mark rode by fortune by a well, in the way where stood a knight errant on horseback, armed at all points, with a great spear in his hand. And when he saw King Mark coming flying he said: Knight, return again for shame and stand with me, and I shall be thy warrant. Ah, fair knight, said King Mark, let me pass, for yonder cometh after me the best knight of the world, with the black bended shield. Fie, for shame, said the knight, he is none of the worthy knights, and if he were Sir Launcelot or Sir Tristram I should not doubt to meet the better of them both. When King Mark heard him say that word, he turned his horse and abode by him. And then that strong knight bare a spear to Dagonet, and smote him so sore that he bare him over his horse's tail, and nigh he had broken his neck. And anon after him came Sir Brandiles, and when he saw Dagonet have that fall he was passing wroth, and cried: Keep thee, knight, and so they hurtled together wonder sore. But the knight smote Sir Brandiles so sore that he went to the earth, horse and man. Sir Uwaine came after and saw all this. Jesu, said he, yonder is a strong knight. And then they feutred their spears, and this knight came so eagerly that he smote down Sir Uwaine. Then came Ozana with the hardy heart, and he was smitten down. Now, said Sir Griflet, by my counsel let us send to yonder errant knight, and wit whether he be of Arthur's court, for as I deem it is Sir Lamorak de Galis. So they sent unto him, and prayed the strange knight to tell his name, and whether he were of Arthur's court or not. As for my name they shall not wit, but tell them I am a knight errant as they are, and let them wit that I am no knight of King Arthur's court; and so the squire rode again unto them and told them his answer of him. By my head, said Sir Agravaine, he is one of the strongest knights that ever I saw, for he hath overthrown three noble knights, and needs we must encounter with him for shame. So Sir Agravaine feutred his spear, and that other was ready, and smote him down over his horse to the earth. And in the same wise he smote Sir Uwaine les Avoutres and also Sir Griflet. Then had he served them all but Sir Dinadan, for he was behind, and Sir Mordred was unarmed, and Dagonet had his harness. So when this was done, this strong knight rode on his way a soft pace, and King Mark rode after him, praising him mickle; but he would answer no words, but sighed wonderly sore, hanging down his head, taking no heed to his words. Thus they rode well a three mile English, and then this knight called to him a varlet, and bade him ride until yonder fair manor, and recommend me to the lady of that castle and place, and pray her to send me refreshing of good meats and drinks. And if she ask thee what I am, tell her that I am the knight that followeth the glatisant beast : that is in English to say the questing beast ; for that beast wheresomever he yede he quested in the belly with such a noise as it had been a thirty couple of hounds. Then the varlet went his way and came to the manor, and saluted the lady, and told her from whence he came. And when she understood that he came from the knight that followed the questing beast : O sweet Lord Jesu, she said, when shall I see that noble knight, my dear son Palomides ? Alas, will he not abide with me ? and therewith she swooned and wept, and made passing great dole. And then also soon as she might she gave the varlet all that he asked. And the varlet returned unto Sir Palomides, for he was a varlet of King Mark. And as soon as he came, he told the knight's name was Sir Palomides. I am well pleased, said King Mark, but hold thee still and say nothing. Then they alit and set them down and reposed them a while. Anon withal King Mark fell on sleep. When Sir Palomides saw him sound asleep he took his horse and rode his way, and said to them : I will not be in the company of a sleeping knight. And so he rode forth a great pace.

CHAPTER XIV

HOW KING MARK AND SIR DINADAN HEARD SIR PALOMIDES MAKING GREAT SORROW AND MOURNING FOR LA BEALE ISOUD

Now turn we unto Sir Dinadan, that found these seven knights passing heavy. And when he wist how that they sped, as heavy was he. My lord Uwaine, said Dinadan, I dare lay my head it is Sir Lamorak de Galis. I promise you all I shall find him an he may be found in this country. And so Sir Dinadan rode after this knight ; and so did King Mark, that sought him through the forest. So as King Mark rode after Sir Palomides he heard the noise of a man that made great dole. Then King Mark rode as nigh that noise as he might and as he durst. Then was he ware of a knight that was descended off his horse, and had put off his helm, and there he made a piteous complaint and a dolorous, of love. Now leave we that, and talk we of Sir Dinadan, that rode to seek Sir Palomides. And as he came within a forest he met with a knight, a chaser of a deer. Sir, said Sir

Dinadan, met ye with a knight with a shield of silver and lions' heads? Yea, fair knight, said the other, with such a knight met I with but a while agone, and straight yonder way he yede. Gramercy, said Sir Dinadan, for might I find the track of his horse I should not fail to find that knight. Right so as Sir Dinadan rode in the even late he heard a doleful noise as it were of a man. Then Sir Dinadan rode toward that noise; and when he came nigh that noise he alit off his horse, and went near him on foot. Then was he ware of a knight that stood under a tree, and his horse tied by him, and the helm off his head; and ever that knight made a doleful complaint as ever made knight. And always he made his complaint of La Beale Isoud, the Queen of Cornwall, and said: Ah, fair lady, why love I thee! for thou art fairest of all other, and yet showest thou never love to me, nor bounty. Alas, yet must I love thee. And I may not blame thee, fair lady, for mine eyen be cause of this sorrow. And yet to love thee I am but a fool, for the best knight of the world loveth thee, and ye him again, that is Sir Tristram de Liones. And the falsest king and knight is your husband, and the most coward and full of treason, is your lord, King Mark. Alas, that ever so fair a lady and peerless of all other should be matched with the most villainous knight of the world. All this language heard King Mark, what Sir Palomides said by him; wherefore he was adread when he saw Sir Dinadan, lest he espied him, that he would tell Sir Palomides that he was King Mark; and therefore he withdrew him, and took his horse and rode to his men, where he commanded them to abide. And so he rode as fast as he might unto Camelot; and the same day he found there Amant, the knight, ready that afore Arthur had appelled him of treason; and so, lightly the king commanded them to do battle. And by misadventure King Mark smote Amant through the body. And yet was Amant in the righteous quarrel. And right so he took his horse and departed from the court for dread of Sir Dinadan, that he would tell Sir Tristram and Sir Palomides what he was. Then were there maidens that La Beale Isoud had sent to Sir Tristram, that knew Sir Amant well.

CHAPTER XV

HOW KING MARK HAD SLAIN SIR AMANT WRONGFULLY TOFORE
KING ARTHUR, AND SIR LAUNCELOT FETCHED KING MARK TO
KING ARTHUR

THEN by the licence of King Arthur they went to him
and spake with him ; for while the truncheon of the spear
stuck in his body he spake : Ah, fair damosels, said Amant,
recommend me unto La Beale Isoud, and tell her that I am
slain for the love of her and of Sir Tristram. And there he
told the damosels how cowardly King Mark had slain him,
and Sir Bersules, his fellow. And for that deed I appelled
him of treason, and here am I slain in a righteous quarrel ;
and all was by cause Sir Bersules and I would not consent
by treason to slay the noble knight, Sir Tristram. Then the
two maidens cried aloud that all the court might hear it, and
said : O sweet Lord Jesu, that knowest all hid things, why
sufferest Thou so false a traitor to vanquish and slay a true
knight that fought in a righteous quarrel ? Then anon it
was spronge to the king, and the queen, and to all the lords,
that it was King Mark that had slain Sir Amant, and Sir
Bersules aforehand ; wherefore they did their battle. Then
was King Arthur wroth out of measure, and so were all the
other knights. But when Sir Tristram knew all the matter
he made great dole and sorrow out of measure, and wept for
sorrow for the loss of the noble knights, Sir Bersules and of
Sir Amant. When Sir Launcelot espied Sir Tristram weep
he went hastily to King Arthur, and said : Sir, I pray you
give me leave to return again to yonder false king and knight.
I pray you, said King Arthur, fetch him again, but I would
not that ye slew him, for my worship. Then Sir Launcelot
armed him in all haste, and mounted upon a great horse, and
took a spear in his hand and rode after King Mark. And
from thence a three mile English Sir Launcelot overtook him,
and bad him : Turn recreant king and knight, for whether
thou wilt or not thou shalt go with me to King Arthur's court.
King Mark returned and looked upon Sir Launcelot, and
said : Fair sir, what is your name ? Wit thou well, said he,
my name is Sir Launcelot, and therefore defend thee. And
when King Mark wist that it was Sir Launcelot, and came
so fast upon him with a spear, he cried then on loud : I yield
me to thee, Sir Launcelot, honourable knight. But Sir

Launcelot would not hear him, but came fast upon him. King Mark saw that, and made no defence, but tumbled adown out of his saddle to the earth as a sack, and there he lay still, and cried Sir Launcelot mercy.   Arise, recreant knight and king.   I will not fight, said King Mark, but whither that ye will I will go with you.   Alas, alas, said Sir Launcelot, that I may not give thee one buffet for the love of Sir Tristram and of La Beale Isoud, and for the two knights that thou hast slain traitorly.   And so he mounted upon his horse and brought him to King Arthur; and there King Mark alit in that same place, and threw his helm from him upon the earth, and his sword, and fell flat to the earth of King Arthur's feet, and put him in his grace and mercy. So God me help, said Arthur, ye are welcome in a manner, and in a manner ye are not welcome.   In this manner ye are welcome, that ye come hither maugre thy head, as I suppose. That is truth, said King Mark, and else I had not been here, for my lord, Sir Launcelot, brought me hither through his fine force, and to him am I yielden to as recreant.   Well, said Arthur, ye understand ye ought to do me service, homage, and fealty.   And never would ye do me none, but ever ye have been against me, and a destroyer of my knights ; now, how will ye acquit you ?   Sir, said King Mark, right as your lordship will require me, unto my power, I will make a large amends.   For he was a fair speaker, and false there-under.   Then for great pleasure of Sir Tristram, to make them twain accorded, the king withheld King Mark as at that time, and made a broken love day between them.

CHAPTER XVI

HOW SIR DINADAN TOLD SIR PALOMIDES OF THE BATTLE BETWEEN SIR LAUNCELOT AND SIR TRISTRAM

Now turn we again unto Sir Palomides, how Sir Dinadan comforted him in all that he might, from his great sorrow. What knight are ye ? said Sir Palomides.   Sir, I am a knight errant as ye be, that hath sought you long by your shield. Here is my shield, said Sir Palomides, wit ye well, an ye will ought, therewith I will defend it.   Nay, said Sir Dinadan, I will not have ado with you but in good manner.   And if ye will, ye shall find me soon ready.   Sir, said Sir Dinadan,

whitherward ride you this way? By my head, said Sir
Palomides, I wot not, but as fortune leadeth me. Heard ye
or saw ye ought of Sir Tristram? So God me help, of Sir
Tristram I both heard and saw, and not for then we loved
not inwardly well together, yet at my mischief Sir Tristram
rescued me from my death; and yet, or he and I departed,
by both our assents we assigned a day that we should have
met at the stony grave that Merlin set beside Camelot, and
there to have done battle together; howbeit I was letted,
said Sir Palomides, that I might not hold my day, the which
grieveth me sore; but I have a large excuse. For I was
prisoner with a lord, and many other more, and that shall
Sir Tristram right well understand, that I brake it not of fear
of cowardice. And then Sir Palomides told Sir Dinadan
the same day that they should have met. So God me help,
said Sir Dinadan, that same day met Sir Launcelot and Sir
Tristram at the same grave of stone. And there was the
most mightiest battle that ever was seen in this land betwixt
two knights, for they fought more than two hours. And
there they both bled so much blood that all men marvelled
that ever they might endure it. And so at the last, by both
their assents, they were made friends and sworn brethren for
ever, and no man can judge the better knight. And now is
Sir Tristram made a knight of the Round Table, and he
sitteth in the siege of the noble knight, Sir Marhaus. By
my head, said Sir Palomides, Sir Tristram is far bigger than
Sir Launcelot, and the hardier knight. Have ye essayed
them both? said Sir Dinadan. I have seen Sir Tristram
fight, said Sir Palomides, but never Sir Launcelot to my
witting. But at the fountain where Sir Launcelot lay on
sleep, there with one spear he smote down Sir Tristram and
me, said Palomides, but at that time they knew not either
other. Fair knight, said Sir Dinadan, as for Sir Launcelot
and Sir Tristram let them be, for the worst of them will not
be lightly matched of no knights that I know living. No,
said Sir Palomides, God defend, but an I had a quarrel to
the better of them both I would with as good a will fight with
him as with you. Sir, I require you tell me your name, and
in good faith I shall hold you company till that we come to
Camelot; and there shall ye have great worship now at this
great tournament; for there shall be the Queen Guenever,
and La Beale Isoud of Cornwall. Wit you well, sir knight,
for the love of La Beale Isoud I will be there, and else not,

but I will not have ado in King Arthur's court. Sir, said
Dinadan, I shall ride with you and do you service, so you
will tell me your name. Sir, ye shall understand my name
is Sir Palomides, brother to Safere, the good and noble
knight. And Sir Segwarides and I, we be Saracens born, of
father and mother. Sir, said Sir Dinadan, I thank you much
for the telling of your name. For I am glad of that I know
your name, and I promise you by the faith of my body, ye
shall not be hurt by me by my will, but rather be advanced.
And thereto will I help you with all my power, I promise
you, doubt ye not. And certainly on my life ye shall win
great worship in the court of King Arthur, and be right
welcome. So then they dressed on their helms and put on
their shields, and mounted upon their horses, and took the
broad way towards Camelot. And then were they ware of
a castle that was fair and rich, and also passing strong as any
was within this realm.

CHAPTER XVII

HOW SIR LAMORAK JOUSTED WITH DIVERS KNIGHTS OF THE
CASTLE WHEREIN WAS MORGAN LE FAY

SIR PALOMIDES, said Dinadan, here is a castle that I
know well, and therein dwelleth Queen Morgan le Fay,
King Arthur's sister; and King Arthur gave her this
castle, the which he hath repented him sythen a thousand
times, for sythen King Arthur and she have been at
debate and strife; but this castle could he never get nor
win of her by no manner of engine; and ever as she
might she made war on King Arthur. And all dangerous knights she withholdeth with her, for to destroy all
these knights that King Arthur loveth. And there shall
no knight pass this way but he must joust with one knight, or
with two, or with three. And if it hap that King Arthur's
knight be beaten, he shall lose his horse and his harness and
all that he hath, and hard if that he escape, but that he shall
be prisoner. So God me help, said Palomides, this is a shameful custom, and a villainous usance for a queen to use, and
namely to make such war upon her own lord, that is called
the flower of chivalry that is christian or heathen; and with
all my heart I would destroy that shameful custom. And I
will that all the world wit she shall have no service of me.

And if she send out any knights, as I suppose she will, for
to joust, they shall have both their hands full. And I shall
not fail you, said Sir Dinadan, unto my puissance, upon my
life. So as they stood on horseback afore the castle, there
came a knight with a red shield, and two squires after him ;
and he came straight unto Sir Palomides, the good knight,
and said to him : Fair and gentle knight errant, I require
thee for the love thou owest unto knighthood, that ye will
not have ado here with these men of this castle ; for this was
Sir Lamorak that thus said. For I came hither to seek this
deed, and it is my request ; and therefore I beseech you,
knight, let me deal, and if I be beaten revenge me. In the
name of God, said Palomides, let see how ye will speed, and
we shall behold you. Then anon came forth a knight of the
castle, and proffered to joust with the knight with the red
shield. Anon they encountered together, and he with the
red shield smote him so hard that he bare him over to the
earth. Therewith anon came another knight of the castle,
and he was smitten so sore that he avoided his saddle.
And forthwithal came the third knight, and the knight with
the red shield smote him to the earth. Then came Sir
Palomides, and besought him that he might help him to
joust. Fair knight, said he unto him, suffer me as at this
time to have my will, for an they were twenty knights I shall
not doubt them. And ever there were upon the walls of the
castle many lords and ladies that cried and said : Well have
ye jousted, knight with the red shield. But as soon as the
knight had smitten them down, his squire took their horses,
and avoided their saddles and bridles of the horses, and
turned them into the forest, and made the knights to be kept
to the end of the jousts. Right so came out of the castle
the fourth knight, and freshly proffered to joust with the
knight with the red shield : and he was ready, and he smote
him so hard that horse and man fell to the earth, and the
knight's back brake with the fall, and his neck also. O Jesu,
said Sir Palomides, that yonder is a passing good knight,
and the best jouster that ever I saw. By my head, said Sir
Dinadan, he is as good as ever was Sir Launcelot or Sir
Tristram, what knight somever he be.

CHAPTER XVIII

HOW SIR PALOMIDES WOULD HAVE JOUSTED FOR SIR LAMORAK
WITH THE KNIGHTS OF THE CASTLE

THEN forthwithal came a knight out of the castle, with a shield bended with black and with white. And anon the knight with the red shield and he encountered so hard that he smote the knight of the castle through the bended shield and through the body, and brake the horse's back. Fair knight, said Sir Palomides, ye have overmuch on hand, therefore I pray you let me joust, for ye had need to be reposed. Why sir, said the knight, seem ye that I am weak and feeble? and sir, methinketh ye proffer me wrong, and to me shame, when I do well enough. I tell you now as I told you erst; for an they were twenty knights I shall beat them, and if I be beaten or slain then may ye revenge me. And if ye think that I be weary, and ye have an appetite to joust with me, I shall find you jousting enough. Sir, said Palomides, I said it not because I would joust with you, but meseemeth that ye have overmuch on hand. And therefore, an ye were gentle, said the knight with the red shield, ye should not proffer me shame; therefore I require you to joust with me, and ye shall find that I am not weary. Sith ye require me, said Sir Palomides, take keep to yourself. Then they two knights came together as fast as their horses might run, and the knight smote Sir Palomides so sore on the shield that the spear went into his side a great wound, and a perilous. And therewithal Sir Palomides avoided his saddle. And that knight turned unto Sir Dinadan; and when he saw him coming he cried aloud, and said: Sir, I will not have ado with you; but for that he let it not, but came straight upon him. So Sir Dinadan for shame put forth his spear and all to shivered it upon the knight. But he smote Sir Dinadan again so hard that he smote him clean from his saddle; but their horses he would not suffer his squires to meddle with, and by cause they were knights errant. Then he dressed him again to the castle, and jousted with seven knights more, and there was none of them might withstand him, but he bare him to the earth. And of these twelve knights he slew in plain jousts four. And the eight knights he made them to swear on the cross of a sword that they should never use the evil customs of the castle. And when he had made them to swear that oath he let them pass. And ever stood the lords and the ladies on the castle walls crying and saying: Knight with the red shield, ye have marvellously well done as ever we saw knight do. And therewith came a knight out of the castle unarmed, and said: Knight with the red shield, overmuch damage hast thou done to us this day, therefore return whither thou wilt, for here are no more will have ado with thee; for we repent sore that ever thou camest here, for by thee is fordone the old custom of this castle. And with that word he turned again into the castle, and shut the gates. Then the knight with the red shield turned and called his squires, and so passed forth on his way, and rode a great pace. And when he was past Sir Palomides went to Sir Dinadan, and said: I had never such a shame of one knight that ever I met; and therefore I cast me to ride after him, and to be revenged with my sword, for ahorseback I deem I shall get no worship of him. Sir Palomides, said Dinadan, ye shall not meddle with him by my counsel, for ye shall get no worship of him; and for this cause, ye have seen him this day have had overmuch to done, and overmuch travailed. By almighty Jesu, said Palomides, I shall never be at ease till that I have had ado with him. Sir, said Dinadan, I shall give you my beholding. Well, said Palomides, then shall ye see how we shall redress our mights. So they took their horses of their varlets, and rode after the knight with the red shield; and down in a valley beside a fountain they were ware where he was alit to repose him, and had done off his helm for to drink at the well.

CHAPTER XIX

HOW SIR LAMORAK JOUSTED WITH SIR PALOMIDES, AND HURT HIM GRIEVOUSLY

THEN Palomides rode fast till he came nigh him. And then he said: Knight, remember ye of the shame ye did to me right now at the castle, therefore dress thee, for I will have ado with thee. Fair knight, said he to Palomides, of me ye win no worship, for ye have seen this day that I have been travailed sore. As for that, said Palomides, I will not let, for wit ye well I will be revenged. Well, said the knight, I may happen to endure you. And therewithal he mounted upon his horse, and took a great spear in his hand ready for to joust. Nay, said Palomides, I will not joust, for I am sure at jousting I get no prize. Fair knight, said that knight, it would beseem a knight to joust and to fight on horseback. Ye shall see what I will do, said Palomides. And therewith he alit down upon foot, and dressed his shield afore him and pulled out his sword. Then the knight with the red shield descended down from his horse, and dressed his shield afore him, and so he drew out his sword. And then they came together a soft pace, and wonderly they lashed together passing thick the mountenance of an hour or ever they breathed. Then they traced and traversed, and waxed wonderly wroth, and either behight other death; they hewed so fast with their swords that they cut in down half their swords and mails, that the bare flesh in some place stood above their harness. And when Sir Palomides beheld his fellow's sword overhylled with his blood it grieved him sore: some while they foined, some while they struck as wild men. But at the last Sir Palomides waxed faint, by cause of his first wound that he had at the castle with a spear, for that wound grieved him wonderly sore. Fair knight, said Palomides, meseemeth we have essayed either other passing sore, and if it may please thee, I require thee of thy knighthood tell me thy name. Sir, said the knight to Palomides, that is me loth to do, for thou hast done me wrong and no knighthood to proffer me battle, considering my great travail, but an thou wilt tell me thy name I will tell thee mine. Sir, said he, wit thou well my name is Palomides. Ah, sir, ye shall understand my name is Sir Lamorak de Galis, son and heir unto the good knight and king, King Pellinore, and Sir Tor, the good knight, is my half brother. When Sir Palomides heard him say so he kneeled down and asked mercy, for outrageously have I done to you this day; considering the great deeds of arms I have seen you do, shamefully and unknightly I have required you to do battle. Ah, Sir Palomides, said Sir Lamorak, overmuch have ye done and said to me. And therewith he embraced him with his both hands, and said, Palomides, the worthy knight, in all this land is no better than ye, nor more of prowess, and me repenteth sore that we should fight together. So it doth not me, said Sir

Palomides, and yet am I sorer wounded than ye be ; but as for that I shall soon thereof be whole. But certainly I would not for the fairest castle in this land, but if thou and I had met, for I shall love you the days of my life afore all other knights except my brother, Sir Safere. I say the same, said Sir Lamorak, except my brother, Sir Tor. Then came Sir Dinadan, and he made great joy of Sir Lamorak. Then their squires dressed both their shields and their harness, and stopped their wounds. And thereby at a priory they rested them all night.

END OF VOL. I.